American Refugee Policy and European Jewry, 1933–45

American Refugee Policy and European Jewry, 1933–1945

Richard Breitman and Alan M. Kraut

INDIANA UNIVERSITY PRESS
Bloomington and Indianapolis

Quotations from Jay Pierrepont Moffat and William Phillips papers
used by permission of the Houghton Library, Harvard University.

Manufactured in the United States of America

Library of Congress Cataloging-in-Publication Data

Breitman, Richard, 1947–
  American refugee policy and European Jewry,
1933–1945.

  Bibliography: p.
  Includes index.
  1. Refugees, Jewish—Government policy—United
States. 2. Jews—Europe—Persecutions. 3. United
States—Emigration and immigration—History—
20th century. 4. Jews—United States—Politics and
government. 5. United States—Ethnic relations.
I. Kraut, Alan M. II. Title.
JV6895.J5B74 1987
ISBN 0-253-30415-6

CONTENTS

PREFACE

This book was a long time in the making. At the beginning we believed that having two authors—one a specialist in European history, the other in American history—would shorten and simplify the process of research and writing. Even so, the subject proved to have many dimensions that we were both unfamiliar with, and there were far more primary source materials (some of them previously unused) than we had imagined. Combining our individual portions of the book took time as well. In the end, the two of us jointly wrote the introduction and merged essays in chapter 2—Alan Kraut on Carr and Richard Breitman on Messersmith. Breitman wrote chapters 1, 3, 7, 8, 9, 10, and 12. Kraut wrote chapters 4, 5, 6, and 11. Each individual is exclusively responsible for what he wrote.

In the midst of our labors appeared a major new work on the subject, David Wyman's *The Abandonment of the Jews, 1941–1945* (New York, 1984). Wyman's work addressed many of the same issues that interested us, and his research was prodigious. His arguments caused us to rethink and rewrite a number of sections. We remained convinced, however, that we had both a different chronological perspective and a different interpretation. If we made a number of critical references to Wyman's views in our text and notes, that is not a sign of lack of appreciation of his book. We both feel that it has significantly advanced scholarly understanding of the subject.

We owe debts to a great many archivists, librarians, and scholars. At the National Archives, the late John Mendelsohn and Robert Wolfe of the Military Reference Branch offered us wise scholarly counsel and friendship as well as manuscripts. So, too, did Sally Marks of the Diplomatic Branch and John Taylor who has charge of the OSS records. H. D. Williams at the Washington National Records Center at Suitland, Maryland, created conditions under which we could see the records of visa files without violating the privacy of visa applicants. Lane Moore, Mike Miller, Fred Pernell, and David Pfeiffer made sure we saw all there was to see at Suitland. Gary Kohn of the Library of Congress Manuscript Division always had helpful suggestions about yet another collection worth seeing. At the Franklin D. Roosevelt Library, Director William R. Emerson and his entire staff were unfailingly cooperative and helped us track down many a lead.

We are especially grateful to William B. Liebmann of the Herbert H. Lehman Collection at the Columbia University School of International Affairs, Jack Sutters of the Archives Division of the American Friends Service Committee, Elizabeth Mann of the Columbia University Oral History Collection, Bernard Wax and Nathan Kaganoff of the American Jewish Historical Society, Ruth Rauch and Helen Ritter of the American Jewish Committee and Cyma Horowitz of the AJC's Blaustein Library, Sybil Milton of the Leo Baeck Institute, Nancy Bressler and J. Holliday of the Seeley G. Mudd Manuscript Library at Princeton University, Marek Web of YIVO, Abraham Peck of the American Jewish Archives in Cincinnati, Mary Odienyc of the Connecticut College Library, Henry Guzda of the United States Labor Department, and Richard Smyser, formerly of the State Department's Bureau of Refugee Affairs. We are also indebted to the staffs of the Columbia University Rare Book and Manuscript Division, the Special Collections Section of the University of Delaware Library, the Houghton Library at Harvard, the Office of the Historian at the United States Department of Justice, the

Jewish Labor Committee Archives, the Zionist Archives and Library, and the B'nai B'rith Archives.

George Lesser, whose father was assistant director of the War Refugee Board, was kind enough to provide us with a copy of the official history of the board. He can now see that we have made frequent use of this unpublished manuscript. Roswell McClelland, the WRB's representative in Switzerland, was kind enough to provide us with documents in his possession. Josiah DuBois, who deserves a great deal of credit for the founding of the board, did the same; we greatly regret that he passed away before this book was completed. The late Charles E. Wyzanski, Jr., made available personal documents that helped clarify his role in the Labor Department's clash with the State Department in the 1930s.

Our special thanks go to the others we interviewed, including Jacob Beam, the late James T. Mann, Dr. Gerhart Riegner, Elbridge Durbrow, Howard Elting, Jr., Arthur Goldberg, Niles Bond, Willard Beaulac, Gary Van Arkel, and Simon Weber.

We received essential financial support from a National Endowment for the Humanities Basic Research Grant and small grants from the Alfred Beveridge Fund of the American Historical Association, the Eleanor Roosevelt Institute, and the faculty development fund of American University. Ann Ferren took particular interest in our study at an early stage and helped us secure university support.

Both of us benefited from the wisdom and warm friendship of our department chairman, Robert Beisner. Our colleagues Allan Lichtman and Roger Brown read portions of the manuscript and gave us useful advice.

Other scholars and staff who provided timely assistance, advice, or both on sources available include Leonard Dinnerstein, Susan Falb, Henry Feingold, Saul Friedman, Thomas Imhoof, Walter Laqueur, Stanley Matelski, Maurice Middleberg, Kenneth Moss, Jennifer Murphy, Beata Ruhm von Oppen, Richard Polenberg, Jordan Schwartz, Barbara McDonald Stewart, Herbert Strauss, the members of the Mid-Atlantic German History Seminar, and Harold Troper. History graduate student Sarah Larson made valuable editorial suggestions. Timothy Newell introduced us to the world of personal computers.

Of course, our greatest debt is to our families for their steadfast support. The contributions of Carol and David Breitman and Deborah and Julia Rose Kraut well exceeded the call of duty.

American Refugee Policy and
European Jewry, 1933–45

Introduction

To commit suicide in front of the British cabinet would have been one of the most grotesque forms of lobbying in history. But by May 1943 what else was there to try? The outside world had done nothing to impede the Nazi slaughter of Polish Jews in the Warsaw Ghetto and in the death camps scattered throughout the country. So the Jewish underground in Poland urged the two Jewish representatives on the Polish National Council in London, Szmul Zygielbojm and Dr. Ignacy Schwarzbart, to kill themselves in the presence of members of the British cabinet in order to draw maximum public attention to the fate of Polish Jewry. Zygielbojm and Schwarzbart, however, lacked entrée to the corridors of power. On May 11 they discussed the hopeless situation of the remaining Polish Jews. Zygielbojm then wrote farewell letters to the press, to the president of the Republic of Poland, and to the Polish commander-in-chief, General Sikorski. He argued that, while the Nazis were directly responsible for the extermination of millions of Polish Jews, the Allied governments bore a share of the responsibility: they had done nothing to stop the massacres, which were still taking place daily. Of nearly 3.5 million Polish Jews and another 700,000 deported to Poland, only some 300,000 were still alive, he wrote.[1] He did not mention that his wife and children were among the dead. The next day he committed suicide. Although his death was widely reported, his motive received little attention.[2] Six months later the last surviving remnants of the Jewish National Committee in underground Warsaw wrote to Schwarzbart and swore revenge not only against the Nazis but also against "those indifferent elements which have contented themselves merely with words but have done nothing to rescue from the hands of beasts a people doomed to extermination."[3]

Even if Zygielbojm had been able to make his case directly to British government officials, it is hardly likely that his sacrifice or similar sacrifices by others would have altered Allied policies. Franklin Roosevelt and Winston Churchill had frequently spoken of the universal, humanitarian ideals their countries were defending. But the United States and Great Britain were striving to dislodge the German hold on Europe and North Africa and to end the suffering of millions of subject peoples, and it was not easy to convict the two western nations of complicity with Nazi mass murder. The morality of western goals and policies, at least by comparison with Nazi barbarism, seemed beyond question.

Zygielbojm's moral protest, however, was not forgotten. Posterity has vindicated him, even if it was not in the way he wanted. We and most others who have written on Allied policies during the Holocaust agree that British and American inaction in the face of what the Nazis called the Final Solution of the Jewish question represented a fundamental failure of western civilized values. The question is how to explain and evaluate that failure.

One way is to condemn most or all of those in positions of power and influence in Great Britain and the United States as "passive accomplices" to murder[4]—self-absorbed and amoral, if not actually evil. Such retrospective moral absolutism can only exist in an oversimplified world. It overlooks the fact that Allied leaders and governments were capable of moral action on some occasions. And to castigate every politician or private citizen who did not "move heaven and earth"[5] in a desperate effort to halt the Final Solution is to condemn virtually the whole world; only the Zygielbojms and the Holocaust victims escape censure. This sweeping judgment may seem morally appropriate, in view of the magnitude of the tragedy, but it obliterates important distinctions of behavior among individuals and among governments.

It also fails to identify those courses of action most likely to have spared Jews from the gas chambers. To reach any judgment of which methods might have saved lives, one has to take into account not only political conditions in the United States and Great Britain but also the policies and ideology of the Third Reich. To condemn the Allies for failure to negotiate with Germany for the release of Jews is hollow criticism unless one can demonstrate that negotiations had some chance of success.

Before one can judge what might have been, the historian needs a careful and balanced analysis of what actually occurred. Nazi persecution and murder of Europe's Jews was one of many world crises during the 1930s and 1940s. Western policies toward Nazi Germany and toward European Jewry must be examined in historical and political context; only then can the observer understand the real constraints and trade-offs faced by government officials. If one wants to understand why the American government made certain choices, rather than simply condemn them, then the historian must re-create the broad sweep of governmental concerns and activities in the Roosevelt era.

The possibility of a refugee policy for European Jewry was discussed at the highest levels of the American government as early as 1933, and it continued to be a subject of debate throughout the 1930s. We argue here that it is possible to understand American policy during the Holocaust and the motives of the policy makers only in light of the earlier debates and outcomes. We seek to describe and to analyze American immigration policy, as well as rescue and relief efforts (which we call together "refugee policy"), directed toward European Jewry between 1933 and 1945. The focal point of this book is the complex interaction of precedent, process, and individual personalities. We contend that U.S. policy was a product of four major variables: preexisting restrictive immigration laws and regulations; an entrenched State Department bureaucracy committed to a narrow interpretation of its functions and to the protection of American interest alone; the American public's opposition to an increase in immigration; and the reluctance of Franklin Delano Roosevelt to accept the inherent political risks of humanitarian measures on behalf of foreign Jews advocated by Secretary of Labor Frances Perkins, representatives of American Jewish organizations, and others.

Among previous scholars who have written on this subject, few if any deny that various motives underlay American restrictionism—fear of introducing new workers into the economy during a depression, antiradical nativism, and bureaucratic inertia. But some still overestimate the influence that individual anti-Semites wielded in shaping American policy. Others have failed to penetrate beneath the broad social forces that encouraged restrictionism. They have not adequately probed the institutional operation or priorities of the government agencies that dealt with the refugee issue. They have underestimated the importance of conflicting perceptions among policy makers of their institutional and moral responsibilities.

Journalist Arthur Morse was the first to publish a full-length study of America's inadequate response to Nazi persecution of European Jews.[6] He charged that, as Hitler "moved systematically toward the total destruction of the Jews, the government and people of the United States remained bystanders." Morse blamed individuals in the State Department for America's restrictive policies, particularly Assistant Secretary of State Breckinridge Long, though Morse stopped just short of labeling Long an anti-Semite.

Historians David Wyman and Henry Feingold added depth to Morse's exposé. In *Paper Walls*, which covered the period from 1938 to 1941, Wyman argued that pervasive anti-Semitism among the American public was a constraining influence upon policy makers. In addition, antirefugee sentiment in the State Department and particularly among American consuls abroad reflected this broader intolerance, both toward Jews and toward foreigners generally.[7] Feingold echoed Wyman in detecting "widespread anti-Semitism in the foreign service." But in his *Politics of Rescue* Feingold identified an anti-Semitic Breckinridge Long as the specific engineer of policies designed to bar the entry of Jewish refugees to the United States in the early 1940s.[8]

In *No Haven for the Oppressed*, however, historian Saul Friedman questioned whether the feisty Long deserved the designation anti-Semite at all. More important, Friedman saw the refugee issue as a crisis of minor proportion to most Americans who were steeped in their own economic crisis and, later, war. Unlike his predecessors, Friedman refused to blame the State Department's unwillingness to help European Jewry on the anti-Semitism of specific policy makers or lower-level administrators. Rather, he cited American resistance to bargaining with the Nazis for lives as reasons why the State Department eschewed a bolder refugee policy. He also criticized the American Jewish leadership, particularly Stephen S. Wise, for putting insufficient pressure upon the American government.[9]

In a more recent article Feingold diminished the importance of Long and the centrality of anti-Semitism in the motivations of American decision makers. Feingold has pointed the way toward revising his original thesis, now arguing for

> the existence of a broad spectrum of opinion on the issue [action to help persecuted Jews escape the Nazis] among decision makers (broader among political leaders than the public at large), and the complex intertwining of personalities, domestic politics, and conflicting views of the world, which fed into the policy-making arena on the question of the Holocaust.[10]

That complex picture sketched in broad outlines by Feingold is one that we have attempted to fill out here.

In his brilliantly researched second book, *The Abandonment of the Jews, 1941–1945,* David Wyman rendered harsh judgment upon American policy makers and American society. Even a number of American Jewish leaders and organizations failed Europe's Jews. Wyman contended that anti-Semitism was a significant determinant of America's response to the refugees' plight before Pearl Harbor and an important factor in the nation's reaction to the Holocaust. He cited opinion polls and even sociologist David Riesman to persuade readers that anti-Semitism rose during the 1940s and reached a historic peak in 1944.[11] Yet he also condemned the mass media for not publishing more about the Nazi war against the Jews, and he scolded American Jewish organizations for the feuds that impaired their effectiveness.

His moral outrage led him to the verge of inconsistency. Would front-page coverage every day and harmonious cooperation among Jewish groups have kindled a passion for rescue among the public at large? And, if the public was as anti-Semitic as Wyman argued, how could he have expected government officials to make exceptions to restrictionist policies for the Jews? Could any politician, even the wily Roosevelt, retain power and effectiveness while defying public opinion on a visceral issue such as Jewish immigration? Wyman seemed more concerned with establishing the immorality of behavior than in explaining it or assessing its impact. And his lambasting of Roosevelt on the basis of limited evidence (this president did not keep many tape recordings or a diary and prohibited the taking of cabinet minutes) represents one of the weaker points of his book.

In basic accord with Wyman, Deborah Lipstadt, in her examination of the American press during the Holocaust, argued that, with few notable exceptions, American journalism did little more than echo the American public's opposition to a lenient refugee policy, especially one that would circumvent America's restrictive immigration quota system.[12] But she, too, failed to explain how even a sympathetic press that paid greater attention to Nazi mass murders could have altered policies so consistent with prejudices and apprehensions ingrained within the American psyche.

A report by the American Jewish Commission on the Holocaust, containing the work of numerous scholars, echoed Wyman's and Friedman's conclusion that American Jews should have done more to save the lives of European Jews. Several authors offered new details about rifts among Jewish organizations over priorities and tactics. David Kranzler praised the Orthodox groups, such as Agudath Israel, who did not consider themselves bound by laws or agreements with the American government when it was a matter of saving lives.[13] In a separate study, Rabbi Haskel Lookstein, a highly respected Orthodox Jewish scholar, used the Jewish press as a prism through which to examine American Jewish efforts to affect government policy on refugees and to bring about private rescue efforts. His conclusion was only slightly less severe than Wyman's: American Jews did not agonize in trying to save their brothers. "The Final Solution may have been *unstoppable* by American Jewry, but it should have been *unbearable* for them. And it wasn't," Lookstein lamented.[14] But none of these studies measured the scale of opportunity open to American Jewry to affect government policy or to carry out independent action.

Those who have studied other governments' responses to Nazi persecution and murder of European Jewry offer some useful comparisons and guidelines for students of the American experience. In two lengthy articles Herbert A. Strauss examined the pressure for Jewish emigration from Nazi Germany from 1933 on and the responses of receiving nations throughout the world. Strauss demonstrated a global pattern of restrictionist measures against Jewish immigration, partly the result of fundamental economic and social constraints. Still, the variations among nations are almost as significant as the similarities. Strauss's study stands out in its careful examination of the interaction of Nazi policies and western responses.[15]

There are works that substantiate the potency of anti-Semitism outside the Greater German Reich. In their meticulously documented study of Vichy France, Michael Marrus and Robert Paxton dealt both with German efforts in France to obtain and deport Jews to the death camps and with the Vichy government's own Jewish policy. They rejected the notion that Vichy simply responded to German pressure in sending more than 75,000 Jews to the death camps in eastern Europe, and they linked Vichy's measures against Jews to anti-Semitic traditions and immediate domestic concerns. The latter included preserving jobs and business opportunities for the dominant national group, expelling a minority regarded as unassimilable, and compelling the assimilation of other groups, thereby ensuring cultural homogeneity.[16]

The Canadian government also feared the breakdown of valued cultural homogeneity that might occur from an influx of Jewish refugees. Irving Abella and Harold Troper demonstrated how government officials consciously used bureaucratic red tape to choke off refugee immigration and confound the efforts of refugee advocates. Canadian officials such as Frederick Blair and Mackenzie King were themselves anti-Semites. The two authors persuasively showed that in Canada there was little sympathy for the Jews and that Canadian policy makers enjoyed widespread public support for their determined restrictionism.[17]

Great Britain's policy, both for itself and for Palestine, was also restrictionist. There was, however, less of an anti-Semitic consensus in Britain than in Canada, and Britain took far more refugees in, particularly during the 1930s, as A. J. Sherman has demonstrated.[18] Looking at British retrenchment during the late 1930s and during the war, Bernard Wasserstein emphasized how higher national priorities—survival and military victory—interfered with refugee policy. All nations, Wasserstein argued, suffer paranoia when engaged in total war, and human imagination often fails when faced with a tragedy of enormous proportion. The "straitjacket of bureaucratic procedure" was itself an obstacle to unchaining humanitarian instincts to benefit Jewish refugees. If Prime Minister Winston Churchill could imagine the extent of the Nazi program of genocide, even that was not enough to overcome bureaucratic resistance.[19] The British experience represents the closest parallel to what occurred in the United States.

Although anti-Semitism was present in the United States, it was not so virulent or corrosive that it dictated the outcome of refugee policy throughout the Roosevelt era. The most unusual feature of American policy toward European Jewry was the fluctuation in government willingness to admit Jews into the United States and to take other steps on their behalf. Feingold mainly attributed "the vacillating, contradictory character of America's rescue activity to Roosevelt himself."[20] That is indeed part of the truth, but only detailed analysis of American political and bureaucratic processes can provide a full explanation of the fluctuations of American refugee policy. And only a study that includes an examination of Nazi policies against European Jewry can establish which American steps might have proved more effective in saving lives.

On January 30, 1933, Adolf Hitler became chancellor of Germany after a series of behind-the-scenes maneuvers. About six weeks later Franklin Delano Roosevelt, two-term governor of New York, took the oath of office as the thirty-second president of the United States. Adolf Hitler was to lead Germany and most of Europe into mobilization and war. FDR would inject confidence into a country bewildered by the collapse of its economy and would gradually extend American support to the foreign enemies of the Nazi regime. Hitler's persecution of political and "racial" enemies began almost immediately after he took power and increased in range and intensity throughout the 1930s. Eventually, he wielded the powers of a police state that terrorized much of the continent and killed millions of civilians whose only crime was their membership in a particular religious group or nationality. Roosevelt, however, was less responsive to the Holocaust than to the danger the Third Reich posed to the United States as a political and military opponent. That was in part because of substantial public and official opposition to providing haven for European victims of persecution to the United States.

The United States had an older tradition of serving as a refuge for European emigrants. Unlike any other country in the world, the United States was not only populated by immigrants; it was also a society that touted itself as a sanctuary for the world's "homeless, tempest-tost." It also possessed land, resources, and civic ideals embracing religious and political freedom. More than 2.5 million Jews had found a haven in the U.S. during the late nineteenth and early twentieth centuries.

The legend of the open or "golden" door was in some ways misleading, however. For a long time American sympathy for the victims of persecution and poverty abroad was expressed not through a positive immigration policy but through one of benign neglect. The vast expanse of the continent and the expanding industrial economy generally made immigrants seem an asset rather than a problem requiring legislative action. Even before the massive immigration from southern and eastern Europe peaked after the turn of the century, however, there were problems. As John Higham and other scholars have observed,[21] nativism was deeply rooted in the loam of American culture. The price of an open society democratically governed has been the recurrent fear of subversion by new arrivals unfamiliar with—and, therefore, possibly unappreciative of—republican ideals. Moreover, part of the white Anglo-Saxon Protestant majority that cast the mold for American values looked with suspicion upon racial and religious minorities already in the United States—blacks, Orientals, Roman Catholics, as well as Jews.

Government began to impose immigration restrictions upon nationalities: first, against the Chinese and Japanese but, later, after World War I, against Europeans as well. The era of mass immigration came to an abrupt halt. The visa system instituted at the end of the war and the new immigration laws of 1921 and 1924 established maximum annual levels of immigration from each European country (quotas) as well as various qualifications for immigrants. The overall yearly ceiling of quota immigrants was 153,774, in 1929, when the new quota system became fully operable. Western hemisphere countries were exempted from the quota system as were certain professionals whose skills were in short supply.

The Great Depression amplified demands for additional requirements and reductions. President Hoover and the State Department took a key step in 1930 without congressional authorization. The State Department was already using a provision of the 1917 Immigration Act to limit immigration from Mexico: any Mexican considered "likely to become a public charge," i.e., unable to support himself, was denied a visa. The public charge clause, first included in an 1882 law, was originally aimed at persons who lacked physical or mental skills required for constructive employment. But there was another way to interpret "likely to become a public charge"—anyone unlikely to obtain a job under current market conditions. In a September 1930 press release, President Hoover announced a new policy of rigorous enforcement of this LPC clause with regard to potential immigrants from Europe.[22] This Hoover barricade in front of the "golden door" was still in place when thousands of Jews began to seek escape from Nazi Germany in 1933.

The LPC clause was among the most potent of the devices that allowed the State Department, acting through American consuls and vice consuls abroad who issued visas to potential immigrants, to regulate the level of immigration administratively. Beginning in 1933 and continuing throughout the 1930s, government agencies and officials debated whether the Roosevelt administration should reverse Hoover's sharp cutback in immigration and whether it should offer special consideration to victims of Nazi persecution.

Congress might have acted on its own, or it might have turned back the administration's initiatives. It was eager to uncover misdeeds by an administration with a penchant for experimentation and extension of executive authority. But there were always divergent voices in Congress on immigration policy. Bills to reduce immigration were introduced, as were bills to increase immigration. They all were debated, shuttled off to committees, or defeated. Although the advocates of immigration restriction usually outnumbered the supporters of liberalization, Congress never actually intervened to pass new immigration laws. The numerous restrictionist voices on Capitol Hill, however, were audible at the White House.

Inertia was on the side of the restrictionists. But there were influential advocates of a positive refugee policy. In April 1933 Supreme Court Justice Louis Brandeis wrote to his friend and political confidant Felix Frankfurter, then a professor at Harvard Law School: "F.D. [Franklin Delano] has shown amply that he has no antisemitism. . . . But this action, or rather determination that there shall be none [i.e., no change in the Hoover immigration policy] is a disgrace to America and to F.D.'s administration."[23] Frankfurter himself, already an informal advisor to the president, professed to be slightly more optimistic about American assistance to those persecuted in Germany. He wrote to Secretary of Labor Frances Perkins on the same day: "My thanks for the memorandum concerning the treatment of political refugees. . . . I shall continue to refuse to believe that, alone of all Western Governments, this Administration will remain without public action or utterance in the face of such [Nazi] assault on the decencies of civilization."[24] Partly through the efforts of Frankfurter, Perkins, and similarly minded people, the number of Jewish refugees admitted to the United States gradually increased through the 1930s. But a new tightening of immigration rules and regulations in 1939–41, the result of wartime fears, reduced the flow of refugees to a trickle, precisely at the time when the Nazis began to practice mass murder against the Jews. The American cutback was in part a reaction to conscious German efforts to stimulate anti-Semitism abroad.

The tightly restrictionist phase of American policy did not change until late in the war. A good part of the reason has to do with bureaucracy. Even those who championed the cause of European Jews found themselves confined to the channels and bound by the procedures of the bureaucratic system. Bureaucracy, as Max Weber observed in a famous essay, was the *sine qua non* of the modern democratic state.[25] Bureaucracies follow precedents and usually restrict themselves to their assigned tasks. The two overriding concerns of the American government in the Roosevelt era were economic recovery and protection of the United States against a hostile fascist coalition. Lacking presidential or congressional backing for a positive refugee policy, few bureaucrats were willing to consider the rescue of persecuted foreigners as compatible with the defense of the national interest.

Our research makes clear that such figures as Assistant Secretaries of State Wilbur Carr, George Messersmith, Breckinridge Long, Commissioner of Immigration Daniel MacCormack, and many other officials at lower levels of authority devised and carried out adjustments to immigration regulations that had a major effect upon the level of immigration to the United States. Although some of these individuals may have been biased against Jews, we find that bureaucratic indifference to moral or humanitarian concerns was a more important obstacle to an active refugee policy.

President Roosevelt's most frequent role was in deciding not to alter the outcome of the bureaucratic process, although he had the power to do so. When he did intervene, he sometimes liberalized immigration policy (1938) but sometimes tightened it as well, particularly as war approached. Knowledge of the Holocaust did not force him to change his view. When several key Treasury Department officials revealed to FDR that American refugee policy had been disastrous, and that a political scandal might erupt, the president shifted course and established a War Refugee Board in January 1944. For the first time, the advocates of humanitarian action had a stronghold within the bureaucracy, and they used it effectively until the end of the war. But it came very late.

In all, just over 120,000 Germans and Austrians were admitted into the U.S. as immigrants between 1933 and 1944, the overwhelming majority (roughly 90 percent) of them Jews. When one takes into account Jewish immigration from other European countries as well as nonquota immigration and visitors, one arrives at a maximum figure of approximately 250,000 refugees from Nazism who entered the United States during those years.[26] The comparable figure for Great Britain, a far smaller country, is about 70,000; that for spacious Canada, however, is less than 5,000.[27] The American record was not the worst. But the United States failed to do even what its own immigration laws allowed. The overall annual quota (153,774) was never filled during this period; immigration never exceeded 54 percent of the quota. Even the quota of 25,957 for Germany was rarely filled. This was not because of lack of demand for immigration visas. Responsible historians estimate that approximately 6 million Jews died in the Holocaust, and many hundreds of thousands of those had applied for American visas even before the outbreak of World War II.

Conscious decisions to apply regulations in a manner to reduce immigration held the flow well below what the quota laws allowed.

It might be neater, and somehow more reassuring, to find simply that anti-Semites within the government and among the public prevented effective American response to the plight of European Jewry. The same political virus that infected Europe would, in milder form, then be responsible for American passivity in the face of the Holocaust. The substantial decline in anti-Semitism since World War II, particularly in the United States, would then suggest that the western democratic countries are better situated and more disposed to act to prevent future calamities of similar nature. Our findings suggest, however, that even in the absence of anti-Semitism, humanitarian considerations are not easily translated into government policy. Official indifference to suffering in faraway lands and unwillingness to take responsibility for persons whose care might require tax dollars is still with us in the 1980s. We hope that our study will help clarify the tension between humanitarian principles and national interest which may develop in times of crisis.

ONE

The Labor Department's Initiative

The new Democratic administration announced a $2 billion relief program for the millions of unemployed workers, and the House of Representatives voted to legalize 3.2 percent beer. The stock exchanges and the banks were still closed after a government-ordered holiday, caused by a run on the banks, but they were about to open again. The president and secretary of agriculture, only ten days after the presidential inauguration, were still working out modifications of an emergency farm relief bill, trying to avoid putting the government in the farm business. The administration also announced that it would ask Congress for authority to declare arms embargoes to any parts of the world where war threatened. This, according to the *New York Times* of the next day, was the major news on a very busy March 14, 1933.

Readers of the *Times* interested enough in foreign affairs to look hard could have learned that Adolf Hitler's government in Germany was prepared to "steam roller" its program through the newly elected parliaments, with the opposition fatally weakened by arrests and repression, and that the director of the Berlin Civic Opera, a prominent Social Democrat, had been removed from his post. But there was no sign that the president of the United States had taken any particular interest in German developments.

On that same day, Judge Irving Lehman talked with his old friend, now President Franklin Delano Roosevelt. A judge on the New York State Court of Appeals, brother to the New York governor Herbert Lehman, and activist in New York Democratic politics, Lehman wanted to raise the issue of what the United States might do about the troubling German situation. The new Nazi government, which had taken power a month and a half earlier, had wasted no time in arresting political opponents and making life more difficult for German Jews, whatever their political allegiance. For Adolf Hitler was convinced that Jews were a threat to the racial and cultural integrity of the German people. Just what Nazi ideology would lead to was unclear in early 1933, but a growing number of German Jews did not want to wait around to find out. Some of those who had read *Mein Kempf* and took Hitler's words seriously were ready to abandon their homes and start life anew elsewhere.

Lehman specifically wanted the United States government to demonstrate its sympathy for the persecuted. He asked the president to modify Herbert Hoover's 1930 order which had tightened enforcement of the clause in the immigration laws that barred anyone likely to become a public charge. Hoover had decided that, in time of massive depression, virtually any immigrant who needed to work for a living was likely to become a public charge. Lehman now wanted Roosevelt to allow increased German immigration to the United States.[1] Lehman's request was in one sense poorly timed; the last thing Franklin Roosevelt needed was more competitors for the dwindling supply of American jobs. From a purely political point of view, there was little or nothing to be gained from presidential intervention—and great risks involved in liberalizing immigration. Apart from noting the obvious risks, the president almost certainly knew little about the visa situation in March 1933. That would change in the course of the year. Judge Lehman, joined by executives of the American Jewish Committee and B'nai B'rith, then tried to persuade Secretary of State Cordell Hull to make additional visas available for German Jews, but their efforts brought no immediate results.[2]

On April 1, 1933, the Nazis carried out a one-day boycott of Jewish businesses throughout the country. Six days later came a new German civil service law, issued by decree, dismissing virtually all civil servants "not of Aryan descent." Unorganized acts of brutality were giving way to officially sanctioned measures against German Jews. Since the German civil service included the schools and universities, a great many distinguished professors of Jewish faith or descent were suddenly without positions.

Perhaps President Roosevelt was notified of Hitler's new move against German Jews, or perhaps it simply took some time for Lehman's arguments to take effect. In any case, on April 7, Roosevelt apparently raised in cabinet the idea of admitting to the United States a small number of prominent individuals whom the Nazis were persecuting as a "moral gesture." Although the evidence is fragmentary, it is clear that the cabinet took up the issue. One second-hand account reported Cordell Hull agreeing with this action. FDR referred this matter to Frances Perkins, the new secretary of labor, and to Hull, the new secretary of state, for investigation and recommendations. Perkins quickly took up the issue and made it her cause.[3]

The first female American cabinet member in history already had plenty to do in the spring of 1933. Her priorities had little to do with immigration; public works, minimum wage, maximum hours, unemployment insurance, and other welfare measures were part of her strategy to combat the effects of the depression.[4] Even in the field of immigration there were serious problems closer to home. She had discovered that her predecessor had left the Bureau of Immigration rife with corruption and prone to abusive treatment of aliens. Perkins's attitude toward immigrants, formed during her years as a settlement worker and as executive secretary of the Council on Immigrant Education, was positive and sympathetic. She also took a broad view of her responsibilities as a government official and human being. If it was legally permissible to modify

American immigration policy to mitigate the suffering of thousands in Germany, Perkins wanted to do something.

For advice and assistance, she turned to Felix Frankfurter, an old ally from her days with the New York Consumers League. More important, Frankfurter was also serving as an unofficial advisor to Roosevelt and recruiter of bright young talent to administer the New Deal. Never reluctant to give his views on political issues, Frankfurter was highly indignant about Nazi persecution of Jews and political opponents and was most eager to bring about changes in American immigration regulations that would benefit German refugees. He had also done some research on immigration laws and procedures.

Frankfurter drafted for Perkins two executive orders to be sent to FDR, either one of which would have helped German Jews to qualify for American visas. The first version directed the secretary of state to instruct American consuls abroad to enforce immigration laws and regulations in the manner applied prior to the Hoover modification of September 8, 1930—but only in those cases where visa applicants were seeking admission to the United States to avoid racial or religious persecution. In effect, this order would have selectively breached the "likely to become a public charge" (LPC) barrier. In case the president wished to avoid any reference to the LPC provision, Frankfurter drafted a second, alternative order that simply and directly gave precedence to visa applicants seeking to avoid racial or religious persecution in the country of their last permanent residence. He sent the two drafts to Perkins and communicated their substance to FDR himself. Frankfurter explained to Assistant Secretary of State Raymond Moley that there was no danger that these changes would lead to mass immigration to the United States and that they in no way constituted interference with Germany's domestic policies.[5]

Frances Perkins carried out her own investigation. Immigration expert Harold Fields told her that through an executive order the U.S. could admit German Jews even if they lacked German passports.[6] This measure would have prevented the German government from blocking the emigration of Jews. Perkins also consulted the Conference on Immigration Policy, a private organization of immigration experts based in New York, which postponed its general meeting and instead held a special luncheon at the Women's University Club for the secretary of labor. The event, in the words of the conference's chairman, was "small, informal, and entirely free from [the] dangers of publicity."

Although the Conference on Immigration Policy had a reputation for favoring liberal immigration policy, the majority of the executive board could not overlook the disastrous economic situation in the United States. Under these circumstances, the board concluded, enforcement of the Hoover executive order, which had reduced immigration sharply in late 1930, was still advisable. Some minor changes might alleviate the worst hardships of the 1930 measure. Spouses, minor children, or parents of current U.S. residents should be treated more leniently if they applied for immigration visas. The conference also suggested a check on the American consul abroad who had to make sensitive visa decisions; a visa applicant should have a right to appeal in cases where an American resident had expressed willingness to support a relative applying for a visa but the consul had denied the visa on LPC grounds.[7]

Frankfurter's proposals would have helped German Jewish refugees to enter the United States; the conference's suggestions would have aided relatives of U.S. citizens and resident aliens. There was undoubtedly some overlap between these two proposals, but each was aimed at an essentially different group. The one common feature of the two recommendations was their implicit criticism and modification of existing State Department policy.

Perkins preferred Frankfurter's position. At the cabinet meeting of April 18, she advocated an executive order on behalf of German Jews. Secretary of State Hull objected; a State Department committee had not yet reached any decision. But the following day someone from the White House telephoned State and asked why it had not sent over the appropriate executive order. Undersecretary of State William Phillips, an old acquaintance of FDR, told the president that such action would be a mistake. He may have referred to likely opposition from the American Federation of Labor, which had already been antagonized by Perkins's appointment, to any increase in immigration.[8] After some discussion, FDR agreed that, since the German quota remained unfilled, there was no need for any action on behalf of refugees. Anyone meeting the qualifications for an American visa could get one in Germany. Phillips agreed to call Perkins and explain the situation.

By now familiar with immigration laws and regulations, Perkins totally rejected Phillips's argument. The problem was not the availability of quota numbers but the strict 1930 interpretation of what constituted likelihood to become a public charge, which prevented a very high percentage of applicants from qualifying, even though the quota was unfilled. Perkins told Phillips that it was in accordance with American traditions and policy to offer entry to refugees of all forms of persecution. Whether it was agreeable to the AFL or whether it would affect American economic conditions was a matter for her to decide, not for the State Department, which should concern itself only with the impact upon foreign relations. Perkins continued as follows, according to the diary of Jay Pierrepont Moffat, chief of the Division of Western European Affairs:

> She said that she was going to press for an immediate decision and if she did not get favorable action by the Administration within a day or two, there would be unleashed upon us [the State Department] the most formidable instance of Jewish pressure. In fact, she quite blew our poor Under Secretary off his end of the telephone.[9]

Perkins may not have spent a great deal of time on immigration issues,[10] but she certainly did not hesitate to press her views.

Perhaps Perkins attacked Phillips sharply because she had learned that State

Department officials in 1930 had orally instructed consuls in Germany to reduce the number of immigration visas issued to 10 percent of the quota levels. (Charles E. Wyzanski, the new solicitor in the Labor Department, heard about the 10 percent guideline during 1933;[11] one may assume that Perkins learned about it as well.) This instruction not only subverted the intent of the Immigration Act of 1924 but also infringed on the role of the Bureau of Immigration, which was now Perkins's territory. In any case, Phillips's argument to FDR that the availability of quota numbers made any action unnecessary was clearly specious.

Alerted to a serious clash between State and Labor, the White House decided to take a look at the evidence itself. On April 20, presidential press secretary Stephen Early called the assistant solicitor of labor and asked for copies of the relevant immigration laws, regulations, and instructions to consuls. Labor quickly complied. Meanwhile, the State Department brought in its own troops to shore up the 1930 ruling. Moffat and A. Dana Hodgdon, chief of the Visa Division, discovered that Woodrow Wilson, in his veto of the 1917 Immigration Act, had stressed the danger to American foreign policy posed by American consuls trying to determine whether or not persecution existed in a foreign country.[12] Assistant Secretary of State Carr used this ammunition in drafting a long memorandum on "the problem of aliens seeking relief in Germany." To grant asylum to aliens subject to religious or political persecution might raise very serious problems of "international justice and comity" between the U.S. and Germany. In other words, the State Department had a responsibility to protect American interests, which meant to abstain from determining whether Germany was persecuting any group of its citizens. (Carr did not mention that Congress had overridden Wilson's veto and included a section exempting refugees from religious persecution from the literacy requirement in the 1917 Immigration Act.) Carr also pointed out that the 1930 LPC standard had prevented approximately one-half million aliens from entering the U.S. at a time when there were twelve million citizens unemployed. Invited to appear at the cabinet meeting of April 21, Carr apparently made effective use of these arguments.[13]

Since cabinet minutes were not kept in the Roosevelt administration, we know only the results—and even there accounts differ. Hull told Carr that Perkins "backed off completely."[14] Perkins wrote to Frankfurter that there was

> no disposition to issue a public statement [executive order regarding refugees]. . . . Confidentially, the Consuls, however, will be instructed to interpret liberally, in cases of this group of people, the provisions of the State Department rule that they are not to issue visas to persons likely to become public charges, and that they are to be liberal also with regard to temporary visitors' visas.

Frankfurter was dissatisfied with this compromise, partly because the administration was unwilling to make a public statement condemning the Nazis, partly because the Nazis were persecuting Jews regardless of their politics.[15] German Jews were not precisely "political" refugees under these circumstances; they were innocent victims of a regime committed to racist doctrines.

Perkins soon turned the refugee issue over to her new commissioner of immigration, Colonel Daniel MacCormack. MacCormack had no previous professional contact with immigration matters, but he did have personal experience. He had been born in Scotland and had come to the U.S. with his parents when he was nine. He had served as an administrator on the Panama Canal construction project, worked as the head of the American Finance Mission to Persia from 1922 to 1927, and moved up the hierarchy of the Fiduciary Trust Company of New York, where he had become president. By 1933 he was out of sympathy with some of the bank's activities and was looking for new vistas. He called Perkins to seek an appointment. Perkins recognized that this man, known for his integrity, administrative competence, and willingness to do public service, might be exactly what was needed for the Bureaus of Immigration and Naturalization, which were badly in need of reorganization and reform. Even though MacCormack lacked political connections and the job normally went to a political appointee, Perkins persuaded FDR to go along.[16]

MacCormack quickly found on his desk a number of requests to relax immigration requirements to permit the admission of German Jews. He concluded that, if the U.S. granted them temporary admission (visitors' visas), there was little likelihood that they would later wish to return to Germany to face persecution. Unless the U.S. forced them to go back, which seemed politically impossible, temporary admission would become permanent admission. That would be a subterfuge of immigration regulations which he did not want to have any part of.

Eliminating visitors' visas as an option, MacCormack went back to immigration visas and to the LPC clause. Taking note of the high percentage of professionals among German Jews and of the difficulties they would have entering overcrowded professions in the United States, MacCormack questioned whether these people would be better off during the depression in the U.S. than they were in Germany.[17] At the time MacCormack expressed these thoughts (June 1933), physical violence against German Jews had abated, and official action was largely confined to economic and social restrictions. It is also worth noting that Charles Wyzanski considered MacCormack "as open-minded a man on immigration issues as one could find then in public life."[18] His views were not a rationalization of personal prejudice. Rather, they represent a telling illustration of just how difficult it was for most Americans to grasp what was taking place and what was to come in Nazi Germany.

Later that summer MacCormack indicated to an inquirer that, to the best of his knowledge, no serious consideration had been given to changing the 1930 LPC interpretation. But he noted that the State Department could relax regulations if it wished to. The only action Labor could take on its own was to extend the visitors' visas of those German Jews already in the U.S., which was being done. MacCormack suggested, however, that the new American ambassador to Germany, William Dodd, might wish to make a report and recommendations on the need for American action to aid German Jews.[19] This would effectively leave the matter to the State Department. Perkins was still expecting prompt action. She asked MacCormack to discuss with the State Department lifting the monthly restriction within the German quota, so that a larger percentage of the quota would be available in the next few months, "when the professors and others begin to come over."[20] Perkins still expected FDR's "moral gesture" to bring a substantial number of intellectuals to the United States. But was State willing to cooperate?

The State Department made one gesture at compromise with Perkins. The head of the Visa Division, A. Dana Hodgdon, had become convinced that some consuls might indeed be applying the regulations too stringently in cases where American citizens had vouched financially for visa applicants who were relatives. What made the issue pressing was that a number of congressmen had become interested in cases of this sort, and Congress was considering a bill to institute an appeals procedure when consuls denied visas to relatives of American citizens or resident aliens. Hodgdon felt that it was very important to avoid such legislation, (particularly if the appeal were to go to the secretary of labor). Therefore, in early July 1933 the Visa Division issued a new instruction to consuls on "public charge provisions of the law." American consuls abroad were informed that U.S. citizens and resident aliens had natural and perhaps legal obligations to prevent their immediate relatives from becoming public charges. Consequently, the LPC clause should not be applied stringently in such cases; the criterion was whether the U.S. relative was willing and able to provide sufficient financial support. In the case of more distant relatives, however, consuls were told that they would have to judge not only the financial resources of the U.S. resident but also whether the resident was likely to provide support for the alien relative if it became necessary. Aliens without a relative's affidavit or without independent means would still fall victim to the LPC barrier.[21] By admitting those refugees with close relatives already in the United States, State Department officials apparently hoped that they would dampen criticism of immigration policy. But such a measure would not aid either political refugees or German Jews unless they already had close relatives in America willing and able to cooperate.

Another barrier to prospective German Jewish immigrants was red tape. Section 7c of the Immigration Act of 1924 required each applicant to submit, "if available," two copies of his police dossier, prison record, and military record, two certified copies of his birth certificate, and two copies of other available government records concerning him by the government to which he owed allegiance. To extract such a mass of material from German government offices quickly would have been difficult in ordinary times. It was even more so for German Jews under the Nazi regime and quite unmanageable for those who had already fled to temporary havens outside of Germany. Yet the State Department was unwilling to waive the documents requirement entirely because of the danger that those with serious criminal records might slip through and emigrate to the U.S. The department instead requested that consuls provide special consideration and "the most favorable treatment permissible under the law" for those experiencing difficulty in obtaining the documents required in American visa applications.[22]

These limited State Department moves did not satisfy American Jewish representatives, who turned to their friends within Roosevelt's inner circle. Henry Morgenthau, Jr., friend and Dutchess County neighbor of FDR and soon to become secretary of the treasury, arranged for a confidential meeting between Judge Irving Lehman and FDR on September 14 regarding the German Jewish situation. Morgenthau accompanied Lehman to the White House. According to Lehman's report of the meeting, his discussion with FDR was wide-ranging and highly satisfactory. The president noted that he had received two letters from the new American ambassador in Berlin, William Dodd, and that both Dodd and Consul General George Messersmith—the source of most of Dodd's information about the Nazi regime—were angry at the Nazi government. FDR said that he shared the feeling. Lehman raised the issue of an American Jewish boycott of German goods but said he personally was opposed to an exclusively Jewish action. FDR agreed that any boycott should enlist non-Jewish support. Lehman made two requests of the president. The judge wanted a presidential statement about the tragic condition of the Jews in Germany, which would help enlist non-Jewish support, and he asked for help on the outstanding points of dispute on visa questions. FDR cautioned that any presidential statement had to avoid the appearance that it represented interference in internal German affairs and suggested that something about denial of human rights in Germany would be preferable to a statement specifically focused on the plight of German Jews. FDR agreed to arrange a conference among Jewish delegates, the State Department experts, and Labor Department representatives.[23]

The presidential statement never materialized. Although he arranged the meeting on visa regulations, which took place six days later, FDR specifically informed his aides that he did not wish to be present. Retired Judge Joseph Proskauer of New York, a leading member of the American Jewish Committee, called upon the State Department to soften the 1930 interpretation of the LPC clause. Judge Julian W. Mack of New York, a man with wide experience in immigration matters, had found a long-overlooked provision of the 1917 Immigration Act that allowed the secretary of labor to accept a bond as a guarantee that a potential immigrant would not become a public charge. Once such a bond had been posted and accepted by the secretary of labor, then the consuls could not bar applicants on the grounds that they would likely become public charges. Proskauer now sought to begin use of this procedure. He also urged the State Department to waive the documents requirement whenever an applicant could satisfactorily explain why documents could not be obtained.[24]

Perkins and MacCormack had mixed reactions. They questioned whether the bonding procedure, already contained in Section 21 of the Immigration Act of 1917, was intended to cover more than occasional hardship cases. MacCormack feared that there might be wholesale bonding for German refugees and others and that the effect of a substantial increase in immigration would be detrimental. Eventually they agreed that the procedure might be used to admit aged persons and children—those who would not compete on the American labor market. By one account, MacCormack estimated that 4,000 refugees might be admitted in fiscal 1934. Perkins took the responsibility upon herself as long as the bonding procedure was found legal. The State Department representatives—Undersecretary William Phillips and Hodgdon, the Visa Division Chief—put up resistance and urged a delay.[25]

During October 1933 the two departments continued to diverge. After a delegation of Jewish judges met with Perkins, she asked Charles Wyzanski, Labor Department solicitor, to work on a plan to admit German Jews to the United States. Perkins believed that the country could absorb more Jewish immigrants without difficulty, except on the Eastern Seaboard.[26] When Judge Mack, serving as liaison to the American Jewish organizations, conferred with Phillips, Carr, Hodgdon, and MacCormack at the end of the month, the State Department was ready to consult the attorney general about the disputed bonding procedure. Although Mack pressed for an arrangement that would benefit "political and religious refugees," Hodgdon argued that this would be giving a certain class undue preference. MacCormack, who apparently had not made up his mind whether to make such a classification, limited himself to the comment that it was a matter solely within Labor's jurisdiction. All of the government officials, according to Mack, feared that liberalization of the regulations would not only increase anti-Semitism but might also provoke Congress to reduce the quotas by 90 percent. MacCormack noted that the American Federation of Labor had already warned against any change in the regulations. Mack responded that a public statement by the president might well prevent hostile action by Congress and swing public opinion around.

MacCormack then invited Mack to lunch to explain his own position more fully. Describing himself as a pro-Semite and a liberal, the commissioner of immigration said:

> ... he had travelled throughout the Middlewest, the Atlantic states and New England and had had many talks with many non-Jewish liberals. He said not only had he not heard and seen one express himself as favorable to the admission of refugees, but that a number had expressed themselves against it. He believes that the sentiment of the country as a whole is overwhelmingly against any relaxation and he had not the slightest doubt that if the Germany quota were filled during these times of depressions and especially if it were filled largely by Jewish refugees, nothing could stop Congressional action against it. He emphasized again and again that he was reporting to me facts, that he had no sympathy with this position, but that it is important that we appreciate this factual situation. . . .
> The second point that he wanted to impress on me was the serious mistake of

continually emphasizing the Jewish side instead of from the beginning getting liberal-minded non-Jews to emphasize the liberal side affecting Jews and non-Jews alike.[27]

Mack apparently took MacCormack's warning to heart. That same afternoon he told Wyzanski that he was anxious to keep the issue out of Congress.[28]

Eventually State and Labor officials pared down their differences. They agreed that consuls could consider a person's documents unavailable when they could be obtained "only at the serious risk of inconvenience, personal injury, financial loss, or the peculiar delay and embarrassment that might attend the request of a political or religious refugee to his former government." But the State Department continued to object to a bonding procedure that would allow the secretary of labor to prevent consuls from declaring an applicant likely to become a public charge, particularly if the procedure was to be used exclusively for refugees.[29]

The disagreement over public charge bonds led to a most unusual legal battle between two branches of government, conducted entirely behind the scenes. Richard W. Flournoy, a patrician Virginian who was legal counsel in the State Department, wrote an opinion that expanded upon the meaning of "likely to become a public charge." Flournoy argued that this was more than a financial criterion; those with criminal tendencies (even if they had no criminal record), moral deficiencies, and mental abnormalities would also be vulnerable and might be disqualified for visas. Only the American consul abroad could carry out an investigation thorough enough to uncover these liabilities.

> In many cases the consul's finding would be based principally upon the mental or physical characteristics of the alien applicant, brought out upon a personal examination and interrogation. . . .

If the secretary of labor had the right to prevent a consul from declaring an applicant a potential public charge, the United States would lose a major safety device. The secretary of labor's power to accept a public charge bond, Flournoy concluded, should be used only on behalf of those immigrants who arrived at American ports with visas—those whom the consuls had already cleared.[30]

Wyzanski, at twenty-seven the improbably young solicitor of labor, wrote the Labor Department's case. He traced the history of public charge bonds and demonstrated that they had been used before for visa applicants. He pointed out that there was nothing in the language of the law that expressly or implicitly limited use of the secretary of labor's discretionary power to accept a bond as a guarantee for those who had already reached American ports (i.e., already received visas). Finally, Wyzanski confronted the political problem as well; the secretary could not admit anyone she pleased but only applicants otherwise admissible. She was not required to accept public charge bonds for applicants; she did so at her discretion. If she made extensive use of her power, Congress could intervene. In short, public charge bonds were not likely to create a flood of immigrants.[31]

After finishing this opinion, Wyanski wrote to his parents:

> The problem is highly technical and in some ways it is easier to say it can't be done than it can. At any rate I have had an uphill fight with my own Assistant Solicitor. . . . I have done my best not to let my emotions sway me, and in this I hope I have been more successful not only than my own co-religionists but the State Department bureaucrats. I have, however, finally concluded that a method of admission for 25,000 refugees (I hope non-Jews as well as Jews) can be satisfactorily worked out.

Wyzanski showed the opinion to Judge Mack, who called it a good job, "though too long for a *judicial* opinion."[32]

Wyzanski gave his opinion to Perkins, who (presumably with some satisfaction) sent it to the president. Whether by prior decision of the two departments or by FDR's own choice,[33] Attorney General Homer Cummings was asked to adjudicate. Cummings turned the matter over to his assistant, Alexander Holtzhoff, who found Wyzanski's interpretation entirely convincing. The formal opinion signed by the attorney general on December 26 referred to the "excellent memorandum prepared by your Solicitor" and authorized Perkins to proceed.[34] Labor had won the legal battle.

When the attorney general's decision arrived, the Visa Division of the State Department threatened to join the effort to reduce the quotas through legislation. One division official, C. Paul Fletcher wrote:

> It now seems that only by quota reduction can the 600,000 Jews in Germany and the 60,000 in France seeking so-called religious refuge be prevented from entering the United States. At the moment the people of the United States are apathetic in immigration matters; they are completely occupied with economic problems. Nevertheless, they look to us to protect their rights, and if ships begin to arrive in New York City laden with Jewish immigrants, the predominant Gentile population of the country will claim they have been betrayed through a "sleeping" State Department.

This comment and hostile ones by other division officials reveal fears that the attorney general's decision had ruptured the dike erected to hold back immigration generally and that an influx of Jewish refugees would be particularly unpopular.[35]

The attorney general's ruling was not the only threat to the State Department. Immigration inspectors were also turning up evidence of unfair application of the LPC clause. MacCormack soon notified Perkins that consuls had transformed the meaning of the LPC clause; if there were a remote possibility that a visa applicant could become a public charge sometime in the future, he was barred. The State Department was at fault, because it had proclaimed a restrictionist move, left the consuls without specific standards, and engendered a competitive spirit to refuse as many applicants as possible. The American consulates in Europe, in particular, discouraged prospective applicants from filing for visas (thereby invalidating American statistics on the percentage of applicants refused visas) and in some cases (e.g., Germany) limited visas to only 10 percent of the quota. All in all, MacCormack concluded, "the present application of the LPC clause is in effect amending the immigration law by administrative fiat. In operation, it is intended to restrict immigration and does so with little regard to whether the alien is actually likely to become a public charge."[36] That was all the more reason for the new bonding arrangement.

Following the attorney general's ruling on December 26, nothing changed immediately. Perkins and MacCormack both were out of town for the holidays. After their return, on January 9, Attorney General Cummings asked Perkins if she had any objection to publication of the decision on the public charge bond. Perkins consulted Wyzanski, who found himself torn. Publication would make the decision binding upon subsequent officeholders and upon the consuls. On the other hand, publication might also bring a wave of publicity against the decision and against the Labor Department. (Although the newspapers initially had only brief pieces on the public charge decision, the Labor Department was already flooded with protests.) In the end, Wyzanski advised going ahead if only not to reveal that Labor, which had sponsored the bonds, was opposed to publicity.[37]

Perkins wanted to push right ahead and entertain applications for bonds up to the limit of the German quota—25,957. She told Wyzanski on January 11 that the United States should do something for those who were suffering, that immigrants had made important contributions before, and that an increase in consumer demand would help the economy. Wyzanski urged her to consult with the president and the cabinet and to exercise judgment and selectivity in accepting the bonds. In part he was concerned about an increasing wave of anti-Semitism that might damage the position of American Jews. He also feared that the president might be damaged politically, especially if he made a public statement about the new policy.[38]

Perkins notified the cabinet the next afternoon of the attorney general's decision and the Labor Department's proposed use of public charge bonds. Beyond her handwritten note that Secretary of State Hull was not present (the State Department was apparently represented by William Phillips), there is no record of what transpired.[39] Judging from subsequent events, Perkins may have been told not to go too far. In a public speech to the Hebrew Immigrant Aid Society on February 4, Wyzanski also stated his personal belief that public charge bonds should not be used on a scale large enough to weaken the restrictionist policy of the United States. He soon recommended to Perkins a limit of 500 immigrants per month from Germany, with no more than half of those using public charge bonds. That would have meant an annual immigration from Germany of about 6,000. In fiscal 1933 only some 1,300 applicants had received immigration visas under the German quota.[40]

Judge Mack continued to press for a presidential statement regarding Jewish refugees in conjunction with the issuance of new regulations. But Wyzanski feared that presidential action would further arouse hostile elements in Congress, the Ku Klux Klan, the AFL, and other restrictionists. As a result, the administration's hands would be tied, and the president would be damaged politically. Restrictionist groups were already becoming a problem for the Labor Department. At the end of January the American Coalition of Patriotic Societies adopted resolutions in favor of continuing restriction and announced to the press that Perkins was not in sympathy with the policy of Congress and the United States.[41]

Wyzanski was not the only one worried about the political repercussions of publicity. When a journalist named Edwin Mims had earlier showed Judge Mack the proofs of his forthcoming article for *Today* magazine, "German Refugees and American Bureaucrats," Mack was taken aback. The piece delivered a loud warning to "Old Deal" bureaucrats in the State Department to adapt themselves to the spirit and ways of the New Deal—specifically, to the attorney general's ruling on public charge bonds. It contained sharp criticism of past State Department and consular visa decisions. Even though Sims claimed that Perkins had read the article and approved of it, and even though he implied that FDR had done so as well, Mack advised against publication on the ground that a "red hot diatribe" would do more harm than good.[42]

Commissioner MacCormack, too, was concerned about publicity. He was initially inclined to limit public charge bonds to perhaps 5,000 cases involving children, the elderly, and persons whose skills were in short supply.[43] But, even as he criticized State Department visa policy, MacCormack wanted to avoid brusque assertion of Labor's authority to accept public charge bonds. He preferred a solution satisfactory to both State and Labor. He again noted the strong opinion in Congress and in the country against relaxation of immigration restrictions and foresaw an increase in anti-Semitism if a large number of Jews were admitted.

MacCormack faced an additional problem. He was about to propose new legislation giving Labor discretionary power not to deport those aliens committing minor offenses and to convert resident aliens to permanent status. (More than 2,000 aliens of good character who had committed technical violations of immigration laws faced mandatory deportation.) In MacCormack's words, "if before this program is presented to Congress we have acted in a manner that they consider contrary to the congressional power on immigration, we will endanger the success of our program."[44]

Thus, MacCormack held off on any decision on the bonding procedure, even after State Department officials proclaimed themselves ready to transmit a new instruction to consuls and even after Judge Mack submitted detailed proposals.[45] In April 1934 a number of immigration experts from Jewish organizations conferred with MacCormack on a program to bring 250 German Jewish children to the United States with the use of public charge bonds. The commissioner asked the group to refrain from any action and from publicity until June, by which time he would have presented his legislative program to Congress. The American Civil Liberties Union repeatedly solicited without success information about when the new instruction regarding public charge bonds would take effect.[46]

MacCormack meanwhile sent out peace signals to the State Department. In a discussion with Wilbur Carr regarding pending legislation, the colonel said that Labor might be willing to agree to a 40 percent reduction of the quotas. He also claimed that he had considered a new formula for reducing immigration but had been unable to find one better than the LPC arrangement.[47] The well-informed Joseph Chamberlain, professor at Columbia University, explained the situation to League of Nations High Commissioner on Refugees James G. McDonald:

> At the last session of the American Congress there was strong opposition to allowing any refugees to come to this country, and while I think the economic reasons were the strongest, there were nevertheless some outcries based on racial ground. The Bureau of Immigration was really alarmed over the demonstration, and is nervous over the possibilities of difficulty being made by the A.F. of L., so that they are treading very cautiously in respect to allowing immigrants to enter. This has been apparent in the negotiations for the admission of the small number of German children. . . .

Both Chamberlain and MacCormack were said to be anxious to keep the arrangements for the 250 children as confidential as possible.[48]

Public willingness to accept aliens into the United States declined sharply during the summer of 1934. One major reason was the San Francisco longshoremen's strike, organized by Harry Bridges, an Australian with leftist views whom the San Francisco press denounced as a communist. Beginning on May 9, the strike expanded to other West Coast ports and, after a clash between strikers and police in which two men were killed, into a general strike throughout the Bay City. Secretary of State Hull and Attorney General Cummings wanted to send in federal troops, but Perkins successfully argued that the strike would die down soon and that presidential intervention carried risks. In the midst of the tumult, General Hugh R. Johnson, the intemperate head of the National Recovery Administration, gave a number of inflammatory speeches in California, helping to stimulate vigilante actions against communists and suspected communists and trampling on the Labor Department's cautious advocacy of immigration and naturalization reform. Johnson told a Los Angeles audience:

> I think it is about time for an America First campaign on this subject. I do not know the accuracy of the statement and I have no means to check it, but it has been

said to me . . . that if the jobs of aliens and non-declarants were given to citizens and the former were deported, the unemployment and destitution problems of the United States would be reduced by at least one-third.[49]

Newspaper magnate William Randolph Hearst and William Green of the AFL quickly demanded widespread deportations, and Perkins came under widespread criticism for her failure to deport troublesome aliens such as Bridges. Back in Washington, Wyzanski feared that this was the beginning of a "wave of hysterical hate" of the foreign born and the descendants of the foreign born.[50] It was not a propitious moment to be advocating liberalization of immigration regulations.

By late summer State Department officials heard through the grapevine that MacCormack had backed away from the use of public charge bonds because of criticism by the AFL. Even the 250 children were to be admitted without the use of bonds, although the State Department forced the Labor Department to take responsibility for the arrangement nonetheless. The first ten children arrived in New York on November 9, 1934, accompanied by considerable publicity, a good deal of it negative. Contributing to the problem, in the eyes of one observer, was a public statement by the American Jewish Congress that 20,000 children were to be brought over. In any case, John B. Trevor, chairman of the American Coalition of Patriotic Societies, officially called for a congressional investigation of violation of the law on the part of the Labor Department and unofficially spread the rumor that the children were from communist families. German Jewish Children's Aid had other problems, too. The number of American families willing to take the children in was far below expectations. In the end, only about 200 children were placed, and the program was suspended after one year. It was not resumed until 1937.[51]

In the meantime, State and Labor had both advised Congress that there was no need to cut the quotas. The House Immigration Committee declined to send any of six proposed immigration reduction measures to the floor of the House, and the number of immigrants from Germany increased from some 1,300 in fiscal 1933 to more than 4,000 in fiscal 1934.[52] According to one report, MacCormack boasted that Labor's pressure upon the State Department to be more lenient in enforcing the LPC clause was the key factor in the increase.[53] MacCormack had obtained much of his objective without use of the politically risky bond arrangement. He was quite reluctant to go any farther in this direction. He cautioned one Jewish congregation that calls for liberalization of immigration laws might actually backfire and produce cuts in the quotas. On another occasion he suggested that Jews fill no more than 40 percent of the German quota. In fact, MacCormack even asked the Committee on German-Jewish Immigration Policy, an outgrowth of the 1933 battle over public charge bonds, whether it would support the Dies bill in 1935, which mandated a 60 percent reduction of the quotas. Rejecting the argument that there might otherwise be even more severe legislation, the Jewish immigration experts declined.[54]

American Jewish immigration experts, most of whom agreed that Congress was more likely to hurt than help,[55] nonetheless found the rate of progress unsatisfactory. Prompted by statistics indicating a slight decline in German Jewish immigration in mid-1935, the revived Committee on German Jewish Immigration Policy decided to try to reach high State and Labor Department authorities and the president. But the members all agreed that they should try not to antagonize the patriotic organizations and the labor unions.[56]

This constraint dictated quiet pressure. Perkins agreed that more German Jewish refugees should be admitted.[57] At a meeting about the immigration situation in June 1935, Judge Mack asked Commissioner MacCormack what had happened to the bond procedure, which had not been used despite the attorney general's decision eighteen months before. MacCormack replied that there had been no need for the bonds, since, as far as Labor knew, visa cases were now being resolved favorably. But Cecilia Razovsky, immigration specialist for the National Council of Jewish Women, made it quite clear that MacCormack was simply uninformed of the many visa rejections still occurring. The commissioner then explained his political difficulties. Labor was still pushing for reform of naturalization and deportation procedures in the form of the Kerr-Coolidge Bill then before Congress. MacCormack regarded this bill as so important that he was unwilling to take any other action that might be detrimental to its passage. He pointed out that a whole bloc of southern congressmen would oppose any immigration measure that would benefit Jews. With the State Department fighting every liberalization of immigration regulations and forcing Labor to take responsibility for them, MacCormack could not afford to strengthen prejudices against Labor, against Perkins, and against himself held by southern congressmen and patriotic organizations. He advised the Jewish leaders to exert their own pressure on the State Department, which was the real obstacle to progress. He suggested that they cite specific cases of injustice or illegality to State and that they exploit State's sensitivity to unfavorable newspaper stories.[58] The Jewish representatives had little choice but to follow this line, but the difficulties with State's visa policy persisted until late 1936.

The Kerr-Coolidge Bill to reform deportation and naturalization remained MacCormack's highest priority for several years. The provisions of the bill closely followed the recommendations of the Ellis Island Committee, whose membership included some of the Jewish immigration experts. The bill would have enabled many aliens (including Jews) who entered the United States illegally during the 1920s to remain and to become citizens. He solicited the support of the Hearst newspapers and the AFL for the bill, but without success. He then delivered a series of speeches throughout much of the country to sympathetic audiences. But the House Rules Committee, prodded by Representative Joseph Starnes of Alabama, refused to send the bill to the floor. Only after MacCormack's death did a diluted substitute pass Congress.[59]

MacCormack cannot be considered an outspoken advocate of a generous refugee policy. He was not dissatisfied with the admission of 4,000 to 5,000 Germans per year, whereas Wyzanski and particularly Perkins had originally contemplated larger numbers. But when MacCormack died in early 1937, at least one Jewish immigration expert (Harold Fields) gave him much of the credit for the increase in visas granted to German Jews since 1933.[60]

The basic obstacle to the admission of German Jewish refugees to the United States in 1933–35 remained the State Department's interpretation of the LPC clause, which was inconsistent and quite possibly illegal. It served as a way to reduce the immigration quotas quietly, selectively, and without legislative approval. Felix Frankfurter attacked this practice directly in April 1933 but made little headway. Judge Mack's plan for public charge bonds represented countervailing administrative action. But high Labor Department officials disagreed on how many bonds they could afford politically to accept and how hard they could press this one issue.

The real problem for Labor, and even more so for American Jewish proponents of increased immigration, was that a sharply restrictionist policy apparently enjoyed widespread public and congressional support. Congress might be too divided to initiate cuts in the immigration quotas, but it would certainly not object to administrative devices to limit immigration. To challenge the State Department's policy involved substantial political risks for the immigration liberals and for the Roosevelt administration generally.

TWO

Guardians of Visa Policy

FROM THE DESK OF WJC

Perhaps no public figure in Washington, D.C., better exemplified the confluence of precedent, process, and personality in the making of American refugee policy in the 1930s than did Wilbur J. Carr. Carr's pen drafted the language of restrictionism during the 1920s. Carr's personality shaped the foreign service that would apply that restrictionist policy toward refugees fleeing Nazi persecution a decade later. Because Carr helped shape as well as administer the policy of exclusion, his desk is an excellent observation post from which to view the State Department's initial response to the plight of Jewish refugees and their American supporters both inside and outside the Roosevelt administration.

Called by one historian the "epitome of the bureaucrat," Wilbur Carr was the heir neither to wealth nor to social position.[1] Carr rose, however, in an ascent reminiscent of Horatio Alger, to a position of power and influence in the State Department, having worked hard to acquire a detailed knowledge of the rules, regulations, and procedures by which the department operated. The son of a poor Ohio farmer, Carr attended commercial college where he mastered bookkeeping and shorthand. In 1892 he passed his civil service exams and was hired by the State Department as a clerk. Diligent and meticulous, Carr was promoted through the ranks to the directorship of the Consular Service by 1909. He was the only individual ever to hold this title because the office was abolished as part of a departmental reorganization when Carr became assistant secretary of state in 1924.

Carr wielded his influence throughout the Consular Service by ensuring that his consuls always felt personally responsible to him. In part, this internal discipline was the product of the inspection corps Carr organized. Inspectors visited consulates at least once every two years with thirty-page standardized schedules drafted by Carr. Each questionnaire required a detailed report of management and expenditures, with inspectors rating officers on a scale of 100 for "honesty, morality, sobriety, standing, force, and loyalty," as well as more tangible performance categories such as numbers of visas issued. Each consul knew that Carr was assessing his performance. Tenure, the merit system, transportation allowances, and a generous pay scale were ample incentives for consuls to curry favor with Carr.[2]

Carr's popularity was hardly universal among his subordinates. Howard Elting, who served in the consular service when Carr was the grand old man of the department, recalled him as "sober-minded and unimaginative."[3] Anecdotes and his own testimony suggest that Carr's attention to intricate detail occasionally reached absurd proportions. He often sat on the oral examination board that tested foreign service applicants. During one such grilling he noticed a young woman candidate's jugular vein thumping in response to the tension; taking out his pocket watch he counted her pulse, later neatly recorded in his diary as one hundred and twenty.[4] Though he rarely lost his temper, Carr could be testy at times. Almost always he attributed his bad spirits to the pressure of his office. He tried to avoid such episodes—not because his "passion" made others ill at ease but because fits of pique were inefficient, yielding only "economic waste."[5]

Carr made himself indispensable to those above him in Washington by eagerly representing the department before congressional committees on fiscal and budgetary matters. By 1920, Secretary of State Bainbridge Colby could describe Carr as the "backbone" of the department.[6] "Punctual, methodical, prudent and disciplined," Carr was a proficient bureaucrat who viewed government as a machine that must be made to run efficiently. In 1924 Carr confided to his diary that he had made the consular service, his cog in that machine, "as near perfection as possible."[7]

In spite of his obvious success, Carr always aspired to the style and education of his Ivy League, more socially prominent, and wealthier colleagues at State. By the time of his appointment as assistant secretary, no one could have better looked the part. He was bald with a graying mustache and large eyes that focused through thick, round wire-framed glasses. Slightly built, Carr's dress was always appropriately conservative and neat. His crisp, dapper appearance helped him blend in with those who could afford to spend much more than he on their suits of dark gray and navy blue. Still, he was sensitive because of what he regarded as a serious gap in his formal preparation. He nonetheless took it as a challenge, writing in his diary that he was "conscious always of an inferiority of preparation and of mind, lacking in information, but by determination and endless hours of labor . . . [he could do] what better educated and more highly placed men had failed to do."[8] He earned law degrees at Georgetown University and Columbian University (later George Washington University) in the evenings, often returning to his office after class to get in several more hours of work. He frequently took instruction in literature and music solely for purposes of self-improvement. Both during his workday and on into the evening, then, Carr worked constantly not only to fit in at State but to be among its guiding lights. He pursued both the polish and the professionalism that he believed necessary to achievement in what one historian described as a "pretty good club."[9]

Prior to World War I, officers in the diplomatic and consular services and their Washington superiors were disproportionately recruited from America's upper crust, the graduates of its most prestigious universities and the scions of its wealthiest families.[10] In this pre-bureaucratic era, it was expected that those most able to serve America's interests abroad were individuals who had "an internalized gentlemanly code"—nonspecialists, nonexperts, who had a reliance on "taste, common sense, intuition, and instinct."[11] Often those who found diplomacy most appealing were those whose breeding and education made them unfit to pursue their fortune in the rough and tumble marketplace. Diplomacy became the chess game of the wealthy and their sons. After World War I, all that changed.

In the postwar world a new bureaucratic orientation displaced courtier diplomacy. "The values of continuity and regularity, functionality and rationality, administration and management set the form of problems and outlined their alternative solutions."[12] The Rogers Act of 1924 codified that new, sleek, professional perspective, provided higher salaries and retirement benefits, and encouraged the promotion of the most capable officers to ministerships. The most important innovation, however, was suggested by Wilbur Carr—a personnel system that integrated consular and diplomatic services, classifying secretaries and consuls together for salary and promotion purposes, while keeping them functionally separate. Carr's bureaucratic solution provided for an interchange of officers between the services and prepared the way for a merger of consular and diplomatic services into one foreign service. From now on individuals could be moved back and forth between the diplomatic and consular services depending on the government's need at the time. Carr's idea, in some ways a forerunner of scientific management techniques, brought efficiency and expertise to the new professionalized State Department.

Despite the claims of some congressmen that the Rogers Act would democratize the diplomatic service, even bureaucratization could not totally destroy the "club" atmosphere of the department. But, then, Carr had never wanted to disband "the club"; he merely wanted to be among its most respected members.[13]

In keeping with the mores of the "club" at State, Carr was a fervent restrictionist. Arguing before the House Committee on Immigration and Naturalization against continued immigration in 1920, he testified that "the unassimilability of these classes . . . is a fact too often proved in the past to bear any argument."[14] Carr's first foray into immigration restriction occurred immediately after World War I when he temporarily suspended the issuance of visas to ensure that there would be sufficient Atlantic shipping to accommodate the thousands of American soldiers eager to return home. This personal expression of gratitude to America's fighting men became a mechanism for more serious and comprehensive restrictions. While there is no conclusive evidence that Carr wrote the text of the 1924 Johnson-Reed Immigration Act that made permanent a national quota system, his office was instrumental in facilitating its application. His subordinates prepared careful tables of statistics with explanations and definitions, including elaborate estimates of the distribution of foreign nationalities in the U.S. at different times calculated by different schemes. The purpose was to ensure the precise administration of the new, restrictive law.[15]

Carr was most directly involved in determining how the new immigration restrictionism would be administered abroad. Since 1913 the Department of Labor had enforced the immigration laws in American ports. After the establishment of the visa system in 1918 and the passage of the first quota act in 1921, there was talk of assigning immigration officers to consulates to process immigrants prior to departure—an idea Carr did not favor.[16] Preferring administrative independence for the Consular Service, he suggested appointing fully qualified immigration officers to be vice consuls abroad, who would serve in the Visa Division. Carr hoped that this arrangement would allow immigrant exclusion but place that procedure in the context of the State Department's larger foreign policy jurisdiction. He worried that, "if the impression is created abroad that we are extending our immigration system into foreign countries and utilizing trained immigration officers there," other countries would complain about the unauthorized use of consular facilities, undercutting the Consular Service's credibility abroad.

The tussle between State and Labor proceeded in the field as well as in Washington. Consuls, such as Thomas Bevan in Hamburg, complained that they were "surprised and nonplused" to learn that applicants to whom they had issued visas were later rejected by immigration officials at Ellis Island in New York harbor and other depots. In a 1925 report to Carr and the secretary of state, Bevan surmised that "the immigration service is beginning to fear that it is losing some of its prestige and wants to show the public that it still makes the final decision as to who shall enter the United States." Bevan observed that consuls, watching their decisions changed by immigration officers after the journey, tended to tighten their own policies, refusing more applicants. The compassionate Hamburg consul thought the overall outcome of the interagency battle was "unjust and unfair to the prospective immigrant."[17] With the end result proving to be even higher rates of exclusion, it is not surprising that Carr did not disapprove of the competition between consuls and immigration officers to turn away immigrants.

Even before the 1930s, then, Carr was involved in a clash between the State and Labor departments over immigration. The State Department defended the independence of its consular operations against incursions from Labor, which was unprepared to abdicate its prerogatives over immigration to consular officials. At a 1922 meeting with Carr, State Department representatives, and Congressman Albert Johnson, Secretary of Labor James W. Davis and Assistant Secretary Edward J. Henning "expressed the wish that the Immigration Bureau be transferred to the State Department because of the fact that it had control of the visa work." According to Carr, "the State Department did not want the work."[18] Carr had preserved the State Department's ability to make administrative decisions affecting immigration from its own independent perspective, a viewpoint that could link domestic welfare to international affairs, including the movement of foreign labor into the American job market.

European Jews comprised a substantial portion of these alien job seekers. A memo that Carr wrote to Congressman Johnson, chairman of the House Committee on Immigration, earned the head of the Consular Service a reputation for anti-Semitism. Carr described the emigrants from Rotterdam as "Russian or Polish Jews of the usual ghetto type. Most of them are more or less directly and frankly getting out of Poland to avoid war conditions. They are filthy, Un-American and often dangerous in their habits." With the Polish Jews, Carr suggested caution because "it is impossible to estimate the peril of the class of emigrants coming from this part of the world and every possible care and safeguard should be used to keep out the undesirables."[19] When Johnson used these phrases in his committee report on the quota act, the congressman as well as the president and the secretary of state were deluged with letters and telegrams of protest. The State Department defended Carr's analysis, observing that the reports were critical of a particular group of immigrants that happened to be Jewish. The department denied having implied that Jews as a class were unclean or inferior, noting the emphasis that the department always placed upon strictly unbiased reporting of conditions. Attorney Louis Marshall, a leader of the American Jewish Committee, was not persuaded. He characterized Carr as "a pronounced anti-semitic," who made appointments within the Consular Service based on whether one's name sounded Jewish. The latter charge was never substantiated.[20]

Entries sprinkled throughout Carr's diary suggest that he harbored anti-Semitic feelings which were exacerbated by social contact with Jews. In early August 1924, during a boat trip to Albany, he wrote in his diary, "Most of the passengers were Jews of one kind or another." His own enjoyment of the scenery was even affected by their presence. He found it "appalling to observe the lack of appreciation of the privilege they are having."[21] Later that month he found Detroit laden with "dust, smoke, dirt, Jews. . . ."[22] Often Carr distinguished between poorer Jews, whom he despised, and the more prosperous who had mastered the social graces. These he could tolerate. Carr disliked the boardwalk at Atlantic City because there were more of the former than the latter: "Jews everywhere and of the commonest kind. Yet most of them were well dressed. . . . The Claridge is filled with them and few presented a good appearance. Only two others besides myself in dinner jacket. Very careless atmosphere in the dining room." His discomfort led him to change hotels where he again found "mostly Jewish guests, but of the higher type than at the Claridge."[23]

It would be fair to conclude that Carr's negative view of Jewish immigrants had much to do with his support for immigration restriction during the 1920s. Yet Carr saw the need for immigration restriction generally. Other groups beside Jews were objectionable, and, in any case, the country could no longer afford to absorb an unlimited number of immigrants. Well before Nazism

TABLE 1

Decline in Quota Immigration to the United States, 1929–1933
(Years Represent Fiscal Year July–June)

	1929	1931	1933
Eastern hemisphere	146,918	54,118	8,220
Germany (including Jews)	48,468	10,100	1,324
Jews (worldwide)	12,479	5,692	2,372
Jewish immigration as percent of eastern hemisphere immigration	8.5	10.5	28.9

This table was compiled from various sources: first row, from *The Statistical History of the United States, from Colonial Times to the Present,* introduction by Ben J. Wattenberg (New York, 1976), p. 105; second and third rows, from monthly and annual reports of the Immigration and Naturalization Service found in American Jewish Committee Archives, RG 1, EXO-29, Waldman Files, Immigration 1940–44; Cecilia Razovsky Papers, Box 3, Relief Work 1941–45, American Jewish Historical Society, Waltham, Massachusetts; and National Refugee Service Statistics on Hebrew Immigration to the United States, December 1942, copy in Joseph Chamberlain Papers, YIVO Institute for Jewish Research, New York. In cases of disagreement between primary and secondary sources, we have chosen the primary data.

These statistics measure the number of quota immigrants actually admitted into the United States. They do not include the relatively small number of very close relatives (e.g., wives and children) of U.S. citizens plus certain professionals who were entitled to nonquota status. The immigration figures vary slightly from State Department statistics on the number of visas issued. One other comment is necessary. The number of Jews is almost certainly too low in each year. Some Jews refused to declare that they were of the "Hebrew" race. Still, the number of self-declared "Hebrews" provides some measure of the number of Jews.

provoked Jewish emigration from Germany, then, the State Department, including Carr, was committed to administering a legislated policy of restrictionism that was antiforeign rather than narrowly anti-Semitic. By 1930 the impact of the depression created public demand for even greater curtailment of immigration than the 1924 legislation could provide.

Carr, like many other State Department officials, readily complied with President Hoover's 1930 request to use administrative prerogatives to reduce immigration.[24] The president hoped to further curb the entry of foreign workers into the United States but did not relish the prospect of a long, divisive congressional debate.[25] Assistant Secretary of State Carr along with Visa Division chief A. Dana Hodgdon were dispatched to Europe to instruct consuls on the new LPC interpretation.[26] Carr had not created the new, more restrictive immigration policy, but in the way he implemented it he sought to make it invulnerable to change.

Not everyone was pleased with the new policy, however. To counter protests and criticism from American ethnic organizations, the State Department advised consuls to be sensitive in dealing with relatives of U.S. citizens and resident aliens.[27] But Carr heartily endorsed the new restrictionism and urged a colleague to ignore "these people's importunities," arguing that the president's policy was in the best interest of the country.[28] Certainly the policy was workable; immigration statistics between 1929 and 1933 reveal a marked decline, though Jewish immigration as a percentage of the total actually rose (see Table 1).

Carr was apprehensive about the election of Franklin Delano Roosevelt. He wrote in his diary, "I like him [Roosevelt], but doubt his capacity and I fear his party more."[29] Carr and Roosevelt had known each other ever since World War I when they had offices on the same corridor. Roosevelt, then a young assistant secretary of the navy, had never forgotten Carr's skill at crisis management and bureaucratic maneuvering when war erupted in August 1914. Still, Carr had not actively supported FDR, and he was surprised when the evening after the inauguration he received a telephone message at 8:30 P.M. to come to the White House. A meeting was already in progress. FDR greeted Carr warmly and introduced him to all present. Most were economic advisers. Roosevelt told Carr, "Wilbur, I am going to do something tomorrow which has never been done in the history of our nation. I am going to close the banks." They had drafted a statement and now wanted Carr to judge whether it should be issued as an executive order or a proclamation. Carr thought it should be a proclamation. Though he echoed the president, saying that there was "no precedent for such a move," he placed aside his personal reservations and, with bureaucratic dispassion, rushed to the State Department and brought back "the executive forms." When Carr returned, FDR handed him a paper with his name and those of Raymond Moley and William Phillips on it. FDR said he intended to send the names to the Senate for approval. Carr respectfully reminded the president that "he did not need to send my name" [since Carr already held his post], but FDR responded, "I know that but I thought you would like a commission from me." Before Carr departed for the evening, Roosevelt wangled a promise for some of the stamps from official correspondence for the presidential stamp collection.[30]

Although Carr did not refuse when the new president asked him to remain at his post, he long remained skeptical of FDR's ability.[31] Well over a year after Roosevelt took office, Carr finally admitted that the president had some of Carr's own appreciation of detail. After a meeting of the Emergency Council, Carr remarked, "The President showed a more alert and agile mind than any of the others; showed an amazing penetration of mind into the subjects discussed; a wonderful facility for making constructive suggestions as to improvements in methods and character of information brought to the Council; a grasp of all these intricate operations and a knowledge of detail very unusual."[32]

Though Carr was flattered by Roosevelt's admiration and his reappointment by the Democratic president, his first loyalty was always to the State Department. And when conflict erupted between Secretary of State Hull and

Secretary of Labor Perkins over the Jewish refugee issue, Carr was a partisan rather than the president's peacemaker. He was quick to defend his department's jurisdiction in refugee matters. Adhering to the law and the administrative procedures he adroitly fashioned at the behest of his superiors, Carr opposed any exemption of refugees from the LPC clause and every effort by Perkins to suggest a compromise for the sake of humanitarianism.

Carr was necessarily a combatant in the ensuing battle for jurisdiction over immigration policy. Little had changed since the clashes of State and Labor in the mid-1920s. The Immigration and Naturalization Service had remained an agency in the Labor Department. But the issuance of visas, handled by American consuls abroad, was still under Carr's jurisdiction in the State Department. The gray areas in the law that left agency responsibilities ambiguous tested Carr and challenged him to exercise his considerable knowledge of regulations and expertise in their manipulation. Carr resisted Perkins's intrusion with the encouragement and assistance of Undersecretary of State William Phillips, who was a personal friend of both Carr and the president, Jay Pierrepont Moffat, who was chief of the Division of Western European Affairs, and A. Dana Hodgdon, the Visa Division chief. Carr crafted a long legalistic memorandum demonstrating how the LPC clause had set the precedent for administrative restrictionism. Carr's handiwork provided Hull with ammunition for the ensuing cabinet-level debate.[33]

The State and Labor departments were left to thrash out how to handle the increased number of visa applications from Germany, especially from German Jews. Alert to increasing pressure from American Jews and the Labor Department, Carr cautioned his consul general in Berlin, George Messersmith, to be sure that consuls were courteous and provided visa applicants with necessary advice but that they always insisted upon compliance with existing American laws. Indeed, before sending his letter to Messersmith, Carr checked with Hodgdon: "As nearly as you can determine will this letter be understood by the men in the field to mean precisely what it says and not be construed as an invitation to relax enforcement of the law?"[34]

Despite Carr's determination not to curtail restriction, the escalating American anxiety about German Jews had its effect. The confrontation between Labor and State altered administrative procedures, allowing aliens without sufficient means of self-support to enter the U.S. provided a close relative was willing and able to offer support. Only a month after his letter to Messersmith, in early July 1933, Carr was forced to modify the Visa Division's position on LPC's.[35]

Carr proceeded by carefully crafting instructions to consuls that would give the appearance of leniency while still holding visa applicants to a strict interpretation of the quota law and procedures for its enforcement. When Jewish representatives complained that the official documents required to accompany visa applications could only be obtained with great difficulty from frequently hostile government officials, Carr cloaked his hard-line position in sympathetic language. He ordered consuls to provide special consideration and "the most favorable treatment permissible under the law" for those experiencing difficulty in obtaining documents. Taking his cue from his superiors at State, Carr sought to quiet Jewish criticism of the State Department while making few substantial concessions.[36]

From Carr's perspective, efforts were being made, consistent with American law and precedent, to ease the plight of foreign nationals fleeing an oppressive government. But, from the viewpoint of American Jewish spokesmen and others concerned with the fate of German Jews, Carr's position and that of others at State seemed at best indifferent and at worst callous.[37] Max Kohler of the American Jewish Committee characterized Carr as "an anti-semite and a trickster, who talks beautifully and contrives to do nothing for us."[38]

Yet the persistence with which Carr resisted special considerations for Jewish refugees was inspired less by anti-Semitism than by his sincere belief that he was the steward of America's restrictive immigration laws and the bearer of responsibility for their enforcement. He and other State Department officials were also incensed by what they regarded as Labor's jurisdictional incursions, so reminiscent of those in the 1920s. The president's unwillingness to take a public stand on the refugee controversy only exacerbated the hostility between Carr and his colleagues at State on one side and the Labor Department bureaucrats, led by Perkins, on the other.

By the autumn of 1933, the interagency war was well under way. Carr and Undersecretary Phillips adamantly opposed any solution that would remove a consul's prerogative to reject visa applicants. Phillips was Carr's superior at State but also his closest ally in the battle for restriction. All the pedigree and education that Carr coveted belonged to Phillips, who was the scion of a family that had included the antislavery reformer Wendell Phillips and, even earlier, the American revolutionary John Jay. During the Wilson administration Phillips met Roosevelt, a fellow Harvard alumnus, who in 1933 called upon Phillips to serve as undersecretary to the diplomatically inexperienced Hull. It was an unfortunate choice for Jewish refugees from Hitler's Reich, because Phillips, even more than Carr, was an immigration restrictionist. While Jewish spokesmen requested leniency from the State Department, Phillips urged that the refugees' advocates be ignored. He also advised Hull against American participation in the League of Nations High Commission for Refugees from Germany because he feared that American Jews might use the commission "as a wedge to break down U.S. immigration policy."[39] Unlike Carr, however, Phillips's attitude was grounded almost exclusively in anti-Semitism rather than in a passion for administrative precision in the enforcement of a legislative mandate.

Phillips hated Jews. His diary contains a number of strongly worded anti-Semitic comments. Like Carr, Phillips was appalled by the Jewish presence in a favorite vacation spot, Atlantic City. He complained that it was "infested with Jews" and that on the weekend the beach disappeared under a swarm of "slightly clothed Jews and Jewesses."[40] Jewish business associates were also privately ridiculed in the pages of Phillips's diary: "Bernard Morrison, my little Jewish friend from Boston, who has a habit of butting into my affairs, called me to suggest that the estate should sell to some Jewish friend of his in New York the Phillips buildings."[41] Phillips was also known by contemporaries for his anti-Jewish comments. James G. McDonald, who became League of Nations High Commissioner for Refugees in 1933, reported to prominent American Jewish spokesmen that Phillips entertained very unfavorable attitudes toward Jews.[42] Justice Brandeis sensed Phillips's views fairly early and correctly predicted that "Phillips's wrong action on Germany's Jews will not end until he leaves the State Department."[43] Phillips's closeness to FDR ensured both his influence and his access to the White House until he received an ambassadorship and left Washington in 1936.

Carr and Phillips proved formidable foes for Perkins. From their perspective, the stake was State Department jurisdiction and the protection of the national interest, which demanded restriction. Capitulation to Labor would be tantamount to a dereliction of State's duty to protect America from a surplus of alien workers. The new chief of the Visa Division, John Farr Simmons, complained to a sympathetic Carr not only that the Labor Department was battling for turf but also that Perkins had a hidden agenda contrary to the national interest—"to give relief in the case of Jewish refugees from Germany. . . .[44] At risk, then, was more than State's prerogatives. Failure to prevail meant that the United States would be submerged by the tide of aliens that the 1924 law had been designed to stem.

Carr's apprehensions about the influence of Jewish lobbyists and the Labor Department were never realized. The LPC clause survived all attacks by opponents and remained the predominant administrative instrument of restriction. Over the next two years, the immigration controversy was handled by State with only minimal modification of its restrictionist policies. A satisfied Carr boasted to a subordinate in early 1936: "We have achieved administratively what is proposed [restriction] and it is for Congress to say whether that should be permanent."[45]

Carr was far from content, nevertheless. Increasingly during the 1930s, he privately expressed his dissatisfaction with the Roosevelt administration. One reason was that, as the department budget officer, Carr was charged with wringing adequate funding from an administration that did not view State and its independent-minded career officers sympathetically. Edith Nourse Rogers, whose husband had sponsored the Rogers Act in Congress, was herself an active and influential minority member of the House Foreign Affairs Committee. In January 1935 she reported to Carr her impressions after a conversation with FDR. According to Rogers, the president had "no clear picture of Foreign Service," but she suspected he was "definitely unfavorable to the diplomatic side but thought consuls were good."[46]

Especially irritating to Carr was the nonhierarchical style that the president encouraged. He objected that the other assistant secretaries, especially seventy-one-year-old Judge Walton Moore, a former Virginia congressman who was close to Hull, and to Roosevelt favorite Sumner Welles, frequently reported to FDR directly, circumventing proper channels—and Carr. He complained that they

> not only have access to the President but discuss all manner of foreign service personnel things with him. Many of them are not reported to me. Hence I can hardly see how I can go on with this work. . . . I do not want to continue in a position if I am not wanted there, and the failure of the President to have any relations with me would seem to indicate that I am not very welcome. I am the only Ass't Sec'y who does not have access to him.[47]

When his confidant, Phillips, was appointed ambassador to Rome in 1936, Carr felt even more isolated. Phillips's departure for his Italian post had the inadvertent effect of removing a key opponent of German Jewish immigration from policy-making councils.[48]

By 1936, Carr was well aware that he and other restrictionists were sailing against the tide. The accord reached with the Labor Department, Phillips's departure, and White House gestures—all seemed indicative of a new spirit. Not until after the election was there any relaxation in the enforcement of visa restrictions. But presidential meetings with important Jewish leaders and public statements sympathetic to Zionism prior to the election suggest that the president's political antennae were raised.[49] So were Wilbur Carr's. Anxious to retain his position at State, Carr, a veteran of many bureaucratic wars, understood when discretion became the better part of valor. Carr would keep step with the administration. In June 1936 Carr forwarded to FDR a response to Herbert Lehman's request for more sympathetic treatment of Jewish refugees. The letter, written under Carr's supervision and approved by him, did not promise any change in policy. The tone, however, sought to pacify Lehman. The letter concluded by assuring Lehman that consular officers were performing their duties "in a considerate and humane manner." The letter conveyed a sympathetic spirit. Lehman was assured that the president would "do everything in his power to be helpful."[50] In late November 1936, Carr suggested to Visa Division Chief E. B. Coulter that new instructions be issued to visa officers "to bring to their attention the unusual features present in the case of German refugees."[51] Carr lent his voice, if not his heart, to the new administrative drift.

The following year, a disappointed Wilbur Carr left Washington. He was sity-six years old, most of his friends had departed Washington, and there appeared no likelihood that he would receive the position of undersecretary of state that he had awaited so long. Instead, he was offered the face-saving option of a ministership. He took it rather than return to private life. Carr served in Prague, Czechoslovakia, from September 9, 1937, until the government of that country was dismembered by the Nazis in the spring of 1939. On July 31 he retired.

The reams of memoranda and instructions that left the State Department bearing the initials WJC, when examined collectively, reveal the profile of an ardent restrictionist. Though Carr's diary entries were laced with anti-Semitism, his restrictionism exceeded the narrower prejudices written in his personal journal. Carr's behavior prior to the 1930s suggests that he hoped to exclude emigrants in general, not just German Jews. Between 1933 and 1936 he tenaciously pursued policies consistent with his belief that increased immigration—of non-Jews as well as Jews—posed social and economic problems for Americans that strict enforcement of existing restrictionist laws could preclude.

Carr may well belong among those "American Christians [who] forgot about the Good Samaritan"; most did according to David Wyman.[52] Much understanding of American policy can be gained, however, from plumbing beneath Carr's social biases to comprehend his behavior. Despite his personal dislike of Jews, Carr did not exercise a double standard in enforcing the law, though he was perhaps restrained only by a bureaucrat's zeal for regulations uniformly applied. Whatever his discomfort in the company of Jews, he also understood that a bureaucrat's success is measured by his longevity in his post. Therefore, he did not hesitate to moderate his stance in 1936 when his sixth sense for Washington politics detected a new inclination toward leniency in the administration of immigration policy within the State Department and elsewhere. Even if he thought the inclination misguided, Wilbur Carr would not feign deafness to the wishes of those above him in the organization that had given him a status neither family nor wealth could bestow. In a lecture at the Foreign Service School that he delivered near the end of his career, Carr preached what he had practiced. " 'It makes no difference whether the President and the Secretary of State, who are your commanding officers,' are Democrats or Republicans. 'Your obligation under your oath of office is to be loyal to them and to carry out with all the ability and conscientiousness you can muster the instructions they give you.' "[53]

Wilbur Carr, then, was a "company man" who implemented the restrictionist policies of those who outranked him at State. But Carr was more than a surrogate. He was a dedicated public servant who felt that he was a steward of the government of the United States and the American people. He regarded immigration restriction as part of a broader national interest which he was bound to defend. Others in Washington, such as Frances Perkins, who indulged themselves in what Carr regarded as naive idealism and challenged the State Department in the interests of foreign nationals, albeit refugees from persecution, could not escape jousting with the bureaucratic windmill he erected.

MESSERSMITH'S FIRST-HAND VIEW

Wilbur Carr was unable to choose his own successor as assistant secretary of state.[54] The man who took over his desk, presumably the choice of the president and secretary of state, was from a similar middle-class background but had somewhat different views from Carr about Jewish refugees. The contrast was partly the result of the new man's years of experience in the field in dealing with Nazi Germany. The new assistant secretary knew from his own observations that some German Jews would make good American citizens.

George S. Messersmith, American consul general in Berlin from 1930 to 1934, was "a dry, drawling, peppery man, his eyes always glinting with the readiness to accept combat, . . . stern and incorruptible in his fight for what he considered right and decent."[55] Messersmith reached the Foreign Service by way of the classroom. Educated at Delaware State College, he became a high school civics teacher and then principal in Fulton, Delaware. He entered the Foreign Service as a consul in 1914—a late starter. By the time he reached Germany, he was forty-seven years old. But Messersmith had assets that allowed him to shine in Berlin. Of German ancestry and fluent in the language, he was able to build up an array of important contacts in the business world and in German politics. Inside information gave him a major advantage in assessing the unpredictable course of Nazi Germany.

He was also strong-willed and independent enough not to wilt when Nazi leaders took exception to his efforts to represent American interests. Reich Marshal Hermann Göring, one of the top Nazi leaders, invited Messersmith to the Air Ministry on April 5 and proceeded to inveigh against American press coverage of Germany regarding the one-day Nazi boycott of Jewish businesses (April 1, 1933). Messersmith responded that the American government had no control over the press but that many Americans, including the newspapers, were concerned about Nazi persecution of the Jews. Meanwhile, as Messersmith reported to Washington, other forms of Nazi persecution and discrimination against Jews continued unabated.[56]

One dissonant report that reached American Jewish organizations claimed that Messersmith had been rude to a German Jewish physician who complained about "atrocities" in the chaotic days before the April 1 boycott. Messersmith allegedly responded, "You Jews are always afraid of your own skins. The important thing is for us to preserve friendly relations between the two countries."[57] It was uncharacteristic for Messersmith to use such an unpleasant tone and stereotype. Stripped of its veneer, however, Messersmith's alleged comment accurately indicated his primary functions. Although there were isolated cases where Messersmith or his chief subordinate, Consul Raymond Geist, intervened to protect German Jews, they had no real authority or mandate and had to operate delicately.[58] The Nazi press nonetheless denounced Messersmith as half-Jewish, a label which even Ambassador Dodd (incorrectly) believed accurate.[59]

Messersmith developed excellent relations with Jewish leaders in Europe and in the U.S. When Jacob Billikopf, one of the leaders of the (American) Federation of Jewish Charities, visited Berlin in September 1933, he found Messersmith understanding and sympathetic.[60] The consul general lacked the genteel anti-Semitism of some of his aristocratic colleagues, and he was genuinely disgusted with the brutality of the Nazis. All of this made an impression on American Jewish visitors. Joseph Hyman, head of the American Jewish Joint Distribution Committee, stated that Messersmith had done a "monumental piece of work in defending the Jews" during the early months of the Nazi regime, and Rabbi Stephen Wise of the American Jewish Congress, correcting early critical reports about the consul general, claimed that he had heard nothing but unlimited praise.[61]

Messersmith's main concerns in 1933 were to prevent physical molestation of American citizens in Germany (especially American Jews) and to protect American investments, which he considered menaced. He labored with considerable difficulty, but with some success, to convince Nazi leaders that transgressions in these areas would injure German interests. Even if he had been inclined to advocate American intercession collectively on behalf of German Jews, he would not have had much effect. The Nazis regarded the Jewish question as an internal matter, a point of view with which Assistant Secretary of State Wilbur Carr concurred.[62]

By July 1933, acts of brutality, particularly on the part of the SA, were restricted more and more to the concentration camps holding more than 25,000 enemies of the Third Reich. The Nazi government had turned to legislation against Jewish professionals, students, and intellectuals.[63] But Messersmith recognized in his conversation with Billikopf during the summer of 1933 that the outlook for German Jews was by no means improved.

> They [the Nazis] did not realize that their Programme, intended to annihilate the Jews at once, would meet with such an unfavorable reception throughout the world; but they are sanguine. They feel that in another month or two or three, the world burdened with more important problems will forget that there are Jews in Germany. There is a point of saturation and news of yesterday ceases to have any value tomorrow. The Nazis will then, in their own sweet way, accelerate the tempo.

Even if one chooses not to take the word annihilate literally, it is clear that Messersmith foresaw that Nazi measures would ultimately become very brutal and that all Jewish property would be confiscated.[64] By September Messersmith had learned that the Nazis also intended to strip Jews of German citizenship (eventually accomplished in September 1935). He also wrote that Hitler was "absolutely implacable" on the Jewish question. Even worse, the Nazis were preparing for war as quickly as possible.[65]

The one optimistic note, in Messersmith's opinion, was the instability of the Nazi regime. Inclined by background and training to stress the importance of economic forces and international trade upon political developments, Messersmith incorrectly concluded that the Nazi leaders could not overcome their economic problems without massive outside assistance.[66] German economic vulnerability, combined with the serious schisms within the party and the growing opposition outside the party, convinced Messersmith that the Third Reich could not last very long. Thus, he began to issue a series of predictions regarding the impending collapse of the regime.[67]

These forecasts were unfortunate because they helped convince key policy makers in Washington that the U.S. role in Europe should be primarily a negative and passive one. The United States should simply avoid any trade agreement likely to assist the Nazi regime; the fact that the Nazi leaders could not be trusted to observe any agreement only strengthened the case for a hands-off policy. But the U.S. could also abstain from politically risky efforts to shore up opposition to Germany. Messersmith's reports were undoubtedly given greater weight in Washington than those of the new ambassador, William Dodd, formerly a history professor at the University of Chicago. (Dodd, who did not arrive until September 1933, quickly proved less than ideal in his role.) Of course, the Roosevelt Administration was focusing on economic recovery in any case and was sensitive to public and congressional opposition to any foreign policy commitments. Messersmith was pushing the administration in the direction it wished to go—or not go.[68]

Messersmith told one British Jewish official that the downfall of the Nazi regime was the only hope not only for Germany but also for all of Europe.[69] Messersmith's anti-Nazi sentiments did not escape the attention of the Nazi leaders. One Nazi official tried to find out from whom he obtained confidential information, and the German government made it clear that his presence was not improving German-American relations.[70]

All of his efforts simply strengthened the view of American Jewish leaders that he was an important ally. When the American minister to Austria died, Judge Julian Mack informally put forward Messersmith's name for the vacancy. (Minister to Austria was the highest American post at the time; today the United States has an ambassador there.) Messersmith had been slated for an appointment to Uruguay. With the aid of lobbying by Ernest Gruening and Felix Frankfurter, however, Messersmith got this important central European post next door to Nazi Germany. Justice Brandeis expressed his pleasure at the result. Mack later praised Messersmith to President Roosevelt, and Roosevelt replied that Messersmith was one of the best men in the whole Foreign Service.[71]

From Vienna, Messersmith continued to send reports to Washington about developments within Nazi Germany, in some cases backed up by detailed information provided by prominent German industrialists and financiers.[72] For a while, he continued to believe that Nazi Germany was headed for a crash and that the U.S. should simply avoid any kind of endorsement of, or aid to, the regime. Messersmith warned that hosting the 1936 Olympics would be excellent propaganda for the Third Reich, which would thoroughly politicize the games. Messersmith urged the United States to boycott the Olympics, but State Department officials decided not to interfere with the positive decision of the U.S. Olympic Committee.[73]

When Britain and France failed to halt the illegal German remilitarization of the Rhineland territory in March 1936, Messersmith turned more pessimistic. He began to realize that the Nazis might go ahead with their expansionist plans unless and until the United States was drawn into a war.[74] Raymond Geist, Messersmith's former subordinate in Berlin, had anticipated this line of analysis.

Geist, too, was of German extraction. Like a good number of Germans, his grandfather had fled to the United States at the time of the unsuccessful 1848 revolutions. He fought and died as a Union officer during the Civil War. Geist's parents settled in Cleveland, where he was born in 1885. He graduated from Columbia University in 1911 and received a Ph.D. in literature from Harvard in 1918. His specialties were German and Romance philology and medieval literature. Geist then served with the American delegation to the Paris Peace Conference in 1919, went from there to assist Herbert Hoover's American Relief Administration in the feeding of starving children in Vienna, and returned to Harvard in 1920 as an instructor in English. But his horizon now extended far beyond the Charles River, and he soon left academic life and entered the Foreign Service. He reached Berlin in 1930 and remained until 1940—the longest span for any American official there. Despite the fact that his promotions came relatively late, his superiors regarded him very highly. Messersmith described him as the most useful officer in Berlin, and Assistant Secretary of State Carr agreed. One reason that he stayed so long in Berlin was that his superiors in Washington thought him irreplaceable.[75]

Although very much a Messersmith protégé, Geist recognized from the beginning that Nazi Germany's economic problems were not insuperable. Geist forecast in 1934 that, if Germany became prosperous under Hitler's rule, Hitler would try to establish a Roman-style empire in Europe, which would change the course of history, perhaps even of civilization. He doubted that economic problems would deter the Nazis from their massive rearmament program, and he predicted an intensification of Nazi anti-Semitism, once the regime had mastered other problems.[76] His letters to Moffat, chief of the Division of Western European Affairs, became so gloomy that he once apologized: "I am very sorry to paint so dark a picture, but I think we might just as well face the facts and direct our policy in dealing with the European situation, with reference to them."[77] The same pessimistic realism was necessary in discussions of the possibility of Germans emigrating to the United States.

Both Messersmith and Geist kept a close watch on the situation of Jews in Germany, in part because both were responsible for implementing the instructions of the State Department's Visa Division. The consul general in Berlin not only supervised the visa interviews and decision by consuls and vice-consuls in Berlin but also checked up on the other American consulates in Germany and administered the immigration quota for the country. Messersmith had of course received instructions in September 1930 to reduce the number of immigration visas granted under the German quota to 10 percent of the quota level, and he had complied promptly and efficiently.[78]

Messersmith was no blind spokesman for the official State Department line on visa policy. For one thing, he personally had been embarrassed when strict instructions from the Visa Division forced the consulate in Berlin to scrutinize and delay the visa application of Albert Einstein in 1932. Einstein had professional reasons for coming to the U.S. temporarily, but his political views were known to be leftist. Since Einstein had academic contacts in the U.S. as well as world renown, he refused to submit to the bureaucratic run-around. The case became public knowledge, and Walter Lippmann denounced Messersmith in a column. But Messersmith was not even present in Berlin when Einstein was interviewed, and Lippmann was forced to issue a grudging apology. Messersmith blamed "stupidity in the Visa Division" for the incident.[79]

His critical attitude toward the Visa Division did not make Messersmith an outspoken reformer. It might have impaired his chances of advancement if he had bluntly challenged existing visa policy. In fact, Messersmith at times seemed to endorse it. One of his early reports to the department in April 1933 emphasized how successful his previous efforts to reduce immigration had been. Although many Jews were said to be leaving Germany, relatively few were asking for visas to the U.S. "due to the fact that the difficulties in securing visas for the United States are well known and the Jews without resources are obliged to remain in the country."[80] Two months later, however, Messersmith noted a great increase in the number of visa applications, reflecting increasing desperation on the part of German Jews. He forecast a continuing interest in emigration, especially among younger German Jews, who would find all avenues closed to them in the Third Reich. He also raised the possibility that, without improvement in the German economic and political situation, as many non-Jews as Jews would be seeking to leave the country.[81] When Jacob Billikopf visited Messersmith in Berlin and urged him to support a modification of the Hoover LPC order, the consul general pointed to the level of unemployment in the United States and argued that any attempt to modify the order would arouse criticism and create unfavorable repercussions throughout the country. Messersmith did, however, imply that the consulates had already begun to shift toward a more lenient interpretation of the LPC requirement "without provoking painful [i.e., public] discussion."[82] This comment showed how well Messersmith understood the State Department's political balancing act.

Messersmith's own views on visa policy were idiosyncratic. He took particular exception to Alvin Johnson's proposed University in Exile, which later became part of the New School for Social Research, which was to employ a number of left-wing and Jewish professors dismissed from their posts in Germany. Messersmith wrote to Carr: "We cannot fill our own universities with foreign professors who are alien to our thought and will influence our youth in a direction not in line with our national policy and our cultural life." He was concerned that leftist intellectuals or others bearing resentments against the state might lack commitment to the American system and might not strengthen the patriotism of American youth. Was this a veiled anti-Semitic tendency? Messersmith proved the contrary by adding, tellingly: "The average Jew, for example, who desires to emigrate to the United States, will be very glad to be able to make a home for himself in our country and to fit himself into our picture; but these professors who feel that they have a mission in life, may potentially be a danger to us. . . ."[83] His criticism of German professors thus was not a disguise for anti-Semitism but an indication of Messersmith's nationalism and his regard for the influence of the professoriate.

The increase in visa applications and inquiries continued at least through the fall of 1933, and 90 percent of the visa applicants in Berlin were said to be of Jewish origin.[84] After a meeting with the other American consul generals in Germany, Messersmith wrote to Assistant Secretary of State Carr that "we are conforming to the principles which you set forth." He also suggested at one point that it might be necessary for the U.S. to take additional protective measures against an influx of immigrants.[85] The main problem was that the potential demand for visas far outstripped what Washington generally and the State Department in particular were willing to grant. Even limited and confidential relaxation of visa regulations[86] was not without adverse political effects.

Messersmith had been willing to tell Billikopf "off the record" that a more liberal interpretation of the LPC clause was in the offing, but, when similar information reached the press through another channel, alarm bells rang in Washington. The American press had carried some items about the new State Department instruction regarding documentary requirements for refugee applicants and the impending authorization of public charge bonds. In response to prodding from his New York office, Max Smolar, the Berlin correspondent of the Jewish Telegraphic Agency, asked Raymond Geist about the new instructions. Geist told Smolar off the record that the American consulates in Germany were not responsible for the fact that only 10 percent of the German quota had been used last year and that, if there was good evidence that an alien would have support in the United States, consuls would not use the LPC clause to deny him a visa. Geist asked Smolar not to quote him or refer to the consulate general in his despatch to New York.

Citing authoritative Jewish sources in Berlin, Smolar then wrote an article suggesting that there had been a shift in American policy and that, if American citizens were to adopt German Jewish visa applicants, that might give the latter a favored position to obtain visas. Smolar also complimented Geist and his subordinate Archie Woodford on the sympathetic manner with which they were carrying out the immigration laws and regulations. He had done Geist and Woodford no favor. When the article hit the press, John B. Trevor, chairman of the Coalition of Patriotic Societies, immediately complained to the State Department, which sent off a stern inquiry to Berlin. Geist was forced into a lengthy explanation of his contacts with, and his statements to, Smolar.[87]

A second incident occurred after *Today Magazine* published Edward Mims's article, "German Refugees and American Bureaucrats,"[88] which was sharply critical of State Department visa policy. Geist felt compelled to write a critique of the article for his superiors in Washington. He argued that the main obstacles to increased German Jewish emigration to the United States were German laws that barred the transfer of property and capital and the inadequate means of poorer Jews. Geist wrote that most would-be immigrants would not wish to be caught in the United States without a livelihood or means to support themselves; they preferred to hope for an improvement of their position in Germany. He conceded that, for German Jews who had already fled to nearby countries, German police officials probably were not supplying documents necessary for visa applications to the United States. But, if Washington eliminated the requirement entirely, some undesirable persons would undoubtedly receive visas. This was indeed what the State Department wished to hear. It hastened to send a copy of Geist's despatch to the Labor Department[89] in the apparent hope that Commissioner MacCormack would ease up.

Geist was not free of departmental scrutiny. The Visa Division remained concerned that many German applicants had found ways to evade American regulations and that the Berlin consulate in particular was granting too many visas to individuals with only distant relatives in the United States. When a vice consul in Berlin made some critical comments about visa policy there and complained also of incomplete German police records, visa official C. Paul Fletcher requested a special instruction to the Berlin consulate to set matters aright. He also claimed that the report strengthened the contention that the United States was becoming the dumping ground for criminals.[90] Such Visa Division views were based more on fears and stereotypes than on any concrete evidence.

All of the regulations, instructions, and guidance from Washington cast added light on frequent accusations, echoed in historical works, that many American consular officers were prejudiced against Jews.[91] The prohibition of anyone likely to become a public charge was inherently ambiguous, and the Visa Division explicitly informed young consuls and vice consuls that it was their job to make a personal judgment about the financial and personal soundness of a visa applicant (and his relatives). One can hardly imagine an arrangement more heavily dependent upon the attitudes of the consuls toward the people they interviewed, and there were bound to be differences in judgment and orientation among consular officials. When Cecilia Razovsky, executive director of the National Coordinating Committee, traveled to Berlin in the fall of 1935, she found that Vice Consul Prescott Childs discounted Jewish fears and criticism of the Nazis; he was insensitive toward Jewish applicants. She handled the arrangements for bringing Jewish students to the United States with Consul Geist instead.[92]

But all Foreign Service officers labored under the same constraint: the system was designed to make it difficult for consular officers to approve too many visas. The consuls and vice consuls could not ignore Washington's feelings without seriously jeopardizing their own careers. The result was that, in cases of doubt, consuls invariably leaned toward refusal. In one documented case in 1934, a Berlin surgeon who was a non-Aryan (part Jewish by descent) applied for an American visa. The German government decided to allow him to take two thousand marks (about eight hundred dollars) with him. The surgeon secured an affidavit of support from a cousin in New York who was a fur dealer and who listed an income of forty dollars per week. After the vice consul (Ware Adams) questioned the affidavit, a representative of the American Friends Service Committee (Quakers) came in to vouch for the surgeon as well. But Adams said (correctly) that the rules did not permit an organization to supply an affidavit. The Quaker observed that Adams was a very nice young fellow and concluded that the restrictions were "very very severe." Two years later another Quaker was told that no affidavits would be acceptable unless they were from close relatives.[93]

The apparent arbitrariness of the process made a lasting impression on a number of German Jews. In one case a nineteen-year-old German Jewish student named Hermann Kilsheimer went to the American consulate in Stuttgart in 1934, accompanied by his sister, to seek an immigration visa. Kilsheimer was well acquainted with American visa requirements, because his sister had emigrated before him and had since married an American citizen. She was back in Germany on a visit and wanted to help her younger brother, one of twelve siblings, to get out. Hermann's sister brought three affidavits of financial support for him—one from her husband, one from Hermann's first cousin (also in the U.S.), and one from another cousin's husband. All of the sponsors owned real estate, but none earned more than one hundred dollars per week. American Consul Charles Teller was dubious. Cousins were not (under the instructions) considered close relatives, and the amount of financial support from the sister and her husband would not be lavish for someone who wanted to attend an American university. After interviewing the brother and sister, he turned down the application. The two left the consulate in tears. As they descended the stairs, a young vice consul named Gray came out and recognized Kilsheimer's sister—she had tutored him in German when he had lived in Washington. Gray asked what was wrong, listened, then asked them to come back into the building. Kilsheimer got his visa, and he left Germany on October 10, 1934.[94] But how many applicants had as many breaks as Hermann Kilsheimer?

There were, nonetheless, some positive changes over time. The implicit compromise between the State Department and the Labor Department regarding refugees, a slight improvement in American economic conditions, an ebbing of anti-Semitic action in Germany, and, consequently, a diminution of the number of applications for American visas reduced the rates of visa refusal and deferral in 1934. In fiscal 1935 (July 1, 1934–June 30, 1935), about 4,500 Germans were granted immigration visas to the United States.[95] On the negative side, a new German law in October 1934 formalized and tightened earlier restrictions on the removal of property from the country. Emigrants were now barred from taking more than ten marks (about four dollars) without written permission, which was often refused.[96] That restriction made it all the more difficult for a visa applicant without American relatives to convince an American consul that he was not likely to become a public charge. In their own separate ways, both Germany and the United States were making it difficult for Germans to immigrate into the United States.

A new wave of anti-Semitic propaganda and violence during the spring and summer of 1935 ended the lull in Germany. Messersmith wrote from Vienna that flagrant violence against Jews was so frequent that there was no point in reporting each incident. He suggested that the State Department warn American Jews to avoid travel in Germany.[97] Then the Nuremberg Laws of September 1935 stripped German Jews of their citizenship and added a host of humiliating restrictions, all of which made it clearer that Jews had a bleak future in Germany. At least one American consulate was immediately inundated with visa inquiries and applications. The American consul general at Stuttgart wrote that, for the first time, Jews of substantial financial resources were willing to sacrifice all of their property just to get out.[98]

In May 1936 Consul General John G. Erhardt in Hamburg predicted that, with all of the pressure on German Jews, American Jewish spokesmen might see the presidential campaign in the U.S. as an opportunity to push for modification of visa regulations. There might also be efforts in Congress to exempt some German Jews from the regulations and the quota. Wilbur Carr praised Erhardt's "timely warning."[99]

In the months before the presidential election President Roosevelt took a more direct interest in Jewish issues. In August 1936, FDR issued a public statement favoring the rebuilding of the ancient Jewish homeland in Palestine, and, after a cabinet discussion on September 2, the United States urged Great Britain not to curtail Jewish immigration to Palestine, a step then under consideration in London.[100] There is no evidence that Roosevelt issued any instructions to the State Department about immigration to the United States,[101] but careful observers could see which way he was leaning.

In late 1936 Foreign Service Inspector Jerome Klahr Huddle visited the American consulates in Germany and reported back to Washington that the character of German Jewish immigration was unusual. Many of the immigrants and would-be immigrants came from better-class families, and even their distant relatives in the United States had a sincere desire to assist them escape persecution.[102] From Vienna, Messersmith added his weight to the forces pushing for change. He had previously prepared a twelve-page, single-spaced memorandum offering detailed guidance on visa decisions for the staff of the legation and consulate in Austria. Messersmith had warned Foreign Service officers not to treat visa decisions as routine or of minor importance and not to read into regulations their own principles or ideas as to what the law should be. In a telling passage, Messersmith analyzed what he called the real object of immigration laws and visa practice:

> Stated briefly, it is to preserve our liberal attitude on immigration and yet at the same time adequately protect the interests of our country and people. The object is not, as some interpret it, to maintain the United States as an asylum or refuge for

dissatisfied and oppressed people in other parts of the world irrespective of their capacity to become good and self-supporting citizens of our country. Their object is also not, as some interpret it, to keep out certain classes of persons on account of their race, religion, or political ideas.

Here Messersmith was carefully marking out a centrist position on visa policy. Immigrants who would make good citizens and would strengthen the country should be admitted, whether or not they were Jewish. On the other hand, if refugees were likely to become public charges or presented other serious problems, they should not be given visas—even though they were the victims of persecution. Of course, it was still a difficult matter to determine just who would make a good citizen and just how many immigrants the United States could profitably absorb. Lacking explicit congressional instructions, the State Department and the consulates had to make their own determination. One can see why Messersmith warned against treating visa decisions as routine.

In November Messersmith sent this memorandum to Washington with the suggestion that it be transmitted to Foreign Service officers elsewhere for their information.[103] What he had written was a little too much for the Visa Division, both in length and in substance. Although C. Paul Fletcher generally approved of the memo, he discouraged the idea of mimeographing it and circulating it throughout the service; certain passages, he wrote, might do more harm than good. One of the marked passages was "their object is also not, as some interpret it, to keep out certain classes of persons on account of their race, religion, or political ideas." Visa Division chief Simmons preferred to have Assistant Secretary of State Carr provide guidance to the consular officials.[104] But a politically weakened Carr was now willing to concede that there were unusual features present in the case of German Jewish refugees. Eliot B. Coulter of the Visa Division suggested one specific change: the acceptance of affidavits from distant relatives because "the Jewish people often have a high sense of responsibility toward their relatives, including distant relatives whom they may not have seen, and . . . they feel keenly the difficult lot of their kin in Germany.[105] Other Visa Division officials expressed varying degrees of concurrence. From all appearances, the president's signal, combined with pressures from those such as Huddle and Messersmith, swayed the old guard.

In late December 1936 the State Department informed certain consulates that they had occasionally interpreted the LPC provision improperly, and a new visa instruction followed on January 5. Consuls were told specifically to make a judgment whether the applicant was "probably" going to become a public charge; if so, they should deny him a visa. But the possibility of becoming a public charge was not sufficient grounds for denial.[106]

John Wiley, consul general in Antwerp, wrote to his counterpart in Rotterdam to ask whether the communications from Washington represented a radical liberalization of visa policy or a concern about inefficiency. Homer Brett replied:

I understand it as a radical change of policy and I am sending an enthusiastic acknowledgement. My guess is that it is not unconnected with the appointment of a new special assistant to the Secretary of State[107] and that it is due to political pressure from jewish organizations. . . . However this may be I personally think that a strained definition of the LPC clause has been enforced ever since September 1930, and that this instruction signifies that "likely" is to mean what is meant when the law was written.[108]

Wiley was not the only one curious about the new instruction. A consul general in Albania wrote personally to Visa Division chief Simmons, stating that the new policy contradicted his training. He conjectured that the instruction was "a reversal for political reasons of a policy which had never been officially stated or put in writing. . . ." But Simmons simply offered a legalistic response.[109] From Vienna, Messersmith wrote to praise Carr for the new instruction. He forecast that it would do a great deal of good.[110]

The increase in European immigration to the United States was dramatic. For example, 6,978 individuals (26.9 percent of the quota) had received visas under the German quota for fiscal 1936 (July 1, 1935–June 30, 1936), but 12,532 were given visas in fiscal 1937. In fiscal 1938 the number jumped to 20,301. In mid-1937, when Congressman Emanuel Celler of New York introduced a bill in the House of Representatives to exempt refugees from the LPC clause, Labor Department officials and immigration expert Cecilia Razovsky advised him that congressional debate might be counterproductive; the visa situation was "as satisfactory as it possibly can be."[111] In late 1937 Geist wrote to Messersmith that the visa situation in Germany was now satisfactory, and Messersmith wrote back that he was pleased.[112] By that time Messersmith was sitting in Wilbur Carr's chair at the State Department.

Shifting currents within the State Department thus managed to bring about what the Labor Department alone had been unable to do in 1933–34—use of a large part of the German quota and a substantial increase in the immigration of German Jews to the United States. The State Department did respond partly to outside forces. Labor's earlier criticism of State Department visa policy undoubtedly had a residual effect after William Phillips abandoned his office and Wilbur Carr his viewpoint. The continuing lobbying efforts of Jewish and nonsectarian organizations, particularly the National Coordinating Committee, also contributed to the change. Finally, one cannot neglect the effect of economic improvement in the United States and the indications of presidential interest in Jewish problems during 1936.

To an advocate of increased immigration such as Cecilia Razovsky, it must have been easy to reach the conclusion in 1937 that the changes in visa policy and State Department personnel had gone far toward meeting the refugee problem. If some 20,000 Germans (largely Jewish or of Jewish descent) could enter the U.S. each year, that would substantially reduce the backlog of those seeking to flee the Third Reich. But Nazi efforts to restrict the role of Jews in the economy and force the sale of Jewish businesses had already begun. Seizures of

Jewish property and prohibitions on a whole range of economic activities followed. Moreover, the German annexations in 1938 forced ever-larger masses of victims to seek refuge in the United States and elsewhere.

The next wave of Nazi persecution laid bare a major disagreement between Messersmith and the supporters of liberalized immigration. For Messersmith, Nazi persecution of the Jews, though deplorable, was only one element of an ever-expanding vortex in Europe. If the United States was to prevent the worst, domination of the continent by the Nazi regime, it would have to protect its own interests first and foremost. That might leave limited scope for humanitarian action.

THREE

A Window of Opportunity?

If Adolf Hitler had a comprehensive plan for the solution of the "Jewish problem" in Germany,[1] he did very little to inform anyone about it during the first four years of his rule. The laws churned out by German bureaucrats and Nazi party experts with little guidance from above severely restricted the legal and economic position of German Jewry, but these discriminatory decrees seemed to provide some protection against arbitrary anti-Jewish activities by Nazi thugs. Some Jews even regarded the Nuremberg Laws of 1935, which stripped Jews of citizenship and barred "interracial" marriage or intercourse between Aryans and Jews, as a stabilization of their situation.[2] A lull in Nazi persecution of the Jews in late 1935 and during much of 1936—an effort to guarantee that Germany would host the 1936 Olympics and make the right impression upon foreign visitors and press[3]—misled many people inside and outside the country. It is easier to see in retrospect that, once it no longer had any need to impress foreigners, the Nazi regime would intensify its anti-Semitic policies.

If leading Nazis believed that German Jewry represented a menace to the "Aryan race" in peacetime, war created an even more dangerous situation. Perhaps, then, it was not quite accidental that Hitler, in the midst of a September 1935 monologue about the danger posed by Jewish assimilation, suddenly began to talk about his plans for war.[4] After the Olympics the German government began war preparations, with the establishment of the Office of the Four-Year Plan, adopted measures designed to separate Jews from German society, and stepped up the Aryanization of Jewish businesses and wealth.[5] In late 1937 or early 1938 (i.e., around the same time that Hitler alerted his top military officials to his plans for the domination of Europe),[6] Hitler made a verbal decision to promote the emigration of Jews from Germany by all possible means, and in 1938 he began to play a more direct role in the formulation of policy on Jews. In February Heinrich Himmler, head of the SS, which was beginning to assume more jurisdiction over Jewish issues, ordered the expulsion from Germany of all Jews who were citizens of the Soviet Union.[7] It was but the first of many arbitrary and increasingly severe Nazi moves against Jews that year. The result was an intensification of pressure upon central Europesan Jewry to leave at all cost any territory under the German sphere of influence. Some were given no choice.

On March 13, 1938, the German army marched into Austria without resistance. Two weeks later, following formal German annexation of the country, Nazi leader Hermann Göring delivered a speech in Vienna, announcing that it was to become a "pure German" city within four years. The Jews must get out. Affected were not only the 170,000 Jews by religion but possibly also the other "non-Aryans" (those part Jewish by descent, who may have numbered 400,000–500,000). The Nazis began to seize Jewish property almost immediately. Some Jews were simply dumped across Austria's borders; many others were given a date by which they had to leave the country. The alternative was a concentration camp; the arrest, imprisonment, and shipment of 1,600 Viennese Jews to Buchenwald and Dachau made that plain.[8] Adolf Eichmann's assembly-line operation in the former Viennese mansion of the Rothschild family made it possible for Austrian Jews to obtain all German documents needed to leave in a single day. Within six months, 50,000 Jews left the new province of Nazi Germany.[9]

As Hermann Göring began to centralize the expropriation of Jewish businesses and property, there were signs of even stronger measures to come. Martin Bormann of the Nazi Party Chancellery told the Gauleiters in August 1938 that Göring intended to have a fundamental cleaning up (*grundlegende Bereinigung*) of the Jewish question that "would satisfy the demands of the party to the fullest measure."[10] Meanwhile, Hitler had chosen his next foreign target—Czechoslovakia. The Munich Conference unexpectedly ended the fall 1938 crisis without war; the British and French agreed to surrender a major chunk of Czechoslovakian territory. After the German annexation of the Sudetenland, Nazi persecution spread to tens of thousands of Jews now stripped of Czech citizenship, and the visa lines lengthened outside the American consulates in rump Czechoslovakia.[11]

Less than a month later the Nazis struck again at foreign Jews in Germany, setting off unforeseen shock waves. Anticipating a decision by Poland to revoke the citizenship of those who had lived many years outside the country, Germany abruptly deported more than 20,000 Jews of Polish origin, dumping them over the border without property or concern for their person. Herschl Grynzspan, a seventeen-year-old Polish Jew living in Paris, whose parents had been among the deportees, made his own protest. Mistaking a third secretary in the German embassy in Paris for the German ambassador, Grynzspan pulled out a revolver and fired. After the official died, Hitler authorized a wave of violence against German Jews. The SA, virtually stripped of its functions since June 1934, was allowed to have a fling. Synagogues all across Germany were set afire, some seven thousand Jewish businesses were destroyed, and the death toll among German Jews exceeded ninety. This event became known as the Night of Broken Glass (*Kristallnacht*).[12] In the aftermath, the Nazis intensified their anti-Semitic program. More than 30,000 Jews were sent to concentration camps, a huge,

immediate levy on Jewish property was imposed, and Jews were prohibited from working for Aryan businesses (except as forced laborers). Along with other restrictions that anticipated Jewish ghettoes, the post-*Kristallnacht* measures completed the separation of Jews from German society. When thousands of Jews were later released from concentration camps, they were desperate to emigrate.

Various Nazi measures during 1938 amounted to a policy of forced emigration. Wherever Nazi Germany could dump Jews, it did so, provided that they surrendered most of their money. Some historians have seen this phase of Nazi policy as evidence that Hitler as yet had no final goal for the Jews in sight[13] and that the Nazis later turned to the Final Solution only because emigration schemes failed: the number of Jews to dispose of was too great, and foreign countries would not take enough in. In other words, the Final Solution later became the only solution remaining for fanatical Nazis committed to eliminating the Jewish presence in their domain.[14]

Although this argument accentuates the moral guilt of western governments for what occurred during the war in Nazi-dominated Europe, it overlooks several facts. There were various reasons why Nazi officials wanted to expel German Jews. In the eyes of SS officials, forced emigration of impoverished Jews not only rid Nazi Germany of its main enemy but also stirred up anti-Semitism and created political strife wherever the Jews landed. The Foreign Office shared this view,[15] as apparently did Hermann Göring. In the summer of 1938 Göring told an astonished American diplomat that within ten years the United States would become the most anti-Semitic country in the world and that the combination of Jews and Negroes raised grave questions about America's future.[16] Hitler told the South African minister of defense in late November 1938 that he was not exporting National Socialism; he was, however, exporting anti-Semitism. (He added that the Jews would one day disappear from Europe.) And the American military attaché in Berlin, Truman Smith, alerted Washington that Nazi anti-Semitism actually promoted German plans for expansion in the east.[17]

Nazi emigration policy was designed to cause trouble for anyone "generous" enough to admit Jews. Conversely, it might create sympathy for Germany's own Jewish policy, and it might well serve as a wedge for future German expansion. The corollary was that the Nazi regime was not terribly interested in promoting *orderly* emigration of Jews. The faster the disposal, and the more chaos abroad, the better.

American Consul General John Wiley in Vienna observed that Nazi officials were not content to wait a number of months until individual Jews received visas to the United States; they insisted on immediate expulsion. Wiley wrote, "One can only perhaps imagine that it is inspired by the possibility of war and the desire to eliminate a hostile element in the population. If there is war, Heaven alone knows what will happen to these unhappy and wretched people."[18]

In Berlin Raymond Geist found that Himmler (who was also chief of all

German police) was not willing to issue instructions to police officials to give German Jews the certificates of good conduct required with the applications for American visas (although the corrupt Berlin police office was willing to do so in exchange for American currency).[19] If he had been interested solely in removing all of the Jews from Germany, Himmler presumably would have cooperated with the paperwork.

Then Geist received information that went beyond conjecture about Nazi intentions. Over a number of years Geist had established contact with an SS official named Karl Hasselbacher, head of Security Service Department II F 2, in charge of Jews, Freemasons, Lodges, and emigrants. Sometime in 1938 Hasselbacher informed Geist that Germany was to be made "judenrein" and that those Jews unable to leave the country would be exterminated.[20] And this was not the only sign of what was to come. As Robert Wolfe has stressed, a careful reading of the minutes of Göring's post-*Kristallnacht* strategy session on the Jewish question leads one to conclude that, by November 12, 1938, high Nazi officials had already decided, in principle, on extermination, embracing a range of measures that would strip Jews of the right and means to exist. Göring also warned at the close of the November meeting that, in case of war, the Nazis would settle accounts with the Jews.[21] The sequence of events leading to the Final Solution was not yet determined, but the idea already hung in the air.

Given what Adolf Hitler himself stated during early 1939, few should doubt what the Führer had in mind for his archenemies. On January 21 he told the Czechoslovakian foreign minister, Frantisek Chvalkowsky, that the Jews in Germany would be destroyed—this would repay them for November 9, 1918 (the revolution that Hitler believed had stabbed the German army in the back). Then on January 30, he made an infamous prophecy to the Reichstag and to the world: "If international finance Jewry in and outside Europe should succeed in forcing the peoples once again into a world war, the result would not be the Bolshevization of the earth and the triumph of Jewry, but the destruction of the Jewish race in Europe."[22]

In a highly secret speech to leading figures in the Nazi Party, business magnates, and high army officials in March 1939, Hitler not only laid out his plan for step-by-step expansion across the European continent but also went further: "With British and French possessions in America as a base we will settle accounts with the 'Jews of the dollar' (dollar Juden) in the United States. We will exterminate this Jewish democracy and Jewish blood will mix itself with the dollars."[23] Here Hitler revealed both a desire for world conquest as well as a thirst for Jewish blood outside of Europe.

This brief survey of Nazi planning reveals a link between the approach of war and intensification of anti-Jewish policies. Whatever one could say about the ability of the outside world to have absorbed impoverished German, Austrian, and Czech Jews, it certainly could not have handled the 3.3 million Jews of Poland. The Nazi leaders knew, regardless of how many Jews left Greater Germany, that when the war began, they would have an opportunity to settle accounts with millions of Jews and to "secure the future" for the Aryan race. Forced emigration and murder of Jews thus were not alternatives for the Nazis. They were complementary.

What Hitler ultimately had in mind and what he could accomplish, however, were two different things. For roughly eighteen months before World War II began, the short-term policy of the Nazi regime was to expel Jews from its territory. The greater the number of Jews who left Nazi-controlled territory and the farther they went, the better their chances of survival. So their fate did depend on the willingness of foreign nations, particularly the United States and Great Britain, to admit refugees from Nazi persecution. To be sure, this mortal danger was not yet widely recognized in the west. To many westerners, the idea of killing off large numbers of people because of their religion or "race" seemed preposterous in the twentieth century.[24] Hitler's speeches and threats seemed mere rhetoric. But by 1939 high American officials did not lack information about Nazi intentions.

PRESIDENTIAL INITIATIVE

The American government considered special measures to assist the victims of Nazi persecution in Austria and Germany during 1938. Part of the reason was a decision by the White House to involve itself openly with the refugee issue for the first time. But the Roosevelt administration and the State Department generally perceived too many drawbacks to initiatives to bring much larger numbers of Jews to the United States. Conflicting American priorities and political constraints, as well as diabolical Nazi exploitation of anti-Semitic sentiment abroad, prevented Washington from going beyond what the quota system already allowed. These factors did not make the Roosevelt administration a passive spectator to Nazi persecution of the Jews in Europe, but they did weaken America's commitment and ability to react effectively.

With the German annexation of Austria, the streets of Vienna were filled with people who needed to get out. Confronted by huge lines of applicants, the visa section at the American legation in Vienna began to work from nine in the morning until ten each evening, seeing about six thousand persons per day, conducting an average of five hundred personal interviews per day. The stepped-up effort was frustrating for the interviewers as well as for the applicants, for the annual quota for Austria was only 1,413.[25]

One of the earliest advocates of some form of emergency response to the plight of Austrian Jews was Herbert Feis, a high-ranking specialist in international trade and economics within the State Department. Feis, a New Dealer and a Jew, began to press for American action almost immediately after the German army marched into Austria on March 13. Feis found that the president was definitely interested in doing something and Hull was acquiescent.[26] One press account reported that Roosevelt was angry at the Nazi mistreatment of the elderly Sigmund Freud and eager to do something. A key lobbyist was the writer Dorothy Thompson (Mrs. Sinclair Lewis), whose article on the refugee problem was to be published in *Foreign Affairs* in March. She spoke with Jay Pierrepont Moffat and also sent her article to Hull and George Messersmith.[27] Four key proposals came from these two sources: merger of the German and Austrian quotas (Feis); streamlining the procedure for consideration of affidavits of support from Americans (Feis); establishment of a new American organization to coordinate the immigration efforts of private agencies and individuals (Feis); and the establishment of a new international organization to deal with the refugee problem on a broad scale (Thompson). Thompson also wanted some kind of bloc legislation for Austrians to enter the U.S., but that of course required congressional action.[28]

According to Feis, one of the real obstacles, surprisingly, was Messersmith, who was "slow to recognize the inadequacy in this instance of the usual method of our immigration arrangements, inclined to fear any new though wholly reasonable and justified flexibility in our laws."[29] Messersmith's reaction was particularly important, because he was considered the State Department expert on Nazi Germany, as well as the man with authority over the Visa Division.

Messersmith continued to follow events in Germany quite closely and believed that the Nazi purge of the Army High Command in early 1938 had removed the last restraining influence upon Hitler's foreign policy.[30] Messersmith's hard-line views on the Nazi regime endeared him to Rabbi Stephen Wise, head of the American Jewish Congress. (After a February 1938 conversation with Messersmith, Wise wrote, "How fortunate that at Hull's side stands a man who has a real understanding of what Fascism means and how in every way it must be resisted by America."[31] Given this endorsement and Messersmith's earlier advocacy of a more lenient immigration policy, we can dismiss the idea that anti-Semitic prejudice hardened Messersmith's feelings. But his awareness of the Nazi menace did not make the assistant secretary a supporter of emergency rescue measures for German Jews in 1938–39. He preferred to let American consuls in Germany and Austria exercise their own judgment on visa applications, under the instructions of the State Department's Visa Division. Messersmith had himself worked under that system, and by 1938 he had improved it considerably.[32] He saw no reason to abandon it, particularly since he now sat in the assistant secretary's chair.

Another skeptic about new measures was Moffat, who preferred to have the refugee bureau of the International Labor Organization expanded rather than to set up any new organization. Messersmith also shared this view. Nonetheless, Messersmith recognized that it was politically important for the State Department not to assume a purely negative position, and he elicited the cooperation of the Department of Labor.[33] In a speech in New York on March 18, Visa Division chief Avra Warren announced that the consuls had been advised to look more leniently upon refugee applications when it was a matter of determining who might become a public charge.[34] But this was probably a reference to the visa instruction of January 1937, which had informed American consuls that American Jewish residents who signed affidavits of financial support to bolster the visa applications of their European relatives could be relied upon to fulfill their commitments.[35]

At the cabinet meeting of March 18, FDR himself raised the question of what the United States could do for Austrian political refugees. Treasury secretary Henry Morgenthau, who was present, recorded the gist of the president's remarks: "After all, America had been a place of refuge for so many fine Germans in the period of 1848 and why couldn't we offer them again a place of refuge at this time." FDR suggested combining the German and Austrian quotas, which would allow the many Austrian applicants a chance at the unused portion of the much larger German quota. (The quota for Germany was 25,957; for Austria, 1,413. Since Germany had formally annexed Austria, there was some justification for FDR's move.) He also asked the cabinet whether an act to increase the German quota would get through Congress. Secretary of the Interior Harold Ickes supported the move, but the consensus was that it would fail. Vice President John Nance Garner said that, if it were left to a secret vote of Congress, *all* immigration would be stopped.[36] The idea of raising the quota was dropped. FDR announced that he hoped to encourage different countries to take anywhere from one hundred to one thousand families, thus finding homes for ten to fifteen thousand Austrian families.[37] That, of course, was a tiny fraction of the number of potential Austrian refugees. In subsequent discussions with Morgenthau and Undersecretary of State Sumner Welles, the president reaffirmed that congressional and public opposition made any new legislation impossible, but the administration could liberalize American immigration procedure and issue an appeal to persuade Latin American countries to accept refugees.[38]

By encouraging the full use of the German-Austrian quota, the administration could actually increase immigration to the United States—a move that was well in advance of American public opinion. A confidential poll on anti-Semitism in the U.S. carried out by the Opinion Research Corporation for the American Jewish Committee in the spring of 1938 noted that 82 percent of those polled were opposed to allowing a large number of Jewish exiles from Germany to immigrate to the U.S. The polling analysts observed that the percentage of negative responses on this question was far higher than the percentage of anti-Semitic responses to other questions: "We should perhaps interpret the question as a question regarding immigration rather than a question regarding the Jews."[39] Clearly, it was politically safer to sponsor resettlement of refugees abroad.

FDR wanted a new organization, not the International Labor Organization, to manage refugee resettlement. Welles went over the ideas with Messersmith and other State Department officials and then with Morgenthau, who found Welles extremely cooperative. Welles and Moffat composed two memoranda and cleared them with Hull the next morning. The documents described the administration's plans: invitations to foreign governments to join a special international committee to facilitate and finance emigration from Germany and Austria; mobilization of private organizations which might finance emigration work; a public appeal to the American people to remind them of the American tradition of providing asylum for refugees. Morgenthau thought that the documents covered the subject admirably and needed no amendment. He found that FDR was also enthusiastic but wanted one key change. The president wished to avoid the words "religious and racial refugees" and to use "political refugees" instead.[40]

One signal of trouble ahead was the decision to reassure foreign governments that no country taking part in the international committee would be expected or asked to receive a greater number of immigrants than was permitted by existing legislation.[41] Herbert Feis also complained two weeks later that the decisive question, intercession with German authorities, was being neglected. He blamed Messersmith, whose "philosophical calm" was disturbing.[42]

In early April the president invited to the White House a group of prominent Americans of various faiths to meet with him and with Undersecretary of State Sumner Welles, Messersmith, and Secretary of Labor Perkins. FDR announced that an international conference would soon take place to consider solutions to the refugee problem and to establish an international committee to deal with refugee resettlement. He asked the group to form a presidential advisory committee on political refugees (PACPR) to provide liaison among the government, private agencies concerned with immigration, and the new international committee once it was established. Professor Joseph Chamberlain of Columbia University proposed that the United States and other governments supply funding for refugee resettlement, but virtually the entire group disagreed because it would involve asking Congress for an appropriation.

Monsignor Michael Ready, general secretary of the National Catholic Welfare Conference, asked whether it was really necessary for each refugee to have two iron-clad affidavits of financial support from American citizens. Perkins pointed out that this requirement stemmed not from the law but from President Hoover's 1930 decision to strengthen the interpretation and enforcement of the LPC provision at a time of widespread unemployment. She urged a change. Messersmith argued that any loosening of regulations would create a storm of protest from "certain circles." Presumably this was a reference to congressional sentiment and to the potency of the patriotic associations. Perkins agreed that it would be wiser not to make any public statement about easing regulations, but she called upon the State Department to issue informal advice to consuls not to be so strict. By one account, she appealed to FDR: "Mr. President, I have no doubt that we will have to relax the regulations with regard to affidavits and that if we really want to be of help, we will have to permit the incoming of refugees without affidavits." Her words challenged Messersmith's view that only those immigrants who would strengthen the United States should be admitted. The experts did not want to burden the president with details, and the meeting adjourned until the afternoon. By then FDR and Perkins were no longer present.[43]

At the next meeting of the committee in May, Messersmith promised somewhat greater leniency with regard to documents required of visa applicants but otherwise stood his ground against any liberalization. He also cautioned against overoptimistic expectations regarding the refugee conference, now scheduled for Evian-les-Bains, France.[44] At least part of the problem was that no one was willing to take a leadership role. The State Department was anxious to avoid the impression that this was to be an American conference. Messersmith's view was that publicity should be kept to a minimum and that discussions should be as confidential as possible, focusing on constructive long-range solutions.[45]

Contrary to Messersmith's hope, the conference that convened on July 6, 1938, in the spa town of Evian on the shore of Lake Geneva became a well-publicized show, with journalists and observers (many from Jewish organizations and refugee associations) joining the official representatives from thirty-two nations. Retired U.S. Steel executive Myron Taylor headed the American delegation. In the first major address, Taylor sensibly pressed for a specialized refugee organization for Germans and Austrians, who posed the most urgent problem. Other refugees would have to wait. He then suggested resettlement efforts both for those who had already left the Reich and for those wishing to leave because of persecution. Following the established line of American policy, Taylor described existing American laws and practices as liberal, indicating that the full German quota of 27,370 would be used.[46]

After Taylor's speech, Lord Winterton presented the British viewpoint. A week earlier Winterton had written to British Foreign Secretary Lord Halifax that only German willingness to allow Jews to take property out of Germany and Austria could make emigration possible. When German foreign minister Joachim von Ribbentrop received this message from London, he refused even to consider allowing Jewish capital out of the country and threatened to retaliate against German Jews for any anti-German propaganda at the conference.[47] Winterton could not have been encouraged. Describing Britain as "not a country of immigration," Winterton told the conference that it could grant asylum only within narrow limits. Moreover, considerations of climate, race, political development, overpopulation, and "local political conditions" ruled out substantial immigration to many British colonies and overseas territories. "Local political conditions" was apparently a reference to Palestine.[48] An August 1937 White Paper had restricted Jewish immigration to Palestine, and Great Britain now had no intention of opening the gates wider.

The representatives of the other thirty nations delivered public statements of their governments' positions. They expressed their concern about persecution and their hope for eventual resettlement of refugees. Most did not even name the country creating the refugee problem. Virtually no one made any commitment to accept refugees, and some delegates went out of their way to explain why their immigration laws could not be changed (in that they were following the American lead) or why Jewish refugees could not be assimilated. A good many speeches were designed more for domestic consumption than for impressing other nations or the United States with their goodwill toward refugees. Thirty-nine different private organizations also had representatives at Evian, and virtually all of them insisted on testifying before one committee or another. The actual work at Evian was carried out by two subcommittees, which listened to the experts and drew up recommendations.[49] The one achievement of the conference was the establishment of a permanent Intergovernmental Committee on Refugees, headquartered in London. Under the leadership of seventy-year-old Washington lawyer George Rublee, the IGCR was given a mandate to negotiate with Germany about the fate of those wishing to leave. This move followed the original American plan.

The Roosevelt administration seems to have had two separate objectives in this initiative. Evian might have produced an organization capable of moving refugees from Germany (after negotiations with the Nazi government) to new places of settlement, perhaps even to mass settlements on large tracts of land in central or southern Africa. The IGCR would have been an international government agency providing a kind of New Deal for substantial numbers of refugees.[50] If the IGCR failed, and the odds were against any negotiations with Nazi Germany succeeding, the Evian Conference might at least have educated various governments about the problem and marshaled opposition to Nazi Germany. White House confidant Ben Cohen told one IGCR official that, if and when negotiations with Germany failed, the world would regard the Nazis as the villains.[51]

The Evian Conference failed to deal concretely with the desperate need of hundreds of thousands who had been heartened by President Roosevelt's initiative. In the words of one Jewish participant, "The little that was achieved bore no relationship to the hopes that were aroused."[52] In that sense, the meeting was a failure. Some insiders, such as American consul general John Wiley in Vienna and PACPR executive secretary George Warren, conscious of the many obstacles to progress and pessimistic about solutions, nonetheless were impressed by the lack of quarreling and by the quick establishment of a new international refugee organization.[53] Of course, they could not foresee that little would follow.

Director George Rublee quickly found that the British government and the American ambassador to Great Britain, Joseph Kennedy, were almost equally uninterested in his work and unwilling to support his efforts to open negotiations with the German government.[54] The other major task, finding places of settlement for the expected flood of Jewish refugees, was equally difficult. Only Generalissimo Rafael Trujillo of the Dominican Republic formally offered to admit large numbers of settlers and actually supplied land; other possibilities such as British Guiana, the Philippines, Madagascar, Angola, and Rhodesia never got beyond the exploratory stage.[55]

RENEWED EFFORTS

The Night of Broken Glass, widely reported in the international press, set off a wave of public revulsion against Germany in the United States and in Great Britain. Pleased with the growing unpopularity of Nazi Germany, Messersmith advised the White House to demonstrate its disapproval of the violence in Germany, recommending the recall of Ambassador Hugh Wilson "for consultation" without further comment. FDR decided to add a strong public statement, voicing his dismay that such things could occur in a twentieth-century civilization.[56] That was a condemnation of Nazism, not a concrete form of assistance for its victims. The British government, however, decided to admit 5,000 German Jewish children as a special measure. This British program was extended, and before the outbreak of war some 20,000 Jewish children came to Britain on special transports.[57]

The State Department remained steadfastly opposed to any attempt to expand the American immigration quotas. Messersmith quickly clashed with an old State Department adversary on immigration policy, Frances Perkins. Messersmith informed her that the State Department strongly opposed and regarded as illegal her plan for an executive order to allow German Jews in the United States on visitors' visas to remain indefinitely.[58] But Perkins won this battle. Although FDR had stated on November 15 that he would not recommend modification of immigration laws to Congress, three days later, at a second press conference, he announced that 12,000 to 15,000 visitors' visas granted to German Jewish refugees would be extended for at least six months.[59] The gesture was a significant bending of immigration regulations, but it paled beside the British response.

FDR, who had not seen his presidential advisory committee since April, met with its chairman, James G. McDonald, and members Hamilton Fish Armstrong and George L. Warren on November 16. The visitors told the president that his March initiative on the refugee problem had broken down and that something ought to be done. The committee delegation also stopped in afterward at the State Department to suggest that Myron Taylor return to London as the president's personal representative; that any negotiating functions be removed from Ambassador Kennedy, who was less than helpful; that FDR consider either a public appeal for funds or a request to Congress for an appropriation for resettlement of refugees; and that the IGCR accept and pursue the Dominican Republic's offer aggressively.[60] FDR apparently agreed, and the instructions drafted for Myron Taylor to take to London gave him enough leeway to bypass Kennedy. Although the State Department left open the possibility of negotiations with Germany, that aim was now played down. Instead, Taylor was to harness all possible efforts toward resettlement.[61]

FDR also considered a public appeal of some kind. In late November, while at Warm Springs, Georgia, he asked Sumner Welles to forward State Department information regarding "possible places for Jewish colonization in any part of the world." FDR also consulted his migration consultant, Professor Isaiah Bowman of John Hopkins University, regarding places of settlement in Latin America and Tanganyika.[62] A handwritten undated draft produced around this time, probably by FDR's speech writer Samuel Rosenman, gives some insight into FDR's thinking. He was to pledge to use his best efforts to raise a sum of money sufficient to buy a homeland or protectorate (for the Jewish people), a land large enough for five million people. This would not be a Zionist movement, but a "movement to find a place of refuge for millions of persecuted people who cannot be absorbed into the economies of other lands." This concept of a substitute for Palestine had attracted FDR earlier that same year.[63] But, in the end, he did not issue a public statement.

Rosenman advised the president against attempts to increase the American quotas. Provided that a large expanse of land could be obtained, colonization was more suited to the dimensions of the refugee problem. Any proposal to stretch the quotas would raise so much domestic opposition that all other proposals would become impossible; an increase in immigration would also aggravate the unemployment situation and produce a "Jewish problem."[64] The Roosevelt administration would become even more vulnerable to attacks by anti-Semites and isolationists, precisely at the time when the president was trying to influence public opinion and Congress against Germany. Just how far did the president's anti-German views go? In December 1938, through a private and confidential channel, Roosevelt told Prime Minister Chamberlain that if conflict broke out, Great Britain would have the industrial resources of the American nation behind it and could count on raw materials from the democracies of the world.[65]

Messersmith was thinking along similar lines. Messersmith was already aiming toward American aid to Britain and France in case war broke out; this aid would require repeal of the Neutrality Laws, which he believed the administration could accomplish. That overriding goal, however, impelled him to measure each new proposal for its possible adverse effects upon the administration's relations with Congress. And Jewish refugees would not win any popularity contest on the Hill. Thus, Messersmith opposed any bargain negotiated by the Intergovernmental Committee on Refugees with Germany if the arrangements gave the Nazis any economic advantage or worked to the detriment of American interests. "There are things in the world today which are of even greater importance than the refugee problem," he wrote to Geist, "and that is major political considerations and sound trading principles."[66] The major political considerations presumably involved the Roosevelt administration's efforts to stiffen British and French resistance to Germany, as well as to persuade Congress to step up defense spending. Messersmith's longtime opposition to any economic arrangements that might bail Germany out of its financial difficulties also played a role in his stance.

Messersmith and others at State argued that excessively liberal immigration measures would bring out and magnify latent American anti-Semitism. In the process they would create serious problems for the administration and its foreign policy. Messersmith was convinced that comments about what the United States owed the world in the way of admitting refugees were already stirring up trouble for the administration, and he took pains to rebut complaints about the prejudiced behavior of certain American consuls. American consuls were responsible for enforcing the law, and the public would not complacently accept laxity on immigration regulations, even under these circumstances. There is some evidence to support Messersmith's view. Although a Gallup poll conducted shortly after the Night of Broken Glass showed that 94 percent of the sample disapproved of Nazi treatment of German Jews, 77 percent of the American public still opposed permitting a "larger number of Jewish exiles to come to the United States to live." Whether or not this restrictionism was fueled by anti-Semitism, Messersmith correctly gauged the public's opposition to additional immigration.[67]

The assistant secretary believed that, for the time being, the United States could absorb the maximum number (27,370) of immigrants permitted under the German quota. When there was so much suffering in the world, he wrote to one Foreign Service officer, it was not the time to take restrictive measures. But he was also convinced that, if Congress went to work on immigration bills, it was much more likely to reduce the quotas than to expand them. Under these conditions, the important thing was for the State Department and Foreign Service to administer the laws and regulations fairly and to demonstrate to American citizens and congressmen that each case was receiving due consideration.[68]

Some administrative changes made it easier for the consulates to grant visas. Consuls were allowed to accept cabled texts of affidavits and cables from banks as evidence of the financial capability of American relatives of visa applicants. Applicants were also allowed to obtain quota numbers through letters of application rather than personal visits to the consulate. But the State Department rejected most suggestions for additional flexibility in visa policy. From Berlin, American consul general Raymond Geist advised not transferring numbers under the German quota to American consulates in other countries where German citizens had applied for visas; Geist's reason was that Jews in Germany were under much greater threat than those outside. But the Visa Division, backed by Messersmith, argued that the system of regulations was designed to equalize the waiting time wherever one applied for a visa under the German quota. No group should enjoy an advantage.[69] Geist also suggested that some of the documents sent by American citizens to support the visa applications of their relatives should be turned over to the applicants. The consulate itself lacked sufficient room to file all the documents, and, when visa applicants could show such documents to the German police, that often convinced the authorities that the applicants were trying to emigrate, which meant that a good number of them escaped arrest and imprisonment in concentration camps. The Visa Division was unmoved. All documents were to be kept in the consulate.[70] On the sticky question of whether affidavits from distant relatives or friends would be acceptable, the Visa Division suggested that such sponsors should set up irrevocable trusts on behalf of visa applicants to meet the LPC problem. Unsupported affidavits remained suspect.[71]

When Geist was allowed freedom to operate, he could perform wonders, for he had established a working relationship with some of the highest officials in the Nazi regime. In late 1938 after the Nazis arrested a number of wealthy Jews who had relatives in the United States, Geist managed to persuade Werner Best of the Gestapo to release twenty individuals from Sachsenhausen, among whom was Fritz Warburg of the prominent Jewish banking family. On occasion, Geist himself went into the camps to get the people out.[72]

Geist had also arranged for temporary havens in Britain, France, and the Netherlands for German applicants whose position on the waiting list was high enough to guarantee them American visas in the near future. Geist simply wrote letters stating that such persons had cleared their preliminary examination and were expected to receive American visas on such and such a date. This assurance alone convinced some German authorities to leave the applicants at liberty and to let them proceed to other European countries. When the Dutch government stated that it regarded such letters from the consulate as a U.S. commitment to admit the refugees in the future, Messersmith abruptly terminated the practice as illegal and damaging to the national interest.

> If through our own action and through the actions of the German government intermediate countries are filled up with large numbers of those refugees looking to this country as a final haven. . ., there is going to be pressure upon us and we, in public opinion, will be held up as the country which is refusing a refuge to these people. I think that we must be careful to avoid doing anything which will serve as any basis for such possible complication of our relations with other countries.[73]

Geist's humanitarian efforts gave way to perceived American foreign policy interests.

In early 1939 Messersmith blocked a proposal by the American Friends Service Committee to supply additional personnel for the visa work in the American consulates in Germany. Unless consulate staffs could file and process the mass of documents, the full quota might not be used. Entrepreneur-philanthropist Marshall Field had offered to cover the salaries of Quakers who would serve in clerical positions. The chief of the Visa Division, Avra Warren, had just returned from an inspection trip in Germany. Well aware of the problems of staffing and work load there, Warren was inclined to accept the proposed arrangement. Messersmith, however, felt that this might represent favoritism to the Quakers over other organizations. More important, he suspected that the employees would have divided loyalties—partly with the consulate, partly with the interests of their organization and the refugees. He turned the American Friends Service Committee down flatly.[74]

State also took steps to choke off visitors' visas at the source. Visa Division chief Avra Warren had been in Europe to survey the needs of the various consulates. He discovered that more than 300,000 persons had applied for visas under the German quota and that the consular staffs were overburdened. He also found that some staff members in Suttgart had sold visas. Warren added fifteen people to the staff of the consulate in Vienna, ten in Berlin, and ten in Stuttgart. In the process, however, he cautioned consuls against granting too many visitors' visas. Messersmith explained the situation to Geist: "Once people are in this country, we can hardly throw them out if they have no place to go except where they may be further persecuted." The department could not approve granting visitors' visas to those who would in effect become permanent immigrants. These people would have to remain in Germany and await their turn for a quota number. Messersmith justified this policy not only with an appeal to the law but also with an attack against Perkins, whose sympathy for the aliens constituted "an element of danger" and whose extraordinary measures represented "hysterical action."[75]

Perkins had not rested with her November 1938 triumph on visitors' visas. She was seeking legislation to permit a set number of children under age eighteen to enter the U.S. outside the quota system, a concept soon embodied in the Wagner-Rogers Bill, which died in Congress in mid-1939. Perkins also favored an additional and separate quota for sparsely settled Alaska that would benefit refugees.[76] Perkins, however, was severely handicapped in 1938–39 by opposition within the Labor Department and by congressional criticism. Commissioner of immigration James Houghteling, whose main qualification for the job was that his wife was FDR's cousin, was not in sympathy with Perkins's views. Following vitriolic right-wing criticism of Perkins, the House judiciary committee even investigated impeaching her because of a number of unpopular deportation and immigration decisions on her part. Charles Wyzanski, no longer solicitor general in the Labor Department but still a Perkins confidant, wrote to Felix Frankfurter in early 1939 in concern about the secretary of labor.

> I was gravely disturbed to see how obsessed she is with what I am sure most people regard as mere factional sally by the anti-Administration forces. Never having withstood the pummelling of an election campaign, and never having been subjected to the rough and tumble of ward politics, Miss Perkins takes much too literally charges which even the proponents would describe as political rather than personal. The result is that she is not concentrating on the program of her Department. . . .

Even Perkins's generous biographer concedes that the continuing slander hampered her effectiveness.[77]

There were few (if any) outspoken humanitarians like Perkins in the State Department. The one dissenting voice among State Department sources was Raymond Geist in Berlin. In a private letter to Messersmith, his former superior and friend, Geist recommended that the U.S. negotiate with Germany on the Jewish question because of the situation's urgency. Geist prophesied:

> The Jews in Germany are being condemned to death and their sentence will be slowly carried out; but probably too fast for the world to save them. . . . After we have saved these refugees, and the Catholics and Protestants have not become new victims of the wrath here, we could break off relations and prepare to join in a war against them [the Germans]. We shall have to do so sooner or later; as France and England will be steadily pushed to the wall and eventually to save ourselves we shall have to save them. The European situation was lost to the democracies at Munich and the final situation is slowly being prepared. The age lying before us will witness great struggles and the outcome when it comes will determine the fate of civilization for a century or more.[78]

Messersmith, who had always rejected any kind of deal that involved U.S. financial concessions to Germany, responded:

> Fundamental issues are at stake. These issues are greater than any individual or any individual suffering. . . . What we must do is maintain our principle in every field and one cannot maintain principle of so fundamental character by making concessions in individual cases or by soft-pedalling our adhesion to these principles. . . . Human ingenuity and the capacity of governments for action are not up to taking care of a refugee movement such as that which is being created by the German government and which may only be in its beginnings if the present movement continues.[79]

Whereas Geist linked humanitarian action to the fundamental principles and interests of the United States and the democracies generally, Messersmith rejected the connection. In fact, he feared that any deal with Nazi Germany regarding refugees might damage American political and economic interests.

NEGOTIATIONS WITH GERMANY

In December 1938 Reichsbank president Hjalmar Schacht surfaced in London under the sponsorship of Montague Norman, governor of the Bank of England. George Rublee of the IGCR finally arranged a meeting with Schacht through his British contacts, and Schacht presented his plan for Jewish emigration, about which rumors had been circulating for some time. The essential element was an orderly exodus over a three-year period of 150,000 Jews between the ages of fifteen and forty-five, to be followed later by their dependents. Some 200,000 Jews would have to remain in Germany. Schacht still retained the notion of a trust fund composed of seized Jewish property in Germany, 25 percent of which could be used for purchases by Jewish emigrants of supplies, equipment, and transportation sold by German companies. But outside (Jewish) interests would have to raise large amounts of capital for resettlement in the form of a bond; the remainder of the German trust fund kept safely in Berlin could supposedly serve as collateral.[80]

Could the rest of the world sanction German confiscation of 75 percent of all Jewish assets? Rublee and Robert Pell, a junior State Department official (and the uncle of current Rhode Island Senator Claiborne Pell), went to Berlin to pursue the negotiations, despite the distasteful features of the Schacht plan. But Schacht's resignation on January 20, 1939, the result of basic economic disagreements within the Nazi regime, left the negotiators stranded. Geist, however, managed to reach Hermann Göring, who expressed a willingness to see Rublee and to reopen the negotiations. Helmut Wohlthat, a mid-level official in the Economics Ministry, took over for Schacht, and the two sides exchanged memoranda of understanding on February 1–2. Rublee and Pell had managed to refashion arrangements so that the German government and the IGCR were each taking certain steps independently, which meant that no formal contract needed to be signed. The western nations were not implicated in Nazi extortion.[81]

The Rublee-Wohlthat agreement never came to fruition. The inactivity of the IGCR and the delayed establishment of the Coordinating Foundation that was supposed to raise hundreds of millions for resettlement has led historian Henry Feingold to question the depth of the commitment to refugee resettlement on the part of the Roosevelt administration and the State Department. It is true that Roosevelt's Evian initiative had bogged down and that the February agreement between Rublee and Wohlthat at least allowed the Americans to salvage a diplomatic achievement.

Where Feingold goes amiss is in implying that the negotiations were a sham.[82] Private letters as well as State Department documents make it clear that the negotiators were trying for the best agreement possible—one that would not benefit the Germany economy at the expense of American interests.[83] One problem that concerned Messersmith and Moffat was that other countries—Italy, Rumania, and above all, Poland (with its huge Jewish population of 3.3 million)—might follow Germany's example and demand resettlement of their Jews. The Polish ambassador to the United States had already hinted at this to Messersmith.[84] All in all, Rublee and the State Department had avoided the obvious pitfalls—allowing the Germans to derive economic benefits and setting a dangerous precedent of paying ransom for refugees—at the cost of acting immediately and decisively.

The president was willing to sanction German confiscation of Jewish assets (and private fund raising in the west for resettlement) provided that the result was mass immigration primarily to countries outside the United States. State Department officials, on the other hand, were concerned about the economic benefits that might accrue to Germany and the danger of other countries treating their Jewish citizens as hostages. Even American Jewish leaders were sharply divided, some accepting the view that the Rublee-Wohlthat agreement would encourage Germany (and Poland) to continue persecution. At one meeting of prominent Jewish spokesmen, Governor Lehman of New York declared that, if he were a free agent, he would throw the whole plan out the window but that "we cannot afford to offend the President or Taylor or Rublee or the world." In the end, the group agreed to cooperate with the establishment of a Coordinating Foundation as long as Jews did not have to sanction German "atrocities" directly or indirectly.[85] Roosevelt was the driving force behind American Jewish approval of the establishment of the Coordinating Foundation.

Once the foundation came into being, the president continued to push its potential to save lives. On May 4, 1939, Jay Pierrepont Moffat of the State Department attended a meeting at the White House with Myron Taylor, James G. McDonald, and a number of Jewish leaders. According to Moffatt, "Sumner Welles . . . read the latest telegram from Geist, indicating that, . . . unless places of settlement opened up very shortly, the radicals would again gain control in Germany and try to solve the Jewish problem their own way." Moffat recorded the president's urging: "We should tell the Germans in a fortnight—not one day longer,—that an organization was in existence which could deal with the German Trust. It was not so much a question of money as it was of actual lives, and FDR was convinced that the warnings given by our Embassy in Berlin were sound and not exaggerated."[86]

Actually, the Nazi radicals had already begun to take control. Reinhard Heydrich, Gestapo chief and SS Gruppenführer, took control of the new Reich Office for Jewish Emigration in February 1939. At the first meeting of its high-level officials, Heydrich announced that the expulsion of Jews from Vienna would serve as a model for similar action in Germany. Heydrich specified that it was not at all clear whether the Rublee plan would work and that his office would promote emigration by all possible means, regardless of the Rublee agreement. The emigration of poor Jews was to receive priority, according to Göring's instructions.[87] Presumably that was a better way to induce anti-Semitic reaction abroad.

The real question, then, is whether Hitler ever took negotiations with the IGCR seriously. For many months Rublee was barred from coming to Berlin; then Schacht broke the ice. In a post-World War II interview, Schacht explained that he had finally gone to Hitler and asked for permission to explore this channel. Hitler agreed but never explained his real thinking or informed Schacht of the other agencies' activities regarding Jewish emigration. Schacht had to fight a running battle with the German Foreign Office even after he received authorization to meet with Rublee. The state secretary in the Foreign Ministry wrote on January 18, 1939:

By direction of the Foreign Minister I told Minister Eisenlohr the following: 1) inialling of any agreements with Mr. Rublee is out of the question: 2) Among the agencies, the Foreign Ministry is to have primary responsibility in this matter, but must not give this impression vis-a-vis foreign countries: 3) no promises are to be given to Mr. Rublee regarding future treatment of the Jews in Germany.[88]

Two days later Schacht's forced resignation removed the one ranking figure who had pushed the project inside the government, and Heydrich told other government officials to proceed as if the Rublee agreement did not exist. For the Nazi leadership, disorderly emigration of impoverished Jews was preferable to well-managed resettlement of them in sparsely populated lands. Once war began, the Nazis would express another preference.

THE ST. LOUIS AFFAIR

Perhaps the most dramatic clash of Nazi emigration policy and American immigration policy occurred in May 1939 with the sailing of the *St. Louis,* a ship of the Hamburg-American Line (Hapag) loaded with 933 passengers, most of them Jewish refugees. These Jews were seeking at least a temporary haven in Havana, Cuba, where there was already a colony of more than 2,500 Jewish refugees. Among the passengers, 743 had applied for American visas and had secured affidavits of support from Americans. In effect, they wished to wait for their turn under the German quota in Havana rather than in Germany—which was perfectly legal under American laws. Many of the refugees already in Cuba were doing the same thing. But it would have been a long wait. The full quota was being used, and those waiting numbered in the hundreds of thousands.

The problem in the first instance was with Cuban law and immigration practice. Common methods of obtaining authorization to enter Cuba included immigration visas and tourist visas. The first required a passport visa and the posting of a five-hundred-dollar bond; the second required, in practice, an unofficial "fee" of one hundred sixty dollars to a private office maintained by the Cuban director general of immigration, Colonel Manuel Benitez Gonzalez, who was close to strongman Colonel Fulgencio Batista. (Benitez was said to have accumulated a fortune estimated at five hundred thousand to one million dollars in this way.) In return, the European "tourist" received a letter, issued by the director general of immigration, authorizing entry into Cuba for such time as was necessary to obtain an American visa. All of this had to occur before the European applicant could obtain passage on a ship. The United States government was well aware of this Cuban practice and not very pleased with it. The greater the number of refugees who entered Cuba, the greater the pressure on U.S. quotas.[89]

After Cuban newspapers and radio stations criticized the admission of Jewish refugees, Cuban president Laredo Bru issued a new decree (number 937) on May 5 requiring a bond of five hundred pesos from all aliens entering Cuba except tourists who were American citizens. Before any alien could disembark in Cuba, he or she also needed the written approval of the Cuban secretaries of state and labor. Transportation lines were made responsible for the expenses of those brought to Cuba without complying with the new regulations, including return passage to Europe.⁹⁰

At the request of the local Hapag agent, the German embassy in Havana requested on May 11 that the decree not apply to those passengers on ships already en route who had obtained tourist letters before May 5. German documents make it clear that the return of the passengers to Germany was considered undesirable.⁹¹ So despite a warning to Hapag by the League of Nations High Commissioner for Refugees,⁹² the *St. Louis* set sail from Hamburg two days later. Most of its passengers had tourist letters, which had been purchased earlier en masse by Hapag and resold to the passengers. The passengers and the captain knew nothing of the potential snag in Havana when they departed Hamburg. They were to learn en route.

As the ship made its way toward Cuba, the Cuban press was filled with anti-Semitic articles, and the pressure on the government to deny entry grew. Nonetheless, Benitez continued to proclaim that the passengers with previously issued tourist letters would be admitted. When the *St. Louis* and the *Orduña,* a much smaller refugee ship, docked in Havana on May 27, however, port authorities were under presidential orders not to honor the tourist letters and not to allow these "tourists" to leave the ship. President Bru was determined to teach Hapag a lesson. The *Orduña* set off, hoping to find a South American port where the seventy-two refugees aboard could disembark. Its passengers sent a telegram to the president of the United States asking for help and pointing out that sixty-seven of those on board held American quota registration numbers. The *St. Louis* remained in Havana harbor. Only twenty-two refugees who had acquired immigration visas were permitted to land. By this time the American press had picked up the story of the ship with no place to go.⁹³

The ship was forced to leave Cuban waters while negotiations were conducted. The captain of the ship, delaying the return to Hamburg as long as possible, maneuvered along the coast of Florida. A U.S. Coast Guard cutter followed, with orders to prevent anyone from trying to swim ashore.⁹⁴

The American consul general and ambassador in Cuba walked a tightrope during the confrontation. They were under instructions not to make official representations to the Cuban government over the *St. Louis.* Both Visa Division chief Avra Warren and Undersecretary Sumner Welles opposed intervention. On the other hand, the consulate was flooded with inquiries, particularly on the part of American relatives of the *St. Louis* passengers. Ambassador J. Butler Wright, therefore, held an informal conversation with the Cuban secretary of state regarding the incident and stressed the humanitarian aspects of the situation and the danger of negative publicity for Cuba. This gentle suasion was not enough to affect the Cuban decision.⁹⁵

Lawrence Berenson, New York lawyer, president of the Cuban Chamber of

Commerce in the U.S., and representative of the American Jewish Joint Distribution Committee, tried unsuccessfully to work out a bonding arrangement—to guarantee that the refugees would not be an economic burden to Cuba—with the Cuban president. According to Berenson, the president made definite promises to admit the passengers on three different occasions, but subordinate officials kept raising the ante. When Berenson turned down their outrageous demands, which ranged as high as a bond of four hundred fifty thousand dollars and approximately the same amount in "gifts," the negotiations ended. The American State Department, too, felt that additional bribery would not be wise.[96]

While negotiations were collapsing, Consul General Coert du Bois received a telephone call from Avra Warren in Washington. Warren said that a number of New York financiers had asked the Havana manager of Chase National Bank to pledge whatever sums the Cuban president considered necessary. They wanted the American ambassador to help arrange an interview with President Bru. Warren went on to say:

> that under no circumstances and in spite of considerable pressure would he or the Secretary of State or the President give me [du Bois] or the American Ambassador in Habana any instructions to intervene in the matter of the landing of the Saint Louis refugees, nor, presumably, of any other European refugees. . . . He said that he had had several interviews with Secretary Hull and that word had come from the White House. . . .[97]

A telegram from the passengers of the St. Louis to the president of the United States went unanswered.[98]

As the St. Louis slowly made its way back toward Hamburg, its passengers terrified of returning to Nazi concentration camps, the Joint Distribution Committee redoubled its efforts. Unable to budge the government agencies in Washington, chairman Paul Baerwald and European director Morris Troper finally succeeded with those in London, Paris, Brussels, and Amsterdam. Reassured by large financial guarantees and impressed by the publicity that the St. Louis had aroused, officials of the four countries agreed that each country would admit a percentage of the passengers. One passenger had died, and another had attempted suicide and had been hospitalized (in Cuba) during the ordeal. The remainder survived—at least until the German conquests in the spring of 1940.[99]

The German embassy in Havana asked the Foreign Office to deliver a note of protest to the Cuban government which stated that, although the embassy could well appreciate Cuba's unwillingness to accept Jews, the German government could not countenance the way a German company and a German ship had been abused. The Foreign Office, however, limited itself to an expression of displeasure (Befremden) rather than a full diplomatic protest.[100] The State Department in Washington had no complaints to make to Cuba.

The passengers of the St. Louis could not have entered the United States legally without new legislation or some kind of executive order. They could not be considered visitors or tourists, for both of these categories had to have a home country to which to return. They could not be given immigration visas without depriving other German applicants, who had registered earlier, of their visas.

If Congress had been capable of action rapid enough to meet the need, would it have taken the refugees in? We can give a probable answer to this question, because, even as the *St. Louis* waited near Cuba, Congress was considering another refugee bill. In February 1939 Senator Robert F. Wagner of New York (Democrat) and Representative Edith Nourse Rogers of Massachusetts (Republican) introduced a bill to bring into the United States 20,000 German refugee children during a two-year period—outside the quota. As David Wyman has noted in his well-researched analysis of the Wagner-Rogers bill, it would have been the first major liberalization of the Immigration Act of 1924.[101] We can use congressional sentiment on the Wagner-Rogers bill to estimate legislators' attitudes regarding the *St. Louis* passengers. (On the one hand, the Wagner-Rogers measure involved more refugees and thus was more controversial, but, on the other, foreign children usually generated more sympathy and less anxiety than adults.) The hearings generated a great deal of positive publicity and labor leaders supported the bill. Among the opponents were John B. Trevor of the American Coalition of Patriotic Societies, the Daughters of the American Revolution, and the American Legion. Senator Robert Reynolds of North Carolina threatened to filibuster against it.[102]

There were two private polls of Senate opinion, one in March and one in July. The first found that twenty-one senators favored the measure, twenty four were opposed, and the rest declined to answer.[103] That was clearly not enough for passage. The Senate Immigration Committee in June amended the bill to count the children as part of the German quota but to give them preference within it. Senator Wagner found this wholly unacceptable—the children would come in at the expense of adults. Even this diluted bill was far from certain to pass. A poll by the American Friends Service Committee found thirty-five senators in favor and thirty-four probably in favor. That might have sufficed, although a filibuster would have caused problems. But the House Immigration Committee never reported the bill out—eleven members were said to be opposed, only eight in favor.[104] The rush to adjourn for the summer ended any chance of passage.

The April 1939 *Fortune* poll listed 83 percent of all Americans opposed to an increase in the quotas; congressional inaction, therefore, was not surprising. Nor was FDR's stance. When he was asked to express his position on the Wagner-Rogers bill on June 1, he simply wrote, "File No Action." But Eleanor Roosevelt expressed support for the bill at a press conference.[105]

There is little question that, in addition to general anti-immigration sentiment, anti-Semitism played a substantial role in the bill's defeat. Messersmith had learned that a group interested in restricting or stopping immigration was approaching various senators and inquiring about the percentage of Jews admitted under the present quota system. The group threatened to emphasize and publicize the high proportion of Jewish immigrants. Messersmith thought this kind of trouble most unfortunate and advised against any effort to amend the quotas.[106] Laura Delano, the wife of immigration commissioner James Houghteling and FDR's first cousin, provided another view, according to Moffat: "Her principal reserve on the Bill was that 20,000 charming children would all too soon grow into 20,000 ugly adults."[107]

CLOSING THE WINDOW

In spite of the *St. Louis* incident, the extinction of the Wagner-Rogers Bill, and the stillborn schemes for refugee settlement in Alaska and the Virgin Islands, the period from March 1938 until September 1939 marked the most liberal phase of American immigration policy between 1931 and 1946.[108] Roughly 20,000 Germans were admitted to the United States per month as immigrants under the quota system, and the overwhelming majority were Jews or of Jewish descent. As many as one-quarter of these immigrants actually resided outside Germany when they obtained American visas, but they had not found permanent homes and, in any case, were still counted under the German quota.[109] A few hundred more individuals, some of them refugees, entered as nonquota immigrants; these individuals fell into special professional categories exempt from the quota.

The United States, it is fair to say, did not turn its back on the problem of Jews in Nazi Germany in the eighteen months before the outbreak of war. But the dimensions of the problem dwarfed the capacity of the United States under American immigration laws. By the end of June 1939, 309,782 Germans (including Austrians and Czechs) had applied for immigration visas under the quota.[110] There was no way for the Roosevelt administration to take in even a substantial fraction of that number without confronting Congress head on.

Nor could the Intergovernmental Committee on Refugees do much beyond cope with a portion of the German Jews who had already left the country—an estimated 150,000, of whom two-fifths were partly or wholly dependent on charity.[111] In July 1939 the British government proposed to speed up the flow of German refugees from "countries of intermediate refuge" (countries outside Germany) to new homes outside Europe by adding government money to private funds. This would have been a major change in the rules, and the British wanted other governments to participate as well. Although part of the reason for the proposal was undoubtedly to reduce the estimated 40,000 refugees in Great Britain, the British offer, combined with the prospect of refugee settlement in British Guiana, raised new possibilities. President Roosevelt invited the officers of the IGCR to meet in Washington in October in order to dramatize the issue again, explore means of intergovernmental cooperation, and check out the possibilities of government funding.[112]

Little more than a month later, the outbreak of war blasted any hopes of progress. Undersecretary Welles had given out the word in late August that Congress's willingness to follow the president's wishes on appropriation matters had diminished; Roosevelt would not ask for an appropriation for refugees unless he thought he had an even chance of winning on the Hill. And, if the worst came to pass in Europe, "all consideration of intergovernmental activity in Europe in behalf of German refugees would be abandoned."[113] The President's Advisory Committee on Political Refugees soon recommended cancelling the Washington IGCR meeting because of the changed situation. The committee foresaw problems:

> The issue of [American] neutrality may also be confused by the injection of the problem of German refugees who are considered by the [American] public to be predominantly Jewish. Anti-Semitic spokesmen may capitalize [on] this opportunity to accuse Jewish circles of a desire to involve the Government at a time of national emergency. Others in no sense anti-Semitic may consider that the problem of German refugees is receiving undue emphasis now that it is but one aspect of the total refugee problem.[114]

If the advocates of refugee immigration had reason to be this pessimistic, the American climate was very hostile indeed. Other nations now found reason to shy away as well. As the October conference approached, the British notified Washington that they would *not* propose adding government funds for refugee resettlement and that emigrants of German citizenship would not be admitted to British colonies during the war. That was the end of the British Guiana project.[115]

The State Department began to take stronger protective measures against a flood of aliens seeking entry. On September 30, it sent out a strongly worded instruction to the consulates not to grant (short-term) visitors' visas to individuals seeking to last out the war in the United States. Visa Division chief Avra Warren followed this up by an inspection tour at various European posts in November in order to tighten standards further.[116] The Visa Division also notified American consuls in Germany not to give visas to Germans without passports or without permission to leave the country. Consular officials in Germany decided, in view of the shortage of transportation out of the country, not to issue immigrant visas to anyone without evidence of a booking on a ship due to sail within four months. In addition, the potential immigrants had to have the ability to pay for passage and affidavits of support from American relatives. In early October only 93 German applicants out of more than 790 whose turn on the waiting list finally came up could qualify for visas.[117]

The result of all the obstacles in Germany was to free up immigration quota numbers for Germans living temporarily in other countries. Whether this was planned State Department policy is unclear. Although State Department officials disputed a deliberate diversion of German quota slots to countries outside

Germany in talks with the American Friends Service Committee, a Visa Division instruction to the field contains self-fulfilling assumptions:

> Presumably only a comparatively few persons are now able to depart from Germany. . . . Under the existing situation, therefore, it is anticipated that the German quota will be absorbed almost entirely by qualified applicants outside of Germany who are able to proceed to the United States. A similar situation is anticipated with respect to the Czechoslovak and Polish quotas and you are requested to inform . . . the officers who return to Warsaw accordingly.[118]

This instruction comes very close to a conscious policy to give preference to refugees who had already made their way to England, The Netherlands, Belgium, France, and the Iberian countries. The shift resulted from a modification in President Roosevelt's approach to the overall refugee problem.

Franklin Roosevelt's grandiose vision of resettling millions of human beings in underpopulated portions of the globe ran into practical difficulties even before September 1939. Given the unwillingness of non-European countries and colonies to admit Jews, the needs of German Jews alone were more than the Intergovernmental Committee and the Coordinating Foundation could handle. Yet FDR had originally taken the view that the Evian Conference and the IGCR should concern themselves not only with the German Jewish situation but also with the millions of potential refugees elsewhere in Europe—people who were unwanted in the country in which they lived and who themselves would prefer to start new lives abroad. The situation of the millions of Polish and Rumanian Jews was particularly noticeable. But the president once estimated that the total number of potential refugees was ten to twenty million.[119] As one skeptical State Department official put it, "We were trying to revive a horse that was ⅞ dead, and, at the same time, we were seeking to increase his burden to the point which would probably kill him if we first successfully revived him."[120]

Although the U.S. was not yet directly involved in the war, the president could easily have dropped the refugee issue entirely for more pressing defense and foreign policy matters. What he did instead was to divide the problem into two parts—long-term and short-term. The long-term goal remained a vast resettlement plan, for which necessary research could continue during the war. But there could obviously be no action until the war ended.

There is enough evidence to indicate that Roosevelt was sincere about this long-range vision. When the British and French governments claimed that, if they won the war, there would be no refugee problem—all refugees would simply be allowed to return to their homes—the president dismissed the argument and insisted that the research continue. When the State Department's Division of European Affairs showed an inclination to drop the IGCR, FDR refused to "put the Intergovernmental Committee quietly to sleep." Roosevelt criticized plans worked up by Belgian official Paul van Zeeland because they consisted only of small individual projects and lacked one or two very large areas for multitudes.[121]

With grand visions temporarily unattainable, one had to concentrate on what limited steps could be taken. The short-range refugee program, as FDR told the officers of the IGCR who met in Washington in October 1939, should be to find permanent homes for those persons who had already fled Nazi territories for temporary refuge in European countries. This would involve resettling *only* 200,000 to 300,000. Since Britain and France were at war, the president expressly stated, the burden of this work would have to fall heavily on the neutral nations.[122] The United States had been taking in substantial numbers of refugees since early 1938. The new American "anticipation" of giving German visas almost exclusively to German applicants already outside the country promised to reduce the refugee burden upon the European countries. If Latin American nations contributed as well, the short-range problem might be solved. But the Nazis had other plans.

BEGINNING THE FINAL SOLUTION

In early September 1939 Adolf Hitler made a special train trip to the war front in order to get a first-hand view of the German conquest of Poland. On September 12, Hitler's train stopped at the Silesian town of Ilnau. The chief of German military intelligence, Admiral Wilhelm Canaris, was delivering a report to General Keitel in one of the cars when Hitler and one of his top military aides, General Jodl, walked in. Hitler soon interrupted Canaris and delivered one of his customary monologues about what the French would do in the west—nothing. He then proceeded to discuss the German options in Poland and went into detail about the need to break all elements of the Polish will to resist. According to Canaris's aide, Erwin Lahousen, who was present:

> He said that it was especially necessary to eliminate the Clergy, the aristocracy, the intelligentsia, and the Jews. Now I don't remember the exact term that he used, but it was not ambiguous and it meant "kill." There is one expression that he used in this connection, which I am sure of, and I want to give it to you here. It is "Political Housecleaning." In German it is "Politische Flurbereinigung."[123]

To be sure, this was Lahousen's recollection in a 1945 interrogation. But it is supported by a variety of contemporary evidence.

Lahousen's memorandum for Canaris on the meeting of September 12, written two days after it took place, does not contain this part of Hitler's monologue. (The fact that Lahousen still remembered Hitler's chilling words in 1945 suggests that he consciously omitted writing them down in 1939.) The Lahousen memorandum does, however, contain Canaris's protest to Keitel against the plans for far-reaching executions in Poland and Keitel's response that the Führer had already made this decision. If the army refused to have anything to do with the executions, the SS and Gestapo would handle them. There would also be a civilian commander in each military district in charge of extermination of alien elements *(volkstümliche Ausrottung)*. Keitel also indicated that Hitler discussed these matters frequently not with him but with Göring. At best, Keitel learned of the results.[124]

On September 14, Heydrich held a meeting in Berlin with some of his important subordinates: Werner Best, Otto Ohlendorf, Heinrich Müller, Arthur Nebe, Walter Rauff, Franz Six, and Neumann. The Gestapo chief described his trip to the front and the impressions he had gained there. He then reported his own views on the Jewish problem in Poland. (Unfortunately, the minutes of the meeting lack any details of Heydrich's opinion.) Heydrich did say that Himmler would take some ideas on the subject to the Führer and that only Hitler himself could make such decisions, since they also had considerable implications for Germany's foreign policy.[125] This was undoubtedly a reference to the widely held belief in the influence of Jews on Germany's enemies. Although Britain and France had declared war against Germany after the invasion of Poland, they had done nothing to force hostilities. The Nazi leaders still hoped for peace in the west. On September 19, General Franz Halder wrote in his diary that Heydrich had reported an imminent political housecleaning in Poland: Jews, intelligentsia, clergy, nobility. The army leaders had insisted that the housecleaning be deferred until the army had withdrawn and the country was turned over to a civilian administration. The next day Halder mentioned a central agency for the housecleaning; the army would have the opportunity to scrutinize the plans.[126]

On September 21, Heydrich held another office conference on a number of issues, including the Jewish question. He reported that the Führer had approved plans for the creation of a foreign-speaking region around Cracow, into which Jews would be deported. Polish Jews would be concentrated in cities, German Jews would be sent to Poland (as would some 30,000 gypsies), and those portions of Poland to be annexed by Germany would also be cleared of Jews. On the same day Heydrich sent an express letter to the Einsatzgruppen commanders regarding the planned anti-Jewish measures. In this letter Heydrich specified that the final goal, which must be held strictly secret (*streng geheim Endziel*), would require considerable time to carry out. But they could move there in stages, which should begin immediately. Heydrich explained that Germany had to attend to economic security in the occupied territories, which might involve noninterference with Jewish merchants and industrialists who were important to the military or to the Office of the Four-Year Plan. Aryanization could be planned now and "emigration" carried out later. He did not spell out what the final goal of Nazi Jewish policy was.[127] He did not have to. When Adolf Eichmann was shown this document at his trial in Israel, he admitted that the term could only mean physical extermination.[128]

On September 22, 1939, Himmler sent Heydrich to meet with General von Brauchitsch, commander in chief of the German army, to respond to the army's expressed concerns. Heydrich agreed to inform the army about all SS commands. He also reported that Hitler had ordered that economic considerations should take priority at this time—thus, no overly rapid elimination of the Jews, and so forth *(keine zu schnelle Beseitigung der Juden, usw)*.[129] But, on October 17, Hitler told the High Command of the Armed Forces that it was necessary to replace the military administration in Poland with a civilian one that would confirm the prior decision [Hitler's decision] for a racial housecleaning *(völkische Flurbereinigung)*—i.e., for cleansing the new areas annexed by Germany of "Poles, Jews, and rabble."[130]

Hitler's decisions of September and October 1939 made it clear that the Government General of Poland would become a temporary dumping ground for Jews from the Warthegau, Posen, and the Reich itself, except for those held to be essential to the war effort. A careful reading of the documents also indicates that Hitler had already made the fundamental decision about the ultimate fate of these Jews. It was no accident that Heydrich used the term "final goal" (to be held strictly secret) on September 21. The timing and method remained to be determined. The Einsatzgruppen began the work of ridding Poland of thousands of nobles, clergy, intellectuals, and Jews in late 1939. But these actions only foreshadowed what was to come.

A combination of factors prevented Hitler from proceeding with the Final Solution at the outset of the war. The army's disinclination to take part in executions of civilians, combined with possible foreign policy repercussions if mass killings became known in the west, suggested that a more private method of disposal was needed. The gassing techniques of the Nazi "euthanasia" program would eventually be used on millions of Jews. Even more important, the German war effort might require the temporary assistance of Jewish businesses and labor. Before the Nazis disposed of millions of Jews, they had to make preparations to avoid excessive disruption of the war economy. Millions of foreign laborers ultimately supplanted Jewish labor.

To non-Nazi eyes, the Final Solution was not only literally incredible but also completely illogical. Germany remained short of labor during the war, and the transportation of Jews from all across Europe to the killing centers in the east clearly interfered with the war effort. The Nazi perspective was quite different. Beyond "revenge," the Nazis were determined to dispose of an unalterably hostile element in Europe, as the American diplomat John Wiley had foreseen in 1938. For Hitler and Himmler believed that the presence of Jews not only interfered with the war effort but also endangered the future of the Aryan race. The Final Solution was worth pursuing even when it became likely that the war itself would be lost.

FOUR

Refugees and American Jewry

Almost forty years after the end of World War II, the role of American Jews in influencing American refugee and rescue policies toward Hitler's victims remains a flash point for guilt, shame, self-castigation, and recriminations. The highly politicized, controversial American Jewish Commission on the Holocaust and numerous independent scholars continue to sift the historical record in the hope of clarifying what American Jews did and did not do for their suffering coreligionists.[1] A final verdict grounded on scholarly investigation rather than on self-serving, accusatory exchanges born of bitter reminiscences and frustrations is probably still years away. Available evidence, however, already suggests the need for a revised perspective on the prewar period.

In the 1950s, historian David Brody argued that during the 1930s there was a "lack of Jewish enthusiasm to liberalize our immigration policy by proximate causes that arose out of conditions peculiar to the time: economic distress, anti-Semitism, popular opposition, and Zionism." He also cited a reluctance among Jews to see a large influx of Jewish immigrants lest their own "Americanism" be called into question.[2] More recently, David Wyman's *Abandonment of the Jews* has dealt with the 1940s, but his assessment of Jewish efforts to modify America's restrictive refugee policy and promote rescue differs little from Brody. According to Wyman, there were two logical steps for American Jews: an "appeal to high government officials" and a "national campaign to publicize the mass killings with a view to directing public pressure on the Roosevelt administration and Congress." Wyman observes that, though they pursued both courses, Jewish leaders' efforts were "importantly diminished by their inability to mount a sustained or unified drive for government action, by diversion of energies into fighting among several organizations, and by failure to assign top priority to the rescue issue." Differences over Zionism emerged as an especially difficult obstacle. Both Wyman and Brody, then, agree that anti-Semitism was virulent and pervasive in the American population. Neither, however, explains how even a coordinated Jewish lobby could have overcome the anti-Jewish consensus.[3]

Other critics of American Jewry's behavior during the 1930s and 1940s merely echo the passionate outcries of contemporary witnesses. Some lament that American Jews did not "shake heaven and earth, echoing the agony of their doomed brothers." Others, however, denounce not only the inadequate effort but also a deficiency in sensibility that allowed Jews who could not stop the Holocaust to make peace with their impotence.[4]

In spite of the accusation that not enough was done and the assumption that if more had been done many Jews who died might have been saved, there is abundant evidence to suggest that, during the 1930s, American Jews did their best, using every means at their disposal, to provide European Jews with a haven. During this critical period, when the Nazi Final Solution was not yet a reality, American Jewish leaders tried private entreaties, mass meetings, public protests, and political pressure both formal and informal to recast American immigration policies and procedures so that European Jews might enter the United States. They met with staunch opposition from the State Department, the Congress, and the public at large. Even President Roosevelt, though generally sympathetic and sometimes helpful, refused to support an assault on the quota system. Some of the opposition was anti-Semitic, but most of it was grounded on the widely held belief that restrictionism was in the national interest, especially in light of the depression. As David Brody has observed, prior to 1933 many Jews did not differ markedly from non-Jews in believing that "the economic situation warrants restrictions."[5] In the 1932 presidential campaign, Roosevelt as well as Hoover favored restrictionism.

Between 1933 and 1939, Jewish groups tried and failed to confront their formidable restrictionist adversaries with a cohesive political force. Though most groups could agree on the goal—the generous admission of Jewish refugees to the United States—profound disagreement permeated the Jewish community on strategy and tactics. The inability of American Jews to successfully petition their government in behalf of their European brothers generated great frustration. Each group blamed the other for the failure, castigating tactics different from their own as wrong and damaging to the cause.

Able to budge American policy makers only slightly, Jewish groups perceived each other as part of the problem rather than as allies. As the position of the Jews in Germany degenerated, Jewish frustrations with their political impotence in the United States boiled over. Passions that could prod neither the State Department nor Roosevelt were turned by Jewish leaders and their groups on each other. Instead of a unified flock, Jews appeared to their fellow Americans to be a gaggle of squabbling factions, squawking shrilly over the credit and blame for actions taken but actions that accomplished little. Through all the sound and fury, however, American Jews were never "docile," consumed only by parochial concern over how more Jewish immigrants might further paralyze the economy, nor cowed by the threat of domestic anti-Semitism, as Brody has suggested. Though anti-Semitism "put Jews in the defensive and kept some from speaking out," David Wyman accurately observes that "many thousands of Jews were publicly vocal on a variety of controversial issues." American Jews of all organizational stripes were more than vocal. They acted, though all of them failed equally to "shake heaven and earth" or even jar the quota system during the 1930s.

The divisions in the American Jewish community were apparent even prior to the 1930s. Although the community could trace its American roots back three centuries, the overwhelming majority of Jews living in the U.S. were recent arrivals, having come during the great wave of immigration between 1880 and 1921. As late as 1880, there were only approximately two hundred fifty thousand Jews in the United States. In the next forty years, over four and one-half million Jews arrived. Even more important than the numbers, though, was the ethnic and religious character of the newcomers. Until the 1880s, the majority of Jews in America were from the German states, with a vestige of Sephardim whose forebears had come to America during the colonial period. These Jews tended to be quite secular, many of the Germans having embraced the reform Judaism that had modified traditional religious observance in their homeland. Many were artisans, craftsmen, and merchants, who brought with them marketable skills, entrepreneurial sensibilities, and, often, modest sums of capital for investment. The new Jewish immigrants, in contrast, were primarily from eastern Europe. They were poorer, and they tended more toward religious orthodoxy than did those who had come from Germany. In the 1880s and early 1890s, most of these new Jewish immigrants were young males seeking economic opportunity, some hoping that after they grew rich in America they could return to the families and communities they had left behind. But, by the turn of the century, an escalation of religious persecution in Russia, including the bloody Kishinev pogrom of 1903 in which forty-nine people were killed and more than five hundred injured, persuaded many Jews to leave. This later group included rabbis, intellectuals, the wealthy, and middle-class businessmen. Gone were the plans to return home eventually.

Although eastern European Jews had their own religious and secular leadership, in America the newcomers were frequently given assistance and advice by German Jews and the philanthropic organizations they had endowed to help poor and unassimilated newcomers. German Jews such as the Schiffs, Lewisohns, and Guggenheims designed their philanthropy to foster rapid assimilation. They hoped to eliminate the embarrassingly scruffy, primitive appearance typical of many eastern European Jews, especially those reluctant to shave their beards and clip their sidelocks. Forced to accept whatever help they could find, Russian Jews were often deeply alienated by the patronizing manners of the yahudim, as the Germans were derogatorily called. One Russian Jew complained in a letter to the *Yiddishe Gazetten* in 1894 that "in the philanthropic institutions of our aristocratic German Jews you see beautiful offices, desks, all decorated, but strict and angry faces. Every poor man is questioned like a criminal, is looked down upon. . . ." But "a Russian Jew . . . in an institution of Russian Jews" received a warmer reception. "He feels at home among his own brothers who speak his tongue, understand his thoughts and feel his heart."[6]

Conflicts over theology, socialism, and Zionism also divided Jews living in America and compounded their differences over assimilation.[7] German Jews tended to favor reform Judaism, oppose socialist politics, and be skeptical of the Zionist movement. Those of Russian heritage frequently supported orthodox religious values and institutions, clung to socialist politics or at least the rhetoric of socialism that they had learned in Russia, and were initially indifferent to Zionism. After World War I, Russian Jews came to see Palestine as the best refuge for those barred from the United States, a view not shared by the Germans. Many acculturated German Jews regarded themselves as merely members of a religious community. Zionism seemed a reactionary philosophy. Perhaps more important than the issues themselves, though, was the profound disagreement over the means by which Jews should choose their representatives to the non-Jewish world and the style of behavior those leaders should assume. In general, eastern European Jews preferred popularly elected representatives and supported the formation of a congress. German Jews, however, generally eschewed that approach in favor of a less representative, self-appointed elite, such as Louis Marshall and the other prominent Jews of the American Jewish Committee. Only one general election for a Jewish congress ever occurred, at the end of World War I. Nevertheless, an organization called the American Jewish Congress, headed by the Hungarian-born Rabbi Stephen Wise, did evolve to compete with the American Jewish Committee for the favor of American Jews.[8] By the 1930s neither the American Jewish Congress nor the American Jewish Committee could legitimately claim to represent a majority of American Jewry. The decentralized structure of American Jewish life that encouraged multiplication of organizations and discouraged unified action made coordination and cooperation impossible when the American Jewish community was faced with the persecution of European Jewry and needed to respond swiftly and effectively.

Consistent with their philosophical differences, American Jews mounted vastly different campaigns to help European Jewry. Some, such as the American Jewish Joint Distribution Committee, dedicated themselves to social programs, raising money and sponsoring direct assistance to refugees. Others, such as the American Jewish Committee and the American Jewish Congress, were defense groups that sought to lobby political leaders and marshal public opinion in pursuit of the community's interest. Still others, such as B'nai B'rith and the Jewish War Veterans, were fraternal organizations largely unconcerned with political matters until the refugee crisis galvanized their leadership. During the 1930s, the fraternal organizations sought to persuade the government of the United States to help European Jewry. They were divided, however, between those who favored "accommodation" and those who chose "protest."[9] The former tended to favor bringing informal influence or personal pressure to bear on individual decision makers; advocates of the latter preferred loud public protest whether in the press, at mass meetings, or through the use of such dramatic tactics as fasts or boycotts.

The American Jewish Committee and its largely German Jewish following usually opted for "accommodation."[10] On February 3, 1906, thirty-four Jews, most of them of German heritage, gathered in New York City to form a defense organization. They were stirred by the Kishinev pogrom, which even appeared on the front pages of the *New York Times*. The committee was itself a synthesis of old and new world notions of leadership and organization. It generally adopted the *shtadlanut* (court Jew) strategy that had been traditional in European Jewish communities since the Middle Ages. Jews of wealth and influence would use their prominence to influence non-Jewish wielders of power to act benevolently toward Jews. Other Jews would defer to their leadership. The committee, however, was also a product of the American social milieu and Progressive notions of political power and rule by educated experts. As such, it took the form of a voluntary association, loosely knit and led by a small group of dedicated activists. As did Americans involved in the Progressive movement, committee members stressed "enlightenment" as their proper function, specifically "scientific inquiry" that could be used for social planning. The offices of the committee often functioned as a research bureau, helping to finance the Jewish Telegraphic Agency and employing a staff to read and translate foreign periodicals. Sometimes criticized by members of the Jewish community for being a "self-appointed, undemocratic group," those prominent in the organization usually preferred discreet, personal interventions with policy makers to shrill threats of mass action.[11] Such committee members as Irving and Herbert Lehman, Joseph Proskauer, Samuel Rosenman, and Sol Stroock were highly regarded and influential political operatives who mixed regularly with those at the highest levels of American government. It was indeed this very influence that made many committee members skeptical of Zionism. They believed that Jews' best opportunity for a peaceful and productive existence was to integrate themselves into the social, economic, and political fabrics of the countries in which they lived and not pursue a separate homeland.

The American Jewish Congress with its sizable eastern European constituency tended to embrace public protest more readily than the American Jewish Committee.[12] The congress was founded in 1915 largely out of the desire of some Jews, especially Zionists, to articulate a separate Jewish political interest. Opponents, such as some members of the American Jewish Committee, feared the fragmentation that a congress of representatives might bring to an already factionalized American Jewish community. They were apprehensive over the alien appearance that Jews might reinforce in the eyes of their non-Jewish neighbors and sought to limit the congress to representing Jewry's interests at the postwar peace conference in Paris. Nothing, however, could prevent the election of delegates that took place in June 1918 and involved over thirty organizations. Some four hundred delegates were elected, 25 percent of whom represented various formal organizations. Members of the congress were in Paris in 1919 and, despite anti-Zionist opposition, supported the demand that the Balfour Declaration of 1917 be implemented. After the peace conference the congress did not disband, as its opponents had hoped, but continued to function as a pro-Zionist defense organization.[13]

The contrasting styles of the American Jewish Committee and the American Jewish Congress should be viewed as poles on a continuum. In between, Jewish groups and individuals adopted whatever tactics or ensemble of tactics that appeared consistent with their perspectives and resources. For instance, the B'nai B'rith (Children of the Covenant) was the oldest of the Jewish fraternal organizations. It was founded in 1843 by a number of German Jewish merchants living in lower Manhattan who believed that an exclusively Jewish fraternal order would be advantageous in ameliorating "the deplorable condition of the Jews in this our newly adopted country." Lodges of the new order sprang up in Jewish communities throughout the U.S., and in 1852 the organization became international with the opening of a Berlin chapter. Though B'nai B'rith occasionally found itself defending Jews against discrimination, it was not founded primarily for such duties. In the 1930s over sixty thousand American Jews belonged to B'nai B'rith. Its national leadership often supported the American Jewish Committee's accommodationist approach, but individual lodges and members exercised great latitude in their own choice of tactics.[14] Often similar tactics were employed simultaneously by different Jewish groups without any prior coordination. This absence of organizational discipline broadcast discordant notes rather than a carefully orchestrated appeal to the White House and State Department.

As early as January 1932, American Jewish Committee and American Jewish Congress representatives met to discuss how best to cope with Nazi anti-Semitic propaganda. Consultation with Jewish groups in Germany, however, suggested that any action by Jews in the United States would be premature and perhaps unnecessarily provocative. European Jews remained confident that the enlightened outlook of modern Germany and civil rights guarantees in the Weimar constitution were adequate defenses against National Socialism.[15] Nevertheless, the American Jewish Congress conducted internal discussions on monitoring the German situation and making known to the Germans that their behavior toward Jews was under surveillance.[16] Nine months later, Rev. John H. Holmes, a founder of both the National Association for the Advancement of Colored People and the American Civil Liberties Union, who had just returned from a trip to Germany, expressed his astonishment to Rabbi Stephen Wise that "the Jewish financial world in America" was permitting the Nazis' "deliberate incitements to pogroms" to "continue without protest." Holmes, according to Wise, observed that American Jewish financiers could launch an "intelligent campaign" that "could play hell with the Nazis, of course not by attacks in Germany but by bringing moral pressure to bear upon this element in the country." He was certain that "the Nazis are sensitive to foreign comment."[17] Still, the major Jewish organizations remained hesitant to intervene.

Hitler was already in power when Roosevelt took the oath of office in March 1933. American Jews immediately converged on the new president.

Among the telegrams of congratulations that FDR received upon his inauguration was one from Harold Debrest of the *Jewish Forum,* who urged the "successor to George Washington, Abraham Lincoln, Theodore Roosevelt and Woodrow Wilson" to reassure American Jews that their "brethren in Germany" would not be "massacred."[18] The White House shunted Debrest's plea to the State Department; there it came to Undersecretary of State Phillips who wrote, "I am happy to inform you that no reports from our representatives in Germany afford any ground for crediting the accuracy of the press dispatches in question." Phillips assured him that "our representatives will continue to be alert to and active in behalf of the rights of American nationals."[19] The State Department consistently took the stance that it had no responsibility for non-Americans in Germany.

Jay Pierrepont Moffat offered an embassy official in Berlin a Washington perspective on Jewish reaction to events in Germany. For a while, according to Moffat, the State Department succeeded in responding only to incidents of mistreatment involving American Jews in Germany, but soon "stories cabled to this country by Jews who succeeded in getting out of Germany" aroused "political pressure of astounding proportion." Moffat observed that "groups headed by Cyrus Adler, Rabbi Wise, Bernard Deutsch, Dr. Cohen, Judge Lehman, etc., came to see the President, the Secretary and Bill Phillips, jointly and severally. Resolutions were introduced in Congress. Mass meetings were called all over the country, and demands were made with varying degrees of emphasis that our government send a sharp protest to Berlin."[20] Moffat's description accurately reflects the flutter of activity among American Jews during March 1933 in the hope that FDR's humanitarianism would be translated into stern warnings to Germany and a generous immigration policy toward refugees.

But the American Jewish community was neither large nor intimidating in 1933. With a total population under five million, Jews accounted for less than 3 percent of the nation's voters. High concentrations of Jewish voters in states having large numbers of electoral votes such as New York, Illinois, and Pennsylvania gave Jews some electoral clout. In 1932 New York City's Jews gave Franklin Roosevelt 72.2 percent of their votes, second only to the Italians (80.5 percent) among the city's major ethnic groups. By 1936 FDR did better among New York's Jews (87.5 percent) than among any of the city's other ethnic blocs.[21] Still, the Jews could hardly claim sufficient numbers at the polls to make or break a national politician.

And not many Jews were in prominent political positions prior to the New Deal. There had never been a Jew in a presidential cabinet until FDR's cousin, Theodore, appointed Oscar Straus secretary of commerce and labor. FDR did no less, inviting Henry Morgenthau, Jr., to head the Treasury Department in late 1933 after William H. Woodin was forced to resign the post because of illness. There were Jews in Congress; ten were seated in the first session of the seventy-fifth Congress and six in the second. A few even held key committee positions. Sol Bloom was chairman of the House Foreign Affairs Committee, Samuel Dickstein was chairman of the House Committee on Immigration and Naturalization, and Emanuel Celler was chairman of the House Judiciary Committee. Jews in Congress as well as those who were close to the president walked a tightrope on issues of concern to Jews, lest they be vulnerable to the charge of using their positions to advance Jewish causes at the expense of the national interest.[22]

Charges that the Jews in America were more loyal to their tribe than to their country abounded in the United States during the 1930s. Prominent Jews and Jewish organizations often found themselves in a fishbowl, closely scrutinized by a society that was already suspicious of Jews. Father Charles E. Coughlin's movement had between 185,000 and 350,000 paid subscribers to its Jew-baiting weekly paper, *Social Justice*. Millions more listened attentively to Coughlin on the radio every Sunday. The Christian Front, largely supported by the "radio priest," became the hub of much anti-Semitic activity in the neighborhoods of cities where Irish Catholics felt threatened by the intrusion of Jewish newcomers from eastern Europe. Fritz Kuhn's German American Bund had approximately 25,000 followers, many of German extraction; about one-third of them clad themselves in the brown shirts that Hitler's storm troopers had popularized in Germany. White sheets with holes for eyes, nose, and mouth characterized the Ku Klux Klan, whose Imperial Wizard could claim a membership of well over a hundred thousand during the 1930s. For over a decade klansmen had included Jews and Catholics in northern cities with southern blacks as targets for abuse.[23]

Many Protestant Americans viewed the depression as a moral and spiritual crisis precipitated by a conspiracy of unchristian subversives, especially Jews. Historian Leo Ribuffo has identified this "old Christian right," including William Dudley Pelley and his Silver Shirts, Gerald P. Winrod, and Gerald L. K. Smith, as "emerging from devout Protestant backgrounds," their politics and prejudices grounded in religious faith. To these right-wing Christians, the New Deal was just the latest form of infidelity to Christian values. Jews and others who supported such sacrilege were fought with "appropriated memories, historical analogies, and formulas as familiar as the frontier thesis and the wrath of God," according to Ribuffo.[24]

In spite of the popularity of hatemongers and their groups, few politicians went so far as congressional candidate Joseph E. McWilliams who boasted that he was the "anti-Jewish candidate for Congress."[25] Many politicians found it advantageous, however, to allude to a clandestine Jewish conspiracy to control America—whether from the bottom up as Bolsheviks or from the top down as the masterminds of Wall Street. Either or both—the point was that the Jews were bad for America.

Those who labored in the vineyards of anti-Semitism found the American population ripe for harvest during the 1930s. Public opinion polls, taken with increasing frequency after 1935 by George Gallup, Elmo Roper, and others, suggest an unmistakable pattern. Anti-Jewish feeling seemed related to apprehensions over wealth and power in the country. A 1938 poll determined that "greed," "dishonesty," and "aggressiveness" were the three "qualities" that America most objected to in Jews. Fully 41 percent of those questioned in March 1938 thought Jews had "too much power in the United States." A poll two months later revealed that one-fifth of those sampled wanted to "drive Jews out of the United States" as a means of reducing their power. Almost one-quarter (24 percent) wanted to keep them out of government and politics, while 18 percent would have restricted them in business.[26]

The intensity and pervasiveness of American anti-Semitism was not lost on Jewish leaders nor on the membership of their organizations. Prudence and a wary appreciation for the marginal place of Jews in American society were ever-present considerations. Even so, David Brody greatly exaggerated when he charged that "the relation between the necessity of German Jewry to emigrate and a more liberal immigration policy was passed over in silence by American Jews."[27] On the contrary, Jewish voices representing many different ideological and tactical preferences were raised on behalf of German Jewish refugees in the 1930s.

Between 1933 and 1936, Jewish "accommodationists" and "protesters" worked tirelessly—sometimes together, more often separately—to command the attention of the hydra-headed government bureaucracy in Washington. Simultaneously, a handful of prominent Jews sought to circumvent the bureaucracy and elicit action directly from Roosevelt. After Roosevelt's re-election in 1936 and until the outbreak of war in Europe, American Jews sought to expand the limited modifications in American visa policy that they had won, even as their frustration with the modesty of their accomplishment led to more virulent charges and countercharges of bungling among the groups.

At the suggestion of the B'nai B'rith in early 1933, the American Jewish Committee, the American Jewish Congress, and the B'nai B'rith met to assess developments and plan a strategy.[28] On February 22, 1933, the three organizations agreed to establish a Joint Conference Committee of six to confer periodically on events in Germany and determine the proper involvement of Jewish organizations. Only three weeks later, in response to the continued mistreatment of Jews in Germany, the American Jewish Congress struck out on its own by endorsing mass meetings and demonstrations across the country. A rally at Madison Square Garden was planned for March 28 in opposition to the judgment of German-American Jewish leaders who continued to advocate cautious watchfulness over precipitate acts of protest.[29]

The unilateral action on the part of the American Jewish Congress troubled the State Department and Jewish leaders in Germany as well as members of the Joint Conference Committee from B'nai B'rith and the American Jewish Committee. Jay Pierrepont Moffat reported that "the agitation, instead of calming, continued to grow in intensity and we were told that unless some good news were forthcoming . . . the speeches and resolutions there [at the rally] might prove exceedingly embarrassing."[30] State sought to calm fears among Jews and avoid a potentially awkward exchange with the German government by sending Rabbi Stephen Wise of the congress and Cyrus Adler of the committee a telegram for presentation to the rally. The message—which had been reviewed by Sol Bloom, Hamilton Fish, Judge Sam McReynolds, and Senator Royall Copeland, "all of whom approved the general tone and expressed the belief that it would enable the leaders to keep the rank and file at the mass meeting . . . from running away"—was intended to be reassuring.[31] It stated that physical mistreatment of Jews "may be considered virtually terminated," that Hitler had called upon his followers to "maintain law and order," and that the State Department would "watch the situation closely, with a sympathetic interest and with a desire to be helpful in whatever way possible."[32] Moffat thought the telegram got "a pretty good press here."[33]

The State Department's message, which had been delivered to the presidents of the American Jewish Congress, the American Jewish Committee, and the B'nai B'rith, though comforting, was insufficient. In reply, Stephen Wise and Bernard Deutsch of the congress made clear that, "until the status of the Jewish citizens of Germany is safeguarded and the position of the non-national Jew is secured, the enlightened opinion of America must watch with profoundest anxiety the development of events in Germany."[34] That anxiety was fed by the mounting reports that the Nazis had no intention of canceling an anti-Jewish boycott that they had been instigating since early March.

Escalating concern over the planned boycott threatened to unleash Jewish protests in the United States more militant than anything even the American Jewish Congress advocated as American Jews called for retaliation in kind.[35] Again, a congress delegation headed by Wise and Deutsch went to the State Department for a discussion with Undersecretary Phillips. Though the details of the discussion on March 30 were never made public, the press reported that the U.S. government would seek to assert its influence in a restrained, quiet manner rather than in formal protest to the German government.[36]

The boycott issue exposed the raw nerves within the American Jewish community, but it also strained relations between American Jews and the Jewish leadership in Germany. Among prominent German Jews, Eric Warburg of the well-known banking family contacted his American cousin, Frederick, to warn American Jews that the German government could probably be dissuaded from permitting an anti-Jewish boycott unless atrocity stories and threats of counter-boycotts continued to appear in print. Cyrus Adler, head of the American Jewish Committee and Frederick Warburg's close friend, agreed to try to calm the situation and assured the Warburgs that "no responsible body in this country had proposed a boycott against Germany and the statements to that effect that had been made were purely sporadic."[37] Morris D. Waldman, executive secretary of the committee, issued a public statement at Adler's suggestion that eschewed once again the threat of a boycott. But he added, "It is impossible to tell, however, what will happen if the threat of boycott against all Jews in Germany is carried out on April 1st."[38]

While the American Jewish Committee limited itself to veiled threats, hoping to defuse the situation, Stephen Wise and the American Jewish Congress were publicly skeptical of German assurances that an officially sanctioned, sustained boycott would not take place. On April 2, Cordell Hull received word from the American chargé d'affaires in Berlin that there had been a one-day anti-Jewish boycott, but that it had occurred quietly and had not triggered an outburst of violence.[39] He passed the word to the Jewish agency presidents promptly along with German promises that the boycott would not be resumed. Wise and Deutsch, risking the ignition of a situation that they correctly assessed as volatile, responded publicly that German assurances "will not deceive anybody interested in the actual plight of the Jews in Germany. The attitude of the German government is more truthfully reflected in the brutality which accompanied the organized execution of the boycott and its humiliating violations of human rights and dignity."[40] Yet, though Wise and Deutsch preferred tougher talk, the congress was initially no more supportive than the committee of an anti-German boycott.[41] It was the independent initiative of some congress constituencies that forced all Jewish agencies to take a public position on the boycott of German goods.

Proposed initially by the Jewish War Veterans (JWV), the anti-German boycott gained support only gradually. Eminent jurist Joseph M. Proskauer reflected the fears of many when he warned that a militant campaign of "marches" and "meetings" and other "unintelligent action" could increase rather than dissipate the troubles suffered by Jews in Germany.[42] Still, by late spring, boycotters had begun to march in parades, distribute fliers, and compose slogans. Leaders made unsubstantiated claims that, within days of the boycott's beginning, orders worth almost two million dollars placed with German firms by Americans had been canceled. On March 30, a delegation even managed to visit the White House and present FDR with a resolution condemning the mistreatment of Jews in Germany.[43] Propelled by the Jewish War Veterans, a new organization called the American League for the Defense of Jewish Rights (ALDJR) was born in late April. The boycott was the main component of its agenda.

The American Jewish Committee continued to oppose the boycott, arguing that "all should entrust the responsibility [of acting for the Jewish people] to recognized organizations like the American Jewish Committee and B'nai B'rith who have been dealing with these problems for many years."[44] But, by August, the American Jewish Congress had begun to question its antiboycott position. Throughout the spring of 1933 Stephen Wise clung to the belief that public protest and private consultation would move FDR to use his influence with the Germans. As it became apparent, however, that neither Roosevelt nor the State Department had been moved to action, Wise turned from his antiboycott stance.

In Prague for the World Zionist Congress, Wise said that, as long as Germany continued persecuting Jews, "decent self-respecting Jews cannot deal with Germany in any way, buy or sell or maintain any manner of commerce with Germany or travel on German boats."[45]

Shocking and alienating its uneasy, accommodationist allies, the American Jewish Congress voted to join the boycott in August 1933. The American Jewish Committee reacted to this sudden change of tactics by regarding cooperation with the congress as virtually impossible. A Conjoint Consultative Council, which had only recently replaced the old Joint Conference Committee, seemed all but dead, and the two major Jewish defense organizations now stood diametrically opposed to each other, a condition that would neither help in the already difficult task of rescuing German Jewry nor dissipate over time.

Groups anxious to forestall destructive "fighting within our own ranks" looked to Jews in the U.S. Congress to coordinate political efforts to rescue European Jewry. But they placed their faith in a weak reed. Stephen Wise colorfully, but dismissively, described the congressmen he encountered:

> Sabath, who is a thick and thin supporter of the President and who I believe did much to nominate him by securing Cermak's support for him; Celler, who is blatant but insignificant; Mrs. Kahn who has probably the best head of the whole crowd—though that does not mean very much; Dickstein, who can best be characterized as Dickstein; Sirevich, a super-articulate charlatan; Bloom, former vaudeville manager and real estate speculator, who as a result of his success in having put George Washington on the map is now become one of the statesmen of Washington; Ellenbogen of Pittsburgh, a Viennese lad who must wait another two months before he can be sworn in, because seven years have not elapsed since he became a citizen.[46]

According to Wise, Ellenbogen reported that FDR told him: "There are two kinds of Jews—those who want me to spread-eagle and those who want me to be silent." Though Wise was surprised to hear "from the lips of the President that there are those who want him to be silent," he was not impressed by the potential of the congressmen he met to break that silence. Indeed, to their report of anti-Semitism even in the halls of Congress, Wise responded that "much of what they imagine to be anti-Semitism in general is nothing more than contempt and loathing for them personally, which of course they rationalize away in the self-protective terms of anti-Semitism." Though Sabath and Bloom attempted to demonstrate their command of the situation and their loyalty to the president, Wise was quite convinced that he and others such as Brandeis and Frankfurter knew much more about "what has been happening." Wise felt that "Bloom and Sabath and those poor little colleagues of theirs, require indoctrination almost as much as C.H. (Cordell Hull) did on other grounds. . . ."[47] Though his assessment of individual Jewish members of Congress smacks of Wise's characteristic hyperbole, the rabbi's criticism of their collective ineffectuality was correct.

"Accommodationists" among organized Jewry and those who remained outside the Jewish organizational network altogether never doubted that personal overtures to Roosevelt would produce the best results. And most agreed with presidential advisor Raymond Moley that Frankfurter "was the person in whom the President put the greatest confidence and that Felix Frankfurter's attitude in this matter would have enormous weight with the President." Some Jewish leaders, however, recognized that his very closeness to FDR made Frankfurter reluctant to impose upon that friendship. Wise perceived that Frankfurter felt "a certain disinclination to step out into the open at this time." And even the assertive rabbi thought that perhaps "his [Frankfurter's] very great influence with the administration ought to be reserved."[48] In fact, Frankfurter had raised the issue with Roosevelt in a meeting on April 7.[49]

Frankfurter waited two weeks for some word of the action that the White House planned to take. Finally, he telegrammed his old friend for "some word of progress" on plans for assisting the refugees, plans that might preempt a politically awkward, direct public appeal from Wise.[50] In return he received a telegram from Raymond Moley to the effect that Moley was taking personal charge of the matter.[51] Several weeks later, Frankfurter received a courteous letter from Hull, assuring the professor that his views had been "carefully noted" and that Hull had met with Wise personally the week before. Hull, however, did not waver from State's insistence that "applicants born in Germany are experiencing no delay in receiving visas as a result of quota limitations, since the quota for Germany is heavily underissued and applicants who can meet the other requirements of the immigration laws may receive visas promptly."[52] Even Frankfurter, the president's personal confidant on so many matters, was shunted into bureaucratic channels when he pressed Roosevelt on the refugee issue.

Cyrus Adler attributed the president's reluctance to deal directly with American Jews to FDR's wish to appear unencumbered by special interests in his conduct of foreign policy. Adler wrote, "I have had no direct relations with the President since he came into office and this at his request. He wished all of our dealings to be with Secretary Hull. Because of the large interests that he was taking up with various foreign nations he did not wish anything to intervene." In June, Adler and Judge Samuel Rosenman, a close friend and advisor to Roosevelt, assured the Executive Committee of the American Jewish Congress "on the basis of direct information" that FDR was "deeply concerned over the German situation" and that he had withheld any public statement only because "his present greatest concern is with the economic and disarmament conferences and he would not do anything that has the slightest possibility of doing injury to those conferences, because if they fail, the results for the world at large and for the Jews in particular would be extremely unfavorable."[53]

Whatever Roosevelt's motivation for his unresponsiveness to Frankfurter, no one was more frustrated by it than the professor himself. Frankfurter, in part, blamed the wrangling within the American Jewish community and especially the equivocating accommodationist leadership of the American Jewish Committee for having derailed "the train for action" he believed he had set in motion. An irritated Frankfurter, concerned with both his own credibility in the White House and the need to approach policy makers with a united front, angrily wrote, "Now I don't give a damn about the internal rows among New York Jewry. But they have much significance to something about which I care profoundly, namely, the realization by this government that there are no real divisions among the ranks of American Jewry in their anxious desire . . . to have the government speak out on . . . 'fundamental human rights.'"[54] Frankfurter confessed to his long-time friend Frances Perkins, "For once in my life I wish that, for a brief period, I were not a Jew. Then I would not have even the appearance of being sectarian. . . ."[55]

In spite of all the obstacles he had encountered, Frankfurter continued to hold FDR blameless, asserting that it was "the formal timidities of the Bill Phillipses" that stymied the president's wise forthrightness."[56] Even as FDR referred his entreaties to the State Department, Frankfurter persisted in believing that State was "frustrating" the White House rather than merely responding to administration mandates to follow a restrictive immigration policy and a low-key foreign policy toward Germany. Moreover, the Harvard professor failed to understand that the "rows" among Jews were not simply spats among petty, selfish, organizational bureaucrats but manifestations of the frustration building within Jewish ranks. Unable to believe they would not be able to marshal American government support for German Jewry, Jewish leaders attributed their lack of progress to the ineffectiveness of each other's tactics and strategies. The "rows" were the product, not the cause, of Jewish disillusionment.

Though patently unable to stop their internal bickering, Jewish leaders were not unaware of the public ramifications of their discord. Cyrus Adler, still fuming in November 1933 over the decision of the American Jewish Congress to support the boycott, wrote:

> The Jews in America are not united; the Jews throughout the world are not united. I do not know any way in which the Jews can be united unless the policy of Germany is followed and they are "coordinated . . . I . . . have the feeling that there is too much public discussion and we Jews are promoting too much of it and that it is not unlikely that our Christian fellow citizens will get tired of us.[57]

Adler feared that anti-Semitism stoked by Nazi propaganda would only be inflamed by "the constant airing of their [the Jewish people's] wrongs and their sorrows and the showing of their sores, wearying people . . . giving the impression that in the world they wish to put themselves forward as the only problem."[58]

Adler's comments are revealing. The American Jewish Committee's leadership denounced the open, public style of the American Jewish Congress. Underlying this criticism, though, simmered frustration over how little attention the refugee issue was attracting among non-Jews generally. Unable to accept the indifference of most Americans, including many Jews, Adler could only rant against the congress's tactics, even complaining that the congress had enjoyed good publicity while "the work of the American Jewish Committee was not widely known."[59] Implicit is the assumption that, if only the committee could have the field to itself, American leaders could be moved to act on the refugees' behalf.

Rabbi Stephen Wise, especially, irritated and embarrassed committee leaders. The outspoken rabbi and honorary president of the congress, with his flair for publicity and personal promotion, provoked conservative committee spokesmen. In April 1933, Joseph M. Proskauer confided to Louis D. Brandeis, the elder statesman of American Jewish leaders, that he considered Wise "temperamentally unable to refrain from raising arguments as to what has been done by the Committee and what has been done by the Congress, a subject which I am sure is of little interest to you and me at this particular crisis."[60] Later Proskauer wrote directly to Wise, "At the present time nothing will prompt me to argue, discuss, or have controversy about any matter as to the past performances of the American Jewish Committee or the American Jewish Congress."[61]

According to the committee, Wise consistently claimed credit for himself and the congress that ought more rightly to have been shared with other leaders and groups (especially the committee), thereby fueling dissension. Morris Waldman circulated a call from the American Jewish Congress to American Jews to participate in national democratic elections but not before he furiously underlined Wise's exaggerated claim that the congress was "the first body to reorganize and to gauge the menace of Hitlerism," "initiating the world-wide protest movement against Hitlerism" and "the great defensive movement against this menace as exemplified in the boycott, as well as exposure of the Nazi invasion of America."[62]

The American Jewish Committee exulted in being able to demonstrate Wise's inconsistencies. In the file that the committee kept on Wise, the committee compared demands that the rabbi "emphatically made" of the German government at the Madison Square Garden rally on March 28, 1933, and those he made before the National Executive Committee of the American Jewish Congress six months later on September 24. Before the throngs and the reporters at the Garden, Wise made bold demands: (1) immediate cessation of anti-Semitic activities in Germany, including an end to the policy of racial discrimination against and economic exclusion of Jews from the life of Germany; (2) revocation of all special measures already taken against Jewish non-nationals and their equal treatment with other non-nationals in Germany; and (3) safeguarding of Jewish lives and Jewish rights. Before his own group, however, Wise's demands were considerably more modest. He wanted means devised (1) to facilitate the emigration of Jews in appreciable numbers from Germany; (2) to enable Jews to take with them their capital in whole or in part; (3) to explore lands of possible emigration; and (4) to reorient Jews economically, industrially, and socially.[63]

If Wise's daring swelled before larger audiences, his personal conceit was nourished by press coverage, according to his adversaries on the American Jewish Committee. Waldman clipped an article from the *New York Herald Tribune* in September 1933 that he felt gave an "insight into his [Wise's] personality of which the newspapermen are not unaware."

> A thousand things seemed to crowd into his mind at once, and about all of them he felt so passionately that frequently he had to stop to suppress his emotion. Then the flight of 'newspaper time' seemed to bother him. Time and again, looking at a watch, he would halt to inquire: 'When does your next edition go to press boys?. . . .' [64]

Several hours later, after assuring the reporters that the situation in Germany was "far graver than has yet been told," the rabbi announced, "Well boys, I must give a 'little time now to the photographers.' He [Wise] stood with his hand on the cardinal's chair. 'It comes from Florence,' he said of the chair. 'It's the finest thing in the room, so don't leave it out of the picture. . . .' "[65]

Members of the American Jewish Committee resented Stephen Wise all the more because their own leadership was at a low ebb. After the death of brilliant, charismatic Louis Marshall, the committee's presidency was filled by Dr. Cyrus Adler, the scholarly president of the Jewish Theological Seminary, a former curator of Oriental antiquities at the National Museum in Washington, and librarian and assistant secretary of the Smithsonian Institution. Adler had spent much of his career soliciting funds for Jewish scholarly projects, many of which he had initiated. A humble man born in Van Buren, Arkansas, Adler felt honored to have been received by five American presidents—Harrison, Taft, Wilson, and both Roosevelts—even as he often felt distant from the eastern European Jews so increasingly important to Jewish organizational life. Adler's humility and his self-conscious concern that a strident word might offend a prominent Washington official was both a contrast to the wrathful, indignant style of Louis Marshall and a handicap in the struggle to win the attention of Washington bureaucrats.

The divisions among American Jews worsened during the mid-1930s, as new groups were formed to combat Nazi persecution. Ironically, each new organization or coalition sought, as one of its announced purposes, the unification of American Jewry against the Nazis. The Jewish Labor Committee (JLC) is a case in point. It was organized on February 25, 1934, at a meeting attended by 1,039 delegates representing the International Ladies' Garment Workers' Union (ILGWU), Amalgamated Clothing Workers' Union of America, United Hatters' Cap and Millinery Workers' International Union, Workmen's Circle, United Hebrew Trades, Forward Association, Jewish Socialist Verband, and the Jewish Workers' Party. The representatives of these groups selected Baruch Charney Vladeck as chairman; David Dubinsky, president of the International Ladies Garment Workers' Union, as treasurer; and Joseph Baskin, executive director of the Workman's Circle, as secretary. The JLC represented the coordinated sentiment of the American Jewish labor force, which accounted for several hundred thousand workers.[66]

Like the American Federation of Labor (AFL), which advocated immigration restriction to keep out cheap foreign labor, Jewish unionists had opposed unrestricted immigration. Nazi persecution, however, put an end to this exclusionary sentiment, at least for Jewish unionists. As early as March 27, 1933, William Green of the AFL joined other non-Jews at the Madison Square Garden rally to denounce Nazi persecution. Green also led the AFL in support of the boycott, emphasizing not only the oppression of German Jews but also the repression of German unions. Immigration reform was another matter. At the 1935 convention of the AFL, delegates of the largely Jewish ILGWU introduced a resolution that recommended easing the immigration quotas, arguing that compassion toward the oppressed "could not be viewed as a deviation from the traditional policies of the A.F.L." Though sympathetic, organized labor was not about to endanger its own interests, and the resolution was killed in committee. Caught in the cross fire, the Jewish Labor Committee did not leave the AFL or publicly denounce it. As with other Jewish organizations, the JLC hoped to avoid alienating non-Jewish allies and isolating themselves and their cause.[67]

Between 1933 and 1938, American Jewish organizations divided their efforts to help German Jews along distinct tactical lines. The American Jewish Committee and the B'nai B'rith continued to place their confidence in personal appeals to policy makers, delivered in restrained and reassuring tones. Cyrus Adler, Joseph Proskauer, and others sought to elicit two concessions from the White House and State Department: a lenient immigration policy that would fill the German quota to capacity with Jews seeking escape and direct intercession with the German government to curb acts of persecution in Germany. The American Jewish Congress, the Jewish War Veterans, and the Jewish Labor Committee hoped that the appeals of Jewish leaders, such as Stephen Wise and Bernard Deutsch, and prominent Jews in public life, such as the Lehmans, Brandeis, and Frankfurter, would spark action. These groups, however, also mounted public protests and continued the boycott of German goods in the belief that quiet conversation alone would neither alter America's restrictive immigration policies nor persuade the Germans to cease persecution.

While some American Jews debated how best to influence policy makers, others organized to assist European Jews directly, especially those prepared to emigrate. Much of this assistance was financed by private philanthropies such as the American Jewish Joint Distribution Committee (AJJDC), founded in 1914 to aid Jews displaced by the turmoil of World War I. Its mission essentially one of rescue and relief, the American Jewish Joint Distribution Committee was run by the same kind of non-Orthodox, highly assimilated, liberal-minded German Jews who founded the American Jewish Committee, most particularly, Felix Warburg, son-in-law of the legendary financier Jacob Schiff.

Unlike the other organizations locked in a competition born of ideological and personality differences, the Joint (as it was affectionately called by those who worked for it) had little rivalry in the field of overseas aid during the 1930s. Between 1929 and 1939, it spent $24.4 million dollars in Europe, primarily in Germany. Only $4.3 million was spent between 1931 and 1935, because the economic depression and hesitation on the part of many German Jews to emigrate circumscribed the Joint's efforts. Expenditures, however, kept pace with the developing crisis; from 1936 through 1938 the organization spent $8.5 million, and almost the same amount was spent just for 1939.[68]

In the spring of 1933, the Joint had begun cooperative efforts with Jewish groups from Argentina (ICA), France (Alliance Israëlite Universal) and Britain (British Board of Deputies) to provide loans and support to individual German Jews seeking emigration and settlement. Members of the Joint were anxious for governments and the League of Nations to address the problem also. After some prodding, the League of Nations formed an international commission on refugees in October 1933, which received substantial financial support from Jewish organizations, including the Joint.

Prominent Jews used their influence to shape this new body. On October 18, Henry Morgenthau, Sr., wrote to Hull suggesting that James G. McDonald be nominated for the post of high commissioner.[69] An eminent journalist and president of the Foreign Policy Association, McDonald was a religious man devoted to humanism and high moral principle, and he was popular among the cosmopolitan German-American Jews.[70] Though the State Department was not anxious for the United States to assume a leadership role, Roosevelt nominated McDonald, who was ratified by the League. The High Commission was now chaired by an American who had the endorsement of powerful Jewish interests. In addition, the U.S. representative to the commission, Professor Joseph Chamberlain of Columbia University, an expert in refugee affairs, also met the approval of Jews. The Joint Distribution Committee paid a major portion of the High Commission's expenses, including McDonald's salary. Even McDonald's secretary was on loan from the Joint's Paris office.[71]

From the time of his appointment until his departure in July 1935, McDonald, with the support of the Joint Distribution Committee, struggled to internationalize the Jewish refugee problem. McDonald and Chamberlain soon came to understand firsthand the frustrations of Jewish groups that had been attempting to influence American immigration policy. It quickly became obvious that other countries were gauging their own acceptance of refugees to that of a reluctant United States.

Between 1934 and 1935, the League High Commission under McDonald struggled to place refugees in countries outside Germany, help alleviate refugee distress, and persuade Germany to allow Jews to leave in peace. Just as energetically, the United States resisted all efforts to include it in a broad international agreement on refugees. The United States did not wish to compromise in any way its own absolute power to admit or expel aliens nor to limit its jurisdiction to issue visas, passports, and re-entry permits. Moreover, all regulation of aid such as welfare, disability, and workmen's compensation were local and state matters in which the federal government did not have the right to interfere. Finally, the State Department believed that American participation in an international agreement would be redundant as refugees were already "handsomely served" by the humanitarianism of American laws and procedures.[72]

After two frustrating years, McDonald resigned. The commission survived but floundered without McDonald's dedicated leadership. Obviously, philanthropically funded efforts to provide direct relief to Jewish refugees were to be no more successful than the political machinations of the American Jewish Committee and the American Jewish Congress.

Shortly after the election of 1936, there was an easing of the rigidity with which visa regulation was enforced. Yet there was no administrative commitment to immigration reform. In January 1936, Stephen Wise reported to Louis Brandeis that he had met with the president personally "for the first time . . . in years." During the conversation Wise was "appalled" by Roosevelt's response to the problem of Jews in Europe. The president threw up his hands and quoted German financier Max Warburg who he said had written to him that things were so bad in Germany that "there is nothing that can be done."[73] Wise and Brandeis had apparently speculated earlier that Roosevelt could have more easily been persuaded to action had it not been for the Warburg interference. Still, Wise felt that, "if we press hard, F.D.R. can be moved to say or do something more."[74]

If the rabbi had his way, some of that pressure would come from a new international Jewish confederation that would act on behalf of Jews without regard to state boundaries or to the parochial interests of one or another nation. Though the idea for such a body had been debated by Jewish leaders for almost twenty years, the pressure of Hitler's persecution lent a new immediacy to the discussion. The American Jewish Congress, especially Wise, was committed to fostering Jewish unity and collective action through a popularly elected, international political assembly, a world Jewish congress. This notion met with stiff opposition from the American Jewish Committee, which clung to its faith in a self-appointed, vaguely defined elite operating within the context and culture of the individual nations in which Jews resided. Committee members also feared that a Jewish political body transcending national boundaries could only feed the anti-Semitic myth of a worldwide Jewish conspiracy.

In spite of all opposition, the World Jewish Congress (WJC) was formed in Geneva, Switzerland, on August 8, 1936, by delegates from Africa, Asia, Europe, and North America. Stephen Wise was unanimously elected chairman of the executive committee, and Nahum Goldmann became chairman of the administrative committee. The new World Jewish Congress sought to dispel non-Jewish suspicions by stating that it would not interfere in routine internal matters affecting all citizens, including Jews, in various countries. It did lobby the League of Nations to facilitate the departure of Jews from Germany, and it developed effective research facilities to monitor Nazi persecution. And, like the

American Jewish Congress, the World Jewish Congress was committed to the public protest of Nazi persecution.

There is no evidence that the World Jewish Congress was more persuasive with Franklin Roosevelt than the American Jewish Congress had been. The new congress, however, did give Jews a voice that its founders hoped would be heard above the din of bickering over national priorities. Jews did not have a homeland, but the people of the diaspora, Wise and Goldmann hoped, could now speak collectively. Without political power, though, there could be no assurance that world leaders would listen to the Jewish voice. In the United States, Jewish leaders continued their efforts to find a means whereby they could assert political influence, either through the informal networks of power or through the electoral process.

With the election of 1936 only months away, some American Jewish leaders tried to get Roosevelt's attention by cloaking their concerns in the mantle of political expediency. Wise wrote to Frankfurter in March 1936, "I am afraid that Republicans are going to make capital out of what they hold as FDR's inaction on Nazism. It is going to make support of FDR unnecessarily difficult on the part of those who, like myself, have some part in the leadership of Jewish affairs and organizations throughout the country. Some dignified, fitting and unobjectionable way must be found in which FDR could express himself." The rabbi urged the professor to go to his personal friend in the White House and ask for some "outspoken word by him at this time." Wise said he knew that Frankfurter shared his conviction that "the SD [State Department] has not played the game along with F.D.R.'s mind" and that Roosevelt abhorred "the Nazi thing" but that now FDR must be made "invulnerable in this matter." Wise wanted "him [FDR] to have the fullest benefit and perhaps the almost complete support of American Jews, excepting, possibly for a handful of millionarish Republicans."[75]

The message must have reached FDR that a gesture to the Jews would be politically astute. But, instead of a dramatic gesture that would substantially alter American refugee policy, FDR sought to pacify American Jews by criticizing British policy in Palestine. In 1936 the British hoped to quiet Arab opposition to Jewish immigration by halting it and appointing a Royal Commission to study the problem. FDR consulted with Secretary of State Cordell Hull and then asked Hull to inform the British that the United States "would regard suspension of immigration as a breach of the Mandate." The British agreed not to suspend immigration until the commission submitted its report. In September, FDR sent a letter for publication in the *United Palestine Yearbook* that reaffirmed his support for a Jewish homeland. He wrote, "It is a source of renewed hope and courage that by international accord and by the moral support of the people of the world, men and women of Jewish faith have a right to resettle the land where their faith was born and from which much of our modern civilization has emanated."[76]

Stephen Wise was again invited to visit the president, this time at Hyde Park, only a month before the election. According to Wise's recollection, the rabbi gently chided the president about the "deserved dose" of criticism he was receiving from the Warburgs who thought that FDR should refrain from commenting upon Nazi treatment of Jews since it was a matter about which the president could do little. But, Wise added, "I know from Felix that you wanted to do the right and strong thing, as evidenced by what you said to Hull and Frances Perkins." Wise reported that Roosevelt criticized Max Warburg for advising Wise and the government on relations with Germany while Warburg remained a loyal citizen of the Reich. FDR also cited reports that "the Synagogues were crowded and apparently there is nothing very wrong in the situation at present." Wise responded that the Germans were on their best behavior before foreigners because of the 1936 Olympics but that conditions were grave. He offered numerous examples but left feeling that Roosevelt still believed that the stories of Nazi persecution were exaggerated.[77]

If Roosevelt thought he had little to worry about in the election, he was correct. In 1936, he won in a landslide victory, running even stronger among Jewish voters than he had in 1932.[78] This was a mixed blessing to American Jewish leaders and their organizations. On the one hand, Roosevelt had heard their appeals on behalf of the refugees. After the election there was some moderation in visa policy. On the other hand, the president would not support fundamental change in the quota system; he would not take on the Congress, the State Department bureaucracy, or American public opinion on behalf of European Jews. And that unwillingness had not cost him Jewish votes at the polls.

Aware that the Nuremberg laws and other acts of repression were increasing the danger to German Jewry, American Jewish leaders were becoming proportionately frustrated. They could not move the American government far enough or fast enough on immigration reform. As Roosevelt's second term began, they could only rail against each other over tactics and strategies, all sides still clinging to the belief that the right approach would galvanize the Roosevelt administration into saving European Jewry. Given the consensus in favor of restrictionism, the undercurrents of anti-Semitism prevalent in many quarters of American society, and the high level of popularity that Roosevelt enjoyed, there seems little basis for the assumption that a more unified Jewish campaign would have unlatched America's doors for the refugees.

After the 1936 election, the struggle resumed to wring concessions for European Jewry from the administration. American Jews both inside and outside the government were returning to the barricades after the brief autumn of agreement when most had supported Roosevelt for another term. But the "Roosevelt recession" of 1936–37 made it even more difficult for Jewish spokesmen and groups to gain a hearing. This setback occurred just at the time when the situation of European Jewry was worsening. The largest Jewish community in Europe—the 3.3 million Jews of Poland—were coming under attack with Polish leaders calling for the emigration of all Jews from the country. As early as April 1937, representatives of the Jewish Labor Committee and the AFL visited Cordell Hull at the State Department to express their concern.[79] The JLC was especially anxious because Poland, unlike Germany, had long been a major center of the Jewish labor movement. Consequently, the JLC passionately argued for the removal of immigration restriction, taking a far more vigorous stance than it had when only German Jewry was involved. But, in addition to the implacable resistance of the State Department, the JLC met with the disapproval of Bundists in Poland who urged Jews to stay in Poland to fight for their honor as Jews and as socialists.[80]

The JLC and other American Jewish organizations found their co-religionists in the U.S. Congress to be of little help. As they had been in the early 1930s, some Jews in Congress continued to be ill informed, and they were often a stumbling block to easing the enforcement of visa procedures. Early in 1938, Stephen Wise reported to Felix Frankfurter that "[Emanuel] Celler, to our amazement and horror, is introducing a resolution into Congress . . . which is very bad, so bad that it almost seems the work of an agent provocateur." The bill's second article proposed that "the quota prescribed in the 1934 [1924?] Act shall be increased to such an extent as may be necessary for the issuance of visas." Wise believed that, if Celler pressed his bill to increase the size of Germany's quota to accommodate Jewish refugees, "the whole country will go down on the President's proposal [for more liberal visa procedures] with a thud. . . ."[81] Celler, who claimed to have Frances Perkins's support, was described by Wise as "not a particularly voracious [sic] or scrupulous person. Even if it were all true and he really were thinking of nothing but November 8, 1938 [upcoming elections], he should have had a non-Jew introduce the measure."[82] Some leaders of Jewish organizations feared that Celler's precipitate action "would merely bring to the surface a great deal of illiberalism and hostility to aliens, and may lead to the failure of even moderate efforts to ease the immigration situation." Members of the American Jewish Committee feared that Celler's bill and the debate that would ensue might discourage FDR from further steps to moderate visa procedures. The knowledgeable Cecilia Razovsky was "prepared to lay before Mr. Celler certain facts with regard to the immigration situation which indicate that the situation is as satisfactory as it can possibly be under present conditions."[83] As Jews in Congress floundered under the critical gaze of the Jewish organizational leadership, Nazi aggression heightened the urgency of action.

Jewish groups applauded FDR's initiative, following Germany's conquest of Austria, in calling for the international conference on refugees that was to be held at Evian in July 1938. In late March Felix Frankfurter congratulated his old friend on the bold stroke, though the Harvard professor acknowledged that most of the Nazi victims "won't find a haven of refuge here or elsewhere. But what you [FDR] have done will help sustain their souls in their material enslavement."[84] FDR confided to Justice Irving Lehman his fears that "narrow isolationists," especially in Congress, would "use this move of ours for purely partisan objectives." Moreover, Roosevelt made clear to Lehman long before the Evian Conference convened that the United States could take only a small proportion of the refugees.[85] Never did he promise or even vaguely suggest that he wanted to change the U.S. quota system. When Governor Herbert Lehman of New York sent a note with the single word "splendid" on it, FDR replied, "I only wish that we could do more."[86] Always the master of elusion, the president purposely left vague what "more" might be without new legislation, always an unlikely possibility.

The president's plan for the Evian Conference seemed especially exciting to Jews within government who knew firsthand how little progress was being made on the refugee issue. Herbert Feis, at the State Department, wrote to Frankfurter of his enthusiasm for this "general public gesture which may have ultimate results."[87] Feis was hopeful because "in the immediate situation we are doing nothing effective, I am sorry to report. No great effort has been taken, and certainly no great achievement shown in ascertaining from the German authorities whether they will permit refugees to leave the country. That whole decisive question is being handled in a lagging way." Feis was troubled especially that in the State Department "it is not appreciated that each day weighs like a season of despair upon the victims who are being cut off from all normal opportunities to communicate with the outside world, and possibly being penalized for any effort."[88]

Frustrations mounted even further in late 1938 with reports of the deteriorating situation in Germany. One recurring topic of discussion was choosing an appropriate area in the world for mass resettlement of the Jews. Wise feared that the discussions of resettlement in terms of "overpopulated lands and unoccupied areas" might offer eastern European countries an opportunity to describe themselves as "overrun with superfluous populations," which would be defined as the Jews. Such an approach would also make most Central and South American countries, already teeming with people, hesitate to accept refugees, Wise thought.[89]

The resettlement issue stirred debate among prominent Jews close to FDR. Wise, Brandeis, and Frankfurter deplored Bernard Baruch's memo to the president arguing that the best alternative to admitting refugees to the U.S. would be "to assist these immigrations to assenting countries whose problem is too little rather than too much immigration."[90] The so-called Baruch Plan called for the establishment of a nondenominational refugee commonwealth—The United States of Africa—to include British possessions such as Kenya, Tanganyika, or Northern Rhodesia, the Belgian Congo, or Portuguese Angola. Baruch did not favor revising U.S. policies toward refugees because of America's strained economy and his desire for "no discrimination in favor of any particular political, religious or racial group."[91]

Certainly Zionists such as Wise were opposed to a national home for the Jews in Africa. But, because of British opposition to any increase in the Palestine immigration schedule, all discussion of British Palestine was excluded from the international conference agenda. Though the majority of the President's Advisory Committee on Political Refugees supported Wise's demand that Palestine be considered at the conference, this suggestion was vetoed by the administration. Moreover, Myron Taylor, the head of the U.S. delegation, refused to endorse demands that Chaim Weizmann, president of the Jewish Agency for Palestine, be allowed to speak either before the assembled delegations or in a private session.[92]

As usual the Jewish agencies were quarreling with each other and were ill prepared for the diplomatic atmosphere of the Evian Conference. Instead of attending the meeting with a single agenda settled beforehand, Jewish groups arrived with a smorgasbord of proposals. Some advocated increasing immigration to Palestine; others were most concerned with readaptation and vocational guidance to foster assimilation in the countries of refuge; there were those who wanted settlement in unpopulated areas and still others who were primarily concerned with protecting minority rights in European countries.[93]

Worse, there was a major clash between pro- and anti-Zionists present at the conference. An effort to draft a joint memorandum recommending the Zionist solution to the refugee problem was undermined by anti-Zionists. While the Zionists were critical of the conference, AJJDC representatives tried to emphasize the "very definite element of usefulness and encouragement" of the conference which "placed the whole question of refugees on [a] humanitarian basis—a unique step forward in international cooperation."[94] The Joint's attempt to shed the best possible light on the conference originated with its hope for large-scale colonization projects, which it expected to help fund in parts of the world other than Palestine. Joint leaders, such as the chairman Paul Baerwald, expressed their satisfaction that "the Conference did not deteriorate . . . into a public discussion of the undesirability of Jews as immigrants and settlers."[95] Ironically, the blatant resistance of most countries to establishing a sanctuary for the Jews within their borders merely strengthened the Zionists' argument that Palestine must be established as a homeland for the Jewish people. The feuding of pro- and anti-Zionist groups, however, only further muddled Jewish efforts to establish clear, achievable goals at Evian.

In addition to their own disarray, Jewish organizations had great difficulty with the unwieldy subcommittee system at Evian. One subcommittee alone heard and received memoranda from thirty-nine private refugee organizations, twenty of them Jewish. S. Adler-Rudel, a participant in those hearings, described the ad hoc arrangements:

> Nobody was prepared for it, neither the members of the Committee, nor the representatives of the various organizations who had to queue up at the door of the meeting room to be called in, one after the others, and to face the 11 members of the Subcommittee, [to] whom they were supposed to tell their tale within ten minutes at most.[96]

When the Evian conference adjourned on July 15, Jewish representatives had little reason for optimism.

In reaction to the conference at Evian, major Jewish organizations made yet another attempt at cooperation. Edgar Kauffman, a leader of the Pittsburgh Jewish community, invited the American Jewish Committee, the American Jewish Congress, the B'nai B'rith, and the Jewish Labor Committee to organize a new cooperative body. The American Jewish Congress indicated its willingness to work with the others by dropping its controversial call for a national Jewish referendum to elect delegates to a special defense conference. And so, in August 1938, the General Jewish Council (GJC) was formed. Though barred from encroaching on the "religious, racial, national or economic philosophies of the member groups," the council was supposed to establish a forum for the coordination of defense policies, including refugee policy. The council, however, did not even engage in joint fund raising and soon foundered on the same distrust and jealous rivalry that had destroyed earlier attempts at cooperation.[97]

Much of the controversy concerned the American Jewish Congress's desire for a plebiscite of all American Jews on a variety of issues of special concern to that group. The American Jewish Committee rejected the idea because it smacked of a Jewish parochialism that committee members deplored and because they feared that such a plebiscite could only alienate non-Jews. Interestingly, presidential advisor Samuel Rosenman, who usually sided with the committee, both brought the plebiscite idea to FDR's attention and signed a committee letter denouncing the plebiscite. Although Stephen Wise wrote that Rosenman's signature eliminated him from being an "impartial and unprejudiced witness," the rabbi was most interested in FDR's response, reported by Rosenman to be negative in the extreme. According to Wise, "The Chief used this term [several times]: 'The whole thing is loaded with dynamite.'" FDR pointed out that a question on the desirability of Palestine as a homeland was especially provocative. Roosevelt asked, rhetorically, "Won't this enable Americans to say that the fellows who wrote the Protocols of the Elders of Zion has some justification?" FDR concluded by advising Rosenman, "And you know, I am a friend of your people and I warn you against it." Rosenman asked whether he could repeat their conversation to Stephen Wise, and FDR encouraged him to repeat it as a message from the president personally. Somewhat taken aback, Wise responded by referring threateningly to "some people who we could not control, who would say that it was none of the Chief's business and they would publicly say so and very unpleasant things would result." Recovering his composure but still in a huff, Wise decided that he would go to Washington to see FDR, though "the Gentleman's mind is made up on this question." In the end, Wise backed down and contented himself with attacking the American Jewish Committee rather than FDR. Once again there was the reminder of Jews' essential powerlessness and vulnerability to anti-Semitism, and once again the reaction was for Jews to criticize each other.[98]

Improbable as was its chance of success, the Intergovernmental Committee on Refugees still became the focus of American Jewish hopes. Once that committee's negotiations with Germany bogged down, the Roosevelt administration itself focused on private groups to hasten the flow of refugees from Germany. Myron Taylor called upon two members of the President's Advisory Committee on Political Refugees, Stephen Wise and Paul Baerwald, "to take steps towards the implementing of a program of orderly migration from Germany through the organization of a Coordinating Foundation."[99] The Foundation's purpose was to coordinate the work of the various agencies and individuals engaged in improving the condition of the refugees and to facilitate "the emigration of involuntary emigrants from Germany."[100] The foundation was, in effect, to purchase the emigration of German Jews. Seventy-five American Jewish leaders were called by Wise and Baerwald on April 15, 1939, to discuss Taylor's initiative. By June 17, the group had agreed to establish the Coordinating Foundation, with the Joint Distribution Committee underwriting up to $1 million.

The new organization was to be administered by a directorate of twenty, consisting of ten Americans and ten Europeans, who were to cooperate with all organizations, governments, and the League of Nations to aid the persecuted in Germany, especially those unable to afford emigration. Those being expelled from the Reich would be helped to leave. Settlement opportunities would be investigated by the foundation, which would also help emigrants transfer their goods and assets for their own personal use. However much money the foundation succeeded in raising, there was always a need for more. Lewis Strauss, longtime activist in Jewish causes and a member of the American Jewish Committee, reminiscing about his work with the foundation, wrote regretfully, "I might have done so much more than I did. I risked only what I thought I could afford. That was not the test which should have been applied, and it is my eternal regret."[101]

The foundation was not, however, universally popular in Jewish organizational circles. The Jewish Labor Committee opposed it because it mistakenly believed that the foundation's purpose was to finance a plan by which the world's Jews would pay huge sums to Germany to finance an elaborate exodus. The JLC, therefore, protested the Joint's financing of the foundation. With the American Jewish Congress acting as an intermediary, assurances were given that the foundation's articles of organization contained nothing that could be interpreted as permitting "funds to be used in any way to pay with foreign exchange for the cost of goods made or purchased in Germany."[102] The Joint assured the JLC that its funds could not and would not be used for colonization or any mechanism by which Jewish money would be funneled into Germany. Once again, the argument had shifted from the absolute ineffectiveness of government relief efforts to the internal antagonisms of the Jewish community.

As Jewish groups squabbled among themselves over the best way to influence government officials, they also kept a sharp eye on the anti-Semitic climate of the country. Though they needed power if they were to help the refugees, American Jews were cautious lest they give the appearance of being too powerful. Stephen Wise, hardly known for his hesitance to wield political influence, wrote to Frances Perkins in January 1937 to express his concern over her choice of a successor to the recently deceased immigration commissioner, Daniel MacCormack. An uncomfortable Wise wrote, "I understand that several Jews have presented their applications for the post. May I say to you in confidence, that it is a post no Jew ought to be called upon to fill. The Commissioner has so much to do with the admission of immigrants, etc. including Jews, that it is really unfair to burden a Jew with that particular post," although Wise assured the secretary that he did not believe that Jews ought to be exempt from "the normal responsibilities of public life and office."[103] Perkins did not recommend a Jew to the White House for the post.

James Sulzberger of the *New York Times* used his connections to communicate to FDR his apprehensions over the selection of a Jew as a Supreme Court justice in late 1938. Sulzberger's efforts were denounced by Felix Frankfurter who was furious over "the number of prominent Jews who are unwittingly embracing Hitlerism by actually sponsoring a position of political inferiority and second-rate citizenship for Jews." The Harvard professor was "shocked out of my boots to learn of the important Jews who voted against [Herbert] Lehman and hoped for his defeat because of their fear of anti-Semitism." Frankfurter said the episode was deeply significant because Sulzberger was the "dominant head of the most powerful newspaper in the land." As for Frankfurter, he preferred to "die standing than live on my knees."[104]

During the early 1930s, Frankfurter had been hesitant to appeal the refugees' case too openly to FDR. He felt self-conscious and did not wish to leave himself open to the charge of special pleading or imposing upon his personal friendship with an old Harvard classmate. As war loomed over Europe, however, Frankfurter wrote literally hundreds of notes to Roosevelt attacking fascism and calling for a more generous refugee policy, though even then he tended to present his appeals as not so much a Jew calling for the relief of his people as a nonsectarian appealing for liberalism and humanitarianism.

Although the Kristallnacht in November 1938 jarred both Jews and non-Jews sympathetic to the refugees, even this catastrophe did not bring down the barricades that separated Jewish organizations. The American Jewish Committee was as opposed to protest and public demonstration in December 1938 as it had been in March 1933. The American Jewish Committee continued to deny the need for militance or even forceful and blunt lobbying. Though Stephen Wise and other protesters were actually no more successful than the committee in changing German policy or modifying America's quota laws, within days after news of the Kristallnacht reached Washington, the rabbi was lunching with Myron Taylor, planning a deputation to "the Big Chief [FDR]," and suggesting that "the Chief send for Dieckhoff [German Ambassador] and lay down the law."[105]

And always in the background could be heard the ever-louder cries of their brothers. Reports filed in December 1938 with the American Friends Service

Committee by non-Jews traveling in Germany were typical of the word reaching all relief groups. One observed that "the suicide rate is so heavy that the Mainz town Authorities have turned off the gas in every Jewish home, I myself was present at an attempted suicide of a woman who was not in any economic plight but just driven to despair by the prospects and fear of the future." The observer concluded, "The Jews are . . . dominated by the one thought of getting out of Germany. Again and again they emphasize that they asked for nothing more than a [refugee] camp and a crust of bread—only to get out of Germany at any price. They see only the possible effects of the present conditions (a) death in a few months or (b) the establishment of Jewish Labour camps by the authorities. Most of the Jews preferred the former to the prospect of a so-called Labour Camp."[106] As the trap closed, the leniency in the issuance of visitors' visas and other concessions on the part of the United States government could not satisfy the frustrations of many American Jews that still more needed to be done.

Uncharacteristically, Jewish organizations in 1939 united in support of the Wagner-Rogers bill to allow, above the annual quota, 20,000 German refugee children, aged fourteen or younger, into the United States over a two-year period. The American Jewish Congress snidely reported that even the cautious American Jewish Committee "has recommended the adoption of the bill and it seems that the cautious restraint on the part of liberal and Jewish groups may be eased in order to help the passing of the Bill in the House."[107] Though historian Saul Friedman has implied that unusual timidity on the part of Stephen Wise contributed to the bill's failure, later studies suggest that the rabbi intentionally curbed his usually flamboyant style in the hope of securing the bill's passage.[108] With the bill's chances for passage recognizably slim, its supporters became overly sensitive to even the hint of bad publicity. Just as the Wagner-Rogers bill was reaching the House floor, a news story was published charging that the Independent Order of B'rith Sholom had arranged to bring fifty children from Germany to Philadelphia in violation of the quota. Though the National Coordinating Committee and the Non-Sectarian Committee for German Refugee Children officially treated the report as absurd, Joseph Chamberlain of the Coordinating Committee denounced the Philadelphia lodge for creating the impression that Jews thought they could circumvent immigration laws with money and influence. In spite of all this uproar, there is no evidence that the incident worsened the bill's already negligible chances of passage.

The bill reported to the House in July had been significantly modified. Visas issued to the children over the next two years were to be issued within, not in addition to, the quota. Saving the children now might mean abandoning an equal number of adults to incarceration in concentration camps. A shaken and disappointed Wagner withdrew the bill, thus sparing its hopeful Jewish and non-Jewish supporters the additional grief of a vituperative debate on the floor and a humiliating defeat.

Compounding the disappointment over the collapse of the Wagner-Rogers bill was news from London that, on May 17, the British had published a White

Paper on Palestine virtually choking off that escape route. Jewish immigration was to be limited to 75,000 over the next five years, with total Jewish population to be maintained at one-third that of the Arabs. Land sales to Jews were to be subject to new restrictions as well. After five years no more Jews would be allowed to settle without the approval of the Arabs in Palestine.

On September 1, 1939, Hitler's army invaded Poland. The beginning of world war in Europe fundamentally altered the possibilities of escape for Jews trapped in countries occupied by the Nazis. Though there was a dramatic decline in the emigration of Jews from Nazi-held territory, Jewish leaders did not call for U.S. participation in the war that Britain and France had now joined. Rabbi Stephen Wise regarded "peace through appeasement and surrender to Hitler . . . deeper and fouler than Hell," but even Wise did not advocate U.S. entry into the war as the best way to save Jewish lives. In spite of his hatred for Hitler, Wise wrote, "Such loathing and my sympathy with England and France will not move me to action in favor of war."[109]

Cyrus Adler of the American Jewish Committee, Wise's old organizational rival, was ill as war broke out across Europe. Like Wise, Adler was careful not to call upon the American people to fight Hitler for the Jews. Adler contented himself with a feeble denunciation of war. He wrote: "While I think probably there ought to be a meeting of our Executive Committee, I confess that I do not see what program it could bring down at the present time, if any. Our business is to protect Jews and Jewish rights wherever they are assaulted, and in time of war nobody has ever been able to do this."[110]

In the autumn of 1939, the major Jewish groups considered the possibility of a complete consolidation. The American Jewish Congress favored it. The American Jewish Committee, however, regarded it as a back-door approach to the kind of representative body it had rejected for so long. Instead, the committee offered a coordination of refugee activities and a strengthening of the Jewish General Council. The legacy of distrust, however, could not be set aside even in the face of disaster. Numbed by years of fruitless lobbying or perhaps just resigned to the ineffectuality of Jewish organizational efforts, the new president of the American Jewish Committee, Sol Stroock, could not find anyone even to attend Jewish General Council meetings for the American Jewish Committee. Overwhelmed by the threat that war posed to European Jewry, many committee members stopped attending meetings, pleading schedule conflicts. In the summer of 1939, Stroock could not hold the Sunday meetings he thought necessary because so many members preferred to spend their weekends in the country.[111]

Frustrated American Jewish leaders reacted to the outbreak of war by further diffusing their own efforts; this time the impetus came from the orthodox sector of the community. Traditionally, orthodox Jews in Europe had not emigrated in great numbers to the west; the secular quality of American society made many doubtful that they could live their daily lives and raise their children in an atmosphere of piety. Apprehensive as they were that western ideas might intrude upon their highly ritualistic lifestyles that were regulated only by the demands of their faith, orthodox Jews were not impervious to political realities. Prior to the war, many orthodox Jews in the United States were content to allocate their money and their support for German Jewry to the American Jewish Joint Distribution Committee. In 1938 the Agudah, a branch of World Agudath Israel, had also begun its work on refugee and immigration issues. A relief organization rather than a political body, the Agudah concentrated on obtaining sponsoring affidavits and visas for orthodox Jews in occupied Europe. But the war created problems of a magnitude beyond the reach of the Joint and the Agudah. Therefore, the Union of Orthodox Rabbis of the U.S. and Canada formed the Vaad Ha-Hatzalah (rescue committee). Rabbi Chaim Ozer Grodzinski, a noted Talmudic scholar of the Vilna orthodox Jewish community, turned to Rabbi Eliezer Silver of Cincinnati, a leader of the union, for assistance in making this new group successful in the United States.[112]

The Vaad was symptomatic of even more disagreement within the Jewish community. With the issue one of rescue and fund raising, the adversaries were the orthodox and the nonorthodox elements of Jewry. The Vaad's specific purpose was to assist rabbis, yeshiva students, and members of their families who were fleeing from their homes in eastern Poland following the Soviet occupation of that area in the fall of 1939. The yeshivot of eastern Europe had long been the hub of the world's Jewish scholarship—a world of letters now facing extinction. But the creation of a separate organization just to rescue scholars at a time when the needs of all European Jews were so great provoked considerable controversy.

Fund raising in the Jewish community of the United States was orchestrated by local community federations and welfare agencies, the work abroad being conducted with the assistance and supervision of the AJJDC. Opponents of the Vaad argued that yet another fund raising campaign would splinter Jewish relief efforts until they mirrored the disarray in the political arena. Though Rabbi Silver and the other leaders of the Vaad insisted that they had nothing but admiration for the Joint and had formed a separate group only out of dire necessity, conflict was unavoidable.

By the winter of 1939, Jewish community organizations throughout the United States were asking AJJDC and its central fund raising organization, the Council of Jewish Federations and Welfare Funds, to explain their relationship to the Vaad Ha-Hatzala. Were not the established organizations already aiding rabbis as well as other Jews? As the Vaad approached each community separately for funds, local orthodox and nonorthodox Jewish groups clashed. The Joint, though irritated and critical of Vaad competition for funds, could not bring itself to publicly denounce a rabbinic rescue organization "in the light of all the tragedies requiring aid."[113] And the Vaad was somewhat successful. From November 1939 until mid-September 1940, the Vaad spent in excess of one hundred five thousand dollars to aid refugee yeshivot. By the time of America's entry into the war, the Vaad had spent over one-quarter of a million dollars on its activities.

But the Vaad raised funds at the expense of the Joint, often leaving the Joint to pay for combined projects. The issue became one of who should be rescued first. Did scholars have a stronger claim to life than other Jews? Without the scholars, could Judaism survive? The rocky relationship between the Vaad and the Joint that began in 1939 continued until the end of the war. As in their political endeavors, American Jews could not achieve unity in their rescue work.

American Jews did not shake heaven and earth between 1936 and 1939 any more than they had prior to 1936. Handicapped in their efforts to modify American immigration policy by the climate of anti-Semitism in the United States, American Jews—though different from one another in ethnic background, religious ideology, attitudes toward Zionism, and socioeconomic class—did, however, use every means of pressure and every source of influence available to a minority population of fewer than five million to change government policy.

The internal bickering that at times almost obscured the efforts of American Jews to save their European brothers has often been mistaken for the cause of Jewish impotence. The evidence suggests, however, that the internecine conflict was a manifestation rather than a cause of Jewish frustration. When Jewish organizations found themselves unable to budge Roosevelt or the State Department on the refugee issue, they blamed each other. They were unable to come to grips with the horrible truth that they were diaspora Jews, powerless on their own to rescue their brothers and insufficiently persuasive to recast American immigration policies. Of far greater significance than the tactical mistakes and blundering on the part of American Jews was the opposition and disregard of an indifferent and often anti-Semitic American society. Public opinion polls of the late 1930s suggest that Jewish leaders could not count on the humanitarian spirit of the American people, many of whom favored excluding Jewish refugees. Roosevelt, on the other hand, could claim popular support for his position. Typical of the letters coming to the White House was one FDR received from the Bronx, New York, in January 1939. A gentleman wrote:

> I realize your debt to Jewish financial backing as a result of your own case and those who you have put into office, and then again those you put into office, who in turn appoint their own "Angels". But as a Christian and an American I must ask that you, who are likewise an American and a Christian exercise a little concern for your own people first and worry about Russian, Roumanian, Polish and German Jews later on. I am deeply sympathetic of their plight. But I am far more gravely concerned about my own kind first.[114]

Such letter writers were also voters. Their fears and resentments determined the lever they pulled in the voting booth. The addressee in the White House needed voters' ballots on election day and the votes of those representatives and senators on the floor of Congress whom concerned citizens elected. Even a well-coordinated regiment of Jewish groups could not have altered the basic political arithmetic that made the millions who opposed a liberal refugee policy more influential with Congress and the White House than Jewish spokesmen. Those who believe that Jews in the 1930s enjoyed a political power far out of proportion to their numbers, contained only by the community's own internal battling, indulge themselves in illusion. Moreover, with the coming of war, Jewish leaders and prominent Jews in government faced a fresh obstacle, widespread fear that among the refugees were fifth columnists, bolshevists, and others who threatened America's security with internal subversion.

FIVE

The Fifth Column Threat

War in Europe multiplied the uncertainties for Jewish refugees fleeing Germany after September 1939. In spite of the State Department's vigorous use of the LPC clause to divert the flow of German refugees away from the United States between 1933 and 1938, there had also been periods of moderation in enforcement. Sometimes the leniency was the by-product of domestic partisan political pressures; other times it was an expression of indignation toward Nazi excesses such as Kristallnacht. Whatever the cause, these interludes had encouraged the refugees' American advocates to persevere in trying to persuade American officials that a humanitarian refugee policy could be reconciled with the national interest. Now, however, the specter of foreign agents intentionally planted among the refugees by the belligerents, especially the Germans, and later their Soviet allies, raised national security concerns in the minds of both policy makers and the general public. Reported confirmation that fifth column subversives in Europe had been instrumental in some fascist successes on the continent precluded dismissing such threats as mere hysteria. The new menace of internal subversion in the United States nourished the restrictionism that long predated it.

The decline in the issuance of American visas was dramatic. The numbers of German and Austrian citizens (or former citizens) given immigration visas to the United States fell from 27,370 in fiscal 1939 (the maximum under the quota law) to 4,883 in 1942.[1] Although the outbreak of war made it more difficult for German and Austrian residents to obtain transportation to the United States, there were many Germans and Austrians who had already fled their native lands and were applying for American visas under the German quota from neutral havens. Jews throughout much of Europe sought to escape from territories conquered by, or under the influence of, the Nazis. Neither a reduced demand nor a shortage of transportation, then, adequately explains the reduction of visas issued by American consuls after 1939, especially the decline of visas granted to Jews in flight. Instead, dark rumors of enemies among the aliens galvanized restrictionists both inside the government and among the public at large.

In Washington, internal subversion by enemy agents among the refugees,

112

particularly among Jewish refugees, did not seem farfetched to either the State Department or the White House. Apprehension over fifth columnists among the refugees sometimes complemented and at other times superseded concern over the predominantly Jewish character of the refugees in the minds of policy makers. But the threat to national security was more than a thinly veiled justification for the anti-Semitism of particular State Department officials or continuation of the government's restrictionist policies, "a device for keeping refugee entry to a minimum," as David Wyman contends.[2] The fear of subversion was more than a calculated ploy to curb refugee admissions. Throughout the government and among the general population there was increasing worry that a number of Jewish refugees placed under duress by America's enemies might permit themselves to be used by their former governments to undermine the United States and sabotage its institutions. Neither the theme of internal subversion nor its link to Jewish radicalism was new in American culture.

Previous flows of immigrants to the United States had frequently set off shock waves of concern about foreign influence and, particularly, foreign radicalism. According to such eminent American historians as Richard Hofstadter and David Brion Davis, one consistent strand of American culture has been a fear that enemies could strangle the American republic from within. Hofstadter called political expressions of this fear "the paranoid style," which, according to John Higham, often fixed upon foreign radicalism.[3] The French Revolution created deep divisions among Americans who supported the Jacobins and those who feared that Europe's disorders might infect the United States. Later, in the 1840s, the arrival of Germans who had participated in the revolutions of 1848 induced concern that alien ideologies could threaten American values and institutions. The Bolshevik revolution and America's participation in World War I contributed to a "red scare" in 1919. Anti-alien and anti-radical sentiment also served as a backdrop to the trial of Sacco and Vanzetti and their execution in 1927. Americans had become aware that the vast Atlantic was not a secure barrier against threatening foreign ideologies.

Long before the 1930s some nativists had equated Jews, especially those from eastern Europe, with radicalism. The formula was derived from the "100 percent Americanism" that became a sine qua non of American life during World War I. Jews with German-sounding last names inspired suspicion. Nativists who opposed American participation in the war often suspected that prominent Jews, such as financier Paul Warburg, were part of a conspiracy to undermine America from the top.[4] Meanwhile, newcomers from eastern Europe were suspected of participating in a conspiracy from the bottom, Bolshevik subversion. For those prepared to believe in it, evidence of a Jewish-radical connection seemed ubiquitous. The strength among Jewish voters of a Socialist party candidate in a New York mayoralty election, Leon Trotsky's friendship with certain New York intellectuals of Jewish background, even the socialist rhetoric of impoverished Jewish tenement dwellers was sufficient to raise eyebrows among self-styled nativist patriots. In the midwest an Iowa association of businessmen went so far as to accuse itinerant Jewish peddlers of selling Marxism wrapped in dry goods.[5]

Many allegations of Jewish radicalism were based upon a hoax perpetrated by anti-Semitic Russians. "The Protocols of the Elders of Zion," a document invented by the Russian secret police at the behest of Tsar Nicholas II's government after 1894, fabricated a worldwide Jewish conspiracy to seize control of all nations. The modus operandi would be terror, war, and revolution fomented by a small coterie of Jewish subversives. The fraud was exported to the United States in 1918 and widely circulated. Though Jewish defense groups scrambled to expose the "Protocols," the document was instrumental in sustaining an anti-radical rationale for anti-Semitism throughout the following decade.

During the 1930s most refugees lining up for visas at American consulates were Jews seeking escape from Germany or German-held territory. How could a consul tell a frightened Jewish refugee from a spy trained to conceal his identity? And what of those refugees forced into becoming subversives through coercion? How could American officials prevent their entry? Closing America's door to all refugees would eliminate the guesswork. Refugee advocates, especially those in the Jewish community, pursued a strategy of education and publicity in an effort to discredit the equation of Jews and radicalism. The door must be kept open, if only a crack.

Jewish organizations, particularly the American Jewish Committee and its self-consciously assimilated leadership, demonstrated their desire to refute vigorously the charges that Jews were committed to any alien ideology, especially Bolshevism. Executive committee minutes suggest the American Jewish Committee's sensitivity on this issue. In May 1934, the committee looked with apprehension upon a forthcoming series of newspaper articles on Jews and communism scheduled for publication by the Hearst syndicate. The committee's president, Cyrus Adler, strongly advocated that his group "take an official stand against communism." But, after considerable debate, the executive body decided against such a statement and, in the fashion characteristic of the committee, sought resolution through informal channels. Henry Ittleson volunteered to speak to Paul Block, "a close friend of Hearst." After learning that Block was in Los Angeles, however, Ittleson and Sol Stroock phoned him directly from the meeting room with all of the others present to request that Block see Hearst and persuade him to cancel the articles or at least delay publication until either Block or a member of the executive committee had spoken to Hearst in New York. It worked. At that same meeting the American Jewish Committee's leadership decided to commission a study to determine the percentage of "deported Reds" who were Jews. Max Kohler, the committee's immigration expert, said he was certain the percentage was "very small."[6]

A Madison Avenue consulting firm compiled a report, "Jews and Communism," which systematically refuted the notion that Jews in Russia, Germany, and the United States were the moving force behind Bolshevism in those countries. The report estimated that in the United States the number of Jews in the American Communist party was a mere "one-tenth of one percent of the total Jewish population," with the highest concentration of Jewish communists in New York City. Nor were Jews prominent among the Communist party (CP) leadership. Neither William Z. Foster nor Earl Browder were Jews, nor was Clarence Hathaway, the editor of the *Daily Worker*. There were only 31 Jews among 224 district and section organizers of the CP across the country. The report concluded with assurance that communist tactics tended to alienate rather than attract Jews because Jews in America tended toward the professions or membership in labor unions that were staunchly anticommunist. Moreover, the CP's anti-religion and anti-Zionist postures only alienated most Jews, according to the report.[7]

Organized Jews sought to join with other religions to denounce atheistic communism. Joseph Proskauer, the influential Democratic judge from New York and a prominent member of the American Jewish Committee, was asked by the executive committee to make an overture to Cardinal Pacelli, then Papal Secretary of State (and later Pope Pius XII), through the brother of Pacelli's American hostess while the cardinal was visiting the U.S. Proskauer was to request some Jewish representation on a Pro-Deo Committee being formed by the Catholics and on which some Protestants had already been invited to serve. The American Jewish Committee also wanted American rabbis to amplify and sharpen their attacks on communism from the pulpit.[8]

In reports and sermons, then, Jews were attacking radicalism as vehemently as they were Nazism. It is all the more ironic, then, that the anti-Nazi overture of an American Jewish congressman should have become twisted, initiating, instead, the formation of a congressional committee that raised fresh suspicions of fifth columnists among the refugees who were fleeing Hitler.

Samuel Dickstein, a Democratic congressman from New York, has been described by one historian as belonging among "the ranks of those public men, from Pyrrhus forward, who have striven and striven and at last succeeded, only to have their triumph turn shortly to gall."[9] Dickstein, an eastern European Jewish immigrant who arrived in America at the age of three, represented a district on New York's Lower East Side composed largely of others from the same background. He served his constituents in the House for twenty-two years, from 1923 to 1944. It was his demand for a legislative investigation of subversive groups, especially the German-American Bund, that led to the founding of a committee with a much broader investigative mandate. Dickstein had supported Hamilton Fish's investigation of domestic communism in 1930, he had introduced Martin Dies's anticommunist bill on the House floor in 1932, and, the following year, called for an investigation of anarchists after the attempted assassination of FDR. As chairman of the House Immigration Committee in 1933, he conducted an unofficial inquiry into Nazi propaganda.

The following January, Dickstein introduced a resolution to investigate Nazi activities in the United States and other potential sources of subversion. In spite of some resistance from congressmen with German-American constituents, the resolution passed by a vote of 168 to 31. John McCormack of Massachusetts chaired the investigating committee so that there could be no accusation of a Jewish vendetta, and Dickstein took the vice chairmanship. The committee's investigation was thorough, but Dickstein wanted an even broader look at un-American propaganda.[10]

Dickstein's bill aroused widespread opposition and was defeated. Even the American Jewish Committee, usually in favor of such investigations, opposed it. The leadership felt that little new information could be revealed, while the "much publicized public hearings" could "stir up animosities and cause ill-advised publicity, without producing any corresponding benefit in actual legis-lation." Moreover, the American Jewish Committee feared that, if the proposed committee recommended no legislation or legislation not quickly enacted, it might "be used unfavorably by the Nazis and anti-Semitic groups, and result in a boomerang."[11]

Three months later Martin Dies, an anti-union, anti-Semitic, anti–New Dealer from Texas, advanced a new version of the Dickstein bill. Once again politics made strange bedfellows. Dickstein campaigned hard for the bill by pointing to Nazi atrocities abroad and warning of the domestic danger of Nazi spies, smugglers, and agitators. Dies, meanwhile, stressed anticommunism in his appeal. Many anti–New Dealers also wanted investigations as a first step in demonstrating that among Roosevelt's men were followers of Stalin. In the end, the Dies bill passed, 191 to 41. Dies got his license to hunt left-wing subver-sives, and a deluded Dickstein was excluded from the committee he had worked so hard to establish.

The investigations of the Dies committee perpetuated and broadened the atmosphere of suspicion and sharpened fears of internal subversion initiated by the McCormack-Dickstein committee. Dies and his associates, however, were more concerned with the spread of a communist conspiracy than they were with Nazi subversion. In these circumstances American Jewish leaders were con-cerned that Adolf Hitler's persistent charges linking Jews to the communist movement in Russia and Germany would cripple Jewish-Christian relations in the United States as well and bolster opposition to the entry of many Jewish refugees.

In the spring of 1938 a report commissioned by the American Jewish Committee, "Confidential Report on [an] Investigation of Anti-Semitism in the United States," was released. The survey was conducted by the Opinion Re-search Corporation, which did field work for the Gallup polls. One question asked was "do you think they [Jews] tend to be more radical in politics than other people?" Of the respondents, 43 percent said yes (24 percent had no opinion). When asked, however, whether Jews were more conservative or more radical than others, 31 percent said more radical and 21 percent said more conservative while 48 percent said about the same. In the public mind, then, Jews were politically different from their neighbors but not necessarily more radical.[12] Still, Jewish leaders continued to denounce communism and any effort to link Jews with the activities of Bolsheviks. On the eve of war in Europe, Henry Monsky, president of B'nai B'rith, said in his July 4th address, "No Jew true to his faith, to his traditions and to his history will ever subscribe to any program calculated to create friction or division between the various groups of our great American citizenship." He declared "Communism, Fascism and Nazism" to be "equally hateful."[13]

In spite of such ringing denunciations of enemy "isms" by American Jews, the onset of war in Europe created new doubts about the potential loyalty of refugees, most of whom were European Jews. In the United States, apprehensions over fifth columnists were extended to individuals other than Jews. Anyone who exhibited unusual behavior became the object of suspicion and the target of accusation. The term "fifth column" originally referred to those individuals in Madrid who aided and supported Francisco Franco against the Spanish Republic during the civil war of 1936–39. Now, however, it was being applied more generally to all those whose behavior aroused suspicions of disloyalty. Those who refused to salute the flag for religious reasons, such as Jehovah's Witnesses, were often mobbed and beaten. One worker in Sparta, Michigan, was murdered by a neighbor for being a fifth columnist, while another in Sapulpa, Oklahoma, was jailed on a similar charge. The self-appointed leader of America's hoboes, Jeff Davis, pledged the cooperation of those who rode the rails daily to watch for fifth columnists. Davis even instructed one of his loyal followers, "One-Eyed" Connolly, to take charge of the surveillance. Near Buffalo, New York, a women's group turned their binoculars skyward and vowed to shoot on sight any German parachutists. In the same county, American Legionnaires assumed the responsibility of keeping fifth columnists from infiltrating across the Niagara River.[14]

In the United States, fifth column fears were not the hallucinations of merely a small cluster of psychopaths. A Roper poll, appearing in *Fortune* in July 1940, found that 71 percent of the respondents were persuaded that Germany had "already started to organize a 'Fifth Column' in this country." In response to another question, 46 percent agreed that the United States government should deport or imprison pro-Nazis. What was perhaps even more ominous was the testimony of respondents that they were keeping neighbors whom they suspected of fifth column sympathies under surveillance.[15]

The suspicions of small-time Nazi- and Red-baiters were titillated by popular magazine articles and movies. Most of the media treatment of the subject was designed to exploit the perceived danger for its commercial value and capitalize on the inherent drama of spies, espionage, etc. Only a few articles and movies attempted to calm fears rather than arouse them. In the summer of 1940 the *American Magazine* published six articles about fifth columnists with such sensational titles as "Hitler's Slave Spies in America," "Treachery in the Air," and "Enemies Within Our Gates." *Reader's Digest* followed suit in the autumn. More serious journals such as the *Nation* and *Fortune* treated the topic with greater concern for accuracy and less for sensationalism, hoping to inform even as they diffused the hysteria. *Fortune,* especially, observed the absurdity of the uncontrolled, almost senseless drone of accusations and counteraccusations. The magazine noted that, while some groups claimed FDR was leading the fifth column, others believed Roosevelt to be the "unwitting dupe of columnists in the government" among whom were the secretary of labor and the attorney general. Meanwhile, the leading communist newspaper, the *Daily Worker,* attributed leadership of the "column" to J. P. Morgan. The German American Bund assured its followers that the Pilgrim Society and the Carnegie Endowment for International Peace camouflaged the culprits.[16]

Even the movies offered no escape. In the movie palaces where Americans sought refuge, if only temporarily, from the grim realities of the depression, silver screen images warned of subversion. In *Confessions of a Nazi Spy* (1939), starring Edward G. Robinson, a weak link in the Nazi spy network is exploited by an FBI agent. *Espionage Agent* (1939) and *Foreign Correspondent* (1940), both starring Joel McCrea, exploited the fifth column theme. In his classic *The Great Dictator* (1940), Charlie Chaplin movingly portrayed the dangers of Nazism to the human spirit everywhere. The theme of Americans with Nazi sympathies tempted moviemakers after America's entry into the war as well. In *Keeper of the Flame* (1942), starring Spencer Tracy and Katherine Hepburn, Tracy is doing an article on the death of a great American when the widow admits that the great man was really a fascist! A movie released as late as 1945, *House on 92nd Street,* still dealt with the theme of internal subversion.

The government never wished to fuel the hysteria, but it did want to alert citizens to what it regarded as a genuine threat. Well before he was recruited to form the Office of Strategic Services, William Donovan was performing sensitive missions for Franklin Roosevelt. In 1940, after a particularly important fact-finding mission to England, FDR and Navy secretary Frank Knox urged Donovan to collaborate with Edgar Ansel Mowrer on a series of newspaper articles alerting the country to fifth column threats. Much of the information on the fifth column was given to Donovan by the British who hoped to arouse American interest in their cause by using every opportunity to kindle fifth column fears. Over the working breakfasts that he preferred to later appointments, Donovan provided the content, and Mowrer did the writing. Their horror stories were published in newspapers and later as a pamphlet, "Fifth Column Lessons for America," with an introduction by Knox. The purpose—to help Americans recognize the methods used by "the totalitarian powers" so that, if and when those methods were tried in America, they would be "recognized for what they are and their effect nullified."[17] Using France as a key example, Donovan and Mowrer described how German agents "went everywhere, saw everybody, came to know everything"—and, of course, preached "hatred of the Jews to all."[18]

Whatever Roosevelt had intended, the articles produced by Donovan and Mowrer only added to the hysteria. Without adequate documentation the authors claimed that the Nazi victories of 1940 had all been made possible by the fifth column organized by the Gestapo and financed by a "$200,000,000" annual budget. As for America, Donovan and Mowrer warned of the thousands of domestic workers of German extraction, including all the "German waiters," who would willingly serve as "snoopers" for the fatherland. Donovan's and Mowrer's conclusion that at least some German-Americans would be willing to "destroy their own country, to sabotage its defenses, weaken its war effort, sink its ships, [perhaps even] kill its soldiers and sailors for the benefit of a foreign dictator and his alien political philosophy" only heightened the frenzy.[19] The government feared that Americans might turn to vigilante tactics to purge the poison. Even J. Edgar Hoover realized the potential for chaos. The FBI director published an article in *American Magazine* in August 1941 asking the public not to assume that any neighbor who behaved suspiciously was a spy. He cautioned readers simply to report those they suspected of disloyalty to his office.[20]

The pressure of international events between 1939 and 1941 only stoked domestic suspicions. The Nazi-Soviet Pact of August 1939 apparently brought the two foreign sponsors of subversion together, and, after the German invasion of Poland in September, a joint partition of the country sealed the unholy alliance. The Russian attack against Finland—followed by the sudden, stunning German victories in Norway, Denmark, The Netherlands, Belgium, and, above all, France—created widespread belief that conspiracies had eased the Germans' path. The Norwegian quislings must have had their counterparts elsewhere.

American officials were neither immune to the anti-radical contagion nor able to remain passive in such a climate. The State Department was prepared. Consuls were told to scrutinize all applications for nonimmigrant and transit visas to weed out any dangers to public safety.[21] Any refugee that a consul suspected of subversive ideas or intentions, whether fascist or communist, was vulnerable. When it appeared that the German government would not grant passports or permission to depart to applicants for American visas, the Visa Division simply concluded that the German quota would now be available to more Germans in neighboring countries such as Switzerland, whose government wished the U.S. to take more Jewish refugees off its hands.[22] Visa Division chief Avra Warren was sent abroad with verbal instructions in November 1939. Consuls were urged to issue many fewer visas and to gather data that might be used in solving the growing problem of adequately restricting immigration.[23]

By the spring of 1940 the press of refugees seeking asylum in the United States stirred the Visa Division to action. It responded to the new problem with an old regulation. The immediate issue was that German police officials were issuing good conduct certificates to at least some visa applicants who had been convicted of crimes. One consul reported that the authorities were using every means to promote the emigration of Jews from Germany. In April 1940 Samuel Honaker, the American consul general in Stuttgart, reported that "a considerable number of visa applicants with criminal records" had been presenting "clear police certificates in support of their applications for immigration visas."

The State Department received similar reports from other consulates and believed that the Germans had "'whitewashed' police certificates to Jews having criminal records which would, if disclosed, preclude the issuance of immigration visas to them at any American consular office." Robert Alexander of the Visa Division expressed concern about a possible influx of criminal aliens; the whole purpose of the regulation requiring applicants to submit police statements with their visa applications was to reject those with a criminal record. If the Germans refused to change their policy, Alexander suggested that the U.S. would need remedial legislation. From Berlin, Consul A. Dana Hodgdon offered one short-term solution; the U.S. could simply cease to issue visas to Germans.[24] A slightly less drastic measure sufficed.

In May 1940 the Visa Division instructed consuls to demand that certificates contain information on all previous convictions as well as crimes covered by amnesties or crimes expunged from the record for whatever reasons. At the end of June the department informed all consuls that an immigration visa should not be issued "if there is any doubt whatsoever concerning the alien." Recognizing that this new instruction would drastically reduce the number of visas, Assistant Secretary of State Breckinridge Long nonetheless stated that it was essential "to take every precaution to safeguard the best interests of the United States."[25] To clarify the intent of the instruction (and some non-European consuls did write to Washington for clarification),[26] Avra Warren returned to Europe yet another time. In September 1940 the Visa Division dealt more specifically with the problem of unreliable German police certificates by requiring German applicants to present affidavits of good character from several responsible, disinterested persons.[27]

The State Department was rapidly reducing the level of immigration to what it had been in the early 1930s, before the crush of refugees and the period of lenient regulation enforcement that had begun in 1936. Strict regulation with the intent of exclusion was thus not a new policy, merely the resumption of an old one. No new laws were enacted; instead, the discreet, less politically volatile path of altering bureaucratic procedure was taken, as it had been before. What had changed was the rationale. Earlier, immigration restriction had been defensible on grounds of economic self-preservation during the depression and enforcement of the even earlier legislative mandate of 1924. Now the State Department cited the danger of subversion by immigrants, the "fifth column" threat, as sufficient reason to reject a liberal refugee policy.

As the State Department bureaucracy bent the regulations to block alleged fifth column infiltration, experienced statesmen, such as Sumner Welles and Roosevelt confidant Adolf Berle, made it known that in their opinions subversion by refugees was more than a rumor. In April 1940 Berle recorded in his diary a brief but embarrassing encounter with Alvin Johnson, head of the New School for Social Research and founder of the New School's University in Exile, who mentioned his desire to bring German poet Bertolt Brecht to the United States. Berle believed that Johnson shared his own concern with "the Trojan horse tactics by which agents go into a country, and being inside, proceed to open the gates." Berle, however, had information that discretion prevented him from sharing with Johnson. Berle had been warned by Erika Mann [Thomas Mann's daughter] via James Rosenberg that Brecht was really a "Communist agent" whom she did not want admitted. Berle diplomatically suggested that Johnson get in touch with Erika Mann but "did not tell him why." Berle went on to reveal that he, too, was "gunshy now, about refugees." He claimed to have received a "rather rude shock" from the admission of some Spanish refugees who after their admission "as friends of democracy . . . spent their time supporting the Russian invasion of Finland."[28]

Berle did not believe himself to be alone in his concern. Sumner Welles, he knew, was "much disturbed about the 'fifth column' activities in Norway" and the sudden and apparently mysterious collapse of France. Welles wanted to take precautions against subversion in the United States, a sentiment that Berle heartily shared.[29]

Even George Messersmith (now the ambassador to Cuba), often praised by Jewish spokesmen for his fairness and sympathy toward Jewish refugees when he was consul general in Berlin, took seriously reports of Jewish loyalty to Germany and treated them as cues to recommend tighter restrictions. From his new post in Havana he cited rumors that some Jewish refugees allegedly celebrated the fall of Paris to the German army. The stories included a naval attaché's report that he heard Ursula Einstein, the scientist's grandniece, herself a refugee in Port-au-Prince, express similar sentiments. Messersmith hoped that Congress would pass legislation permitting consular officials to assess whether the admission of each applicant to the U.S. would be "in the public interest." For national security reasons, Messersmith argued, "our government can no longer delay giving very specific instructions to consular officials with respect to the degree to which they must go into the character and opinions of aliens desiring to secure immigration visas and visas for a temporary stay in the United States."[30]

Several months later William C. Bullitt, former ambassador to France, further fueled concern by telling a Philadelphia audience that "more than one half the spies captured doing actual military spy work against the French army were refugees from Germany."[31] Though Bullitt's contention was unconfirmed and contradicted by others, it added to the general apprehension that had already reached as far as the White House.[32]

The president did not hesitate to state publicly that he was haunted by the specter of a fifth column whose members included some of the refugees. At a June press conference, Roosevelt responded to a question about how refugees already in the U.S. could be protected from unwarranted suspicions that they were subversives. The president spoke sympathetically of the refugees but added, "Now, of course, the refugee has got to be checked because, unfortunately, among the refugees there are some spies, as has been found in other countries. And not all of them are voluntary spies—it is rather a horrible story but in some of the other countries that refugees out of Germany have gone to, especially Jewish refugees, they have found a number of definitely proven spies." According to the president, these refugee spies had been recruited by the German government through threats, such as "you have got to conduct this particular spy work and if you don't make your reports regularly back to some definite agent in the country you are going to—we are frightfully sorry, but your old father and mother will be taken out and shot." Though Roosevelt conceded that such cases involved "a very, very small percentage of refugees coming out of Germany," he nevertheless insisted that "it is something we have got to watch."[33]

American officials did much more than watch, of course. Secretary of War Henry Stimson conducted meetings with J. Edgar Hoover of the FBI and representatives of the Justice and Navy departments to launch a coordinated response to the fifth column.[34] In the cabinet, according to Stimson, there was a discussion of the selective service law and the possibility that "the communists intended to register fully and get their men called into service with a view to possible Fifth Column work."[35] Stimson later called the selective service director, alerting him to instruct local boards to be on the lookout. Stimson also discussed with Assistant Secretary John J. McCloy an educational drive against subversive activities. McCloy advocated an offensive drive against the fifth column to be pursued in Latin America and even France.[36]

Fifth column apprehensions even spurred the bureaucratic reorganization that moved the Immigration and Naturalization Service from Labor to the Justice Department. The reason for the shift was that those in State close to the president had finally succeeded in persuading him that Labor was lax in its supervision and treatment of immigrants, which was potentially detrimental to the national security in these times. Indeed, the day before FDR sent Congress his reorganization plan, he told a press conference that the shift was necessary as part of the broader plan to halt spying and sabotage.[37] Later Roosevelt attributed the change to the dangers from abroad posed by "fifth column and other activities."[38] At a conference on national defense, the president made his point to the cabinet members and congressional leaders present. Warning that "we have got to be pretty darned careful" in hiring federal employees, he offered an anecdote, very likely exaggerated for emphasis. According to FDR, Secretary of Labor Frances Perkins had been on the verge of appointing a man to deal with unemployment issues when she discovered that he was "100% affiliated and associated with the Communist movement. . . ." Concluding his story, Roosevelt observed, "You have to be careful on that. Also be careful not to get pro-Germans. There are a good many Americans who love efficiency and are pro-Germans for that reason."[39]

Some in the State Department believed, however, that there was a motive besides inefficiency and "soft-headed foolishness" for Labor's laxity. Adolf Berle thought the Labor Department "so honeycombed with Left Wing and Communist intrigue that you can never quite trust what they are doing." Though Berle did not think there was great disloyalty at Labor, he did "suspect there is some." He was equally perturbed, though, by the fact "the older men who knew their business, have in some measure been superseded by the youngsters."⁴⁰ In the mind of a veteran diplomat sensitive about his age, the generation gap at Labor did not appear unrelated to a widening ideological split. Roosevelt's decision could only have warmed the hearts of Frances Perkins's adversaries at State.

With official concern mounting over a fifth column element among the refugees, the Roosevelt administration and the Congress acted in the spring of 1940 to curb the opportunity for subversion by fifth columnists who managed to enter the U.S. In March 1940, Roosevelt approved Secretary of State Cordell Hull's recommendation that all aliens applying for temporary visas be fingerprinted. Congress did its part by passing the Smith Act in June 1940 which imposed additional restrictions on immigrants. It provided that the 4.9 million aliens in the country be registered, fingerprinted, and made to list, in writing, any organizations in which they held membership. Those who were found to have belonged to either a communist or a fascist organization "at any time, of no matter how short duration or how far in the past," could be deported. The rationale was succinctly explained by Attorney General Frank Murphy: "Unless we are pudding headed we will drive from the land the hirelings here to undo the labors of our Fathers."⁴¹

To subdue those disloyal elements that had already managed to penetrate America's borders, FDR approved the placing of wiretaps on the telephones of those the attorney general suspected of "subversive activities." The Smith Act, though primarily directed at alien subversives, contained language sufficiently broad to forbid the native born as well as the foreigner from conspiring to teach or advocate the violent overthrow of the government. Later, in October 1940, Congress required the registration of any organization that was "subject to foreign control" or that favored violent revolution. But the federal government had no jurisdiction over which groups or parties could appear on ballots because each state governs its own electoral procedures and regulations. Therefore, it was left to state legislatures to exclude radical groups from the ballot. Several states, including California, barred the Communist party and affiliate parties from the ballot. Meanwhile, the Justice Department used whatever pretext available to pressure fifth communists, right and left, usually by imprisoning their leadership. Fritz Kuhn, head of the German American Bund, was sentenced to several years in New York's Sing Sing prison for misappropriating five hundred dollars of his group's funds. Equally inconsequential was the charge of passport fraud that placed Communist party head Earl Browder behind bars for two to four years.⁴²

Reports from abroad in late 1940 suggest that suspicions of fifth columnists among the refugees were the product not of anti-Semitic bigotry but of a genuine concern that careless visa policy might endanger national security. Ambassador Laurence Steinhardt, one of the few Jews in a high-level foreign service position, reported to Washington that, despite the assurance that State had received from sponsoring organizations, most of the sponsored applicants for visitors' visas were not "well known intellectuals or labor leaders." Examinations by consular officials had revealed "misrepresentations . . . on such a scale that they could not have been inadvertent." Moreover, Steinhardt reported that "most of them [applicants for visitors' visas] are unable to convince the examining officer that they have the slightest intention of ever leaving the United States." The ambassador was especially indignant over what he regarded as a shift in the burden of proof from the applicant to the consular officer to establish the admissibility of the alien (especially as regarding the alien's "future activities in the United States"). Such a shift was directly contrary to the intention of the 1924 immigration act, Steinhardt contended. Hull quickly responded in support of Steinhardt's objections, emphatically stating the department's position that the burden of proof rested upon the applicant and that, if a consul "has reasonable ground for doubt," the case in question should be resolved in favor of the United States. Still, Hull was cognizant that the possibility of consular abuse existed, and he cautioned Steinhardt that "social status, wealth or other artificial standards have no bearing on any case but that the man himself, his character, his spirit, his general or particular reputation and his intentions . . . are important . . . and . . . should be most strictly interpreted."[43]

Determined to persuade his superiors of the seriousness of the threat of infiltration, Steinhardt, in a later telegram, offered the example of a visa applicant who testified that "he was in considerable disfavor with the local authorities in the town of his residence in Soviet occupied Poland because he had refused to accept repeated offers from them to issue to him the desired exit visa and to facilitate his departure from the Soviet Union in every possible way and even to pay him substantial and regular compensation in the United States provided he would sign an agreement to undertake espionage work in the United States." The applicant said that Soviet authorities claimed they already had "many new agents working for them in the United States" and seemed confident that it would only be a short time before the Soviets would "take over the Government of the United States." Steinhardt was persuaded that this applicant's experience was not unique and that those with relatives still in Soviet territory were especially subject to coercion if they failed to carry out their agreement with Soviet officials.[44]

Reports such as Steinhardt's contributed to the alarm that many American officials felt as they contemplated the arrival of refugees. There is little evidence, however, that German or Soviet political activities in the United States depended upon information from agents among the refugees. Fewer than one-half of one percent of all refugees arriving from Nazi-Soviet territory in 1940 (23,000) were ever taken into custody for questioning. Only a fraction were ever indicted on any charge, and most of those were violations of immigration regulations rather than espionage. Later, after America's entry into the war, hundreds of thousands of these refugees served in the armed services and in defense-related industries.[45] State Department suspicions that, during the early years of the war, Jewish refugee organizations such as the Hebrew Immigrant Aid Society (HIAS), its European counterpart, HICEM, and even the highly respected Jewish Joint Distribution Committee were being used to funnel German agents into the west were equally misplaced. The allegations, however, appear to have been based upon faulty surveillance and errant leaps of logic rather than a predetermined scheme to scuttle Jewish refugees by smearing those who sought to help them.[46]

Now more than ever, State Department officials stiffened their resolve not to allow a misplaced humanitarianism to interfere with their duty and tarnish the department's reputation or their own. State took as a gesture of approval from the White House the transfer of the Immigration and Naturalization Service from Labor to Justice. Pressure, however, especially from Jewish organizations, often left State Department officials in a defensive posture, denying that "national security" was a euphemism for callous indifference to the Jews' plight.

The national security issue was not a public relations device formulated by the State Department to manipulate public opinion in behalf of restriction. In spite of later Treasury Department suggestions that the security issue was a restrictionist ruse and that restrictions were "not essential for security reasons," there is no evidence that policy makers contrived the security issue or colluded to exploit unscrupulously the public fears of internal subversion.[47] Officials in the State Department and the White House were convinced that a fifth column element could undermine the government of the United States as they believed it had subverted governments across Europe. Therefore, they turned to visa policy as they had so frequently during the 1930s as the best weapon with which to defend the national interest.

Besides the career bureaucrats at State who had upheld restrictionism during the previous decade, there were now political appointees that the president had commissioned to aid the State Department with its new responsibilities in a world at war. Breckinridge Long, one recipient of FDR's patronage, was charged with the task of administering refugee policy. An ardent opponent of subversion in the United States, Long's name became synonymous with State Department opposition to a generous refugee policy between 1940 and 1944.

SIX

Breckinridge Long and the Jewish Refugees

In the spring of 1940, Breckinridge Long was the head of the Special War Problems Division of the State Department. He held the rank of assistant secretary of state, filling the post vacated by George Messersmith when he became ambassador to Cuba. Established in January 1940, well before Pearl Harbor turned the U.S. into a belligerent, the War Problems Division included supervision of the Visa Division. The new assistant secretary thus had jurisdiction over refugee matters. It was his burden to formulate administrative policies that would determine which and how many aliens would have the opportunity to take refuge from persecution in the United States. As did Wilbur Carr in the previous decade, Breckinridge Long sat at the vortex of the controversy over how much America ought to moderate its refugee policy in a humanitarian gesture toward European Jewry.

A political appointee rather than a State Department fixture, Long's memos soon droned on in State Department bureaucratese, and his personal style reflected the aloofness *de rigueur* at State, though he never became proficient at either. Nor did he ever completely transfer the partisan loyalty and personal admiration he felt toward Roosevelt to the impersonal regulations and procedures that Wilbur Carr and other career bureaucrats at State venerated. Still Long's desk, like Carr's, can be treated as an observation post from which to chart department policy until the creation of the War Refugee Board in 1944 removed refugee affairs from the assistant secretary's responsibilities.

Appointed by a president known for his close personal and political ties to prominent American Jews, Breckinridge Long's reputation as an anti-Semite is gradually being revised by historians.[1] Certainly Long's references to refugee advocates as "Frankfurter's boys" or "New York liberals" ring of anti-Semitic feelings.[2] Long's diary, however, echoes a more general "paranoiac tone" that exceeds an exclusively anti-Jewish bias, and historians are finding it "increasingly difficult to answer the question [of Long's anti-Semitism] with certainty."[3] The uncertainty is shared by David Wyman, to whom it is "not clear" that Long was an anti-Semite. More important, perhaps, Long, though an ardent nativist and restrictionist, does not appear to Wyman "overtly negative toward Jews simply because they were Jews."[4] Long was more consumed with fears of conspiracies against himself and his country than with an antagonism toward Jews per se.

As early as 1938, Long recorded his suspicions of a subversive conspiracy in his diary. Two years later, he was convinced that he, personally, was one of its main targets: "The attacks in the newspapers still seem to continue against me little by little and indicate that the wild-eyed elements have marked me out as their objective." And barely nine months after that, Long wrote of "wolves" bent upon wrecking his political career.[5] Long's own words seem to justify his reputation for seeing himself as the target of conspiracies. But any portrait of the suspicious, misanthropic Long as using his position to exercise a special anti-Semitism by deliberately barring Jews from the United States is overly simplistic.

Breckinridge Long can best be understood against the backdrop of pre-existing refugee policy and the cross pressures to which he was subjected by virtue of his appointment. He was conscious of State's mandate to enforce America's restrictive laws rigorously. As a politician he was equally aware of appearing responsive to the appeals of desperate refugees and their supporters, who lobbied in the halls of the State Department. Long always yearned for influence and personal prestige, especially the admiration of Roosevelt, his patron. The scion of a distinguished political family, Long bore the burden of living up to his heritage and surmounting a reputation for clumsy, undisciplined performance earned during an earlier term of service as ambassador to Italy.

Blessed with a name that reflected his venerable family pedigree, Breckinridge Long was born in St. Louis in 1881. He was descended from southern aristocratic stock—the Long family of North Carolina and the Breckinridge family of Kentucky. As had many other southerners of distinguished lineage, Long attended Princeton University. Later he studied law at Washington University in St. Louis and was admitted to the Missouri bar in 1906. In 1912 he married another descendant of southern wealth and Democratic heritage. Christine Graham was the granddaughter of Francis Preston Blair, Democratic nominee for vice president in 1868.

Breckinridge Long, or "Breck" as he was called by most of his colleagues in government, came to the State Department through the vicissitudes of politics rather than the rigors of the foreign service ranks. He was a politician whose support of Woodrow Wilson in Missouri in 1912 earned him the patronage post of third assistant secretary of State. Although he enjoyed his uneventful tenure in State, Long resigned in 1920 and ran unsuccessfully for the Senate. He never again ran for political office, but he did remain an active participant of some influence in Missouri politics.

Throughout the 1920s, Long practiced international law but with considerably less enthusiasm than he displayed in working for Franklin Roosevelt's candidacy in 1932. For serving as floor manager at the Democratic convention and a large contribution to the Democratic war chest, Long was rewarded with the ambassadorship to Italy.

At first Long was enamored of the fascists and Mussolini. He saw Fascist rule as a powerful force enacting badly needed modernization and reform. By 1935, however, Long was becoming disillusioned. He described Italian Fascists as "deliberate, determined, obdurate, ruthless and vicious."[6] He reported pointedly on Mussolini's militarism and the dangerous implications of the Ethiopian invasion. Severe stomach ulcers and perhaps a falling-out with the State Department officials caused Long's resignation in 1935. He had presented Mussolini with a plan for ending the Ethiopian war without consulting Cordell Hull. Because the plan would have strengthened Germany's position among the European powers, the State Department repudiated Long's initiative.[7] Franklin Roosevelt accepted Long's resignation with regret, assuring him that "after November I shall want you again to be part of the Administration."[8] Nevertheless, Long remained in semiretirement for the next three years. But, with the outbreak of World War II in 1939, FDR appointed Long to the position of special assistant secretary of state in charge of emergency war matters (which later became the Special War Problems Division). Suddenly the southern gentleman so loyal to the "party of secession" and the presidency of a fellow aristocrat, albeit a northern one, was burdened with deciding the fate of masses of common men and from one of Europe's most despised groups. Squarely in the middle of his desk, Breck Long found the issue of visas for Jewish refugees.

Long perceived himself as the "policy making officer and executive agent of the Government" on the subject of refugees.[9] As such, he viewed himself as the first line of defense against the infiltration of fifth columnists among the refugees. It was up to him to take a hard line against those who would make America vulnerable to her enemies for the sake of a naive humanitarianism. His perspective brought Long into confrontation with the President's Advisory Committee on Political Refugees, the attorney general's office, and those individuals within government and the private sector who championed the refugees' cause. Between 1940 and America's entry into the war in 1941, Long opposed a liberalization of America's restrictive policies because he believed that with the newcomers would come spies and saboteurs.[10]

In the summer of 1940 the desire of the State Department to exclude refugees that might pose a security risk clashed with the concern of the President's Advisory Committee on Political Refugees to rescue "intellectuals and others [political refugees] now in unoccupied France, Spain, Portugal and England, whose lives were in danger and who should be taken to a place of safety." State Department officials such as Sumner Welles bristled at the suggestion that they had been "stymieing" efforts to help the refugees, including children. PACPR's secretary, George Warren, suggested that the conflict could be resolved if a group, such as PACPR, could help screen lists of worthy refugees submitted by interested parties prior to the filing of visa requests by the individual applicants. The PACPR chairman James McDonald also expressed

his hope that State would show "some latitude in the interpretation of administrative regulations" to expedite the admission of those screened.[11]

On July 26, representatives of PACPR, State, and Justice agreed to cooperate on the issuance of immigration visas, visitors' visas, and transit certificates to
political, intellectual, and other refugees who were imperiled in Spain, Portugal,
southern France, and the French African colonies of Morocco, Algeria, and
Tunis. PACPR was to act as a "conduit" to State and Justice for all names
submitted as prospective refugees. The advisory body was to recommend that
visas be issued to specific refugees only after full investigation into the character
and activities of the refugee. All affidavits and assurances were to be verified by
PACPR. Thus, PACPR was to assist in the process of protecting the national
security even as it facilitated the admission of certain designated refugees. No
immigrant was to be admitted if there existed any evidence that he or she might
engage in activities "inimical to the United States." Intellectuals, such as those
stranded in France and in imminent danger of arrest by the Gestapo, were to be
granted visas without delay. Soon the American Federation of Labor, the Jewish
Labor Committee, the American Jewish Congress, and Orthodox rabbinic
scholars were submitting lists to Breckinridge Long of those who should be
granted special emergency visitors' visas. Such visas were granted to over seven
hundred rabbinic students and scholars from the Baltic area alone.[12]

Though consuls still had the final word on all applicants, almost from the
beginning of the new tripartite agreement the State Department engaged in
obstructionism. A letter to Eleanor Roosevelt from the representative of the
Emergency Rescue Committee, a coordinating body organized in June 1940 to
synchronize the various rescue efforts of American groups, complained that the
consul in France had received new instructions and had stopped granting visas
to all those recommended by PACPR unless they already were in possession of
French exit permits, a clear violation of the agreement.[13] By September, PACPR
had recommended 567 names to State and Justice, which had approved them,
but only 15 visas had actually been issued. As a result of the protests of PACPR
and Justice, State reversed its instruction. It was also clear, however, that State
was applying the agreement of July 26 only to prominent writers and labor
leaders, thus unilaterally narrowing the group that the arrangement was intended to affect. It was the consensus of those at the September PACPR meeting
that a conference with State and possibly the president would be essential.[14]

When the meeting at State finally occurred, the members of the PACPR,
and especially James G. McDonald, found themselves confronting Assistant
Secretary of State Breckinridge Long. The assistant secretary of state leaped to
the defense of the department's policies. Long investigated the number of visas
issued to those on the PACPR's lists of distinguished refugees in need of special
consideration. He hoped to establish that there had been a breach of the
agreement of July 26 and that individuals potentially dangerous to the national
security had been recommended by PACPR for visas. He also perused the lists of
visas issued to prominent European labor leaders whose names had been

submitted by the AFL and those of Jewish intellectuals designated by various rabbis, including Rabbi Stephen Wise, as requiring immediate sanctuary. Long's inquiries to Visa Division chief Eliot Coulter were answered by Coulter's complaint that "a limited number of names were submitted at first but additional lists amounting to several hundred names, possibly a thousand, have been subsequently submitted as coming within the same categories and entitled to the same consideration." Coulter suggested to Long that State take the initiative in altering the terms of the agreement with PACPR and the Justice Department concerning priority treatment of important individuals. The Visa Division chief urged that "no new names . . . be submitted than those now approved by the organizations, except that if an exceptional case should arise, it may be submitted." He pressed Long to support the Visa Division in encouraging consuls to "exercise their discretion in holding up any case in which any doubt exists as to [a refugee's] activity in the past and possible activity in the United States."[15]

Although Long agreed with Coulter that a modification would be desirable, he first had to persuade Cordell Hull. The secretary of state insisted that since the PACPR was involved the president must approve. Long reported to FDR that among the PACPR's recommended visa applicants were "a number of persons who our officers abroad feel are not of the desirable element and against whom there is evident ground for doubt as to the propriety of their admissibility." He offered the president the example of a certain "German citizen," a woman. The woman, recommended by the PACPR, was suspect, Long said, because of "various circumstances of her past activity." Told by a consul that she needed evidence that she could proceed to some country outside the U.S. at the expiration of her temporary visitor's visa, she returned with a letter from the German legation in Lisbon stating that she would be able to return to Germany at the end of the period. The consul, however, now suspected that, since the woman could so easily produce the document he had requested, she was either "not a refugee and in imminent danger or she was acting in the interests of the German Government."

Long concluded from this and several other instances that "a more careful examination of the individuals abroad would contribute largely to closing the loopholes against the penetration of German agents or the use of the courtesy and hospitality of the United States for ulterior purposes." Having authorized 2,583 visitors' visas over and above the quota (though not that many individuals actually made it to the U.S.) the assistant secretary now urged that all lists be closed for "unlimited recommendation" except for a few exceptions in "imminent danger."

Long asked the president to place his faith in the consuls abroad to "exercise their judgment as to whether or not the person desiring to come to the United States is, as a matter of fact, within the category you had in mind in setting up the President's Advisory Committee on Political Refugees." He preferred consular discretion to sending the consuls "mandatory instructions from here to admit persons who are known to very few people in this country and about whom there is no record of their past activity." Cordell Hull, satisfied that Long had kept his promise to inform Roosevelt, now wrote to McDonald in support of his assistant secretary's position.[16]

McDonald, altruistically devoted to the refugees' cause, was outraged by State's behavior. On September 24, he and George Warren wrote to Cordell Hull protesting State's modification of the original arrangement "without previous notice to the Department of Justice or to the President's Advisory Committee on Political Refugees." McDonald and Warren wanted all procedures to conform to the agreement of July 26 and the president to be informed of all that transpired to correct any "erroneous impression" that might have been conveyed to FDR as to the behavior of the PACPR. They did not know that State was unintimidated by the threat of an appeal to Roosevelt because Long had already made his case to FDR.[17]

There is some evidence that Roosevelt supported State's position. In a letter quoted by Clarence Pickett, executive secretary of the American Friends Service Committee, Margaret Jones, who represented the AFSC in Vienna, said that after a conference with Avra Warren she was convinced that "FDR doesn't want any more aliens from Europe—refugees have been implicated in espionage—and so forth. All part of the spy hysteria."[18] However Roosevelt chose to make his position known to Long, the assistant secretary did not buckle when his adversaries threatened to go over his head. After a long evening session with McDonald, Warren, and Sumner Welles, a confident Long acknowledged in his diary that McDonald regarded him as an "obstructionist and was very bitter and somewhat denunciatory." Still, Long had not protested when the head of the PACPR said he wished to take their differences to Roosevelt. Instead, a smug Long wrote, "I said I hoped he would and would lay the whole matter before him [FDR]."[19]

While Long and the attorney general discussed the possibility of drafting a law that would forbid an immigration visa or other travel document to an alien whose admission to the U.S. "would be contrary to public safety," McDonald turned to Eleanor Roosevelt to get him a prompt and sympathetic hearing from the president. The first lady did not refuse. She urged FDR to meet with McDonald and think of "these poor people who may die at any time and who are asking only to come here on transit visas." She hoped he would "get this cleared up quickly."[20]

The president agreed to see the chairman of his advisory committee. But, even before McDonald's appointment at the White House, Long managed to give Roosevelt some of the cables State had received from Ambassador Laurence Steinhardt in Moscow. Steinhardt, who was Jewish, charged that many of the so-called intellectuals and labor leaders endorsed for visas by the PACPR were neither and that the PACPR was intentionally deceiving the department. The ambassador especially objected to what he regarded as a shifting of responsibility from the alien to the consular official in proving the alien admissible under the provisions of the 1924 act and all subsequent operable instructions implementing it. Steinhardt said that he still regarded admission to the United States as a "privilege, not a right," and he objected to the misrepresentations that he felt were the responsibility of sponsoring organizations (such as the PACPR).[21]

On October 8, McDonald and Warren sent a memorandum to Roosevelt outlining their complaints against the State Department. The two leaders of the PACPR acknowledged that the "consuls must be the final judges" but contended that, from the PACPR's knowledge of those sponsoring the persons recommended, they could not "believe that those still without visas present threats to the national interest." They contended that State's assessment of the character of the "masses of refugees who have burst across European borders" ought not to be applied to those nominated by persons known to the PACPR and recommended "only after reasonable precaution has been taken." McDonald and Warren stressed the urgency of the refugees' plight, pointing out that the Spanish border was not closed and that only Lisbon remained as a place of exit from Europe. Thus, to delay would be "to condemn many scientists, scholars, writers, labor leaders and other refugees to further sacrifices for their belief in democracy. . . ."[22]

Roosevelt handled the dispute between the PACPR and State as he often treated internal conflicts in his administration. He told both sides what they wanted to hear, thereby retaining the loyalty of both groups, and insisted that they work out a compromise. The president, Long claimed, had defended his loyal undersecretary of state and told McDonald "not to 'pull any sob stuff' on him." Roosevelt assured Long that he warned McDonald that, as President, "he could not agree with any plan which would allow any organization in this country, whether it be Rabbi Wise, or McDonald, or William Green, to recommend finally that any person abroad whom they had not seen be admitted to this country." According to Long, FDR then ordered McDonald

> to wait in town a few days until Mr. Biddle of the Department of Justice could confer with Mr. Welles and me and come to some understanding on the matter . . . and then that Mr. McDonald could understand from Mr. Biddle what he was to do in the future.[23]

Not surprisingly, McDonald also thought he had won FDR's support. In an almost Rashomon-like episode, McDonald reported to Felix Frankfurter, his friend, a very different account of his meeting with Roosevelt. "The conference yesterday was, I think, satisfactory. The Chief was most cordial at the very beginning, throughout the conference, and at the end." McDonald thought Roosevelt was well informed on the issue, suggesting that "he had gone through the dossier including his wife's pertinent comments on our Mr. Warren's memorandum." He concluded that, "at the end, he [FDR] must have known who are responsible for thwarting his will." Even Roosevelt's demand for resolution pleased McDonald who looked forward to working with the Justice Department's representative. In a thank-you note to Eleanor Roosevelt, McDonald summed up his satisfaction with the meeting, "It was a relief, though I was not surprised, to have the President indicate by his whole manner during the conference that he realizes that we, the members of his Advisory Committee, have throughout been motivated solely by two considerations, our obligations to our consciences and our loyalty to him."[24]

In spite of McDonald's expressions of satisfaction with his White House meeting, PACPR and State remained at loggerheads. At a dinner meeting on October 14, the members of the PACPR said that though they regarded Sumner Welles as "fair and objective when actually confronted with a situation . . . he will not make an initial move."[25] Their expectation of cooperation from Long was perhaps best expressed by its omission.

The committee did feel that it had found an ally in the Justice Department, which it thought was "thoroughly disgusted" with State's obstructionism.[26] Four days later, at a luncheon meeting, representatives of State and Justice tried to reach agreement among themselves on the proper role of the PACPR with respect to their agencies. They agreed that the PACPR should indeed have preference over other committees in securing departure of their sponsored refugees from Europe; that State would honor its original agreement and waive the requirement for exit permits prior to visa issuance; that the selection of visa recipients be based solely on merit and meritorious qualification rather than on numbers; that visa applicants should be presented individually rather than by group; and, finally, that consuls would not be hampered in the exercise of their judgment of refugees' qualifications but that, if an individual recommended by the PACPR were rejected, the consul must cable his reasons to the department and follow with a mail despatch.[27]

While Breckinridge Long and his adversaries played billiard-ball politics, caroming the refugee issue from office to office in Washington, consuls abroad remained puzzled. How were they to judge the intellectual merits of applicants? In Algiers, the American consul general, Felix Cole, asked:

> Is an "intellectual" more worthy of consideration than a working man, or a small time merchant, who has left behind all his meager belongings and has once started in again, in a strange country, under new conditions, at a pittance and who is now forced to attempt at least to begin all over again and is refused on L.P.C. grounds while the University professor is welcomed and supported because of his education, his fluent speech or pen, and his appeal to wealthy individuals?[28]

Cole said he meant merely to raise the question. The question he raised, however, reflects the uneasiness of consuls with their instructions and the anti-refugee bias that the entire national security issue had stirred at all levels of the bureaucracy.

In Budapest, Consul Howard Travers believed that "after the election [the] political pressure will be reduced."[29] Even as Roosevelt heard complaints that State's bureaucracy was obfuscating and obstructing, consular officials blamed the president for playing electoral politics at their expense.

Mutual distrust and bitterness among agencies and individuals continued to block the escape of Jewish refugees attempting to use the American visa process. But the interagency conflict of 1940 was resolved, at least on paper, with the formation of the Inter-Departmental Committee, an interagency committee consisting of representatives of State, Justice, and the PACPR, who would consider negative reports by consuls on refugees and whose recommendation would be binding on consuls.[30]

Even as the warring agencies were moving toward reconciliation, however, Long was plotting to pack the new Inter-Departmental Committee. In his diary, Long recorded his desire to overcome Justice Department objections and persuade Attorney General Robert Jackson to appoint a representative from the FBI (whom Long assumed would be a restrictionist on national security grounds), in addition to a member of the Immigration and Naturalization Service as one of Justice's two members on the new committee.[31]

The State Department hoped to structure the new committee to its own best interests, but, should that fail, the department took the precaution of again tinkering with consular procedures to undermine any efforts to admit more refugees than it chose. According to Long, Visa Division chief Avra Warren had already orally instructed consuls to drop from the visa waiting list all those lacking "travel documents and exit permits and steamship accommodations."[32] By quietly manipulating procedure, State had once again managed to violate the spirit of its agreement with Justice and the PACPR.

Long was equally delighted to learn that Secretary of the Interior Harold Ickes, a New Deal refugee advocate, had raised the president's ire. Ickes had not reprimanded the governor general of the Virgin Islands for announcing his intention to give refugees special permission in selected cases to be temporary visitors (thirty days) on the islands if they were unable to obtain visitors' visas from the consular service.[33] In a memo to Ickes, Roosevelt fumed:

> The fact remains that the Secretary of State and the President must determine all matters relating to the foreign relations of each and every portion of the United States including its insular possessions. That means that no other department of the Government and no Governor of an Insular Possession may make a decision or issue a proclamation which involves foreign policy without the approval of the State Department and the White House.[34]

After the governor's resignation, newspaper columnist Pat Frank shrewdly assessed the episode as "a sad record of the effect of the failure of groups interested in refugees to get together. The setup was ideal." As for Roosevelt, Frank believed that the president's reaction could be explained by the fact that the matter reached his desk "shortly after Army and Navy intelligence had put a bee in his ear regarding the planting of Nazi agents among emigrating refugee groups."[35]

The fifth column threat and the stiff opposition of the State Department to any leniency that would diminish its own jurisdiction and prerogatives sent the refugees' advocates into retreat even before the war stopped the exodus from Nazi-occupied Europe. The fears of internal subversion became arrows in State's quiver capable of piercing the consciousness of both policy makers and public alike. In December 1940 the State Department capped its victory by persuading FDR to permit it to issue a press release in response to what it regarded as "adverse publicity"—publicity that had characterized State as "either negligent of the recommendations made to it by the President's Advisory Committee on Political Refugees or callous to the plight of those endangered by reason of their religious or political views."[36] Arguing that the actions of consuls had been made uniformly consistent with State Department policy in recent months and that "more liberal interpretations might be made of the term political refugee with respect to those who had reached Lisbon," State even persuaded the PACPR of the futility of continuing to act as a "channel for recommendations for the issuance of emergency visas." The PACPR's vote to terminate its list making was unanimous.[37] Long had won another round.

In a nation at peace choking with the fear of war and subversion, State won the battle of bureaucracies that had begun years earlier. It could not, however, completely camouflage its resistance to humanitarianism. In an article for the *Louisville Courier-Journal,* Herbert Agar angered the State Department by calling for its reform. Among some at State, he saw "a maze of jealousy and cross purposes." Overall, the country seemed to be the victim not of a fifth column but of a department that combined "the bad features of a permanent civil service with the bad features of patronage appointments and of government by presidential favorites."[38] Could Agar's oblique description have referred to the loyal southern Democrat whom FDR rewarded with an appointment at State?

In the spring of 1941, the State Department, especially an eager Breckinridge Long, hurried to bolt the door it had all but closed the previous year. Once again citing the dangers of subversives among the refugees, State instructed consuls to reject applicants if they had "children, parents, spouse, brothers or sisters" still residing in the ever-widening territories under Nazi domination.[39] Thousands of Jewish refugees were stranded in Lisbon because apprehensive consuls now considered them potential security threats. On June 20, 1941, FDR signed the Bloom–Van Nuys bill, which authorized American consular officials to withhold any type of visa from an alien seeking admission to the United States "if the official knows or has reason to believe" that the applicant might engage in activities that would "endanger the public safety."[40]

In addition, the State Department instituted a new procedure for issuing visas that included participation by the FBI, just as Long had wanted. Each applicant would have to undergo not only an examination by an American consul abroad but also a review in Washington by the Primary (Visa) Committee, the Interdepartmental Visa Review Board, and, when necessary, the Appeals Committee. The applicant began with a four-sided form, six copies of which had to be sent to the Visa Division in Washington. That office distributed the

copies to the Immigration and Naturalization Service, the FBI, Army intelligence, Navy intelligence, and the State Department. Three to six weeks later
these agencies reported back on the applicant's suitability for admission. A
favorable report from the Primary Committee meant advisory approval, but the
American consul abroad could still deny the visa, in which case the matter
returned to Washington. But the visa was valid only for the remainder of the
fiscal year, and, if the applicant could not get transportation to the U.S. during
that time, he or she had to reapply and begin the whole process *de novo*.

If the Primary Committee rejected the application, the applicant's American sponsor could appeal and appear before the Interdepartmental Visa Review Board. The review board might overrule the Primary Committee. If the
cleared applicants were of nationalities regarded as friendly, such as French,
Belgian, Dutch, or Czech, there was no need for further appeal. All applicants
classified as enemy aliens, however, automatically went to the Appeals Committee, even if they had cleared the review board. The Appeals Committee as
originally constituted tended to be more sympathetic to refugees than the review
boards that were top-heavy with military and FBI personnel. Members of the
Appeals Committee such as Dr. Frederick P. Keppel, a former president of the
Carnegie Corporation, and former Ohio senator Robert J. Bulkley, were often
more moved by humanitarianism than by an agency's agenda. Though reluctant
to discredit themselves in the eyes of the State Department and White House by
"run[ning] our percentage of reversals too high," the Appeals Committee
reversed approximately 25 percent of the visa denials that emerged from the
review boards. Still, Long and his fellow restrictionists had their way 75 percent
of the time.[41]

Just as he sought to minimize domestic interference with the State Department's restrictionism, Long successfully curbed any possibility of international
interventions. By the spring of 1941, Long's snipping opposition to the activities of the Intergovernmental Committee on Refugees paid a dividend in the
resignation of Robert T. Pell, who had been the alternate U.S. delegate to the
IGCR and the liaison between the IGCR and the State Department. Pell,
explaining his decision to Myron Taylor, the regular U.S. delegate, cited Long's
opposition to having "any Intergovernmental Committee around the Department." The indignant Pell saw "no use in going on" because of Long's "unre-
lenting attack on the work and officers [of the IGCR]." Pell was not exaggerat-
ing. Long had bureaucratically boxed his ears. He had fired Pell's trusted
assistant, Alfred Wagg, without cause by simply discontinuing the position; he
reassigned Pell's refugee responsibilities to the notoriously anti-refugee European Division and the beleagured Visa Division; and Long failed to include in
his annual budget request the twenty-six thousand dollars needed for the
IGCR's work.[42]

As the glut of applications and meetings clogged schedules in Washington,
the admission of refugees ground to a halt. Moreover, the new American

barriers had repercussions elsewhere, too. Messersmith told a Cuban official that 80 percent of the European-born immigrants admitted to Cuba, but now applying for American visas, would be unable to qualify under the new regulations and procedure. He advised the Cuban minister to revise Cuban immigration regulations.[43] Breckinridge Long and his fellow restrictionists at State, with their bureaucratic weaponry, had succeeded not only in closing the United States to the refugees but also in closing the hemisphere to them as well.

In December 1941, less than six months after the establishment of the elaborate new review procedures, the United States went to war. For the next four years all the moral and material resources of America and its allies were marshaled for one purpose, quick and total victory over the Axis powers. This new commitment, however, did not include an open door for those most victimized by the enemy. Indeed, the priority of military victory lent a new legitimacy to government officials' unwillingness to make special provision for European Jews and other refugees. Those in the State Department and the Roosevelt administration who had been opposed to the refugees for national security reasons could now use yet another reason—wartime exigency.

With America in the fray, Breckinridge Long's responsibility was to protect the United States not only from its declared enemies but also from all who might adversely affect the war effort. At times that mission ran at cross purposes with strictly humanitarian ends and even, occasionally, with the preservation of comity among the allies. Long adamantly refused to make exceptions to American immigration laws and procedures for Jews in flight. From his perspective, he was seeking to reconcile existing restrictionist laws with the demands of groups who sought sanctuary in the United States without exposing American society to the dangers of imported radicalism and sabotage. He insisted that "discrimination must not be practiced." Restrictionism through administrative measures had to apply to the British as well as to the Germans, and even the Canadians could only be handled through a special "exception to the general rule."[44]

Although Long shunned exceptions to laws and regulations, he did want to be helpful in individual cases of rescue where possible. Prior to America's entry into the war, Long instructed Avra Warren of the Visa Division to begin expediting the issuance of visas to one group of rabbis and rabbinical students from Lithuania, adding, "I want to do everything we legitimately can to help these people out of the predicaments they find themselves in, at the same time observing the requirements of our law."[45] As the Nazi pressure upon European Jewry escalated, however, so did Jewish requests for visas. Long began to stiffen under pressures.

By July 1941, the problem seemed overwhelming. After visits from several Hasidic leaders, Long noted how many rabbis had been to the State Department "time and again during the last twelve months." Their demands seemed only to mount.

In all, they have submitted to the Department in the neighborhood of 10,000 names. In many instances, the name of the individual does not include the persons of his household who desire to accompany him and for whom application is automatically made. Relatives include wife, children, children-in-law, brothers and sisters-in-law and persons of varying other degrees of consanguinity or relationship by marriage.[46]

As charges and countercharges were hurled at Long and his department for not doing enough for Jewish refugees, he remained consistent in his insistence upon adherence to existing laws. "No single group of these persons [refugees]," he insisted, "can be segregated from another group and made an exception without extending the exception to each member of each other group."[47]

Though Breckinridge Long occasionally cooperated to admit Jewish leaders whose lives were in immediate danger, he often expressed concern that the pressure of the American Jewish community in behalf of their persecuted coreligionists might boomerang and also adversely affect the war effort. Long expressed his concern that Jewish pressure, especially the dynamic "leadership of Rabbi Stephen Wise" with whom Long often disagreed but for whom he also had grudging admiration, might produce an anti-Semitic backlash. More immediately upsetting to Long was that such a "reaction against their [the Jews'] interest" might dampen enthusiasm for the war in Europe. Americans might recoil at the sacrifices the war demanded if they believed Hitler's charges that the U.S. had gone to war "at the instigation and direction of our Jewish citizens."[48] The assistant secretary of state was concerned that any diminution in the general public's enthusiasm for the war might be attributed by his adversaries to Long's concessions to Jewish groups asking for visa policy exceptions.

Much of the criticism leveled at Long was the result of the complex visa application and appeal procedure he had helped establish in 1940. What few understood, however, was that, after he set his new bureaucratic structure in motion, the momentum of bureaucracy carried Long's creation beyond even his control. Though Long had won often at bureaucratic games, his mastery of procedures and regulations was never as thorough as Wilbur Carr's. His frustrations often resulted in clumsy acts taken in haste. He recorded in his diary:

> The Visa Procedure is getting to the fore again—much criticism. The lower committees are very strict. The Bd. of Appeals—liberal. I can't get them reconciled in regular course so I may have to do a bit of surgery. The refugee problem is a thorny one—and there is plenty of criticism either way the decision lies. One side is dissatisfied in any case. But I weather that—and try to play it safe against any possible Fifth Column.[49]

Long's fear of spies among the refugees and his refusal to allow Jewish refugees a special exemption from rules and procedures left him with the reputation of being "a narrow, limited man, whose wealth and inclination have kept him from having any sympathy for the people who get pushed around."[50] In the early fall of 1942, however, Long endorsed a proposal to rescue 1,000 Jewish children from France (described at length in chapter seven). He found "the appeal for asylum . . . irresistible to any human instinct and the act of [Nazi] barbarity just as repulsive."[51] He was moved, but even his moral indignation could not overcome a perception of his duty that demanded resisting the impassioned appeals of Jewish groups who criticized him. Long believed that their own parochial interests did not permit such petitioners to appreciate that his unswerving commitment to restrictionism was in the national interest—and, he might have added, his own.

Of even greater irritation to Long than the American Jewish community was the British government. The Bermuda Conference between Great Britain and the United States in late April 1943 produced no tangible movement by either country to facilitate the rescue of Jews. Long's diary entries, however, suggest that he distrusted Britain's enthusiasm for the meeting because he thought it largely derived from a desire to dump "responsibility and embarrassment" for the refugee problem "in our laps."[52] To counter these perceived machinations and to protect the internal security of the U.S., Long assumed a highly defensive posture. Long did not go to Bermuda, but he handpicked delegates. Most of those he picked shared his reticence to commit the U.S. to anything more than "rescue through victory," an increasingly popular slogan among opponents of more aggressive rescue efforts.

An admirer of clever political machinations, Long decided to involve sympathetic members of Congress in the Bermuda deliberations. He realized that Congress would have to be involved in the implementation of any plan that involved funds for refugee assistance or the stretching of immigration quotas beyond the level mandated by the Johnson-Reed Act of 1924. Therefore, he appointed two certain allies to the Bermuda delegation: Congressman Sol Bloom, chairman of the House Foreign Affairs Committee, and Senator Scott Lucas, the assistant majority leader in the Senate.[53] To lead the delegation, Long promised to appoint an individual of "eminent reputation for vigorous and honest mentality."[54] He proposed the name of U.S. Supreme Court Associate Justice Owen J. Roberts. In the role of support personnel, Long, after being placed under considerable political pressure, chose George Warren, the executive secretary of the PACPR, and Long's own immediate assistant Robert Alexander. The latter had only recently expressed his opinion that refugee matters must be "considered not only from the standpoint of possible benefits to the immigrants but primarily from the viewpoint of any benefits to the country receiving the immigrants." To ensure that all would go smoothly, as he defined it, Long added to the delegation the name of a personal friend, Robert Borden Reams, then acting as secretary to the executive committee of the Intergovernmental Committee on Refugees. Reams, an ardent opponent of immigration, was to be secretary to the U.S. delegation.

Long had crafted a delegation that reflected his own commitment to restrictionism. Even Sol Bloom, the Jewish congressman from New York, had a reputation among Jews and non-Jews as fearful of rocking the State Department boat. He was considered, generally, insufficiently aggressive on the refugee issue and "too susceptible to State Department influence." Some Jewish leaders such as Stephen Wise criticized Bloom privately, but the Yiddish press, which never allowed Anglo-Saxon restraint to temper its wrath, characterized Bloom as "a shabbas goy," an expression used to describe non-Jews hired in orthodox communities to complete the tasks that were forbidden to observant Jews on the Sabbath. Others called him the "State Department's Jew."[55] Long did not defend Bloom to the Yiddish press, but to Stephen Wise he wrote that "the composition of the group as a whole is such as to justify that any matter which comes before them will be intelligently considered."[56] As for Bloom's fitness to represent American Jewry, Long's parting shot was that the congressman was "a representative of America."[57] Another of Long's Jewish critics, Congressman Samuel Dickstein, chairman of the House Committee on Immigration and Naturalization, wrote directly to FDR. He asked to join the delegation based on his experience and his committee position. He also claimed that his selection would be politically astute because, unlike Bloom, he was acceptable to "the Orthodox branch of the religion."[58] Neither FDR nor Long shared Dickstein's enthusiasm for such an appointment.

Long had difficulty finding individuals who met his personal criteria, were acceptable to Roosevelt, and were willing to serve. Roberts's position as leader of the delegation had originally been offered to Myron C. Taylor, who had refused the opportunity because he was preoccupied with the business of the President's Advisory Commission on Postwar Foreign Policy. Any delay disturbed Long, who feared that even the appearance of an unwillingness to act might bring down on his head an "unfortunate repercussion of organized public opinion." For Long, this apprehension made even worse Justice Roberts's decision to decline leadership of the delegation. Roberts wrote to the president that Chief Justice Harlan Stone felt the court was "in such shape that I should not leave it until the date about June 1st."[59] Long's third choice, Charles Seymour, the president of Yale, also initially accepted the assignment and then turned it down when his trustees objected to his participation. Seymour said he would only reconsider if "no other qualified person was available" to the State Department.[60] What one Ivy Leaguer turned down, another finally accepted. A personal friend of Long's, Dr. Harold Willis Dodds, Princeton's president, agreed at the last minute (only four days before the conference was to open) to lead the Americans in Bermuda.

Even as Long was struggling to assemble a delegation, the British raised as a problem the number of American representatives. After all, they intended sending only Richard Law. Would not such a disparity appear "odd?"[61] Long would not reduce the size of the delegation he had worked so hard to assemble. Then, while Long was trying to persuade American Jewish leaders not to regard this conference as concerned only with Jews, the British, at the last minute, tried to get an invitation for the British Jewish Board of Deputies to attend the conference. Long protested any such invitation since it might create an "embarrassing" situation for both nations, and especially for him if no American Jewish groups were invited.[62] Even the location and timing of the conference had to be defended by Long. Some, including Rabbi Stephen Wise and Phillip Murray, president of the Congress of Industrial Organizations (CIO), charged that the United States and the British were conducting a secret conference in the hope that the whole refugee issue could be swept under the rug.[63] Others feared just the opposite, that the State Department would try to defy immigration restrictions under the veil of secrecy. Long, besieged on all sides, was determined to orchestrate this potentially humiliating meeting of the two so-called allies.

Breckinridge Long worked hard with others at State on the official memorandum for the guidance of the delegates. It reflects the cautious and generally negative posture that Long adopted toward Bermuda's bilateral approach. The delegates were especially cautioned not to emphasize the Jewish identity of so many of the refugees so as not to lend credence to Nazi charges that the allies were surrogates for the Jews. No transportation facilities were to be made available that might delay wartime shipping. No special funds were to be pledged. Most of all, there were to be no arrangements that would conflict with existing immigration laws which were described in the memorandum as "extremely liberal as they now stand."[64] Long and his colleagues left little room for maneuver on behalf of the refugees.

Not all refugee advocates in government were prepared to adhere to the low-key approach to Bermuda that Long advised. In Congress a debate over the Bermuda meeting produced a resolution more positive in sentiment and tone than anything that had emerged from State. In an address on April 16 to his colleagues, Senator Edwin C. Johnson of Colorado introduced a resolution supported by the Committee for a Jewish Army of Stateless and Palestinian Jews. It read:

> Whereas a conference of importance and far-reaching implications is now under way in Bermuda for the purpose of exploring the refugee problem emanating from the chaos and confusion brought about by Hitler's mad attempt to impose his new order upon the people of Europe; and
>
> Whereas under a program of planned mass murder 2,000,000 defenseless Jews have already been brutally massacred by the Nazi hordes and a damnable policy of extermination has been proclaimed by Hitler against the Jewish people; and
>
> Whereas this vile policy has uprooted and made destitute and stateless the remaining European Jews who are not only marked for slaughter but are abandoned with no one to speak and act on their behalf; and
>
> Whereas the American traditions of justice and humanity demand that we extend the helping hand to every victim of cruel oppression; Now, therefore, be it
>
> Resolved, That the Bermuda Conference be advised that the Senate of the United States advocates an immediate and stern policy of action to save the remaining millions of the Jewish people in Europe, and that such a humanitarian objective be consummated speedily in a manner which will restore to those helpless victims of Hitler the rights and dignity of a free people.[65]

Johnson's colleagues, especially those close to the administration, tabled the resolution. Long dismissed it as a production by backstage Jewish lobbyists.[66] The American delegation left with vague instructions and a mandate to do almost nothing—except not violate the integrity of America's restrictive legislation. In that its success was marked.

When the Bermuda conference ended, all those connected with it rushed to vindicate themselves and to justify the role each had played in the farce. While Rabbi Stephen Wise requested an interview with FDR to inquire into the "inexplicable absence of active measures to save those who can still be saved," Breckinridge Long made certain that FDR heard his own carefully crafted version, which he submitted nine months after the conference. His report included some vastly inflated and distorted estimates of how many refugees had actually been admitted to the United States since 1933.[67]

As weeks and months passed and little was said about the Bermuda meeting, Long received a letter of concern from the delegation chairman, Harold Dodds. Dodds protested the policy of official silence on the meeting. His letter reveals where Long was placing the blame for inaction: "You told me that the difficulty was across the water, but that doesn't obscure the fact that we shall soon be charged with misleading the public and that our report is not being implemented."[68]

Other voices of protest were less measured in their tone. The Committee for a Jewish Army of Stateless and Palestinian Jews opened a campaign to discredit the Bermuda Conference and to lay the blame squarely at the door of the State Department. On May 4, 1943, the group placed a full-page advertisement in the *New York Times:* "To 5,000,000 Jews In The Nazi Death Trap—Bermuda Was A Cruel Mockery."[69] Its campaign against State became known as the "action—not pity" drive. Though the attack was discredited when it was revealed that the committee's leader, Peter Bergson, had printed the endorsement of thirty-three Senators without getting official authorization, Breckinridge Long took little comfort from the fact that the group was denounced repeatedly from the Senate floor.[70] The criticism of him continued. And, always convinced that his enemies hated him because he could see to the heart of their subversive aims, Long wrote in his diary that his "defeatist" and "emotionalist" detractors were using a slogan ("action—not pity") that resembled Hitler's own words in 1937. The familiarity hardly seemed a coincidence to the beleagured Long; he remained thoroughly persuaded that the Gestapo "created and instigated certain organizations for their own ulterior motives. . . ."[71]

Long hoped to strike back at his adversaries by engineering some highly positive publicity about himself and his department. He hoped to plant an article in some popular magazine or newspaper that would "present the refugee problem as a whole and the favorable attitude of the Department of State toward it." Some positive public relations, Long thought, could "correct the criticism" that had been aimed at State. But such an article never appeared. Instead, State hoped that a joint communique with the British would reverse the criticism.

The two countries, however, could not reach agreement. Privately, Long was disturbed and frustrated that even the limited agreements of the Bermuda talks had not been implemented.[72] With the British continuing to resist the establishment of temporary refugee camps in North Africa, Long could only scribble the frustration of a stymied bureaucrat, lamenting the power vacuum that rendered him unable to act and unable to duck the responsibility for the state of inaction on refugee matters: "The truth of the whole thing is that there is no authority in this government that can make commitments to take the refugees in groups and that there are no funds out of which the expenses of refugees could be paid for safe keeping in other localities."[73]

But, even with all other avenues of escape closed, Long would not abandon the responsibility he felt to administer the laws as they stood, and he doubted that lawmakers would change them. If the British would not relent and help alleviate his burden, neither did he anticipate relief from Congress: "The immigration laws stand as a bar to admission of persons unless certain requirements are met, and there is no chance on earth to change those laws in favor of refugees at this time."[74]

In the early summer of 1943, Long again demonstrated his unwillingness to assume a greater humanitarian burden than the Congress had been willing to bear. Peter Bergson's Committee for a Jewish Army responded to the disappointment of the Bermuda Conference with another meeting, the Emergency Conference to Save the Jewish People of Europe. It met July 20–25, at the Hotel Commodore. The Emergency Committee to Save the Jewish People of Europe, a product of the gathering, persuaded Cordell Hull to facilitate the overseas travel of six Emergency Committee representatives going to Turkey, Spain, and Palestine to promote rescue efforts. Hull asked Long to make the arrangements. Persuaded that the Secretary of State had agreed to support an effort duplicative of what the IGCR and the American government were already doing, Long obstructed the mission. Only two Emergency Committee representatives ever got to Europe, and Long managed to delay the departure of Bloomingdale Department Store executive Ira Hirschmann for months. Long refused to allow the State Department to facilitate and thereby legitimize private groups' rescue plans. Long saw himself resisting an interest group's manipulation of a government agency for its own ends, however humane those ends might be. It was a matter of jurisdiction and prerogative. Congress, not eloquent lobbyists and compliant administrators, ought to set policy. And Congress had not changed the law.[75]

Believing that his hands were tied, Long continued to try and put the best face possible on the behavior of the United States toward the refugees. In late 1943, however, the glare of publicity cast a shadow over Long's professions of humanitarian concern for the refugees. His own erroneous testimony before the House Foreign Affairs Committee publicly exposed him as, at the very least, misinformed and lent credence to his adversaries' charges that he was ignorant of the facts and insensitive to the refugees behind the numbers in his reports.

Long's inattention to detail, his shortcoming as a bureaucrat, was the start of his undoing.

The House committee was considering a resolution "urging the creation by the President of a commission of diplomatic, economic and military experts to formulate and effectuate a plan for immediate action designed to save the surviving Jewish people of Europe from extinction at the hands of Nazi Germany." Long denied the need for such a body because the State Department was already engaged in such rescue work, including the resuscitation of the Intergovernmental Committee. He claimed that the U.S. alone had accepted approximately 580,000 refugees "since the beginning of the Hitler regime [1933]."[76]

Long's data were grossly distorted. First, he had confused the total number of visas issued to all categories of aliens (quota immigrants, refugees, etc.) with the number of refugee visas. Then he confused the number of visas issued and the number of refugees who actually arrived in the United States. In contrast to the figure of 580,000 cited by Long, data extracted from reports by the Labor Department and the Immigration and Naturalization Service indicated that 476,930 immigrants (quota immigrants, nonquota immigrants, and visitors) had arrived from all countries, including 296,032 from Europe. The estimated number of refugees from all countries numbered only 218,069, most of them (201,664) from Europe. As for Jews, an estimated 165,756 came from all the European nations combined; ony 138,089 were Jewish refugees. Long's statistics offered a greatly exaggerated profile of America's generosity toward refugees.[77]

Long was unaware of his error. But, even before Long's testimony was made public on December 10, Congressman Emanuel Celler circulated it as an example of State's dishonesty on the refugee issue. Upon its release, the Jewish community raised its voice in protest. Congressman Celler accused Long of shedding "crocodile tears" and blamed him for the "tragic" visa "bottleneck." The American Jewish Conference drafted a point-by-point refutation of Long's testimony.[78]

Long never completely understood what had happened or how negative an impression he had made. He blamed "a serious internal pressure based on humanitarian impulse and surrounded with doubt, uncertainty and suspicion on the part of high officials and a large part of the public including groups naturally interested on account of race and religion." He well knew that Jews had been his harshest critics, but he never believed that their criticisms were justified.[79]

In his testimony before the House committee, Long assured the members that "we did every legitimate thing we could and we observed the laws of the United States." He could never fully comprehend how loyal Americans could object to their "servants" fairly enforcing the law of the land. Moreover, he could even assure the committee that the United States was not breaking from its tradition of welcoming the world's huddled masses. "The point is," he said, "that the historic attitude of the United States as a haven for the oppressed has not changed. The Department of State has kept the door open. It has been carefully screened but the door is open. . . ."[80] Long's obtuse imagination was such that he could not appreciate how outraged American Jews could be by hearing him draw the analogy between a screened door prepared to repulse flies in the summertime and the visa regulations that State was using to bar their suffering European brothers.

When FDR announced the formation of the War Refugee Board on January 24, 1944, Long wrote that it "is good news for me." When the new director was selected, he would take over, which, Long wrote, "insures me of staying out." In a tone of hurt pride, he wondered, "What they can do that I have not done I cannot imagine. However, they can try." And he concluded, "In my opinion, the Board will not save any persecuted people I could not save under my recent and long suffering administration."[81]

Breckinridge Long was an outspoken man of strong prejudices, deep suspicions, personal ambition, and heart-felt patriotism who had been thrust into the State Department bureaucracy by Roosevelt's act of political patronage. Though his diary contains anti-Semitic entries, he was more fearful of internal subversion by fifth columnists than he was of Jews per se; still, on occasion he equated the two. Long's restrictionism was steeped in anti-radicalism. His policies and behavior were derived from his belief that he must rigorously enforce America's restrictive immigration laws in defense of national security and, of course, to nurture his own career. Long persisted in believing it unfair for Jews to ask for special favors which could, in his view, only come at a cost to other refugees. He was equally adamant, though, in rejecting special favors for other groups as well.

Long's stubborn embrace of law and regulation in the light of the Holocaust's reality was typical of a public servant wearing the blinders of bureaucratic responsibility. Only his loyalty to the agency, as expressed by his commitment to its mission, mattered. Professional reward, personal fulfillment, and duty demanded the faithful administration of policies created by those above him. Unlike Wilbur Carr, however, whose performance reflected a high degree of professionalism and a sincere stewardship for both his agency and the nation, Long was a political appointee who had exchanged party discipline for another brand of organizational loyalty. When he allowed himself to be overcome by his own initiative in fascist Italy, he paid the price of exceeding his organizational authority. His open-handed contributions to the Democratic party bought him a second chance, one he did not intend to fumble. At times his diary and letters allow a glimpse of the frustration that the politician in Long felt with the slow, plodding, passionless grind of the bureaucratic gears at State. At such times a few kind words from Roosevelt seemed a gratifying endorsement and a reward for all the criticism that Long believed had been so unfairly leveled against him.

Occasionally Long extended himself and saved a handful of rabbis or talmudic students. Such actions were often undertaken with the self-conscious paternalism of the politician. Long could never completely escape his background. From his perspective, he was doing the maximum he believed fair to relieve misery that neither he nor the United States had created.

SEVEN

A Message to Rabbi Wise

Early on the morning of June 22, 1941, three million German soldiers, stretched from the Baltic Sea to the Black Sea, opened fire on Russian positions and crossed Greater Germany's eastern border. The German armies caught the Russian troops unprepared; Stalin had been convinced that all the rumors of an impending attack were western inventions. So the German juggernaut advanced more quickly and inflicted more casualties than any army in history. Hitler's long-established plan, to destroy the center of the "Jewish-Bolshevik" world conspiracy and gain adequate "living space" for the Aryan race, was well launched.

Was it coincidental that some five weeks after the German attack on the Soviet Union, in accordance with Hitler's orally stated wish,[1] Hermann Göring instructed Reich Security Main Office chief Reinhard Heydrich to make necessary preparations for a "complete solution of the Jewish question in the German sphere of influence in Europe"?[2] Heydrich was to bring about the deportation of Jews from all over Europe to the killing centers.

Sometime that summer SS leader Heinrich Himmler also summoned Rudolf Höss to Berlin for a private conference. Himmler told Höss that Hitler had ordered the solution of the Jewish question once and for all and that the existing extermination facilities in the east were inadequate. The large concentration camp at Auschwitz was, under Höss's direction, to receive a new function, namely, the destruction "of every Jew we can lay our hands on."[3] Auschwitz was ideal, because there was good access by rail and because there was enough land to ensure secrecy. Höss was to direct the gassing at Auschwitz, while Christian Wirth from the Führer's chancellery arranged installation of gas chambers elsewhere. The infamous Wannsee Conference of January 20, 1942, was for the purpose of informing affected government agencies and securing necessary assistance in implementation.

Höss decided against the use of carbon monoxide, employed elsewhere, which required engines constantly in operation, too many buildings, and too much time to reach lethal concentration. Instead, he selected Zyklon B, a commercial pesticide derived from prussic acid. Zyklon B had worked well enough when an enterprising subordinate to Höss had used it to kill some

Russian prisoners of war in the fall of 1942, but they had had to be squeezed into underground detention cells. This was an inadequate arrangement for disposing of millions of human beings. The first above-ground gas chambers at Auschwitz were two converted peasant houses at nearby Birkenau, which were sealed to make them airtight. These houses were put into operation during January 1942, and Jews deported from Upper Silesia were among their first guests.[4]

Trainloads of Jews from western Europe began to arrive at selected sites such as Auschwitz in the spring of 1942. On July 16, Himmler's aide Karl Wolff called the Transport Ministry in Berlin to inquire about the availability of trains to move Jews to the killing centers. On the same day, Himmler, in the midst of a visit to Hitler's eastern headquarters at Vinnitsa in the Ukraine, spoke with Wolff by phone. We may deduce that Himmler discussed the removal of Jews to the killing centers with Hitler.[5] Perhaps there was some question about which method of gassing would prove most efficient.

The next day Himmler came to Auschwitz for an inspection. Arriving with the Reich Führer SS were the Gauleiter and *Oberpräsident* of Upper Silesia, Fritz Bracht, and Superior SS and Police Commander Ernst Heinrich Schmauser. Himmler and the others received a two-day tour of the entire camp—the old concentration camp at Auschwitz, the new killing houses, and the I. G. Farben factory installation attached to the camp. Himmler listened with great interest to Höss's explanation of how everything worked and watched the selection of able-bodied Jews from a transport of Dutch Jews. Those not selected for labor were sent to the gas chambers, and Himmler watched that, too. He said very little at first. Höss later told Adolf Eichmann that Himmler commented that these were battles that the coming generation would not have to fight.[6]

When Höss complained about difficulties at the camp and miserable conditions, Himmler cut him off: "I want to hear no more about difficulties! An SS officer does not recognize difficulties; when they arise, his task is to remove them at once by his own efforts. *How* this is to be done is your worry and not mine!"

At the end of the second day Himmler instructed the Auschwitz commandant to build up the extermination facilities at Auschwitz swiftly and proceed with the destruction of gypsies and those Jews unfit for labor. The deportations of Jews from Nazi-controlled territories would soon be increased. Himmler expressed his satisfaction with what Höss had already done and promoted him to SS-Lieutenant Colonel *(Obersturmbannführer)*.[7]

The Auschwitz method of killing with Zyklon B was now officially endorsed. New buildings were constructed at nearby Birkenau, with the gas chambers disguised as shower rooms. Work also began on a number of crematoria. The rate and level of murder were about to increase dramatically. On July 19, Himmler issued an order to Superior SS and Police Commander Friedrich-Wilhelm Krüger in Cracow. The "resettlement" of the entire Jewish population in the Government General of Poland was to be carried out and completed by December 31, 1942, in the interest of German "security and cleanliness." Jewish laborers could continue to work only in factories attached to concentration camps.[8] They would be the exceptions; most Jews would arrive at the camps and be sent straight to the gas chambers.

On July 30, 1942, a prominent and well-connected German industrialist named Eduard Schulte met with a Swiss business associate, Isidor Koppelmann, in Zurich. Schulte revealed that, at Hitler's headquarters, a plan was being considered to concentrate, in the fall, all Jews from Germany and German-occupied territories in the east and to exterminate them through the use of prussic acid. All together, some three and one-half to four million Jews would be killed in this operation.[9]

Certain parts of the information were inaccurate or obsolete. The plan was not under consideration; it had already begun. The undertaking was so vast that it could not occur suddenly, as Schulte thought, but only over many months. Nonetheless, the Breslau industrialist, whose company had mines not far from Auschwitz, had uncovered one of the greatest secrets in Nazi Germany. Adolf Hitler's Final Solution of the Jewish question was to kill all the Jews in gas chambers. With Schulte's approval, Koppelmann passed the information to Benjamin Sagalowitz, press officer of the Jewish communities of Zurich. Through Koppelmann, Schulte urged Sagalowitz to inform Churchill and Roosevelt immediately. After insisting that his name remain a secret, Schulte then returned to Germany.[10]

Sagalowitz had no way to reach the Allied leaders, but he knew someone who had a chance of getting through. Gerhart Riegner, the Swiss representative of the World Jewish Congress, could reach Rabbi Stephen Wise, head of the American Jewish Congress, in New York. It would then be up to Wise to go to Franklin Roosevelt, a pilgrimage he had made several times before.

Riegner was then a young German Jew who had recognized the dangers of Nazism even before 1933 and had left Germany shortly after Hitler took power. He went to Geneva, where he studied law under a trio of distinguished scholars at the Graduate Institute of International Studies: Hans Kelsen, William Rappard, and Paul Guggenheim. When Stephen Wise and Nahum Goldmann organized the World Jewish Congress in 1936 and were looking for a Swiss representative with a background in international law, the scholars recommended Riegner.[11]

Riegner, who had not met the industrialist and was not initially given his name, needed to know more before he could have confidence in the report, which was bound to be questioned. Riegner learned that the industrialist had twice before provided key intelligence to the Allies, once regarding the planned German invasion of the Soviet Union and once regarding changes in the German High Command.[12] Looking at all of the evidence, Riegner concluded that the report of mass extermination was accurate. It complemented information that he had received from other sources about the brutality of the deportations. He thought over his course of action and then consulted Paul

Guggenheim, his mentor. Guggenheim was a bit skeptical and urged Riegner to tell Wise that the information was unverified. Guggenheim edited the text of the message that Riegner intended to send to Wise, inserting a note of doubt. But Guggenheim also assisted Riegner by giving him a letter of introduction to the American consul in Geneva, Paul Squire, whom Guggenheim knew socially.[13]

As Riegner walked into the American consulate, he was met by a tall, pleasant young man named Howard Elting, Jr., who, he learned, was Squire's subordinate. Elting told Riegner that the information seemed fantastic, but Riegner pointed out that reports from Paris, Holland, Berlin, Vienna, and Prague had all confirmed the fact that large numbers of Jews were being brutally deported. Riegner then requested that the Allied governments be informed, that they make every effort to obtain confirmation or denial, and that the message also be sent to Rabbi Stephen Wise in New York. On the same day Riegner asked the British consulate to transmit the same message to Sidney Silverman, a Labour member of the House of Commons who was also the British representative of the World Jewish Congress. Riegner feared that Washington might not pass the telegram on to Wise, but he believed that the British Foreign Office would not dare suppress a telegram to an M.P. He was correct on both counts.[14]

Although he was skeptical of the revelation, Elting dutifully wrote up a memo of his conversation with Riegner. In it he assessed Riegner as a serious and balanced individual who would not have come forward with the information if he did not believe it. Elting recommended that the legation send Riegner's message to Washington, and legation officials complied.[15] But, in an accompanying despatch, Minister Leland Harrison questioned the accuracy of the information. The State Department summarized the message in Washington and passed a copy to the OSS. The summary described the Riegner message as a "wild rumor inspired by Jewish fears."[16]

Paul Culbertson of the Division of European Affairs pointed out that Rabbi Wise might later "kick up a fuss" if he found out that the State Department had withheld the information. But the dominant view was to wait for further evidence before releasing such a horrendous report from the confidential quarters of the State Department. Elbridge Durbrow of the European Division stated the case most bluntly in an internal memorandum: "It does not appear advisable in view of the Legation's comments, the fantastic nature of the allegation, and the impossibility of our being of any assistance if such action were taken, to transmit the information to Dr. Stephen Wise as suggested."

The European Division then cautioned Harrison in no uncertain terms not to place the department in such an awkward spot. After explaining that State had not passed on the "fantastic" message to Wise, Durbrow formulated the European Division's position:

> The Department feels that it would be unfair to the American public if stories of this kind are given publicity unless careful efforts by our officers abroad have been made to obtain confirmation at least tending to support them. It is suggested,

therefore, that in the future the Legation refrain from accepting information of this kind for possible transmission to third parties unless, after thorough investigation, there is reason to believe that such a fantastic report has in the opinion of the Legation some foundation or unless the report involves definite American inter-ests.[17]

The telegram was passed around the department for approval and initialing. Ray Atherton, head of the division, initialed it, as did James Dunn of Political Affairs. Undersecretary of State Sumner Welles approved it, too. Somewhere along the route, however, the last paragraph (quoted above) was crossed off. In addition, the word "fantastic" was replaced with the word "unsubstantiated." Clearly, someone did not think Schulte's information was fantastic. Since Hull's signature on the telegram was probably only a formality, the most likely candidate is Sumner Welles, who would have received the document last.

The changes made a considerable difference. In the original version, the telegram would have been an order to Harrison to cease such reporting. But the final version was simply a comment that State had not seen fit to forward an unsubstantiated report to a third party. After receiving the shortened telegram, the counselor of the legation, Jerome Huddle, then wrote to Elting, suggesting that, if Riegner could find corroborating information, the department would reconsider. Elting passed the decision along to Riegner, who accepted it with as much grace as possible under the circumstances.[18]

On the very same day that Huddle told Elting of the State Department's decision, Franklin D. Roosevelt held a press conference. The president sum-marized for the White House press corps a document that he had recently received from the governments in exile of the Netherlands, Yugoslavia, and Luxembourg about barbaric Nazi occupation policies in Europe that "may even lead to the extermination of certain populations." He then defined his own official stance:

Our Government has constantly received additional information from dependable sources, and it welcomes reports from any trustworthy source which would assist in keeping our Government—our growing fund of information and evidence up to date and reliable. In other words, we want news—from any source that is reliable—of the continuation of atrocities.[19]

The news of the Final Solution had *already* come from a trustworthy source in Breslau to the American capital, but it had been rejected, and the president had not even been told.

Riegner had better luck with the British, but not because London was more perceptive or more sympathetic. Riegner had calculated the odds correctly. Rabbi Wise was a private citizen; the State Department might not want to do him any favors. But Sidney Silverman was not only the British representative of the World Jewish Congress but also a member of Parliament and a well-known barrister. For a Foreign Office bureaucrat to withhold an important message to a member of Parliament would have been both improper and risky.

In London, as in Washington, the foreign policy experts were skeptical and disinclined to act. Under-Secretary of State for Foreign Affairs Richard Law asked for background on Riegner, but the Refugee Department knew nothing. On August 15, a bureaucrat named Frank Roberts, who became one of Britain's leading diplomats after the war, wrote: "I do not see how we can hold up this message much longer, although I fear it may provoke embarrassing repercussions. Naturally we have no information bearing on the story." Two days later Silverman received the telegram from Riegner. Silverman sent the cable on to Wise via the Western Union office, as Riegner had asked him to do.[20]

Even before hearing Washington's response to Schulte's news, Riegner had set out to buttress his case. On August 13, he supplied Elting with a confidential report about the arrest of 28,000 Jews in German-occupied France. Three days later he added that only 33,000 Jews remained in the Protectorate of Bohemia-Moravia; the rest had been deported to Theresienstadt or to Poland. Moreover, Elting was beginning to receive reports from other sources that supported Schulte's message. Donald Lowrie, an American representative of the YMCA in Switzerland, sent in a detailed analysis of the deportation of foreign Jews from occupied France in which he pointed out that the German need for laborers did not explain Nazi insistence on the inclusion of children, the aged, and the ill in the deportations. Lowrie suggested that the German plan for a new Europe might well include "purification" of undesirable elements. In his cover letter to the legation, Elting highlighted the similarity of Riegner's and Lowrie's conclusions.[21]

Nevertheless, in late August the American legation in Bern still resisted the conclusion that the Nazis were seeking to round up and murder all Jews. Huddle scrawled a comment on one document that he passed to Harrison: "Something should go to the Department on this refugee matter. The recent agitation indicates that there may be a big play soon to get all these people to the U.S.A." In effect, Huddle thought that Jewish officials were orchestrating the atrocity reports for their own purposes. When Paul Squire transmitted to Bern a report based on the testimony of a German diplomat that native French Jews as well as German Jews in France were being systematically transported to the east, Harrison placed a big question mark in the margin, and the military attaché, Colonel Legge, wrote "no confirmation to date."[22]

But Squire was convinced of the Final Solution. When he heard that one of his informants, a German Jew living in Switzerland, had been told that he must leave the country by the end of the year, Squire wrote that he was "unable to believe that in the final analysis the Swiss authorities will force a legally admitted German Jew, with family . . . into a situation that can only mean death." Two American Quakers who had been in Vichy during the summer, Roswell and Marjorie McClelland, told Harrison on September 10 that they believed the deported Jews were to be exterminated; few of the deported, in any case, were fit for labor. Now, finally, Huddle found the reports credible. After Squire reported that the Cardinal Archbishop of Lyon was offering shelter to persecuted Jews in France, Huddle mused on this medieval tradition of sanctuary, lamenting that "the civilized modern world seems bereft of refuge."[23]

Washington did not yet grasp how uncivilized that world was. On August 28, Wise finally received the information from Silverman that Riegner had sent three weeks earlier. Welles, whom Wise contacted on September 2, was the best bet for Wise to get action from the State Department. The wealthy and dapper undersecretary, the image of the old-line diplomat, was a personal friend of the president. Moreover, he was more adept and energetic than his superior, Cordell Hull, a former senator from Tennessee. For years it had been Harvard versus Nashville—and Harvard had been winning the battle for FDR's ear.

It was just as well for Wise. Despite the fact that Hull's wife was Jewish, the secretary had always refused to bow to "special interests" and concerned himself with general issues of foreign policy, particularly economic relations. Perhaps he knew too well what many southern congressmen thought about the admission of Jews to the United States. Welles, however, had a humanitarian streak and was friendly with Eleanor Roosevelt, who had long demonstrated her concern about Nazi persecution of the Jews.[24] Welles might not do all that Wise wanted, but he would certainly not ignore the rabbi.

The undersecretary conceded that Riegner's information could be correct but argued that it would be illogical for the Nazis to kill large numbers of Jews when they needed laborers. He also reminded Wise of the atrocity reports fabricated during World War I. Wise agreed to avoid publicity in the press until Welles returned from vacation and the report was investigated further.[25] But another shattering message came to Wise on September 4, through Dr. Jacob Rosenheim of Agudath Israel. This time the source was the Agudath Israel representative in Bern. The cable revealed that the Nazis had murdered about one hundred thousand Jews from the Warsaw ghetto, and the carnage was said to be continuing. A similar fate awaited those being deported to Poland from other countries. The cable also claimed (inaccurately) that the corpses were used for the manufacture of soap and artificial fertilizers. A stricken Wise immediately wrote Felix Frankfurter and asked him to lay the cables before FDR.[26]

Some contemporaries and some scholars have criticized Wise for agreeing to avoid publicity until the report of the Final Solution was confirmed.[27] But the critics seem to have assumed that Wise kept the information to himself. In actuality, the Union of Orthodox Rabbis called a meeting of leading representatives of the major Jewish organizations: the American Jewish Committee, Wise's American Jewish Congress, the Jewish Labor Committee, B'nai B'rith, Agudath Israel, Mizrachi, Poale Zion, and a number of others. Wise, who chaired the meeting, informed the delegates of the two reports and of the State Department's request for no publicity. The group proposed that FDR appeal to Germany to stop the killing, that he warn German leaders that they would be held responsible for their crimes, that neutral countries be asked to intervene, and that the U.S. threaten Germany with reprisals against German aliens held in the States. In addition, the group would seek congressional and church support. But the first order of business was for Wise to meet again with the State Department.[28] Thus, Wise did not withhold the information from everyone, only from the press.[29]

Wise resumed his inquiries and conferences with government authorities. He saw Welles, Vice President Wallace, Secretary of the Interior Harold Ickes, presidential assistant David Niles, and Secretary of the Treasury Henry Morgenthau. Morgenthau later reported that he would never forget the day in 1942 "when Dr. Wise and his son James came to call on me and read me that unbelievable cable telling about the crematoriums in Europe. I think that that day changed my life."[30] But Wise continued to hear—from the ambassador of the Polish government in exile, among others—that Hitler might conceivably destroy Europe's Jews, but for the moment they were being sent to the Russo-Polish frontier to build fortifications. There were some constructive suggestions in Washington. Assistant Solicitor General Oscar Cox thought the two cables might be "the [last] straw" to bring about the creation of a United Nations Atrocities Commission.[31]

On September 28, roughly one month after receiving the Riegner telegram, Wise spoke at a rally held at Madison Square Garden against Nazi atrocities. Wise was by this time none too optimistic. He wrote to a confidant in London immediately afterward:

> Yes, it was a great Madison Square Garden demonstration, but . . . in time of war it is very difficult to get people excited, generally speaking, about atrocities. All of war is basically such an atrocity that it is difficult to move people with respect to special atrocities, even though they are special and, in the case of the atrocities practiced against us, unbelievable.[32]

CONFIRMATION

The president and undersecretary of state had already instructed Myron Taylor, FDR's personal representative to the Vatican, to consult with the papal authorities about Nazi mass killings. In mid-September, Wise received a horrible new report, this time from Richard Lichtheim, the Geneva representative of the Jewish Agency for Palestine. According to two men (one Jew and one non-Jew) who had recently come from Poland, the Nazis were moving the inhabitants of the Warsaw ghetto to special camps and shooting them. Belzec was mentioned by name. Deportations of Jews from various European nations were for the same purpose, while Aryans deported from France and Holland were to be used as laborers. Lichtheim pointed out that this report was consistent with Hitler's own threat to destroy European Jewry.[33] On September 23, Wise gave the new information to Welles, who telegraphed Lichtheim's despatch from Geneva about Belzec—triple priority—back to Bern, from where it went by diplomatic pouch to Taylor at the Vatican.[34] The State Department now was taking this seriously.

Taylor had already spoken with Secretary of State Cardinal Maglione on

September 25, requesting that the Pope speak out publicly against inhumane treatment of refugees and hostages—especially Jews—in the German-occupied territories. Maglione recited what the Vatican and church officials had already done. The Pope had threatened that God would bless or condemn rulers according to the way they treated their subjects. The cardinal stated that this was as far as the Pope could go without "descending to particulars," which would be a political step and would require documentary proof. The next day Taylor also incorporated the information from Lichtheim's despatch into a letter to the cardinal. Three weeks later the Vatican admitted that it, too, had received unverified reports of "severe measures against non-Aryans." The Holy See had no practical suggestions to make; only physical force from the outside could end Nazi barbarities. Several months later Pope Pius XII himself told another American diplomat that he could not condemn Nazi killings explicitly without condemning the "Bolsheviks," too.[35]

In the meantime, Adolf Hitler helped convince some skeptics through a passage in his speech of September 30, given in the Berlin Sport Stadium, which was broadcast on radio and reported in the press. "In my speech of September 1, 1939 I . . . [warned that] if Jewry should plot another world war in order to exterminate the Aryan peoples of Europe, it would not be the Aryan peoples which would be exterminated, but Jewry. . . . I shall be right also in that prophecy."[36]

To receive a triple priority message from the State Department on Nazi killings of Jews must have startled American Minister Leland Harrison in Bern, for the European Division had not shown great interest in the issue previously. In early October Welles added a personal message to the minister requesting him to meet with Riegner or Lichtheim and see what additional evidence they had.[37] Welles's repeated interest broke the logjam in Bern and Washington. Harrison alerted Welles the very next day that numerous reports from Jewish and non-Jewish sources, supplemented by information from Paul Squire in Geneva, indicated that the Nazis were indeed sending Jews from western Europe to an unknown fate in the east. Polish diplomats confirmed that the Warsaw ghetto was being emptied. Harrison now was willing to assist Riegner and Lichtheim, and he passed word to Squire that the two would be welcome at the legation. Counselor Huddle even told Squire that the matter was urgent. Meanwhile, Welles showed Harrison's ominous cable to Wise.[38]

On October 7, the White House issued a press release indicating that Nazi war crimes were continuing. FDR declared that war criminals would be punished at the end of the war, and toward this purpose the U.S., Britain, and other governments were establishing a United Nations Commission for the Investigation of War Crimes. That was little enough but still a small step forward.[39] It was also a sign that FDR had seen some of the information from Switzerland about the Final Solution.

Riegner and Lichtheim came to the legation on October 22 and presented Harrison with a set of documents they had written and collected about the Nazi policy of extermination. They watched as Harrison opened the cover sheet and read on the first page:

> Four million Jews are on the verge of complete annihilation by a deliberate policy consisting of starvation, the Ghetto-system slave labour, deportation under inhuman conditions, and organized mass-murder by shooting, poisoning and other methods. This policy of total destruction has repeatedly been proclaimed by Hitler and is now being carried out.

The Riegner-Lichtheim report called for the collection of specific evidence against those responsible for the killing and for the punishment of the guilty. More important, it urged that the strongest possible pressure be brought on the partly independent governments of Italy, Hungary, Rumania, Bulgaria, and Vichy France not to cooperate in the deportations, and it suggested that the Vatican might be of service.

Harrison read further and found a country-by-country breakdown of estimated Jewish mortality. He had some doubts about the figures compiled there and later put question marks in the margin.

Then came the crucial part—the section about a reliable German source who claimed that Hitler's headquarters had considered and accepted a plan for the extermination of three and one-half to four million Jews. Riegner and Lichtheim had not spared the State Department. Their report summarized how they had delivered this information to the American consulate at Geneva on August 8 and how they were later informed that the State Department had refused to deliver it to Stephen Wise because it was unsubstantiated.

Harrison finished reading the last part of the nearly thirty-page report—some letters from Poland received by Agudath Israel representatives in Bern as well as an eyewitness account of mass killings of Jews in Latvia. Although he had been reading for twenty minutes already in the presence of his guests, he began to reread some of the key sections. Then, with a face almost without expression (Lichtheim called it a poker face), he began to ask questions.

Harrison wanted to know the sources for each of the documents that Riegner and Lichtheim had appended to their report. He particularly wanted to know the name of the German who had supplied the information about Hitler's headquarters and the Final Solution. Although they had not yet met the industrialist, Riegner and Lichtheim by then knew the man's name—Sagalowitz had given it to them in a sealed envelope. Lichtheim had opened the envelope, and now they faced a moral dilemma. To reveal Schulte's name might cost him his life, for the Germans were quite capable of intercepting and decoding diplomatic transmissions. Not to reveal the name meant that Harrison and the State Department would be less likely to credit their information, and more time would be lost. In the end they gave in. The slip of paper read: "Managing director Dr. Schulte, mining industry. In close or closest contact with dominant figures in the war economy." They asked Harrison not to send this name to Washington, and Harrison complied.

Riegner also told Harrison about new, independent confirmation of the Final Solution order that he had recently received from Paul Guggenheim, who had gotten it from a high official of the International Red Cross (IRC). Harrison wanted more details as soon as possible. The two Jewish officials promised to get proof and more specifics. Harrison expressed his thanks.[40]

Harrison consulted Squire about the Riegner-Lichtheim evidence and gave Squire the task of obtaining sworn statements from those individuals in Switzerland who had supplied the information to Riegner and Lichtheim. On October 24, Harrison wrote a personal letter to Undersecretary Welles, describing his meeting with Riegner and Lichtheim. Harrison informed Welles that he had the name of the German industrialist. He also stated that the International Red Cross official mentioned by Riegner and Lichtheim was probably Carl Burckhardt. At a luncheon Harrison had overheard Burckhardt discuss a Final Solution order with Guggenheim. Harrison promised to send sworn statements as soon as they were obtained.[41]

When Riegner ran into Paul Squire at a bazaar on October 25, Riegner asked if the consulate could supply him with a picture of President Roosevelt to hang in the office of the World Jewish Congress. Squire gladly complied, and the picture went up immediately in order to show, as Riegner wrote, "[our] great admiration [for] . . . one of the most farsighted statesmen of our time . . . [and] one of the most comprehensive friends of our people [who are] going through hard trials."[42]

Squire soon persuaded Guggenheim to write and sign a detailed statement, provided that Burckhardt's name was not used. Guggenheim had learned from "a citizen of Switzerland" that Hitler had allegedly issued an order for the extermination (*Ausrottung*) of all Jews in Nazi-controlled territories. Hans Frank and even Heinrich Himmler were said to have opposed the plan on practical grounds, but Hitler had repeated his order in September 1942. The information about the order allegedly came from two independent sources: an official of the German Foreign Ministry in Berlin and an official in the Ministry of War. Moreover, other sources had provided information that was consistent with the Final Solution plan. By this time Squire had also obtained a sworn affidavit about the execution of the Jews of Riga from a Latvian Jew who had escaped to Switzerland. Harrison sent both affidavits to Welles, warning him to keep the names confidential and promising to send a statement from Burckhardt himself if it could be obtained.[43]

Burckhardt had met with Adolf Hitler in August 1939 in an unsuccessful attempt to settle disputes over the Polish corridor and Danzig. He got a rude awakening; the Führer did not particularly want a peaceful settlement and threatened to wipe Poland off the map. Hitler told Burckhardt bluntly that Germany wanted to go to war in the east to obtain vast stretches of land. But, if the western nations insisted on declaring war to defend Poland, Germany would beat them first and attack Russia later. Beyond his firsthand knowledge of Hitler, Burckhardt enjoyed close contacts with many other high German officials, some of whom he had known since his university days. His Red Cross organization also had sources in Germany.[44] It would be difficult for the State Department to dismiss whatever Burckhardt put on the record about Nazi killings of Jews.

Squire finally collared Burckhardt on November 7. He confirmed privately and not for publication what he had earlier told Guggenheim, although he admitted that he had not actually seen the order itself. Squire asked whether the order explicitly used the word "extermination." Guggenheim replied that the order had required the territories to be "free of Jews." But since there was no place to put the Jews, it was quite clear what the result would be.[45]

Burckhardt told Squire that he had tried to get the International Red Cross to make a public appeal to the world on the question of Jews and hostages in Nazi Germany. The executive committee of the IRC, however, had rejected the idea on October 14, 1942, on the grounds that it would serve no purpose, make the situation more difficult, and jeopardize Red Cross work on behalf of prisoners of war and civil internees—"the real task of the Red Cross."[46] The Nazis considered the Jews political enemies *tout court,* but no other government considered them worthy of special protection. They were not POWs, not civilians, not Americans, not Britons. Only the governments in exile of countries conquered by Germany intervened for their Jewish citizens, and these governments had little leverage. Burckhardt's information, sent to Harrison on November 9, confirmed Schulte's original report.

After the new information went to Washington on November 23, Welles could no longer withhold judgment. He summoned Stephen Wise to Washington the next day and told the rabbi that he regretted to confirm Wise's deepest fears. Wise arranged for press conferences in Washington and New York and made public what he knew. The Associated Press carried the story, which appeared in the *New York Herald Tribune* under the headline "Wise Says Hitler Has Ordered 4,000,000 Jews Slain in 1942." The publicity was far greater than anything generated previously.[47]

To the added irritation of State Department officials in the European Division, Wise disclosed that he had received the information about the Final Solution through channels provided by the State Department, and he alluded to State Department confirmation as well. But Welles must have thought it undesirable to notify his faction-ridden department of what he had told Wise. He wrote no official memorandum of his conversation with Wise. And, despite all of the time and effort devoted to confirming Schulte's original report, a number of State Department officials continued to deny knowledge of a Final Solution and to maintain that Wise's information was purely unofficial.[48]

The result of Wise's actions, as one State Department official soon complained, was "a flood of mail to the President and the State Department aimed at 1) procuring a joint declaration by the United States and the United Kingdom censuring barbarism and promising retribution; 2) opening Palestine to the Jews; 3) removing all barriers to the immigration of Jewish children; and

4) exchanging Jews in occupied Europe for interned Axis nationals."[49] With considerable difficulty, Wise also obtained an appointment for himself and four other Jewish leaders at the White House on December 8. The Jewish officials gave the president a memorandum entitled "Blue Print for Extermination" drawn from the Riegner-Lichtheim memorandum to Harrison and other sources. It included a special section on Hitler's extermination order, and it quoted sections of Riegner's telegram. The report correctly noted the essential point: for most Jews, deportation was just a euphemism for death.[50]

Did Roosevelt believe the report? There is no record of his thoughts on the matter, so we can only make an informed guess. In September and October 1942, he may have thought the Schulte-Riegner report to be dubious. If Felix Frankfurter could not at first accept the reality of an assembly-line operation to destroy millions of his fellow Jews, Franklin Roosevelt may have reacted in a similar way.[51] But by December the evidence was overwhelming.

Wise appealed to FDR to bring the extermination program to the world's attention and to make an effort to stop it. Roosevelt said that the government was familiar with most of the facts, but it was hard to find a suitable course of action. The Allies could not make it appear that the entire German people were murderers or were in agreement with Hitler's actions. He agreed to release another statement denouncing mass killings.[52]

With German forces stretching from the Atlantic to the Volga, from the northern tip of Norway to the desert wastes around El Alamein in North Africa, no power on earth could then stop the Nazi death mills in Poland. But the best chance for countermeasures of some kind lay in Washington. Could not the president at least give a speech that would rivet the world's attention on the problem? Could Congress be moved to act?

In early November FDR had asked Congress to approve a Third War Powers Act that included a provision allowing the president to suspend laws hampering "the free movement of persons, property and information into and out of the United States." Breckinridge Long believed that Roosevelt had no intention of using this power to admit more refugees from Europe to the United States. Some conservatives in Congress and the press, however, thought otherwise, and they may have been right.[53]

Two days after Stephen Wise's press conference, Franklin Roosevelt held a meeting with Vice President Wallace and Sam Rayburn, speaker of the House. According to Wallace's brief account, the president spoke chiefly about the need for legislation to loosen restrictions on immigration and imports. Rayburn, however, pointed out that there was great congressional opposition to this move, particularly in the Ways and Means Committee. Roosevelt then appeared to retreat, stating that this was Congress's responsibility to decide.[54] It is possible that the president's lobbying had little or nothing to do with the Riegner telegram, but he was a master at concealing his true intentions.

In any case, conservative members of the Ways and Means Committee first deleted the word "persons" from the provision and then held up passage of the entire war powers bill until it died. Hostility to increased Jewish immigration was a major factor in the president's defeat. It is not surprising, then, that FDR was not particularly eager to wage a major political battle over the desperate plight of European Jews.[55]

In the end, the initiative came from London. Several committees of British Jews had lobbied persuasively with the American ambassador to Great Britain, John Winant, to bring the Nazi plan to the attention of the Foreign Office. Winant spoke to Foreign Minister Eden, but the initial British response was that they had no definite information about a mass extermination plan. Then Hitler's speech of September 30 intensified perceptions of impending mass murder. In early December, Polish Foreign Minister Count Raczynski laid out the evidence for Eden of a "twin policy of murder on a mass scale and transference of whole communities to the bare eastern territories." The evidence from all occupied territories was that each country had a deadline to clear out its Jews and transport them to the east. Eden began to look favorably upon a proposed joint declaration of the big three powers against German atrocities.[56]

Part of the reason was that Winston Churchill had taken a personal interest in the various reports about Nazi extermination policies. The British cabinet approved the text of a declaration confirming Hitler's intention to exterminate the Jewish people, condemning cold-blooded murder, and promising punishment of those responsible. Eden read the cabinet statement to the House of Commons, which stood in silence as a token of respect for the victims.[57]

As late as December 10, State Department refugee specialist Robert Borden Reams tried his best to halt any proposed joint declaration:

> While deeply deploring the unhappy plight of the Jewish people of occupied Europe the Department is inclined to doubt the advisability of issuing a statement . . . [which] would tend to give official confirmation to reports which are not confirmed by any official information available to the American Government and would augment the grief and uncertainties of the Jewish people outside the occupied areas. If any possibility, however remote, existed that this statement might induce an alteration in the present brutal policy of the German Government the adverse considerations should be waived but in fact the effect might well be an intensification of the barbarities now practiced.[58]

Reams thus repeated the arguments made by the Division of European Affairs in August: there was no real proof of a Final Solution, and, in any case, nothing that the Allies could do would force Germany to change its policy. His concern about the "grief and uncertainties of the Jewish people" outside Nazi territories was linked to potential political repercussions.

The matter, however, had reached higher levels of authority. The State Department dragged its feet up to the last moment, but, in the end, the United States, Great Britain, and ten Allied governments in exile joined to make a declaration on December 17 denouncing Nazi implementation of "Hitler's oft-repeated intention to exterminate the Jewish people in Europe."

From all the occupied countries Jews are being transported in conditions of appalling horror and brutality to Eastern Europe. . . . The above-mentioned Governments and the French National Committee condemn in the strongest possible terms this bestial policy of cold-blooded extermination. They declare that such events can only strengthen the resolve of all freedom loving peoples to overthrow the barbarous Hiterlite tyranny. They re-affirm their solemn resolution to ensure that those responsible for these crimes shall not escape retribution. . . .[59]

There was as yet no acceptance of the notion that the Nazis had established special death camps where poison gas was being used, even though the Polish government had already pointed this out.[60] But it was the first time that the United States government had made or participated in a declaration about Nazi mass killings of Jews. Rabbi Wise proclaimed that this historic statement "will bring solace to, and hearten Jewish people throughout the world as a reaffirmation of the determination of the free people that Axis murderers cannot . . . destroy any race or faith of people."[61]

In the three months since the mysterious industrialist exposed Nazi Germany's genocidal intentions to the world, American Jewish leaders had expressed their grief and helplessness, called anxiously upon their government for information and assistance, and awaited the confirmation they did not want to receive. Their efforts won them the support of Sumner Welles, probably the most influential figure in the State Department. Given the fact that only the United States government had any chance of inducing Nazi Germany to reverse its policy of mass extermination, their approach had obvious advantages. But it helped bring about only one humanitarian gesture.

INTERVENTION AT VICHY

From the beginning of the Nazi regime, official American reaction to Nazi persecution of the Jews had been limited to protection and defense of the rights of American citizens in Germany or German-occupied territory. FDR's condemnation of Germany after *Kristallnacht* was an isolated exception. After the outbreak of the war, the State Department continued to remonstrate against any European discrimination against Jews that applied to American citizens there.[62] There was only one brief effort, in 1940, to develop broader American responsibility. After reading cables from the embassy in Berlin and articles in the *New York Times* regarding deportation of Jews to the Lublin area, Assistant Secretary of State Adolf Berle urged the European desk and Secretary of State Hull to deliver a complaint, in the form of an aide mémoire, to the German foreign minister. He also wanted to release the text publicly in the United States. Berle's argument was that the United States had a right to take a position "based on straight humanity" and that it could do little harm to make clear American rejection of "cruelty on an organized scale." But Berle, despite his title, did not carry great weight in the State Department. Breckinridge Long responded that public expression of American shock and repulsion was hardly necessary and that interference in internal German affairs should be avoided. His real fear seemed to be that any statement critical of Germany would bring the United States one step closer to the Allied camp and to the war. John Hickerson of the European Division agreed with Long.[63] Sumner Welles, who might have shared Berle's views, was off on a peace-making mission in Europe. Thus, the initiative collapsed. After the United States entered the war, there were no major changes in the American position. In the face of information reaching Washington in 1942 about Nazi killings of Jews, the United States government was prepared to stretch its definition of "American interests" slightly but not to embrace the cause of European Jews generally.

The most obvious spot for American intercession on behalf of threatened European Jews in the second half of 1942 was Vichy France. Unlike most of the nations conquered by Germany, France was able to maintain an independent government, albeit at the cost of an unfavorable armistice, German occupation of the northern part of the country, and many other hardships. Nonetheless, the new French government headquartered at Vichy was by no means the puppet of the Nazis. Insofar as the Vichy regime pursued collaboration with Nazi Germany, it did so because it thought the policy advantageous.[64] Hoping to persuade the French leaders not to support Nazi Germany, the United States government ignored a host of distasteful French moves and retained its diplomatic representation in France. When news reached Washington that French Jews were being deported to eastern Europe, therefore, the State Department was in a position to demand a hearing and to make its views known. Moreover, a number of American relief organizations also had representatives in unoccupied France who reacted vigorously against the deportations.

After learning that deportations of foreign Jews from the unoccupied zone were imminent, a coordinating committee of the various relief agencies operating in France managed to obtain an interview with Vichy's prime minister, Pierre Laval, on August 6. Laval launched into a tirade against the foreign Jews; France, he said, was glad to be rid of them. His desire coincided nicely with the German policy of establishing an ethnic reservation in Poland. One of the representatives, however, claimed that the real German purpose was extermination. Laval rejected the idea as "preposterous, pure fiction." He asked scornfully why the United States and Great Britain did not take in these refugees, instead of criticizing France. He said that words did not concern him, only actions. Laval agreed to consider only the exemption of those foreign Jews who held immigration visas to the United States and were scheduled to leave within six weeks. Donald Lowrie of the YMCA raised the same idea with the aged president, Philippe Petain, on the same day. Petain, too, described the Jews' destination as a place near Cracow (it was Auschwitz), but he gave Lowrie a more respectful hearing and promised to speak to Laval about exemptions.[65]

The relief agencies, which included the YMCA, the American Friends Service Committee, and the Unitarian Service Committee, alerted American diplomatic officials to the situation, and the State Department responded with a gesture on behalf of those who had cleared the immigration barriers and were awaiting transportation.[66] The State Department began to notify interested organizations that the chargé d'affaires, S. Pinkney Tuck, was asking French authorities to suspend deportation of three hundred children and of those with immigration visas.[67]

Given some leeway by the department, Tuck proceeded to use it aggressively. In a conversation with Laval on August 25, Tuck protested against the inhumane treatment of foreign Jews, which, he said, had shocked public opinion throughout the world. He also made a personal appeal on humanitarian grounds on behalf of some four thousand children between the ages of two and fifteen, who had been separated from their deported parents. Laval denied that such action had taken place and showed little interest in, or sympathy for, the foreign Jews. Tuck soon concluded that the only possible way to change the situation was for Washington to make a concrete proposal to admit these children to the United States. Laval might accept it in order to lessen the criticism throughout France of the deportations. Tuck made the situation as clear as possible for Washington:

> As it appears to be the intention of the Nazi authorities that their deported parents should not survive the treatment they are now undergoing many of these children may already be considered orphans. To leave them in France is to expose them to the threat of possible Nazi aggression (even against Jewish children). . . . I fully realize the difficulties which such a proposal entails particularly insofar as transportation and funds are concerned. Nothing, however, can alter the fact that the fate of these little people hangs in the balance. Should the Germans decide to order them over the demarcation line into the occupied zone they may be considered as lost.[68]

Breckinridge Long, believing that the Germans were using the deported Jews as laborers, suggested a protest against France's aid to the Axis in excess of the terms of the armistice. But Ray Atherton, head of the European Division, argued that U.S. intercession should be limited to those foreigners who already had visas. He also commented that Tuck had already exceeded his instructions.[69] Tuck's forcefulness clearly had ruffled some feelings in the department.

Tuck's proposal did have support outside the State Department, however. The United States Committee for the Care of European Children, a nonprofit organization that listed Eleanor Roosevelt as honorary chairman, sought to make arrangements for the entrance of one thousand children from France, and the President's Advisory Committee for Political Refugees also pushed the project. Commissioner of Immigration and Naturalization Earl Harrison and Attorney General Francis Biddle were both responsive and sympathetic.[70] The State Department executed a strategic retreat. Long approved the project, although Visa Division chief Howard Travers tried to persuade the organizers to accept visitors' visas (which were temporary) instead of immigration visas. The argument was that immigration visas required full investigations and documentation, as well as medical examinations, and the delay would be considerable.

This factor convinced Dr. Joseph Schwartz of the American Jewish Joint Distribution Committee, which was heavily involved in the project. Official clearance came on September 24.[71]

On the same day Emanuel Celler introduced a bill into the House of Representatives offering asylum in the United States to all French residents fleeing Nazi or French persecution. This would have meant an abandonment of the quota system and the tight immigration regulations in force ever since 1941. The State Department instead extended its offer. If the organizers could arrange for another five thousand children to come from France, they would be given visas also. Although the documentation is incomplete, it appears that FDR personally made the decision to admit five thousand children. The president requested that any public statement regarding this decision be avoided.[72] Perhaps he was again concerned about domestic reaction, but there was another good reason, it turned out, for such secrecy.

Laval's preferred solution for the problem of separated children was for the Nazis to deport the children along with the parents. When Tuck relayed the American offer to Laval on September 30, the premier agreed in principle but alluded to certain administrative difficulties. It quickly became apparent that the difficulties involved the German officials, who complained that the shipment of children to the U.S. might be used for anti-German propaganda. Laval began to stall. The exit visas required by French law were not forthcoming.[73]

On October 15, 1942, Sumner Welles had a press conference. When he was asked whether Vichy had accepted a United States offer to admit five thousand Jewish refugee children for the duration of the war, Welles was caught in a delicate position. He had to explain and justify the decision, but, at the same time, he could not alienate the French without jeopardizing the arrangement. He claimed that the children were not necessarily of any particular race or nationality, that they were completely destitute with no one to look after them. The U.S. government was facilitating the efforts of private organizations to bring the children here under the terms of existing immigration laws. Welles declined to confirm that five thousand children were involved.[74]

According to Tuck, Laval read Welles's statements in the press and became angry. At first, the police in Marseilles were left without instructions, which prevented the shipping of the children. When the instructions finally arrived, they were crafted with malice. Only "bona fide orphans" would be allowed to leave; those whose parents had been deported were not considered to be orphans. There were fewer than one hundred "bona fide" orphans. Tuck appealed to Laval, who raised the number to five hundred. The Quakers handling the preparations in Marseille strove to satisfy all the administrative requirements for this group.[75]

But it was too late. November 9, 1942, Allied troops landed in French North Africa. Two days later, to meet the military threat, the Germans moved troops into the unoccupied zone. With the Nazis in control, there was no longer any chance to ship the children out of France directly. The relief workers did manage to smuggle some of the children—estimates range from 200 to 350—to Spain and Portugal. Sumner Welles agreed to use a portion of the five thousand visas for these children and also authorized admission of their mothers, when they, too, were available. But the Visa Division ruled that only children were admissible without the usual investigation, and a number of mothers sent young children to the United States while they themselves remained in Spain or Portugal.[76] Meanwhile, the State Department asked the Swiss government to intervene with French and German authorities to request permission for the remainder of the children to depart from France. That was done, but to no avail. Some of these remaining children probably were successfully hidden inside France, but many were not.[77]

With the Germans now in control of all of France, the initiative on future deportations lay fully with Berlin. And there, unlike in Washington, there was little question about which authority would prevail. On December 10, Heinrich Himmler consulted his Führer on what should be done with assorted enemies of the Third Reich now in the Nazis' grasp in France. There are two records of the meeting, one handwritten by Himmler, the second typed later by a Himmler staff member with the initials RF and signed (HH) by Himmler. Both documents are dated December 10, and it appears from both that Himmler and Hitler were the only ones present.[78]

Himmler apparently brought to the meeting a third document. He had already drafted an order (dated December 1942) to Gruppenführer Heinrich Müller of the Reich Main Security Office to establish a special camp for those Jews in France, Hungary, and Rumania who had influential relatives in the United States. Himmler described these Jews, whose number he estimated at ten thousand, as valuable hostages (*wertvolle Geiseln*). They would work in the camp, but under conditions that would allow them to remain alive ("Dort sollen sie zwar arbeiten, jedoch unter Bedingungen, dass sie gesund sind und am Leben bleiben").[79]

Himmler's handwritten notes of his meeting with Hitler show that the Führer approved this proposal. Next to Himmler's "Sonderlager für Juden mit Anhang in Amerika," there appear two check marks indicating Hitler's positive response. Himmler's typewritten memorandum also notes that Hitler ordered (*der Führer hat die Anweisung gegeben*) that the Jews and other enemies in France be arrested and deported (*abtransportiert werden*). Only after Hitler had spoken with Laval would Himmler implement the plan. The number of Jews was estimated (incorrectly) at six to seven hundred thousand. If ten thousand Jews were to be kept alive in a special camp, and six hundred thousand were to be deported, there is little doubt about the intended fate of the deportees. These Jews in France were in fact sent to Auschwitz. There they caused no particular complications for the Allies.

German Foreign Minister Joachim von Ribbentrop soon warned Himmler that the deportation of Jews with *foreign citizenship* from France might cause complications for German foreign policy. Himmler insisted that Germany deport those Jews who had taken refuge in the small Italian zone of occupation—even Italian Jews. If the Italians refused to cooperate with Nazi policy, then others in France and Europe generally might begin to cause trouble.[80] In the end, however, many Jews with foreign citizenship were deported not to the death camps but to concentration camps at Buchenwald, Ravensbruck, and Bergen-Belsen, where they had a better chance of remaining alive and eventually being exchanged.[81]

In late 1942, however, there was little sign of outside interest in Jews of Spanish, Turkish, Rumanian, or other nationalities. Most neutrals and satellites were trying to avoid antagonizing Germany. The Allies had their own concerns, one of which was with the Nazi practice of keeping some Jews alive and holding them for possible ransom to be paid by relatives abroad. Washington and London both reacted angrily. The British government took the initiative: the Allies had to denounce this practice and punish anyone implicated in it, because the enemy was deriving "marked benefit" from this scheme.[82] Washington agreed that the best means of dealing with the extortion was to prevent the Germans from collecting any funds from it. Anyone who paid or passed on money for this purpose would be treated as an enemy.

The justification used by Great Britain, the United States, and the Dutch government in exile, however, for cracking down on the individuals involved in making payments to save relatives in the Netherlands showed either extreme ignorance or conscious deception. In a public statement on November 24, 1942, the State Department announced: "If the Germans can be prevented from obtaining the sums they are demanding for the release of hostages, their incentive to find new victims will be removed. Yielding to these attempts at extortion merely encourages the Nazis to employ them against other helpless victims."[83]

But the real situation of Jewish captives in Nazi-dominated territory was that the Nazis would keep them alive only as long as there seemed to be a possibility of gaining something from doing so. And the Nazis did not need encouragement to seek out new Jewish victims. Ironically, this State Department statement was made public on the same day that Stephen Wise held his press conferences about the Nazi Final Solution. Even though Undersecretary Welles had now confirmed Riegner's telegram, the State Department had learned nothing from it.

For Adolf Hitler and his trusted right-hand man Heinrich Himmler, the destruction of the Jewish "race" was of vital importance for the future of the Aryan people. Even the needs of the war could not block the implementation of the Final Solution. And in France, as in all too many European countries, Nazi officials found government officials, police officers, and political organizations willing to cooperate with the Nazi program. The now famous Danish evacuation of Danish Jews to Sweden in 1943 became, unfortunately, the exception to the general pattern.

The odds, then, were loaded against those who wished to rescue Europe's

Jews, because the west lacked the military means (until at least 1944) to force a change in German policy. Still, the contrast between the handling of the Jewish question in Washington and Berlin is glaring. A high-level official such as Sumner Welles might approve a specific plan for the rescue of a group of children; a courageous diplomat such as Pinkney Tuck might use what little influence he had to make Pierre Laval think twice about cooperating with the Germans. But the State Department as a whole found little reason to concern itself with the fate of foreign Jews in the midst of a war when so many people were suffering. In fact, there were key officials—assistant secretaries, experts in the European Division, political counselors, and lower-level personnel in the Visa Division—who found positive danger in any public involvement in attempts to assist European Jews. And the State Department was not the only obstacle.

EIGHT

War Propaganda and the Jews

During World War II the major powers generally succeeded in mobilizing and motivating their own citizens through positive declarations of principles as well as negative information about the enemy. But to influence enemy public opinion was more difficult for technical, as well as ideological, reasons. The struggle for "hearts and minds" was contested more closely in some neutral European countries and outside of the developed countries. In spite of its crude assertions of Aryan racial superiority, Nazi Germany managed to send out propaganda that elicited some support in critical strategic areas.

On November 28, 1941, Adolf Hitler met with Grand Mufti Haj Amin El Husseini of Jerusalem at the Reich Chancellery in Berlin. Husseini thanked Hitler for his interest in Arab affairs and termed the Arabs natural allies of Germany: both were opposed to Britain, the Jews, and the communists. He asked for a public declaration of German support for Arab independence and for the elimination of a Jewish national homeland.

Hitler explained to the Arab leader that the current war represented a political conflict of interest between Germany and Great Britain but an ideological conflict between National Socialism and Judaism. He pledged to carry on the fight until the last traces of Jewish communist hegemony in Europe were destroyed. He forecast a German breakout through the Caucasus mountains into the Middle East, which would bring the hour of liberation for the Arabs. "Thereafter, Germany's only remaining objective in the region would be limited to the annihilation of the Jews living under British protection in the region."[1]

Hitler's comments were by no means insincere. German military plans for 1942 indeed called for a southeastern thrust in Russia to capture the Caucasus, and the army had formed a special unit under General Helmuth Felmy to collect intelligence about the Middle East and train Arabs for subversion.[2] Meanwhile, the construction of extermination camps in eastern Europe had already begun, and less than two months later Reinhard Heydrich, at the infamous Wannsee Conference, set in motion the secret arrangements for deporting European Jews to the gas chambers.

To the Arab world, Hitler and other Nazi leaders veiled only their exact plans for the Jews, not their ideological war. The Final Solution was a state

167

secret of the highest order, but the fact that the Nazis were seeking to destroy Jewish influence throughout the world was not. German radio broadcasts to the Middle East constantly played on the theme that the Allies were fighting the war on behalf of the Jews and that Germany alone could liberate the Arabs from British-Jewish oppression.[3]

Nazi officials went out of their way to publicize this campaign. The Nazi Gauleiter of Upper Silesia, Fritz Bracht, actually wished to rename the world war itself. Bracht wrote to Reich Führer SS Heinrich Himmler in late 1942:

> I suggest "the Jewish war." It revolves in the final analysis around the power of Judah. The outbreak of the war also was to a great extent influenced by American Jewry, which not only abandoned all restraint in inciting others against Germany, but also through its [sic] President Roosevelt, his diplomats and agents, stiffened the backs of all the anti-German peoples of Europe. If this designation "Jewish War" were well launched in the press a number of times or even used by the Führer himself, the press could very soon be instructed to speak exclusively of the Jewish war. It will have a good propagandistic effect upon all peoples in the range of European culture, including the Anglo-Saxons, if the radio and press speak only of the Jewish war. Deep in their hearts they are all inclined to be anti-Semites, especially the North Americans.

Himmler's response was short and to the point. "I would regard it as a mistake . . . . because we would thereby make [the name] Jewry eternal."[4] With the increase in the killing in Auschwitz-Birkenau and other camps, Himmler could foresee the complete disappearance of European Jewry and, eventually, of the term "Jew."

The Nazi viewpoint that Jews were hated throughout the world was certainly exaggerated, but it was no doubt true that Nazi anti-Semitism was an advantage, rather than a disadvantage, for Germany in some parts of the world. That was particularly true for the Middle East and North Africa, whose strategic value was critical. By mid-1942, the combination of German military victories in North Africa (Rommel took Tobruk on June 21) and a constant barrage of Nazi propaganda directed at the Arabs made a number of American civilian and military officials particularly sensitive to Arab opinion. This concern made them wary of publicly associating the United States not only with Zionist aspirations but also with any specifically "Jewish" issue. The result was a bureaucratic consensus to avoid any mention of the Nazi Final Solution, let alone consider any plans to hinder Nazi killing.

In July 1942 the Military Intelligence Section of the War Department sponsored a conference at Yale University on "German Victory in Egypt and the Mohammedan World." One of the academicians participating, Nicholas Spykman, favored a bold propaganda offensive to win Arab support. He urged the United States to exploit Arab nationalism and to make a distinction between Palestine as a cultural center for the Jews and Palestine as a national home. In order to avoid losing the Middle East, he suggested that the U.S. repudiate political Zionism, which he called a magnificent luxury "that one can afford under certain circumstances, but not under others." War Department officials found Spykman's presentation compelling and submitted a transcript to the State Department. An official in the Division of Near Eastern Affairs commented that a statement repudiating Zionism was unlikely unless the war went very badly; the Zionist faction (in the United States) would prevent such action. He nonetheless concluded: "The discussion showed that a group of intelligent, well-informed and unofficial Americans with no axe to grind, hold views and reach conclusions on much the same lines that we do in the Department. That is quite encouraging."[5] The dominant view in the State Department clearly was to adopt a practical policy that would not alienate, and might attract, the Arabs.

In December 1942, Paul West, head of the Cairo outpost of the Office of War Information (OWI), alerted his superiors and State Department officials to the dangerous repercussions of Zionist activities in the Middle East. West feared Arab unrest not only in Palestine, Syria, Iraq, and Egypt but also in North Africa, which might endanger the American troops that had landed there in November. State Department political advisor Wallace Murray noted that the three agencies most directly involved were the State Department, the War Department, and OWI. He suggested a joint presentation of their common views to the president and urged West to speak to Sumner Welles before Welles went to FDR.[6] Perhaps Murray sensed that Welles and the president would not be moved easily. In a conversation with Morgenthau in December 1942, the president actually contemplated moving most Arabs out of Palestine to other parts of the Middle East. Jewish immigrants would take their place. For FDR, however, this clearly represented a postwar solution.[7] Palestine would not be available as a refuge for very many European Jews during the war.

The Division of Near Eastern Affairs prepared a memorandum on North Africa that warned of additional German propaganda to the effect that the United Nations were fighting the war for the Jews.[8] FDR also heard similar warnings from high military authorities whose advice he could not afford to ignore. On November 22, General George Patton wrote to Dwight D. Eisenhower about the Arab-Jewish situation in French North Africa. After a brief description of French policy, Patton proposed to leave the Jewish question to the sultan of Morocco. He claimed that there was no real discrimination against Jews in the area. Patton then added a handwritten note—handwritten, he said, because his stenographer was a Jew.

> Arabs don't mind Christians, but they utterly despise Jews. The French fear that the local Jews knowing how high their side is riding in the U.S. will try to take the lead here. If they do the Arabs will murder them and there will be a local state of disorder. . . . I suggest that you write Gen. Marshall and inform him of the situation so that if some State Department fool tries to foist . . . Jews on Morocco, we will stop it at the source. If we get orders to favor the Jews we will precipitate trouble and possibly civil war.

Patton then passed along a report originating with Admiral Darlan, who had joined the Allies in North Africa and abandoned the Vichy government. A section of the reports on the racial question in North Africa defended the existing restrictions on Jews.[9]

Eisenhower apparently sent the material to Marshall, for a copy soon reached Secretary of War Henry Stimson. Stimson may have gone first to Secretary of State Hull to prevent the State Department from doing what Patton feared. Hull soon told the British ambassador in Washington, Lord Halifax, that the Jewish situation might set the various North African tribes on the rampage, that the danger was acute.[10] In late December, Stimson emphasized to FDR the vulnerability of the United States to German propaganda. Stimson pointed out that in French North Africa, where Allied troops had recently begun their offensive, there were 25 million Arabs and only 350,000 Jews. The Axis powers were telling the Arabs that the Allies intended to turn North Africa over to the Jews. Stimson observed that Darlan had avoided a general emancipation of the North African Jews as likely to stir up a civil war. FDR expressed interest and wanted to read Eisenhower's despatch.[11]

The president was the ultimate arbiter of policy. But he could not take the opinion of his generals in North Africa lightly. Who was in a better position to determine what might cause difficulties for the army? FDR's reading may have made him reluctant to establish refugee camps in American-controlled territory in North Africa during 1943.[12] Despite his undoubted sympathy for those persecuted by the Nazis, the war always came first for FDR.

There were some countervailing pressures from the Allied governments in exile to take up the cause of the Nazi victims. On June 22, 1942, General Wladyslaw Sikorski, the prime minister of the Polish government in exile, wrote to President Roosevelt about a new German wave of terrorism in Poland. Sikorski called for the United States and Great Britain to join in signing the St. James Declaration issued in January 1942 by the governments in exile against Nazi acts of violence in occupied countries. To halt the Germans he also recommended retaliatory measures against German citizens under the control of the United Nations and bombing of the civilian population of Germany. FDR responded with a copy of Secretary of State Hull's condemnation of the Nazi massacre at Lidice, Czechoslovakia. He declined, however, to punish enemy civilians held in the United States or to undertake punitive bombing of civilians in Germany.[13]

In mid-July the Polish National Council in London asked its executive committee (cabinet) to reveal to the parliaments of all free nations the facts of the "systematic destruction of the vital strength of the Polish nation and the planned slaughter of practically the whole Jewish population." The council asked the Allied governments "to find means of halting the German terror, even while the war continued, by adequate retaliation."[14] On July 30, 1942, representatives of the Netherlands, Yugoslavia, and Luxembourg presented Secretary of State Hull with a joint request from nine governments in exile to deliver an American warning to Germany about war crimes against civilians in occupied territories and a promise that criminal acts would be punished.[15]

The State Department responded by preparing a statement for the president condemning "murder for murder's sake; torture for torture's sake; massacre of hostages and revolting cruelties carried out for political ends, and inflicted in a spirit of total depravity." Germans, Italians, and Japanese involved in such practices would be brought to justice. Toward that end the United States had begun collecting evidence of Axis crimes against humanity. FDR issued the statement on August 22. Another presidential statement in October pledged the United States to cooperation with the British and other governments in establishing a United Nations Commission for the Investigation of War Crimes, which would try those "ringleaders" responsible for the organized murder of thousands of innocent persons and the commission of atrocities that violated every tenet of the Christian faith.[16] The word "Jews" appeared in neither statement. Only the Allied Declaration of December 17 explicitly condemned Nazi mass killings of Jews, and that statement emanated from London's initiative.[17]

The Middle East and North Africa were not the only reasons for American reluctance to spell out publicly what the Nazis were doing to Europe's Jews. Many experts were convinced that to condemn Nazi killing of Jews publicly carried serious political and military liabilities in Europe. A survey, taken by an American military attaché,[18] of twenty Americans, mostly journalists, who had spent considerable time as visitors and prisoners in Germany, concluded that the United States should avoid "vehement or sentimental defense of Jews" in its broadcasts to Europe.

> Anti-Semitism has become firmly implanted in Germany and many of the occupied areas. It is therefore inadvisable for Jews to be in conspicuous positions in directing United Nations propaganda or to use them in the preparation or delivery of material which would reveal their race. For the same reason, it is also deemed inadvisable to defend or champion the Jewish cause vigorously. . . . If real atrocities occur they should be revealed, but the evidence and proof should be so convincing that there should be no doubt as to their authenticity. In general, I believe it would be better to ignore the atrocity idea because it became quite generally discredited as a result of world war [I] practices.[19]

Although these observations preceded the specific reports of the Final Solution, the same views persisted in Washington throughout 1942 and 1943.

In an OWI broadcast to Germany in November 1942, theologian Paul Tillich, a native of Germany, tried to warn the German people against participation in the persecution of the Jews. The gist of his warning was that, if persecution of the Jews did not cease, the Germans might be treated similarly. OWI censors barred him from making the statement. On November 27, 1942, a

Yugoslavian national submitted to OWI broadcast control the text of a message dealing with the Jewish question designed for broadcast to Yugoslavia. He was forced to delete key passages, including:

> There is no Jewish race. Goebbels invented lies about race and Aryan blood. . . . In America President Roosevelt was presented with a report by outstanding medical authorities who conducted researches on the blood of all nations. They found no difference in human blood, not even between the blood of Negroes and white people.

The Yugoslavian broadcaster also had to drop references to Rabbi Wise's charges that Nazi policy toward the Jews was mass extermination. (The control officer who insisted on the changes was Jewish.) CBS broadcasts to Germany, also supervised by OWI, underwent similar transformations. A passage dealing with Nazi measures against the Jews in Poland was eliminated because atrocity tales were not to be credited.[20]

A Committee on War Information Policy, consisting of high-level representatives of various government agencies, had been established in early 1942 to advise the Office of War Information. On September 2, 1942, the committee discussed the "thorny" question of atrocities, which required "careful handling." The minutes contain the following explanation of policy:

> It is questionable whether the government, in pursuit of a policy of informational candor, has the right to withhold authenticated information about atrocities to American citizens. But in view of the fact that this has been called repeatedly a United Nations war, it would seem to follow that the same considerations would apply to authenticated atrocity information bearing upon atrocities to the peoples or the soldiers of our allies. On the other hand, it is generally agreed that atrocity material relating to atrocities perpetrated upon citizens of other countries may produce in the minds of our people morbid results rather than desirable results. . . . Under such a policy as this, barbarous actions and cruelties not serving directly to illuminate the nature of the enemy, but merely to excite horror and hatred of all members of the races guilty of such actions, would not be released.[21]

In other words, if the Germans would react angrily to the publication or broadcast of certain Nazi atrocities against foreigners, and if Americans would not be inspired to fight harder, the information should be suppressed. The committee avoided spelling out that emphasis of the atrocities against Jews might have negative domestic and diplomatic repercussions, but the Nazi Gauleiter Fritz Bracht would certainly have understood why German propaganda emphasized anti-Semitism and why American officials played down Allied opposition to Nazi mass killings of Jews.

Another example of selective American information policy concerned a War Department training film for soldiers entitled "Prelude to War," part of a series called "Why We Fight." President Roosevelt and several senators saw the movie and were impressed; they suggested showing it to the general public.

When the War Department consulted the Office of War Information, however, OWI officials objected that the film duplicated material in privately produced pictures and that it contained details "unsuitable for public information." Angered, the War Department brought out heavy bureaucratic artillery. Under-secretary of War Robert P. Patterson wrote OWI Director Elmer Davis that it would be embarrassing to release the film in a different form from the one shown to the soldiers. Assistant Secretary of War John J. McCloy also passed along to Davis the comment of a young officer in the army, a friend of McCloy:

> There is one persistent worry I have had from the first day I got into the Army. It involves the fundamental principle of do the American people know what they are fighting for. . . . In the majority of the soldiers' minds lie only deep mistrust of England even more than Russia, as well as the Hitlerian idea that the whole war was started by Jewish capitalists. It is unbelievable that Americans should believe these things, but they do, and are willing to believe anything involving race prejudice. Isolationism is so deep rooted.

McCloy then added his own endorsement:

> . . . While this is perhaps primarily an Army problem and one that I hope we shall be able to deal with, I do not believe that we can divorce Army thinking from national thinking. The idea we should educate the Army by the Prelude-to-Victory [sic] series and not the public generally, seems to me to be completely unsound. If the men come into the Army with these prejudices, it is going to be hard to eradicate them.[22]

Davis's reply, if any, does not survive, but OWI policy was unaffected. He might well have argued that the time to pursue eradication of prejudice was after the war.

ALLIED COOPERATION

By December 1942 the United States and Great Britain faced a similar problem and similar pressures on refugee policy. The reports about the Final Solution could no longer be dismissed or ignored. Moreover, the governments in exile of nations conquered by Germany were calling for action on behalf of their suffering citizens. Finally, both Congress and Parliament were showing signs of greater interest in refugee questions, as were liberal newspapers and interest groups. These developments were all the more embarrassing to the State Department and the Foreign Office because both governments had already established tight immigration restrictions (on entry into the U.S., Britain, and Palestine), which they did not think it wise to alter. German military strength had already crested, but the outcome of the war was still far from certain.

Since European Jews were not universally popular, and since Nazi propaganda featured alleged ties between international Jewry and the Allies, Washington and London saw little to be gained militarily or politically in assisting the most prominent victims of Nazi persecution. In several cases, official disinclination to provide humanitarian assistance was marked by personal sentiment against Jews. In others, one finds that bureaucrats and politicians simply shied away from risky moves that might have had an adverse effect upon the course of the war.

British public opinion would not let the issue disappear, however. Indeed, one effect of the Allied declaration of December 17, Foreign Minister Eden wrote later, was to stimulate complaints about the inadequacy of government efforts to save those threatened by Nazi persecutions.[23] A Jewish delegation asked Eden on December 23 to seek the assistance of the Red Cross and the Vatican and to admit Jewish refugees to every Allied and neutral country, especially Palestine. It also called for the dropping of leaflets in Germany denouncing atrocities. On January 11, 1943, the cabinet accepted Eden's view that Britain should not distinguish between Jews and other refugees in any rescue efforts.[24] Pending negotiations with the United States, the cabinet had approved only one specific proposal, to allow 4,500 Jewish children in Bulgaria, accompanied by 500 adults, to enter Palestine under the White Paper quota. The colonial secretary announced in the House of Commons on February 3 that 500 children from Rumania and Hungary would also be admitted and that others might enter as well, provided that the practical difficulties could be resolved. They could not. The Turkish government objected to overcrowding its railway system, and the Germans put strong pressure on Bulgaria not to cooperate.[25]

The British government, meanwhile, turned to its American ally, which had similar problems with public criticism of its refugee policy. Together the two nations might be able to agree upon some positive steps on refugee policy and thereby dampen the criticism. The British government's statement to Parliament on January 19 made it clear, however, that it had no great hopes for arresting, blocking, or mitigating the Final Solution.

> They are . . . conscious of the fact that the only real remedy for the consistent Nazi Policy of Racial and Religious persecution lies in an Allied victory. Every resource of all the Allied Nations must be bent towards this supreme object, measures for the rescue and relief of such refugees as succeed in escaping from German Occupied Territory cannot be exclusively British, and His Majesty's Government are now engaged in consultations with the other Governments most immediately concerned with a view to seeing what further measures it is possible to take as soon as possible to assist those who make their way to countries beyond German control. These consultations are necessarily confidential and it would not be in the interest of the refugees themselves to enter upon any discussion on them at the present juncture.[26]

It is tempting to view the British reference to confidential negotiations with other governments as a way to buy time against further parliamentary criticism.

The British aide mémoire on refugees from Nazi-occupied territory, sent to the State Department on January 20, eliminated at the start, either explicitly or implicitly, many of the proposals considered objectionable by the British and American governments. The British government argued that it would be unwise to treat the refugee problem wholly as a Jewish problem; there were other refugees and many other groups suffering. Palestine, for security reasons, could not receive adult males from enemy territories but might take children up to the limits of the White Paper quotas. Britain could take at most only a very limited number of refugees and could only accommodate them on the Isle of Man. London also recognized the importance of American security restrictions on entry into the country and on immigration. That did not leave a great deal still on the table.

Still, the British note contained some positive suggestions. Most of the refugees who escaped from German territories landed on the doorstep of neutral countries with limited absorptive capacities. Some kind of outside assurance that the United Nations would help to resettle the refugees after the war would make the neutrals far more willing to help. One specific suggestion was the removal of refugees from Spain and Portugal to Allied territory in North Africa. The aide mémoire concluded with questions such as whether the U.S. thought joint action advisable and whether it would participate in a private and informal United Nations conference.[27]

State Department advisor on political relations and Near Eastern specialist Wallace Murray sensed a British trap. He urged George Brandt, Breckinridge Long's executive assistant, to remind the British of the many thousands of Italian prisoners that they had already foisted on the United States. Murray also suggested a campaign to rally public opinion in the United States against a deluge of refugees, which would aggravate the shortage of food. Murray also argued that, through the occupation of North Africa, America had acquired an impressive stake in Muslim countries and a need to respect Muslim sensitivities. He noted that the Egyptian and Iraqi governments had recently objected to Zionist activities in the U.S., and several congressmen had supposedly expressed doubts about the wisdom of supporting Zionist activities at this time. Murray concluded that the American Zionist movement was in "a bear market phase."[28] He wrote as if he personally had been selling short. The State Department took no immediate action on the British aide mémoire.

When Samuel Merlin, one of the associates of Jewish activist Peter Bergson, later announced plans for a mass rally in Madison Square Garden on behalf of the moral rights of the stateless and Palestinian Jews, Murray asked Secretary Hull, Undersecretary Welles, and Assistant Secretary Berle to take steps to prevent the meeting. Otherwise, the Axis propaganda machine would certainly exploit the event and exaggerate its implications. Murray did not spell out just how American citizens were to be prevented from assembling.[29]

On February 20, Richard Law, British parliamentary undersecretary of state for foreign affairs, told the American chargé d'affaires in London that, while he was not sure that much practical help could be given to these "unfortunate people," His Majesty's Government could no longer postpone some reply in the House of Commons to persistent demands for information about government efforts to help the Jews. The American response was finally given to the British embassy in Washington on February 25. After listing many measures already taken by the United States on behalf of refugees, the American aide mémoire picked up the British proposal for a refugee conference and some kind of resettlement guarantee to countries receiving refugees and to consider North Africa as a haven.[30] The American aide mémoire had a number of unusual features. It not only claimed credit for past moves in refugee policy; it was drafted to resemble an original proposal, not a response.

The reasons for Washington's behavior soon became apparent. On March 1, 1943, American Jewish spokesmen called upon twenty-two thousand people assembled in Madison Square Garden (and at least fifteen thousand more outside) to "stop Hitler now." The American Jewish Congress, the AFL, the CIO, the Church Peace Union, and the Free World Association sponsored the rally. Stephen Wise pointed out to the audience that, if the United Nations simply pursued their course of winning the war, there might be no Jews left to save by the time victory arrived. The archbishop of Canterbury sent his own encouragement to the meeting: "I trust that our two nations may unite in offering all possible aid and place of refuge for Jews now threatened with massacre and so do what we can to mitigate the most appalling horror in recorded history."[31] On March 3, without prior notice to London, the State Department released to the press the note it had sent to the British government.[32] Just as the British had tried to defuse public criticism by suggesting a conference, the State Department now tried the same tactic with the American public.

Foreign Minister Anthony Eden tried to clear up any misunderstandings when he arrived in Washington later in March. In a conference with Cordell Hull and the British ambassador, Lord Halifax, Eden spoke of British efforts to move 30,000 Jews from eastern Europe to Palestine. When Hull inquired about Arab reaction, Eden explained that these Jews fell under the White Paper quota already announced. Eden pressed for assurances to Spain, Portugal, Switzerland, and Sweden that they would not have to support refugees indefinitely. The British also wanted to release an announcement regarding the forthcoming conference on refugees. William Strang of the British Foreign Office and Ray Atherton, chief of the Division of European Affairs in the State Department, met with Assistant Secretary Long to draft an appropriate statement.[33] The conference was set for Bermuda in the second half of April. The resort island was now the home of the Imperial Censorship Office, where all transatlantic mail was examined, censored, and forwarded. Communication to and from the island was, not coincidentally, strictly controlled.

The next day the House of Lords debated a motion offered by the archbishop of Canterbury supporting "immediate measures on the largest and most generous scale compatible with the requirements of military operations and security" for assistance to Jews and others in danger of massacre and starvation in enemy territory. The archbishop noted that the arguments in support of current policy were disproportionate to the scale of the evil. He called for the admission of all refugees able to reach Britain and for prompt action. Speaking for the government, Lord Cranbourne rejected unilateral British action, emphasized the key constraints of limited food and shipping, and read the joint memorandum, which had just arrived from Washington. American-British collaboration on refugee policy would be discussed at the Bermuda Conference.[34] Eden's work in Washington had served its purpose.

Four days later Eden met with Stephen Wise and Joseph Proskauer, cochairmen of the Joint Emergency Committee for European Jewish Affairs, at the British embassy in Washington. Wise and Proskauer suggested that the United Nations issue a public declaration to Hitler, asking him to give Jews permission to leave occupied Europe. Eden replied that this was "fantastically impossible." He also found impossible the sending of refugees from Spain and Portugal to Palestine and the extraction of adult Jews from Bulgaria. Eden bluntly observed: "Turkey does not want any more of your people." The discouraged Wise and Proskauer then went to see Sumner Welles, who promised to do what he could for the Jewish proposals. Welles also agreed to have the President's Advisory Committee on Political Refugees represented at the Bermuda Conference.[35]

That same day Eden and Hull met again, this time with FDR, Sumner Welles, Harry Hopkins, Lord Halifax, and Strang. Hull urged Eden to do something about the sixty or seventy thousand Bulgarian Jews threatened with extermination. Eden responded that the Allies had to move very cautiously; if they set a precedent, then Jews throughout the world would demand similar action for Polish and German Jews. Eden warned: "Hitler might well take us up on any such offer and there simply are not enough ships and means of transportation in the world to handle them." Although Eden claimed the British were ready to take sixty thousand more Jews to Palestine, transportation and security posed great problems. The Germans would be certain to place agents among the refugees. Eden urged American officials not to make "too expansive promises" that could not be fulfilled because of lack of shipping. A month later Eden's private secretary, Oliver Harvey, wrote in his diary: "Unfortunately, A.E. is immovable on the subject of Palestine. He loves Arabs and hates Jews."[36]

Eden had little need to worry. Breckinridge Long's instructions to the American delegation warned against playing into the hands of Nazi propaganda through sole interest in certain minorities. The guidelines stressed the shortage of shipping and the prior claims of wounded Americans and Axis prisoners. Long argued falsely that American immigration policy was expressed (solely) in the laws enacted by Congress, which the executive branch had no power to alter. He also told reporters that the conference would be exploratory.[37]

April 19, 1943, was the eve of Passover, the festival in which Jews celebrate the escape of their ancestors from slavery in Egypt. On April 19, 1943, a

German SS commander led his troops and accompanying Latvian, Ukrainian, and Polish police into the Warsaw ghetto. The Jewish resistance opened up with its one machine gun, assorted rifles, grenades, and Molotov cocktails. The Nazis fled, and the Warsaw Ghetto uprising had begun.

The Bermuda Conference also opened on April 19, with all but the opening ceremonies held in confidential sessions. Richard Law, parliamentary undersecretary in the Foreign Office, led the assault on proposals for refugee assistance. Law announced British opposition to negotiations with Germany for the release of Jews and other refugees, to exchange of German nationals in Allied hands for refugees, and to shipment of food through the blockade to persecuted persons in Europe. Although Congressman Sol Bloom (of Brooklyn), chairman of the House Foreign Affairs Committee, raised some objections, Law pointed out the folly of offering to take responsibility for any sizeable portion of 20 to 30 million "useless" people, who were a liability to Hitler. The head of the American delegation, Princeton University president Harold Dodds, finally curbed Bloom, and discussion moved to narrower issues.[38]

With an American shipping expert ruling out use of Allied ships for refugee transportation for many months, and with the steady flow of refugees clogging neutral countries such as Switzerland, Spain, and Portugal, the delegates necessarily focused on havens in or near Europe. One promising spot was French territory in northwest Africa, now occupied by American troops, which the British found infinitely better than Palestine. President Dodds supported the British push for refugee camps in French North Africa. Other American officials, including the Joint Chiefs of Staff, looked askance at the idea of Jewish refugee camps in the midst of Muslim Africa.[39] Secretary of State Hull declined to make any commitment before consulting the Free French government. In the end, the conference decided only to let the British write up a detailed proposal for the American government. Hull and the American delegates also requested a quid pro quo from the British—a refugee camp in British-controlled territory in Africa.[40]

The Visa Division of the State Department heard later that Eisenhower had opposed the North African plan and that the president had to intervene personally to approve it. Following Churchill's personal appeal to Roosevelt, and FDR's request to Eisenhower, the Americans did establish camps at Fedhala and Philippeville in French Morocco. No more than 630 Jewish refugees were transported to Fedhala; Philippeville, apparently, was better populated. Free French officials successfully resisted British efforts to establish a refugee camp in Madagascar, one quid pro quo that the Americans at Bermuda had wanted. British military and civilian officials also fought a plan to establish a British camp for refugees in Libya, but FDR and Treasury secretary Henry Morgenthau finally called for Great Britain to fulfill its part of the Bermuda bargain. In June 1944 the British cabinet approved a proposal for a camp for no more than 1,500 Yugoslavian refugees. The number of Jews among them is unclear.[41]

The Bermuda Conference also considered the possibilities of resettlement from eastern Europe. British representatives announced their government's willingness in principle to admit 29,000 Jews to Palestine, the number remaining under the White Paper limit. But because of security concerns only children, with some accompanying adults, were acceptable now. Britain again offered to take the 4,000 Jewish children from Bulgaria, although Law pointed out that the Turks had limited rail transit. He now raised an alternative: two Rumanian ships could take refugees from Istanbul to Palestine. But the British asked the United States to share the cost of chartering the ships. In the past, the State Department had consistently replied that only Congress could appropriate money for refugee resettlement. Whether the British intended to blame the collapse of the scheme on the United States is unclear. Sumner Welles soon pointedly remarked to the British ambassador that delay might be fatal and the United Nations might then be held responsible for the failure. In any case, Washington acted positively. The matter reached FDR, who quickly ordered the use of up to one-half million dollars from the President's Emergency Fund. Meanwhile, the Rumanian ships had become unavailable. The International Red Cross later complained that the British government had not responded to opportunities and had made infeasible proposals.[42]

The Nazis closed the escape route. Reich Führer SS Heinrich Himmler decided that Germany could not allow the emigration of Jewish children from the German sphere of influence except in return for young Germans (capable of reproduction) interned in Allied countries. He suggested a ratio of four Germans for every Jew. Himmler and Foreign Minister Joachim von Ribbentrop then added conditions to maximize the propaganda value of the deal. The Jews could not go to Palestine, only to England. Moreover, the House of Commons would have to sanction the arrangement with a resolution. All of this would demonstrate to the world Germany's pro-Arab attitude and the pro-Jewish stance of the British. A German Foreign Office official minuted:

> Though one must count on the British Government refusing to comply with the German demands, the Reich Führer SS should be asked, as a precautionary measure, that the barter objects which might under given circumstances be required should not be evacuated to the Eastern territories for the time being.

The unsuccessful negotiations, conducted through the auspices of the Swiss legation in Berlin, dragged into 1944.[43] The Bermuda conferees might have been spared the fear that Hitler would release too many useless Jews. On the other hand, Allied concern over Nazi propaganda on the Jewish question was not totally unjustified.

The British government had suggested a declaration reassuring neutrals that the United Nations would repatriate refugees at the end of the war. Although the Americans agreed with the general idea, Hull had some difficulties with the text worked out by the Bermuda Conference. The idea of a United Nations declaration eventually had to be dropped because of difficulties with the Soviet Union. Nonetheless, Britain and the United States did inform neutral nations of their concern for refugees and their willingness to provide financial assistance. This had some effect, particularly on Switzerland and Sweden.[44] This diplomatic initiative proved to be perhaps the most significant life-saving measure initiated by the conference—accomplished perhaps because it obligated neither Britain nor the U.S. to take in refugees. Thus, it could not hamper the war effort.

The Bermuda Conference of course discussed both British and American immigration policy, but with little impact upon entrenched positions. The American delegation had agreed to hear a presentation by George Backer, president of the American Organization for Rehabilitation through Training (ORT), an American Jew who was allowed to attend the conference. Backer bluntly challenged the security rationale for denying immigrants and urged the use of a larger percentage of the American quotas. "If 100,000 Germans would offer to surrender," he observed, "we would find some way to get them out [and take them in]." Senator Scott Lucas of Illinois, a member of the American delegation, delivered one rebuttal:

> I am not only thinking about persecuted peoples in Europe but I am thinking about the millions of boys in this country who are fighting on every front in this war. I am thinking of the mothers. . . . [I am thinking] about casualty lists and the thousands and thousands that are going to return to be charges of this Government after the war is over. Every day you postpone bringing this war to a conclusion you just take upon your hands the blood of American boys. That is the thing in back of my mind all the time.

That was a consideration few politicians dared challenge. Robert Borden Reams added that, if one Nazi spy or saboteur entered the country as the result of refugee admission, the result would be a cutoff of all refugees in the future. Backer countered bitterly that the number now entering was so small that a complete stoppage would not make much difference.[45]

Diplomatic pressure from the Allied governments in exile and domestic criticism of government refugee policy drove Great Britain and the United States to the Bermuda Conference. But the essential stipulation remained: steps to aid refugees that might interfere with the war effort were forbidden. Churchill and Roosevelt had both approved this policy. It made considerable sense, if sensibly applied.

But the war effort was not only the highest priority; it was also an all-inclusive and elastic standard. The war effort required ships and food; tight security in Britain, Palestine, and the United States; a calm Arab population in North Africa and the Middle East; sympathetic support of the United Nations from the populations of nations occupied by Germany; even properly motivated soldiers and citizens at home. In the eyes of some officials in both London and Washington, virtually any publicized assistance or attention to European Jews jeopardized some requisite of the war effort. Too many people in too many places would object to, or take offense at, Allied solicitude for the Jews. Persons who readily perceived anti-Semitic currents elsewhere, such as General Patton, Wallace Murray, and Borden Reams of the State Department, took this view almost instinctively. There were others, however, who simply saw involvement with the Jewish question as a risk to be avoided as long as the war remained in doubt. There is little question that OWI Director Elmer Davis, Secretary of State Hull, and FDR fell into this category.

The existence of a large number of Jewish refugees was, in purely practical terms, a political liability for the American and British governments. The prevalence of anti-Semitism in many neutral nations, and particularly in the Middle East, made open Allied support for European Jews risky. Vicious Nazi anti-Semitic propaganda added to the danger. Western humanitarian values were unable to prevail over the anti-Semites and pragmatists who stressed the risks of taking any action that might lend support to German charges. To a remarkable degree, Adolf Hitler had succeeded in devaluing the lives of European Jews in the eyes of the rest of the world.

NINE

On a Broad Humanitarian Basis

The meager results of the Bermuda Conference left many observers with the impression that the United States and Great Britain would do virtually nothing for European Jewry as long as the war lasted. Then came a surprising chain of events, filled with ironies. The sequence really originated in August 1942 when Gerhart Riegner sent Rabbi Stephen Wise a telegram through the State Department, which doubted the information therein and suppressed it. State Department officials did something more in early 1943; they tried to prevent Riegner from sending any more messages to Wise through official channels. The undersecretary of state, apparently not a party to the effort, unwittingly exposed it.

High-level officials in the Treasury Department, persuaded to authorize relief and rescue operations for Jews in Rumania and France, were frustrated by the State Department. Then they discovered the State Department's attempt to cut off the flow of information about the Final Solution. In the midst of everything, the British Foreign Office stated its own fears too baldly: its primary concern was what to do if the Germans released too many Jews. This British cable was so offensive that the State Department could no longer use the British as an excuse for inaction. A State Department official tried to cover up what his colleagues had done. The Treasury Department men, no mean historians, documented everything. The result was the removal of refugee problems from the jurisdiction of the State Department and the creation of a new War Refugee Board in January 1944. There was a certain pattern to the process: each action produced a corresponding and more extreme reaction until high authorities had to step in.

This chain of events cannot, of course, be viewed in isolation. It would not have occurred without other important developments. During 1943, in spite of their continuing divisions and disagreements, American Jewish organizations began to focus on measures to save Europe's remaining Jews. Increasingly vocal Jewish and non-Jewish advocates of humanitarian measures for Jewish refugees won some additional support in Congress and in the press, which added considerably to the pressure on the State Department. (Other specialized works have gone into such detail on these developments that we shall do little more than make reference to them here.)[1] Finally, a near-continuous string of Allied military victories improved the climate for proposals designed to save civilian lives. But without the Treasury's unraveling of the State Department's policy toward European Jews, the War Refugee Board would not have come into existence as soon as it did (!)—if at all—which would have meant even more missed opportunities and greater loss of life. There is good reason, then, to concentrate on the continuing reverberations of Riegner's telegrams and their effect on the American government.

On January 20, 1943, the American consul in Geneva, Paul Squire, had another visit from Lichtheim and Riegner, who again brought news of the Holocaust, compiled from various sources. From these sources they had now confirmed that mass executions, as many as 6,000 daily, were taking place in Poland, and they had detailed information about deportations in various countries. They asked Squire to send the information immediately to Bern and Washington and on to Rabbi Wise in New York. They even included, for Harrison's benefit only, the general identities (but not the specific names) of their sources. Riegner added that the information was for the use of the government, but, if the message was not considered official, he was prepared to pay for the telegram. Harrison considered the telegram of great interest,[2] and he sent it to Washington to Welles's attention, but the reaction of the European Division of the State Department to telegram no. 482 from Bern was quite different.

In an internal memorandum, Elbridge Durbrow pointed out that Wise had once before received similar information through department facilities; he had then indicated publicly that the State Department stood behind the information. Durbrow thought someone should take up this "misrepresentation" with Wise and should let him know that information given to him was a courtesy and an exception. Durbrow also noted that the department continued to receive inquiries from outside parties whether the department had confirmed Wise's information. Visa Division chief Ray Atherton sent the statement on to Welles with a handwritten addition: "This memo explains the predicament we are in because of many requests for 'official data.' "[3]

Welles's method of dealing with Rabbi Wise and with his own colleagues now came back to haunt him. Perhaps sensing State Department skepticism about the Final Solution and antagonism toward Wise, Welles had privately given Wise confirmation of the August 1942 telegram from Riegner. That allowed Wise to go public, but it increased the resistance to him at State, where virtually everyone was unaware of Welles's intervention. The State Department's predicament was that it did not want to issue official confirmation of the Final Solution. That would have increased the pressure on the United States to do something to hinder the Germans, and virtually all such proposals, from the State Department's perspective, had drawbacks.[4]

Durbrow drafted a telegram (no. 354) to Bern, discouraging the legation from accepting reports for transmission to private parties in the future. Making specific reference to telegram no. 482, Durbrow argued:

It is felt that by sending such private messages which circumvent neutral countries' censorship we risk the possibility that neutral countries might find it necessary to take steps to curtail or abolish our official secret means of communication.5

This telegram overlooked the fact that Welles had specifically instructed Harrison, and Harrison had instructed Squire (in October 1942), to make transmission facilities available to Riegner.6

Durbrow's draft was initialed by other members of the European Division (Hickerson and Atherton), by James Clement Dunn of Political Affairs, *and* by Welles. In all likelihood, Welles simply initialed the cable without realizing its significance; he would have had to look up telegram no. 482 to figure out that the European Division was trying to cut off Riegner's contact with Wise.7 Off it went to Bern, where it must have taken Harrison aback.

When the next two reports from Riegner arrived at the legation in March, Harrison was forced to inform Squire that, "under terms of the instructions which I have recently received from the Department, this message is not deemed of such nature that it may be transmitted to Dr. Wise as such." Harrison wanted Riegner's permission to keep sending his information to the State Department, but he suggested that Riegner telegraph Wise directly.8 Riegner sensibly responded that the telegrams contained such highly confidential information (including sources of information) that he could not risk an uncoded telegram that the Germans might get hold of.9 Finally, Harrison admitted that there was some confusion about what type of information Riegner might send and said that he was trying to clarify the matter in Washington.10

To the State Department, Harrison indicated that some of Riegner's messages to Wise were routine and could be sent through regular channels. But Riegner's messages frequently contained helpful information, Harrison told Washington, and he recommended that messages of this type *not* be subjected to the restriction imposed by telegram no. 354. The department gave Harrison the go-ahead but urged him to reach an understanding with Riegner: only at the State Department's discretion would it transmit Riegner's messages to Wise.11 On the same day Welles wrote Wise about the latest message from Riegner, which, Welles said, the legation had accepted "in an exceptional way." Wise was told not to make reference to the source or means of transmission if he made the information public.12 That letter clearly indicates that Welles was now fully informed of the dispute and that he was trying to strike a balance between Riegner's requests and the position of the European Division. Welles had serious problems of his own. His rivalry with Hull was escalating, and within six months it would cost him his job. Perhaps he felt he could not take too great a risk for Wise.

Riegner's telegram of April 20 to Wise recommended relief and rescue activities by the World Jewish Congress on behalf of Rumanian Jews, particularly those who had been deported to Transnistria, territory conquered from Russia beyond the Dniester River. The Rumanian Jewish leadership had just won Rumania's permission for 5,000 orphans and children there to be allowed to emigrate to Palestine. There were plenty of orphans in Transnistria. In the fall of 1941, Rumania had deported approximately 130,000 Jews to Transnistria. The harsh forced marches, the primitive conditions in Transnistria, the severity of the winter, and, last but not least, Rumanian and German execution squads within a year cut the number of Jews to approximately 70,000. But the Rumanian government had also allowed some Jews to buy their way out of the deportations, which set a precedent for later developments.[13]

By late 1942 the fortunes of war had shifted enough that dictator Marshal Antonescu and the anti-Semitic commissar for Jewish affairs, Radu Lecca, were willing to allow the surviving Transnistrian Jews to go to Palestine for a hefty price—up to one hundred million dollars.[14] This plan fell through because of German objections; the Germans protested that it violated their agreements with the Arabs.[15] The Allies, of course, were unwilling anyway to pay ransom to an Axis satellite, and the British were opposed to mass emigration to Palestine.[16] But Transnistria was one area in Europe where it was possible to get at least some Jews out of Axis territory. They had to get enough food and clothing, in the meantime, to survive.

There was also, Riegner wrote, great need for funds to support children being kept in hiding in France or looking to escape from France to Spain. World Jewish Congress officials had found persons in Rumania and France willing to lend funds for these purposes provided that equal amounts of money were placed in blocked accounts in the U.S. or in Switzerland. Repayment of these loans would not occur until the end of the war, which meant that no funds had to be transferred illegally to Axis countries now. Welles cautiously told Wise to take up the whole matter with the Treasury Department, which was in charge of enforcing the Trading with the Enemy Act.[17] That was the beginning of the Treasury's involvement with Riegner's telegrams. It also put the World Jewish Congress and eventually the Treasury Department on a collision course with the British Foreign Office.

The British had previously opposed virtually all proposals for shipping relief supplies to enemy-controlled territories.[18] There was little change in the British position during 1943. Even when President Roosevelt personally tried to persuade Churchill that the Allies could now afford to send some shipments of food to suffering Europeans, Churchill would not budge.[19] Moreover, the Foreign Funds Control Division of the State Department, as well as the Treasury Department, argued against the authorization of funds for relief purposes on the grounds that it would create "an embarrassing precedent" and make it difficult to deny similar requests by others. But Bernard Meltzer of Foreign Funds Control saw no reason why the U.S. should not release funds to blocked accounts for the "evacuation" of Jews to Palestine and France.[20] (This meant, ironically, that, in both Washington and Berlin, officials were writing at this time about the evacuation of Jews; in Germany, evacuation was one of the euphemisms used by Nazi leaders for the deportations to the death camps.)[21]

On July 22, Stephen Wise consulted President Roosevelt personally about Riegner's proposal and received FDR's endorsement: "Stephen, why don't you go ahead and do it." When Wise expressed doubt about Morgenthau's approval, FDR phoned his friend and advocated support. Treasury officials quickly overcame their doubts and approved both rescue operations in Rumania and France. Morgenthau wrote Hull directly and got his permission.[22] All that remained, apparently, was to ask the legation in Bern and Riegner whether the Treasury's stipulations (blocked accounts in the U.S. only) were feasible.

But the battle was still raging in the State Department. There were three men at State who supported the proposal: Bernard Meltzer and W. J. Hull, both of Foreign Funds Control; and Herbert Feis, advisor on international economic affairs, later a Pulitzer Prize-winning historian. Meltzer and Feis were Jewish. (According to Meltzer, some others in the department—Dean Acheson, Donald Hiss, and Thomas Finletter—might have joined the fight in favor of rescue-relief proposals, but such matters normally did not reach them.) Against them ranged the European Division's refugee specialist, Robert Borden Reams, and George Brandt, Breckinridge Long's executive assistant. Also involved, behind the scenes, were Ray Atherton of the European Division, Wallace Murray, a Near Eastern specialist, and James Dunn of Political Affairs. That was a powerful coalition. In the end, Feis had to take the proposed telegram to Bern to Secretary of State Hull to get it approved, and it was written up as a Treasury Department proposal, not a State Department initiative.[23]

In September the Treasury Department reconsidered the issue of relief payments and decided, subject to the same safeguards (blocked accounts in the U.S., repayment of loans after the war), that Jewish organizations could also use money for relief purposes in France.[24] That new move only added to the disagreements between State and Treasury. Although Assistant Secretary of State Adolf Berle now agreed that it was time to permit food shipments to occupied territories—the blockade was hurting American friends more than enemies[25]— others in the State Department did not.

Unlike many of the unrealistic rescue and relief proposals made in the past year, the World Jewish Congress effort and a relief operation in Rumania mounted by the American Jewish Joint Distribution Committee through its Swiss representative had real chances of success, because Rumanian ruler Marshal Antonescu had changed his line of policy drastically. At the council of ministers meeting of November 17, 1943, Antonescu called for the shipping of the Transnistrian Jews—except for the communists and criminals—back across the Dniester. He wanted to warn Germany not to kill those Rumanian Jews it had taken over. Then he added that foreign nations should send food and clothing for the Jews, for he could not divert what was necessary for Rumanian soldiers, workers, and officials.[26] But the Jewish organizations could save thousands of Rumanian Jews only if they got funds from outside Europe.

In Bern, however, British protests managed to persuade Harrison not to issue the necessary license to Riegner without specific instructions from the

State Department.[27] Harrison knew he was not working for the Treasury. Meanwhile, after Treasury officials complained to Hull about the runaround, they received a State Department memorandum arguing that Riegner had not consulted promptly with his Rumanian sources and that the Treasury Department had never formulated a feasible plan or consulted the British. State was blaming Riegner and Treasury for the delay! Josiah DuBois, the Treasury's assistant general counsel, heard from State Department sources that Ray Atherton and Wallace Murray were the prime forces in the State Department's delaying maneuvers. (Breckinridge Long had approved the license to Riegner because he had heard FDR favored it.)[28]

When Treasury Department officials tried to get the American ambassador to Great Britain, John Winant, to intercede in London and clear away British obstructions, they got a truly shocking reply:

> The Foreign Office are concerned with the difficulties of disposing of any considerable number of Jews should they be rescued from enemy-occupied territory. . . . They foresee that it is likely to prove almost if not quite impossible to deal with anything like the number of 70,000 refugees whose rescue is envisaged by the Riegner plan. For this reason they are reluctant to agree to any approval being expressed even of the preliminary financial arrangements.[29]

This was equivalent to saying that the British preferred these Jews to die. And their objection was not even based on the facts—Riegner's plan did not call for the emigration of anything like 70,000 Jews.[30]

The effect of the British response upon the Treasury's "war council"—Morgenthau, Treasury's general counsel Randolph Paul, Foreign Funds Control chief John Pehle, Treasury's assistant general counsel Josiah DuBois, Jr., and Ansel Luxford—was galvanizing. They had wasted much time trying to cooperate; now they would attack not only the British but also the State Department, which had been working hand-in-hand with the British. They discussed strategy on Saturday afternoon, December 18. Pehle pressed for a presidential commission of sympathetic people to handle refugee problems.[31] Morgenthau quite correctly observed that Roosevelt would want to get Hull's reaction before taking such a move, so Morgenthau had to go to the secretary of state first. But the subject of discussion would no longer be a license for the World Jewish Congress.

> H. M. Jr.: I want to go as Secretary of the Treasury. Just because I am a Jew, why shouldn't I look after the Jews, or the Catholics, or the Armenians. . . .
> Mr. Paul: You are talking on a broad humanitarian basis—talking as a Cabinet member.
> Mr. Pehle: I think that is the term.
> Mr. Luxford: They are not facing up. The issue is very simple for Hull. That is, you can find a million reasons why you can't get them out of Europe, but if somebody put their mind to getting them out, you can then spend the next ten years on what you are going to do with them. . . .

H. M. Jr.: I would like to say to Mr. Hull, "After all, if you were a member of the Cabinet in Germany today, you would be, most likely, in a prison camp, and your wife would be God knows where," because Mrs. Hull is a Jewess, you know.[32]

Morgenthau telephoned and made an appointment with Hull for Monday morning.

The next evening (Sunday evening) the strategy discussion resumed with the addition of Oscar Cox of the Lend-Lease Administration. For some time Cox had been pushing the idea of a special refugee commission without much success. Cox said that the president favored it, but that the State Department had blocked action. Now the Treasury officials had gathered enough evidence to make an overwhelming case for removing jurisdiction from State. Cox added: "When you see specific cases like this one, then you realize that the failure of action means that hundreds of thousands of people are being killed."[33] Morgenthau was convinced to "marry" the Treasury's issue and Cox's plan.[34]

One way or another (partly through Morgenthau's call for an appointment with Hull), the State Department caught wind of the impending Treasury attack. When Morgenthau arrived at State on Monday morning, Breckinridge Long was with Hull. Morgenthau learned that the State Department had taken a number of sudden actions over the weekend, sending a cable to Ambassador Winant expressing astonishment over the British view and instructing Winant to press the matter with Foreign Minister Eden. It also sent off on Saturday night, and without clearance from Treasury, a cable to Harrison instructing him to issue the license to Riegner and the World Jewish Congress. As Morgenthau told the Treasury group that afternoon, "When I walked in there Monday morning, the decks were clear." Hull blamed "the fellows down the line" for the previous difficulties, which was accurate enough. Breckinridge Long told Morgenthau privately that the same fellows had been making trouble for Meltzer (who by this time had left State for the Navy), who in turn had been accusing Long of anti-Semitism, which Long denied. Morgenthau stated that the Treasury had received the impression that the State Department's view was just about the same as that expressed in the infamous British cable.[35]

What made matters worse for Long was that he had not been able to clear the decks entirely. Morgenthau's staff had by this time uncovered the reference in Harrison's cable of April 20, 1943, to the State Department's telegram no. 354 of February 10, 1943, which had instructed Harrison not to send more messages like Riegner's telegram to Stephen Wise about the death of Jews in Poland and Rumania. Josiah DuBois had secretly obtained copies of both cables from his friend Donald Hiss of the State Department, who had told DuBois: "it had been made clear to him [Hiss] that cable 354 was none of Treasury's business and that in no event should it be shown to Treasury. He added that if it were known that he had shown me [DuBois] this cable he might well lose his job." DuBois had copied the two telegrams by hand in Hiss's office.[36]

At the meeting of December 20, Morgenthau had asked Long for a copy of telegram 354. When he received it and brought it back to the Treasury, however, his staff noticed that the reference to telegram 482 was missing, and, without it, there was no way to tell that State had tried to cut off Riegner's access to Wise. Randolph Paul went back to Long's office and got the original unparaphrased text of telegram 354. He then pointed out the reference to telegram 482 and asked for a copy of telegram 482. It took some time, but he got what he wanted. The Treasury group now wrote a secret memorandum to Morgenthau documenting the State Department's attempt to prevent Riegner from sending information to Wise and to cover up the evidence that it had done so. Morgenthau said later that this was the most shocking instance of dishonesty in his entire career. In Paul's words, it was "one of the cleverest conspiracies of silence and suppression."[37] To make matters worse, the State Department now delegated one of its young new employees, who just happened to be Morgenthau's second cousin, to handle contacts with Treasury on Jewish issues.

Dubois, a Protestant, spent much of Christmas Day drafting a report that Morgenthau could use with Hull and with the president. The final version dated January 13, 1944, which went out under Randolph Paul's signature, was eighteen pages long. DuBois discharged his anger in carefully measured prose. He titled the piece "Report to the Secretary on the Acquiescence of this Government in the Murder of the Jews." He laid the blame directly upon the State Department:

> This Government has for a long time maintained that its policy is to work out programs to save those Jews of Europe who could be saved. I am convinced on the basis of the information which is available to me that certain officials in our State Department, which is charged with carrying out this policy, have been guilty not only of gross procrastination and wilful failure to act, but even of wilful attempts to prevent action from being taken to rescue Jews from Hitler. . . . Unless remedial steps of a drastic nature are taken, and taken immediately, I am certain that no effective action will be taken by this Government to prevent the complete extermination of the Jews in German controlled Europe, and that this Government will have to share for all time responsibility for this extermination.

DuBois charged that the bottleneck in granting visas to Jews was the work of Breckinridge Long. He also revealed in the report the Dunn-Atherton effort to suppress cables from Switzerland to Rabbi Wise about the Final Solution.[38] In a conversation with the secretary of the treasury, DuBois suggested that Morgenthau inform the president that action was imperative. If FDR failed to provide a remedy, DuBois would resign and make the story public.[39]

Morgenthau probably did not pass this specific threat on to the president. According to one of Morgenthau's subordinates, the most important thing in his life was his relationship with FDR. He had deep respect, almost reverence, for his friend and Dutchess County neighbor, who shouldered the burdens of the entire world. Morgenthau had always wished to avoid being known as the "Jewish secretary of the treasury." But the news of the Final Solution that

Stephen Wise had brought him in September 1942 had shaken Morgenthau considerably.[40] A number of times during 1943 Peter Bergson had come to Morgenthau and pointed out measures that the United States government might take to save lives. Bergson had urged Morgenthau to press for the establishment of a top-level presidential committee to advise the government on aspects of the war refugee problem that were not the responsibility of the State Department. Influenced by the official line that only military victory would solve the problem, which his staff shared, Morgenthau held back.[41] But his willingness to give several hearings to Bergson, an activist inclined toward loud public agitation, and a man whom the Jewish establishment detested, indicated that Morgenthau was tempted to become more active. The discovery that he could not trust the integrity of State Department officials provided the final impetus. Morgenthau gave the DuBois-Paul report the less jarring title "Personal Report to the President." But he was no longer prepared to temporize either. The substance of the report remained essentially the same. Morgenthau also proposed to bring to FDR an executive order establishing a War Refugee Board and to warn him of the political danger, if not exactly in the manner suggested by DuBois. The revised report observed that a growing number of people now saw anti-Semitism as the motivation of certain State Department officials and warned that there might soon be a nasty political scandal.[42]

On January 16, 1944, Morgenthau, Pehle, and Paul met with FDR at the White House. FDR preferred to hear a summary of the report, rather than read it through, and Morgenthau and Pehle explained Treasury's findings about the State Department. FDR was disinclined to believe that Breckinridge Long wanted to prevent action to save refugees but admitted that Long had "soured" on refugees, allegedly because some of those admitted turned out to be undesirable. Morgenthau reminded the president that Attorney General Biddle had reported to the cabinet that only three Jews admitted during the war fell into this category. In any case, FDR approved the concept of a War Refugee Board, suggested the secretary of war as a member, and urged Morgenthau to consult with the new undersecretary of state, Edward Stettinius, Sumner Welles's replacement, and with FDR's advisor and speechwriter Samuel Rosenman. The president and Morgenthau then discussed the possibilities of getting Jews into Turkey, Spain, and Switzerland.

When Morgenthau contacted Stettinius, the undersecretary listened to the whole story, criticized Long's work in other areas, and announced that the new reorganization of the department would strip Long of most of his functions. Ironically, Long was left with congressional relations. As FDR had forecast, the sympathetic Stettinius supported the establishment of the new body.[43] Although some Justice Department officials worried that a three-man board might be stacked against Morgenthau, Treasury officials expected Stettinius to serve for Hull, which made a considerable difference.[44] The third board member, the Republican Secretary of War Henry Stimson, was no liberal. Still, the prospects of building an effective organization were reasonably good.

Executive Order 9417, dated January 22, 1944, established the War Refugee Board (WRB), which was instructed to take "all measures within its [U.S.] policy to rescue victims of enemy oppression in imminent danger of death" and to provide "relief and assistance consistent with the successful prosecution of the war." The president instructed State, Treasury, and War to execute the plans, programs, and measures formulated by the board as well as to supply the board with information and assistance. The WRB could also accept the services or contributions of private persons and organizations. That turned out to be an essential provision.

Although the board received an appropriation of one million dollars from the presidential emergency fund, which more than covered salaries in Washington and administrative expenses, Jewish organizations financed most of its operations in Europe. John Pehle was quite conscious of the need to use private financing whenever possible. At one staff meeting, he observed, "The last thing I think you want to do is go to Congress."45 Although the response of some congressmen in 1943 had shifted in favor of action on behalf of Jewish refugees, the overall attitude of the Congress was still negative. And appropriations could be blocked just by a determined minority.

John Pehle was the Treasury group's original candidate for executive director of the new board. Morgenthau's only reservation was whether Pehle was indispensable at Treasury. But there was some pressure for a "big name" director, so John Pehle began serving as acting executive director. At the time he was only thirty-five, a graduate of Creighton University and Yale Law School. Like many bright young lawyers, he had gone to Washington and found a place in the expanding government bureaucracy. Treasury secretary Morgenthau soon made him his special assistant and director of the Foreign Funds Control Division, a formidable task. But the difficulties of his Treasury functions were minimal in comparison to what Pehle now undertook. The War Refugee Board first had to fight through layers of bureaucratic resistance in several government agencies; only then could it go about the actual rescue of Jewish refugees. Pehle quickly demonstrated the necessary energy and motivation. After Frank Graham, president of the University of North Carolina proved unavailable, Pehle won the job. His appointment, Randolph Paul wrote a friend, "gives us reason to hope that the Board isn't going to be another stuffed-shirt ladies' aid society. . . . The Treasury is in this business to the hilt and intends to see that something is done even if people have to be run over."46

WRB officials quickly drafted their first cable to American officials abroad and ran into their first bureaucratic roadblock. The WRB had to notify American personnel abroad that they were expected to help save refugees—this had never been a formal function of their jobs before. State Department officials, including James Dunn, Green Hackworth, and Secretary of State Hull, were not pleased with the forceful tone of the WRB draft and insisted on several modifications. Stettinius went along but asked State Department officials to clear the changes with the WRB. DuBois, in turn, found the deletions and substitutions to be a weakening of the instructions. He particularly questioned the removal of the sentence "the [State] Department is determined to do everything in its power to carry out this Government's policy." Visa Division chief Travers explained that the change put the cable in the usual State Department language; nonetheless, the cable was one of the strongest ever sent out by the department. James Dunn, once the protégé of William Phillips and now perhaps the most influential man in the State Department, exclaimed to another State Department official, "That Jew Morgenthau and his Jewish assistants like DuBois are trying to take over this place."[47] Pehle and DuBois were both Protestants.

The much-disputed cable went out to London at midnight, January 25, announcing that the president had instructed the State, Treasury, and War departments to take action for the immediate rescue and relief of the Jews of Europe and other victims of enemy persecution. It explained the creation of the War Refugee Board and added:

> You should do everything possible to effectuate this policy of this Government, bearing in mind that time is of the essence. . . . You are requested to render an immediate report concerning the actual situation as it exists today in the country to which you are accredited. . . . You should include in your report your recommendations. . . . You are requested to approach the Government to which you are accredited, explain the policy expressed in the President's Executive Order referred to above, and ascertain from such Government the extent to which it is prepared to cooperate.[48]

The American embassy in London then relayed the cable to the affected missions in Europe. The next day the State Department sent a circular airgram to all American missions, alerting them to the change in policy. That raised more than a few eyebrows, particularly in places where the instructions seemed irrelevant. An American diplomat in Saudi Arabia telegrammed, for the amusement of his superiors, the following response:

> There are no Jews in Saudi Arabia, . . . and no Jew will be permitted to enter . . . unless a special reason exists for doing so. . . . In the past two years one Jew is known to have come to Saudi Arabia. He was British, and a salesman of woolen textiles. That he ever came to Arabia is believed to have been due to a misconception of where Jidda is on his part, and to ignorance on the part of the Saudi officials that he was a Jew. . . . In view of the special hostility toward Zionism held in Saudi Arabia, both officially and privately, it is believed inadvisable for this Legation to explain the President's policy to the Saudi Arabian Government. . . .[49]

This may have been humorous—and even true—but it was also a sign that not all members of the Foreign Service would willingly accept War Refugee Board intrusion into foreign policy.

The same general instructions, except for the part regarding diplomatic intercession, went to the War Department to be sent to the appropriate theater commanders, but Assistant Secretary of War John J. McCloy replied that only the Joint Chiefs of Staff and the Combined (American-British) Chiefs of Staff could issue such instructions.[50] Pehle wanted the State Department to ask the British to send the same instructions to their missions, but Stettinius said that he would have to check with Hull first. He had gotten into trouble with Hull over the first cable. Charles P. Taft, brother of Senator Robert Taft and acting head of the President's War Relief Control Board, wrote that Pehle was "starting out like a bull in a china shop."[51]

The State Department picked up signals almost immediately that the British and Canadians were not enthusiastic about the War Refugee Board. They were said to fear that it might impair the functions of the Intergovernmental Committee on Refugees. Since the British had opposed the revival of the IGCR in 1943, this complaint was a transparent cover for other objections, mainly, the effect of rescue operations on Palestinian immigration.[52] On February 5, a British embassy official delivered a Foreign Office telegram, dated January 25, to the State Department. The Foreign Office and the British government generally were disinclined to grant a World Jewish Congress request for a new United Nations declaration against Nazi extermination of Jews. Not only was the original United Nations declaration of December 17, 1942, unsuccessful; it had also caused embarrassment for the Allies and aroused excessive expectations among the Jews. The British suspected World Jewish Congress representatives of seeking another declaration as evidence of diplomatic recognition of separate national status for Jews. Before rejecting the World Jewish Congress request, however, His Majesty's Government wished to obtain U.S. views and, if possible, some assurance of support if a similar request reached Washington during what the British noted was an election year.[53] In other words, the British government was inquiring whether Washington still held to the Bermuda Conference line. If so, the creation of the War Refugee Board was primarily an election maneuver that made little practical difference.[54] If not, then the British wished to raise a number of objections immediately.[55] The War Refugee Board and the State Department reassured the British that Washington had no intention of using combat units of the armed forces to rescue victims of enemy persecution, unless such rescue was a by-product of a military operation. Washington, however, would view with favor a British declaration of policy similar to FDR's and British instructions to their missions similar to the U.S. cable of January 25.[56]

The board quickly abandoned the American-British practice of playing down Nazi persecution of the Jews. Anticipating criticism, the assistant director, Lawrence Lesser, wrote up a justification for special WRB attention to the Jews. Many of the Jews were stateless and lacking even the protection of a government in exile, and only the Jews were marked out for complete extermination. Although the board needed to assist other groups of refugees as well, it could not legitimately avoid devoting particular attention to the Jewish tragedy.[57] Consequently, the board composed a presidential declaration on the Nazi killings of Jews. It pulled no punches.

One of the blackest crimes in history, the systematic murder of the Jews of Europe, continues unabated. . . . More than two million [sic] men, women and children already have been put to death solely because they were Jews. . . . The world will not forget the murder of the Jews. . . . He who takes part in the deportation of Jews to their death in Poland is equally guilty with the executioner. All who share the guilt shall share the punishment. . . . In so far as the necessities of military operations permit, this Government will use all means at its command to aid the escape of the Jews and other intended victims of the Nazi executioner. We call upon all the peoples of Europe to lend assistance to this task. . . . In the name of justice and humanity let all freedom-loving nations rally to this righteous undertaking.[58]

This would have been the bluntest possible response to the British discouragement of any new atrocity declaration.

The WRB draft still had to survive the bureaucratic and political obstacle course that had defeated so many proposals for assistance to Jewish refugees. John J. McCloy asked for a few minor changes to make the declaration a little "less lurid," and Pehle agreed. The text also went to the White House, where the presidential press secretary, Stephen Early, approved it. Then came the biggest test, the State Department. Pehle gave it to Stettinius, who had seen the original version. Knowing that department sentiment would be negative, a Stettinius assistant sent a copy to Secretary of State Hull, who was out of Washington. He simultaneously distributed copies to Green Hackworth, Breckinridge Long, and James Dunn and asked for a prompt reply. Legal advisor Hackworth hinted that the statement was inadvisable; it would offer German propaganda additional evidence that Germans must fight to the end. Long apparently turned the draft over to Borden Reams, who sharply criticized the declaration. After citing the British contention that the declaration of December 17, 1942, had only accelerated Nazi persecution of the Jews, Reams also issued the familiar warning that German propaganda would emphasize that the Allies were fighting the war on behalf of the Jews. He also described one paragraph as hysterical in tone and pointless. Rather than try to kill the declaration outright, Reams suggested that any such statement had to be cleared with the British and the Soviet Union. Undoubtedly aware of the momentum behind the declaration, Dunn did not offer specific comments of his own. He forwarded the others' remarks and advised that the State Department should make no comment whatsoever; the War Refugee Board should be forced to take full responsibility. Meanwhile, however, Hull sent back his approval of the declaration as written. Stettinius could sign off in good conscience.[59]

That was not the end of the matter. The board's various rivals managed to join together for a meeting on March 2, to which they invited Pehle and DuBois. Myron Taylor, American representative on the executive committee of the Intergovernmental Committee on Refugees, complained that the WRB had stepped into its territory and that nothing effective could be done without the cooperation of the British. Charles Taft, acting chairman of the War Relief Control Board, argued that private agencies contributing funds to the War

Refugee Board required the permission of the War Relief Control Board. His organization was taking the issue of overlapping jurisdiction to the president. Robert Pell, representing the State Department, challenged the wisdom of the board's plans for a propaganda offensive against Germany and the satellite countries. Pell claimed that the Nazis would simply kill the Jews all the quicker if the U.S. publicly denounced Nazi measures. Pehle and DuBois strongly disagreed. Assistant Secretary of State Berle suggested that both sides had a case; more consideration of the issue was needed. After a discussion of other subjects, including the IGCR's previous failures, the meeting concluded with an understanding that the board and the State Department would meet and try to agree on the issue of public condemnation of Nazi atrocities.[60]

Pehle was apparently alarmed, and he alerted Morgenthau to the danger. Morgenthau quickly called Stettinius. We found no record of Morgenthau's comments, but the secretary of the treasury was apparently in no mood to be diplomatic. When Myron Taylor learned of Morgenthau's intervention, he thought it best to explain his role to FDR, who he expected would also hear from Morgenthau. Taylor wrote a personal memorandum to the president, explaining that his objective was to coordinate activities, not to oppose any helpful action. He also suggested that Pehle go to London to clear up uncertainties with the British Foreign Office and the IGCR.[61] That would have slowed Pehle down considerably. Morgenthau's political weight, however, sustained the declaration on atrocities.

Morgenthau signed the proposed presidential declaration on Sunday, March 5, and Stettinius brought it to Stephen Early at the White House the next day. Although not opposed to the declaration, Stettinius was mindful of lower-level objections. He wrote a postscript on the cover letter to Early: "We in the State Department feel that in issuing this statement the President is taking a very important step and we hope he will have an opportunity to study it with great care."[62] That warning guaranteed that the declaration would not go through routinely.

On March 7, in the midst of a discussion with FDR on Palestine, Morgenthau commented that Pehle and "his boys" had done a fine job and inquired about the declaration. FDR responded that it had not yet reached him. Morgenthau repeated three times that FDR should ask Early for the declaration.[63] The next day a State Department policy committee debated the elements of the War Refugee Board program and questioned the wisdom of a presidential statement not cleared with the British. Some of the specific objections by now had reached FDR, for he told Stettinius on March 8 that the declaration referred to the atrocities against the Jews in too pointed a manner. He wished to avoid the term declaration; he customarily issued "statements." He also wanted to clear this step with the British. Stettinius and presidential confidant Samuel Rosenman were assigned to rewrite the draft. Stettinius told Pehle the next day that he was uncertain whether any statement would be issued. Pehle was left with the feeling that nothing more could be done right now.[64]

But he did not give up. On March 10, he emphasized to Morgenthau that the board needed a presidential statement as a base for a campaign of psychological warfare against the Germans by the Office of War Information. Pehle could live with the changes suggested by Stettinius and Rosenman. The secretary of the treasury called the White House on March 22 to say that the time was particularly appropriate for such a public statement; Germany had just sent troops into Hungary, where nearly one million Jews were now imperiled. Morgenthau also recommended that FDR name Pehle as permanent director of the WRB. Both Hull and Stimson had already approved. FDR now authorized the move. Thus, the president finally came to issue a statement at his press conference on March 24, denouncing systematic torture and murder of civilians by the Nazis and Japanese. The "wholesale systematic murder of the Jews of Europe" was relegated to the fourth paragraph, but it still retained the description of "one of the blackest crimes of all history." And the new draft retained the warning that those who took part in the deportations would share the punishment.[65]

The OWI branch in London decided that it was necessary to offer special guidance to OWI editors and broadcasters on the president's statement: "In regard to the President's special reference . . . to persecution of the Jews, do not give the impression that his denunciation was limited to this subject alone or that it was especially aimed at."[66] Such underplaying of Nazi killings of Jews made it less likely that the threats of punishment would be effective.

To convince Europeans that the United States meant what it said, the War Refugee Board felt that it was essential to set the proper example, in spite of the fact that shipping remained a problem, in spite of the absence of an American diplomatic presence in Germany and in the satellite countries, and in spite of the cumbersome visa review procedure in Washington. DuBois argued:

> The enemy must not be given the pretense of justification that the Allies, while speaking in horrified terms of the Nazi treatment of the Jews, never once offered to receive these people if the Germans released them. The moral aspect of the problem is pre-eminent. . . . The willingness of the United Nations to receive these people could be brought home with such force to every German and to every man in German controlled territory that the Nazis, even if reluctant to desist from their massacres, may feel a pressure difficult to resist.

Dismissing the likelihood of prompt British action, DuBois forcefully proposed that the United States establish temporary havens of refuge in this country for all potential Nazi victims who could escape. In effect, they would be interned in camps and treated as prisoners of war. Prisoners of war did not require immigration or visitors' visas, and refugees certainly represented far less of a security risk than the hundreds of thousands of German and Italian prisoners already in the U.S.[67] It was impossible to remove Jews from German territory to the United States (except by negotiated exchange of prisoners). Still, the evacuation of refugees from neutral countries such as Turkey, Switzerland, Spain, and Portugal, as well from Allied-controlled territory in Italy, would clear the way for other escapees from the Nazi empire. If the U.S. did not undertake some kind of evacuation, the neutrals, already clogged with refugees, might turn back new ones, as had already occurred in Turkey and Switzerland. American and British military authorities also were finding it a burden to cope with the flow of refugees into newly reconquered areas.

New York Post columnist Samuel Grafton labelled the plan "free ports" for refugees,[68] which helped it to obtain some public support, since Americans were already familiar with the concept of free ports for merchandise. On March 9, 1944, Pehle raised the idea of free ports with Secretary of War Henry Stimson. As an internationalist, supporter of a strong military, and interventionist in World War II, the Republican Stimson had basically agreed with FDR's own foreign policy instincts. Stimson's appointment as secretary of war in 1940 had helped broaden FDR's political base as well as public support for aid to Great Britain. Stimson, however, lacked sympathy for many aspects of the New Deal. The product of Andover, Yale, Harvard Law School, and Theodore Roosevelt's progressivism, Stimson had little appreciation for the ethnic and labor coalition which Teddy's cousin had fashioned.[69] He and Pehle, as he wrote in his diary, had "quite a long talk." Stimson warned that Congress and some segments of the public would oppose the proposal out of fear that the Jews would remain in this country after the war. Stimson reviewed the history of the "Jewish problem" in the United States and the reasons for "the growing opposition to unrestricted immigration of Jews," which (he said) had resulted in the post-World War I quota system. In effect, Stimson said that European Jews did not assimilate well in the United States, which caused their unpopularity. But he could not dissuade Pehle from bringing the proposal to the next meeting of the War Refugee Board (Morgenthau, Stimson, Hull). There Stimson again pointed out the dangers and expressed his support for the quota system. Hull apparently supported the proposal but suggested that FDR would have to resolve the issue. Stimson agreed.[70]

Pehle wrote up the WRB staff's position and informed Stimson that this was the most important step the United States could now take to assist refugees. Stimson based his rebuttal on the 1920s quota laws.

> Our people then showed that they strongly feared that an uncontrolled immigration from such countries would modify the proportion of the racial stocks already existing in our own population and would introduce into the United States many people who would with difficulty be assimilated into our own population and brought into conformity with our own institutions and traditions.
>
> I fear that your proposal would meet with a similar reaction from our people today who would feel that it was merely the beginning of permanent immigration. This would be accentuated if it was carried through by Executive authority alone and without the assent of Congress. . . . The mere introduction of these people today on such a scale and for humanitarian purposes alone would be contrary to American law. In this connection I am not at all clear that the war power of the

President would be held to cover a transaction like this which has no direct connection with the prosecution of the war.

Although suggesting that Pehle might still take the proposal to Congress, Stimson clearly hoped to kill the idea.[71]

The lobbying continued through April. Clarence Pickett of the American Friends Service Committee and presidential statistician and advisor Isador Lubin were enlisted to convince FDR to go ahead. Stimson apparently worked on Hull to kill the plan. On May 8, Hull told Stimson that it would be unwise to go ahead without congressional approval.[72]

Three days later Pehle met with the president and conveyed the divergent views of the three board members. FDR did not like the term "free port" because it did not indicate clearly that the refugees would return home at the end of the war. He wished to use army camps somewhere on the Eastern Seaboard. But, despite the favorable publicity, FDR was reluctant to approve the admission of large numbers of refugees without congressional approval. He suggested that he might in an emergency situation allow one thousand to enter and send a message to Congress, explaining what he had done and why. Pehle took what he could get. He told the president that the number of refugees pouring into Allied-controlled territory in southern Italy from Yugoslavia was becoming a burden to the military and, thus, a barrier to the escape of additional refugees. FDR agreed that it would be unwise for the military to cut off or discourage the flow of refugees, a move that the Joint Chiefs of Staff had proposed as early as December 1943. The president concluded that the U.S. should move some of the refugees in southern Italy elsewhere.[73]

The cabinet discussed the plan on May 26 and gave the go-ahead. In late May, FDR mentioned the plan in a press conference. On June 8, the president directed Ambassador Robert Murphy in Algiers to make the arrangements to bring approximately one thousand refugees in southern Italy to Fort Ontario, an unused army camp near Oswego, New York. Four days later FDR sent a formal message to Congress that included a direct reference to the Final Solution:

> As the hour of the final defeat of the Hitlerite forces draws closer, the fury of their insane desire to wipe out the Jewish race in Europe continues undiminished. This is but one example: many Christian groups also are being murdered. Knowing that they have lost the war, the Nazis are determined to complete their program of mass extermination.

The president praised the work of the War Refugee Board, explained the Oswego arrangements, and pledged that the refugees, predominantly women and children, would return home to their native countries at the end of the war.[74]

Congressional opposition to relaxation of immigration barriers had diminished slightly but certainly had not disappeared. Senator Robert Reynolds of

North Carolina, longtime spokesman for the extreme restrictionists, wrote the attorney general to ask under what authority the president acted to admit the one thousand refugees. The attorney general pointed out that, even under the immigration laws, the secretary of state and the attorney general had the power to waive documentary requirements and grounds of inadmissibility in an emergency. Nonetheless, the president preferred to regard the refugees as a group interned in the U.S., like Axis POWs and nationals. The immigration laws simply did not apply.[75]

In the end, the Displaced Persons Subcommittee of the Allied Control Commission selected 983 persons to proceed to Oswego: 369 Yugoslavs, 237 Austrians, 146 Poles, 96 Germans, and 41 Czechs. Some 918 were Jewish. Many had relatives already living in the United States. They arrived in Oswego in August 1944.[76] This "free port" provided evidence to other countries that the United States had some interest in the welfare of refugees, but it hardly made a dent in the problem.

The board had better success in persuading the State Department to change its visa policy, although it took a tragedy and some unorthodox methods to bring about the shift. German officials had never deported all Jews indiscriminately to the gas chambers. The Nazi government had separated out those Jews who were citizens of countries not under Nazi control, and in some cases even noncitizens who had visas to foreign countries, and had kept them in concentration camps, pending some decision on how to dispose of them. They were considered of diplomatic value.[77]

There were a substantial number of Jews in German hands, however, with documents whose validity was in question. Some Latin American diplomats in Europe had issued visas rather freely during various stages of the war, either for humanitarian reasons or for financial gain. If the Germans concluded that these papers were inauthentic, these Jews would be deported to the death camps in the east.

The Germans had captured in France one group of Polish Jews, including many rabbis, with Latin American passports. They were held in Camp Vittel, near Paris. In February 1944 the War Refugee Board discovered that the Germans were questioning these documents, partly because the Swiss government was prosecuting those who had a role in issuing and distributing them. The board immediately sent a cable to the State Department for transmission to Minister Harrison in Bern. The WRB wanted Harrison to ask the Swiss government not to prosecute those connected with the issuance of the passports and, instead, to persuade the Germans to recognize their validity. The European Division and the Passport Division of the State Department held up the cable, insisting on letting Harrison and the Swiss know that the U.S. did not condone the use of false passports. Although the War Refugee Board tried to redraft the cable to meet State Department objections, State Department officials still balked. The standoff continued through March.[78]

Rabbi Baruch Korff called Henry Morgenthau on a Friday afternoon in late

March or early April to alert him to the situation. Accompanied by a number of other rabbis, Korff came into Morgenthau's office, where DuBois was also present, and told the story. Morgenthau was so shaken that he had to walk out of the room to regain his composure. DuBois had an idea. He called columnist Drew Pearson and invited him to lunch the next day. DuBois told the scoop-hungry Pearson all about the Polish Latin Americans and the State Department. On his Sunday night radio program, Pearson lambasted those State Department officials responsible. The next morning at 9 A.M., Secretary of State Hull called the board to say that the department was transmitting the cable to Bern. The State Department policy committee concurred on April 7. But it was too late for this particular group of Polish Jews. The Germans had transferred them to their transit camp at Drancy. Their next stop was Auschwitz. Subsequent Swiss intervention brought the German response that none of the 239 persons had proof of foreign nationality; therefore, Germany considered this an internal matter.[79]

The tragedy had one favorable repercussion. The War Refugee Board had not only brought the State Department's bureaucratic warfare to the attention of upper-level officials in State; it had also shown that State might well receive a black eye if it continued. That made a considerable difference to officials such as Stettinius and Assistant Secretary of State Berle, who now supervised the Visa Division.

The State Department now sent out board cables to Latin American countries, urging them not to cancel documents issued previously by their diplomats. It also asked the Swiss government to notify the Germans that the Latin American countries would consider exchanging the internees for German citizens held in the western hemisphere. The U.S. reassured the Latin countries that they would not actually have to admit these persons; a refuge would be found elsewhere. On May 11, 1944, after the Swiss government had made representations on behalf of those with Latin American documents, the Nazis agreed to cease deporting Jews with Latin American passports or visas. The Swiss also followed American instructions to intercede on behalf of any internee who claimed United States citizenship.[80]

Pehle even convinced Berle to ask a representative of the Dominican Republic if his government would issue protective letters (that would be distributed through clandestine channels) for "new" applicants for passports. The Dominicans, however, agreed to go along only if the United States and other American republics adopted it as a joint policy, which did not occur. In any case, it is doubtful whether the German government would have recognized the new applications and papers. The German Foreign Office, the department most directly concerned with Germany's diplomatic relations, had limited influence over the Reich Main Security Office (RSHA), which carried out the Final Solution. Nonetheless, the idea of distributing protective papers to Jews soon proved very effective in special circumstances in Hungary.[81]

Pehle persuaded the Visa Division and Berle to go along with another Swiss gambit. This time the Swiss government would pass along American concern for anyone who had received an American visa after July 1, 1941, but who had been unable to use it. Even though these visas had expired, the United States indicated that the holders would likely receive new visas once they could present themselves to appropriate American consuls.[82] In 1938 Assistant Secretary of State George Messersmith had instructed Consul General Raymond Geist not to issue any letters to German applicants for American visas, indicating that they would probably receive their quota numbers soon.[83] Now, largely because of the pressure of the War Refugee Board, Berle agreed to something very similar to what Geist had done. The presence of a government agency assigned the specific function of promoting humanitarian rescue efforts in Europe made a great deal of difference in Washington, since the State Department had never taken that goal seriously.

In spite of the demotion of Breckinridge Long and the advent of the generally sympathetic Edward Stettinius as undersecretary, the State Department continued to oppose American rescue and relief efforts on behalf of European Jews. And the State Department was not the only opponent of the War Refugee Board. Two examples from later in 1944 show reluctance of other high officials to follow the board's initiatives on behalf of Jewish refugees. On September 28, Pehle asked John J. McCloy if General Eisenhower would be willing to issue a statement warning Germans not to exterminate persons held in forced-labor battalions and in concentration camps. Pehle and Joseph Proskauer of the American Jewish Committee agreed that an Eisenhower statement would be even better than a presidential statement, because the former would not be discounted as a political gesture and because Eisenhower was expected to be in charge of American-occupied Germany.[84] President Roosevelt approved the War Refugee Board draft, which warned Germans not to harm citizens of the United Nations and stateless persons "whether they are Jewish or otherwise." Eisenhower asked for a change in the proclamation to "without regard to their nationality or religious faith." He also wanted the Combined Chiefs of Staff to direct him to issue the statement. All of this took time. Eisenhower released the amended statement on October 30.[85] Omission of specific mention of Jews came at a time when the Nazi leaders were trying to complete the Final Solution before military defeat halted their murderous activity.

The second example concerned the Office of War Information, whose previous policy had been to shy away from atrocity stories in its broadcasts overseas. In November 1944 the War Refugee Board received through the diplomatic pouch from Switzerland a detailed description of the gas-chamber operation in Auschwitz-Birkenau, written by two Slovakian Jews, Rudolf Vrba and Alfred Wetzlar, who had escaped from the camp after two years as prisoners there. Pehle and the WRB staff decided to issue the document to the press, along with a statement vouching for its authenticity. The board was not aware that, in 1942, OWI director Elmer Davis had issued an order that all news releases relating to the war effort must have OWI approval. When he learned of the Auschwitz document, Davis summoned Pehle to his office.

Pehle explained that War Refugee Board representative Roswell McClelland in Switzerland, a veteran observer of the Nazi regime, vouched for the authenticity of the document. Davis's staff all thought the release was a mistake, that the reaction overseas would be bad, that the timing was bad, that certain items seemed planted, etc. Davis also complained that the release should not have been sent all over the country, only to the Washington bureaus. Davis conceded, however, that the head of his Polish desk had read the document carefully and had stated that the events described might well have occurred. Nonetheless, he severely criticized the board for issuing the story without clearance from OWI, the State Department, the War Department, and other interested agencies, and he insisted on WRB compliance thereafter. Davis asked for a WRB supplementary statement, including a caveat that the validity of the document rested with the credibility of the men who wrote it. The board declined to issue it. But the War Department also warned Pehle to be very careful with such horrifying reports.[86] This concern was partly for accuracy and partly for public reaction. Even after the release of the board's story, the American public still had little sense of just how dreadful the slaughter was. Only 19 percent of a national sample thought that the Nazis had murdered 500,000 people or more, while 27 percent thought that the total was 100,00 or less.[87]

Despite the various problems, the director and staff of the board learned how to deal with bureaucratic infighting. Morgenthau's close relationship with the president and the power of the press were key assets that they did not hesitate to make use of. During 1944 the War Refugee Board provided concrete evidence that the United States was not indifferent to the Final Solution. Those countries and officials who wished to gain favor with the United States, which was expected to be the dominant force in the peace settlement, learned to pay attention to life-saving measures on behalf of European Jews. The War Refugee Board's representatives abroad indicated just which projects were likely to be feasible and effective. Even though not all its plans found the necessary backing in Washington, the activities of the board in 1944 and 1945 would save many thousands of lives.

TEN

The War Refugee Board in Europe

Neither the War Refugee Board nor any other power could bring a halt to the gassings at the extermination camps through any combination of threats and offers to negotiate with Germany on the release of Jews.[1] Throughout much of 1944 the Auschwitz death factory continued to operate at full speed, in spite of the fact that the German armies were now giving ground instead of taking it. Only very late in the war did the combination of Allied warnings about the murder of civilians and the undeniable impact of impending military defeat make some Nazi leaders (e.g., Himmler) reconsider the Final Solution. And as his last will and testament demonstrated, Hitler never wavered on the necessity of his anti-Jewish policies.[2]

The board, however, made a major impact upon Axis satellites and upon neutral nations in Europe. The governments of Rumania, Bulgaria, and Hungary adjusted their behavior to the likely outcome of the war earlier than the Nazi ideologues in Germany, and American expressions of concern for the fate of European Jewry resonated into eastern Europe. Neutral nations such as Spain, Turkey, and Switzerland showed greater willingness to provide temporary accommodations or transit rights to Jews fleeing from Nazi murderers once the Allies stressed the importance of rescue policies and provided financial assistance.

The War Refugee Board nonetheless faced more problems than opportunities. It was difficult enough to work out plans to rescue thousands from the hands of the Nazis or Fascist collaborators in western and eastern Europe. If one had to fight local battles over policy or jurisdiction first, the task became almost impossible. The loss of time alone was tantamount to defeat. The extent to which the board succeeded depended in part upon its ability to elicit the cooperation of others. As representatives of a new and small organization with ill-defined authority, WRB officials had to lean heavily on American diplomatic missions, the military, neutral governments and emissaries, and international organizations.

Bureaucratic resistance within the American government to humanitarian missions continued to limit the effectiveness of American measures against the Final Solution during 1944 and 1945. Space precludes an analysis of the activities and difficulties of all of the WRB representatives in Europe.[3] But three case studies—Spain, Hungary, and Switzerland—illustrate the problems that WRB officials encountered and the results that they were able to obtain.

SPAIN

Spain was largely a case of missed opportunity, partly the result of the delicate diplomatic situation there. Spain had not joined the Axis powers, because Generalissimo Francisco Franco wanted time for his civil war-torn land to recover and because he did not wish to stake the fate of his regime on the outcome of the war. Nonetheless, Franco had reason to be grateful to Germany and Italy, which had backed him and supplied arms and troops to him during the Spanish civil war. He resisted Hitler's overtures for a formal alliance but allowed seventeen thousand volunteers to fight with Germany on the Russian front. At the same time he refrained from actions that would have irrevocably alienated Britain and the United States.

The Spanish government had not been friendly to refugees who, from the summer of 1940 on, straggled through the Pyrenees mountains from France, but it had given transit visas to those who qualified, including Jews. In the summer of 1942, however, the Vichy government in France required everyone leaving the country to obtain an exit visa, a regulation Spain recognized. Jews could not obtain visas, since the Nazis had other plans for them. Nonetheless, French Jews, as well as others from eastern and central Europe who had found refuge in France until the German conquest, continued to enter Spain illegally.

The fate of those refugees apprehended depended first on local authorities. Those who had influential contacts or who were in a position to offer bribes sometimes made it through to Portugal, and from there they could apply for American visas and hope for transportation. Most, however, were neither freed nor turned back to the Nazis, who occupied the rest of France in November 1942. Instead, Spain imprisoned them in a special camp for political prisoners at Miranda del Ebro, near Burgos. After Miranda overflowed with refugees, authorities used regular prisons as well. The greater the number of refugees became, the greater the burden of supporting them, and the greater the temptation for the Spanish to give in to Nazi pressure, seal the border tightly, and hand back anyone who came through illegally. High officials in the Falangist party, sympathetic to Germany, advocated this course for political reasons anyway.[4]

For a time the United States had taken an interest in all of the refugees. The wife of the American ambassador, Virginia Chase Weddell, had agreed to represent several relief agencies in Spain, which were supplementing the minimal food and clothing supplies that the Spaniards gave to refugees. This was particularly fortunate for the American Jewish Joint Distribution Committee, which was not authorized to operate in the country. Through Virginia Weddell, however, the AJJDC spent one hundred eighty-three thousand dollars in 1941 and the first quarter of 1942 to support the substantial number of Jewish refugees in the country.[5] By that time a Portuguese Jew named Samuel Sequerra had arrived in Barcelona, where he unofficially represented the AJJDC.

The period of active American assistance to Jewish refugees ended with the appointment of Carlton J. H. Hayes as ambassador to Spain in April 1942. On the surface, Hayes looked to be a fortunate choice for the AJJDC and the Jewish refugees. A distinguished professor of history at Columbia, Hayes was Catholic, politically liberal, and a former cochairman of the National Conference of Christians and Jews. He also read Spanish and was familiar with Spanish history and traditions.[6]

Before Hayes left for Spain, the president and Sumner Welles made him aware of the importance of his mission—to keep Spain neutral and out of the war, thereby allowing the Allies to hold Gibraltar and to operate in the western Mediterranean. In his memoirs Hayes credits Welles, James Dunn, Ray Atherton, Herbert Feis, Charles Thomson, and particularly W. Perry George for giving him guidance before he left for Spain. George, in charge of the Spanish desk of the State Department, provided "inside" information not obtainable from written documents.[7] One of the key pieces of inside information was that the department had ordered the American embassy to cut itself off from relief work because of criticism by the Falangists. In fact, department officials told Hayes that Virginia Weddell's activities and the resulting Spanish criticism were the chief reasons for Ambassador Weddell's recall. Hayes told Clarence Pickett of the American Friends Service Committee that, "if he was to be effective in putting into operation the new policy . . . which is designed primarily to carry through a successful execution of the war, he could be a party to no relief operations of any kind."[8]

After the Allied landing in North Africa, however, Hayes discovered that there were advantages to the flow of refugees into Spain. Allied pilots shot down over enemy territory, Poles of military age, and members of the French resistance all wished to join the Allied forces and reenter the fray. Hayes pointed out to the State Department and the president that the United States could not very well ignore thousands of French refugees who would be useful in North Africa at a time when it sought to win the cooperation of the French people. This was, in Hayes's words, "much more than a simple matter of humanitarian relief."[9]

The altered balance of power in the area and the appointment of Count Francisco Gomez Jordana y Sousa as Spanish foreign minister made Spain more receptive to refugees (and to the United States). Despite the increasing number of refugees coming into the country, Spain decided not to turn them back. It imprisoned men of an age for military service in Miranda until it could determine their status. Officers on active service were held on a military base. Others were released if they could support themselves or if someone offered to care for them. The American embassy assumed responsibility for supporting (and later transporting) American and French nationals; the British took care of those from the Commonwealth nations and certain other Allied nations. That left really only the stateless—primarily Jews. In January 1943, two American

Quakers, David Blickenstaff and his wife, were admitted to operate on behalf of the American Friends Service Committee, the Unitarian Service Committee, and the American Jewish Joint Distribution Committee after Hayes made an express request to the Spanish government.[10]

In March 1943 German pressure induced Spain to close its border to refugees without legal transit papers and to reinforce its border patrols. The British and American governments immediately protested, warning that this move would destroy good relations. Spain did a quick about-face. Spanish Foreign Minister Jordana notified Hayes that Spain would allow all refugees who reached Spain to stay temporarily, until they could make arrangements to proceed to their final destination. Spain did not want long-term guests. According to the Spanish chief of the European section of the Ministry of Foreign Affairs, refugees who were released and who did not leave Spain within three months would either be expelled or imprisoned.[11]

The possible destinations for the stateless (those deprived of citizenship by their native countries) were limited. Officials of the Jewish Agency for Palestine were able to give immigration permits into Palestine to fewer than one thousand refugees in Spain during 1943 and 1944.[12] As we have seen,[13] at the Bermuda Conference the British had suggested a refugee camp in North Africa under American control, but more than a year transpired before any sizeable number of refugees were brought from Spain to North Africa. The best possibility for resettlement was in the United States, for, as the American consul general in Barcelona noted, nearly all of the Jews had friends or relatives in the U.S. and wished to proceed there. In September 1943, Hayes estimated that 80 percent of the stateless were Jews.[14]

Because of German sensitivities, Spain would not permit any of the refugees to depart directly from its ports. They had to go to Portugal first. The process of acquiring an American visa, a Portuguese transit visa, and transportation across the Atlantic was long, time-consuming, and highly uncertain. Officials in the American embassy in Madrid, meanwhile, did not feel that the U.S. should have to take all of the stateless refugees. At least one official resented the AJJDC's knowledge of visa rules and regulations and its skill at putting pressure on the State Department, and thereby on American consuls, to issue visas. He accused the AJJDC of trying to get as many Jews to the U.S. as possible, failing to discriminate between worthy and unworthy cases, and not considering the welfare of the U.S. at all.[15]

Some of these attitudes, no doubt, rubbed off on Ambassador Hayes, who refused to raise with Spanish authorities repeated AJJDC requests to send an American to Barcelona to run the Joint's office there. Hayes thought that the Blickenstaffs in Madrid already represented the AJJDC adequately.[16] More of the agency's officials in Barcelona would probably mean more visa applications to the United States. Hayes did raise with Foreign Minister Jordana the need to evacuate refugees directly from Spanish ports rather than from Portugal, but Jordana pointed to German protests. The refugees had become a headache for

Hayes, Jordana, and both governments. Hayes placated Jordana, stating that British and American radio broadcasts had urged all potential refugees to stay in France, where they were more useful to the Allies than in North Africa. Only a small percentage of them were of military age, and, by the time they were trained and equipped, they would be "of slight use" to the United Nations. Jordana agreed to raise the use of Spanish ports with Generalissimo Franco once again. This time he succeeded, and by November the Allies had plans to evacuate fifteen hundred persons every ten days from Malaga. That would have removed an estimated twenty-five thousand refugees from Spain in short order.[17]

Just when Hayes had succeeded in reducing the scope of the refugee problem, the War Refugee Board came into existence. In its first cable to Madrid, the WRB asked Hayes to explain the new American policy on refugees to the Spanish government and ascertain the extent to which Spain would cooperate.[18] Hayes was caught by surprise. He also found the timing inopportune, since he was in the midst of a Washington-ordered campaign to induce Spain to embargo all shipments of wolfram (the ore from which tungsten is made) to Germany. Hayes had had a number of "painful" conversations with Foreign Minister Jordana regarding Washington's demands for the embargo, which Hayes himself found unreasonable. (The wolfram crisis was not resolved until the end of April and then with a compromise.)[19] Hayes replied to the War Refugee Board that he did not consider it opportune to approach the Spanish government as suggested. He also suggested that David Blickenstaff could handle whatever refugee problems came up; there was no need for the Intergovernmental Committee on Refugees to open a separate office in Spain.[20] Hayes mistook the War Refugee board for the long-dormant IGCR.

Hayes's response went to WRB officials who were already angry at the State Department's lack of cooperation. They apparently prepared a blistering cable, which, however, James Dunn of the State Department refused to send. At a conference chaired by Undersecretary of State Stettinius, Dunn made the case against the cable. He claimed that Spain would not be sympathetic to refugee proposals and that raising the issue might disrupt the wolfram negotiations. He also pointed out the limited size of the refugee camps in North Africa. He added that interested people in his division might have additional objections. Dunn offered the suggestion that the WRB send out the cable on its own responsibility; that way the State Department would not have to clear it. But Pehle objected that ministers and ambassadors paid a lot more attention to a State Department cable than to one from another agency.[21]

The board managed to gain clearance for a modified version of its cable, asking Hayes to request that Spain relax its border controls, openly welcome refugees through a public statement, and establish reception camps. The board pledged to take care of the financing and the transfer of refugees to North Africa. But, based on his previous discussions with Spanish officials, Hayes sensed trouble. Again he declined to take the steps suggested by the board. He also suggested that Spain would need reassurance about the ultimate destination of these refugees before it would admit them. The American camps in North Africa were limited in size. (The WRB could only inform Hayes that negotiations for other havens were in progress and that he could assure Spain that all refugees would be removed.) Knowing that the agency lacked the full support of the State Department, Hayes continued to battle the board on a number of other proposals, such as a WRB request that Spain establish refugee reception camps inside its border, where American personnel could screen and care for refugees and debrief them. The board also complained that Hayes had not played up the president's denunciation of Nazi atrocities on March 24.[22] The fact that Hayes received careful briefings from the State Department, and that State Department officials blocked the War Refugee Board from giving Hayes instructions for a humanitarian policy, helps explain what David Wyman termed the "riddle" of Hayes's behavior.[23]

The WRB decided to finance rescue activities of refugee children in France, hiring guides to conduct them through the Pyrenees to Spain. Hayes expressed early opposition to the idea on the grounds that it might impede the rescue of Allied military personnel. The board refused to halt its plans because of a mere hypothetical possibility. But the War Department backed Hayes up, pointing out to Pehle the undesirability of refugee operations if they interfered in any way with existing facilities for rescuing Allied airmen. The State Department, meanwhile, agreed to authorize the issuance of 1,000 visas for children reaching Spain and Portugal during the first six months of 1944.[24]

Under the circumstances, the board needed someone in Spain who had detailed knowledge of the circumstances there. After an early attempt to send James G. McDonald of the PACPR to Spain fell through, the WRB sent a young former Foreign Service officer named James Mann. In Madrid, Mann quickly learned from Covey Oliver, special assistant to the ambassador for economic warfare, that Hayes and the embassy considered the War Refugee Board an "unrealistic organization." Hayes had also become reluctant to allow independent (American) agencies to operate in Spain because of previous unfortunate experiences with the Office of Strategic Services, the Office of War Information, and the Foreign Economic Administration. Oliver also identified Willard Beaulac, former counselor of the embassy (who had just been named ambassador to Paraguay), as an anti-Semite.

Mann heard a more favorable report on Niles Bond, the junior embassy official who handled refugee matters. But Bond pointed out to Mann that WRB cables and State Department cables sometimes were in direct contradiction. On May 26 the board had cabled the embassy to urge Spain to increase its representation in Hungary—neutral Spanish representatives might be able to perform services for the many Jews threatened there. But the State Department had recently discouraged relations between Spain and the Hungarian puppet regime. Mann could only say that State cleared the WRB cables and that State did not keep the WRB informed of its political cables.[25]

Bond did not have a high opinion of the AJJDC's Sequerra in Barcelona and pointed to evidence that civilian refugee traffic had interfered with the escape of pilots. Hayes also told Mann that WRB policies were inconsistent with what the U.S. was attempting to do in Spain—stop shipments of wolfram and keep German agents out. Hayes, like Bond, wanted to revoke Sequerra's license to distribute American funds. Mann consulted with American intelligence and security officers, who also stressed the danger of German agents coming in with refugees and of interference with more important traffic:

> They automatically took the position that any other traffic across the border other than on the part of their intelligence couriers jeopardized the chances of their agents passing back and forth. The security officers were not particularly concerned by the fact that the Board was attempting to save the lives of innocent people. They seemed to feel that refugees were expendable.

Mann heard a different story from an American official in the consulate general in Barcelona who was in charge of refugee matters and who had seen the rescue operation close up. This man named Forsythe praised the AJJDC's Sequerra and stated that there were no recent problems of civilian refugees interfering with the escape of military personnel. (There was now a surplus of guides and a dearth of German patrols on the French side of the border. Convoys through the Pyrenees were generally kept segregated—civilians separate from military men.) Forsythe reported the same finding to the embassy. He was, Mann wrote, the only American Foreign Service officer in Spain with a real understanding of the problem and a willingness to do something about it. Upon his return to Madrid, Mann conferred again with Hayes, who remained opposed to any War Refugee Board appointee being sent to Spain.[26]

The WRB had, however, taken steps to get its message to the Spanish government through another channel. Pehle must have complained about Hayes to Morgenthau in March, for the treasury secretary talked to FDR then about the need to send someone to Spain on the refugee problem. Morgenthau originally suggested FDR's legislative specialist Tommy Corcoran, but Morgenthau or FDR eventually found a more efficient solution. Daniel Heinemann, a prominent businessman with international investments and excellent government contacts, happened to be going to Spain on his own account. Heinemann was friendly with both Morgenthau and Roosevelt and held numerous conversations with the War Refugee Board staff, particularly Lawrence Lesser, before he left. With the knowledge of the State Department, he tried to get the War Refugee Board's message to Franco. On the trip to Lisbon, he consulted his fellow passenger James Mann about the line he should take with the Spanish government. Heinemann then took up the refugee problem with a close contact, the Marquis de Foronda, who was very close to Foreign Minister Jordana. Heinemann urged the Spanish government to take the initiative in saving refugees. Jordana supposedly took the matter up with Franco personally.

Heinemann was then informed that the Spanish government would cooperate but preferred not to take the initiative; it wished instead to accede to a formal request from the American ambassador. Hayes finally called on Jordana and for the first time mentioned the WRB and its program.[27] It was better late than never.

Responding to a request from the American embassy, Spanish representatives provided life-saving Spanish passports and letters of patronage to more than 2,000 Jews in Hungary during the fall of 1944.[28] But the need for a refugee escape route from France diminished sharply after D-Day (June 6, 1944) and the progress of the Allied armies through France. In that sphere, Hayes's opposition had cost the War Refugee Board and the refugees a great deal of time. By the time the Spanish government became convinced that the United States was seriously interested in saving stateless refugees, there was very little need for rescue through Spain.

HUNGARY

Spain was the best example of how little the War Refugee Board could accomplish when it lacked the support of other American agencies and Foreign Service officials. In the case of Hungary the War Refugee Board was more successful—even though there were no American officials in this Nazi satellite. In Hungary the board had the advantage of working in conjunction with a number of representatives of other governments—particularly Sweden and Switzerland—who devoted themselves to the task of saving lives now that the end of the war was approaching. Had it not been for the German occupation of Hungary during 1944, the combined efforts of the War Refugee Board and various neutral nations probably would have saved the lives of most of the more than 800,000 Jews there—the largest concentration of Jews left in Europe.

During much of the war, Hungary was an oasis, at least in relative terms, for European Jews. Hungary's anti-Semitic legislation stretched back to the immediate post-World War I period. But, despite German pressure on the Hungarian government presided over by Admiral Horthy, the regent (and the last commander of the Hapsburg navy), Hungarian killing and deportation of Jews occurred only sporadically until 1944. Horthy distinguished sharply between foreign Jews, whom he detested, and loyal, assimilated Hungarian Jews. Many thousands of Jews from nearby Slovakia, Poland, and even Rumania (another Nazi satellite) had fled to Hungary to escape Nazi brutality during the early 1940s. It was easier for the Germans to get the Hungarian government to turn over foreign Jews than Hungarian ones, but the Final Solution proceeded slowly in Hungary until 1944.[29] By that time the War Refugee Board represented a countervailing force.

Shortly after its creation, the War Refugee Board worked out a program with the Union of Orthodox Rabbis in the U.S. and Canada to smuggle Jews hiding in Poland into Hungary.[30] At the time it seemed to be a promising operation. Late in February 1944, however, the board heard rumors that the Hungarian government might yield to German pressure for the mass deportation of Jews in Hungary. The board quickly asked the American legations in Switzerland and Portugal to communicate a warning to the Hungarian government.

> The Government of the United States is determined to do everything it can to rescue such unfortunates who are in danger of losing their lives and to find for them havens of refuge. Any continuation by . . . [the Hungarian Government] of the execution of these policies of Hitlerite persecutions is viewed with great seriousness by this Government and will be kept in mind. . . . The Government of the United States takes the view that . . . [the Hungarian government], as well as . . . [its] subordinates and functionaries, are fully responsible for the actions of persecution committed on their territories and in the interests of humanity they should desist immediately.[31]

Although this message was delivered by March 11, and FDR reinforced the warning in his statement of March 24 (which specifically mentioned Hungary),[32] the Hungarians by then had to face more tangible pressure.

On March 18, Hitler summoned Admiral Horthy to a meeting at Schloss Klessheim, near Salzburg. After the meeting ended, RHSA chief Ernest Kaltenbrunner "escorted" Horthy back to Budapest as German troops took over key locations throughout the country. A special paratroop regiment seized key points around Budapest. The Nazis then forced Admiral Horthy to appoint a new government headed by Dome Sztojay, the former Hungarian ambassador in Berlin, who was sympathetic to Germany. SS and Foreign Ministry official Edmund Veesenmayer, SS Obergruppenführer Otto Winckelmann, and the German Special Command, headed by the RSHA's Jewish specialist Adolf Eichmann, skillfully worked out arrangements for bringing Hungarian Jews under German control with newly appointed anti-Semitic Hungarian officials in the Ministry of the Interior. Immediate concentration of Hungarian Jews in ghettos was only the first step; deportations of Jews began in May. With the Hungarian government maintaining nominal control of the deportations, the gendarmerie and police were eager to cooperate with the wishes of their Nazi allies. Officially, Hungary was clearing Jews from the northeastern parts of the country, which had been declared military operational zones, and delivering Jews to Germany for war production purposes under the terms of an agreement between Hungary and Germany. But high Hungarian officials knew what the real fate of these Jews was—a one-way trip to Auschwitz.[33]

The War Refugee Board tried various stopgaps even before the deportations began. It arranged for continued broadcasts of the presidential statement warning Hungary against persecuting the Jews and for similar leaflets dropped over Hungary by planes. Members of the Senate Foreign Relations Committee, the House Foreign Affairs Committee, Archbishop Francis Spellman of New York, and other prominent Americans also issued public warnings to Hungary to desist from persecution of the Jews. The board asked the International Red Cross and neutral nations to increase their representation in Hungary, hoping that their presence might deter the Hungarian government from acts of brutality. It lobbied with the Vatican to take a more active role in Hungary, and it negotiated with representatives of Marshal Tito an escape route for Jewish refugees through Yugoslavia. The board also encouraged Swiss AJJDC representative Saly Mayer to explore with a German contact the possibility of arranging evacuations from Hungary to neutral countries and of halting the deportations in return for cash. (These negotiations later led to the release of several groups of Jews as a "gesture of sincerity" on the part of the Nazis.) The WRB prevailed upon the Latin American countries to postpone any checking of the validity of their passports or visas held by persons in German-controlled territory until these persons were free of the Nazis. At the same time, the U.S. demanded that Hungary recognize these documents.[34] None of these moves prevented the start of the deportations in May or significantly reduced the deadly traffic to Auschwitz between May and July, but all of them had an impact upon later events.

The most dramatic and successful episode in the effort to save the Hungarian Jews was the mission of Raoul Wallenberg to Budapest. Member of a prominent Swedish industrialist family, Wallenberg had accumulated experience in international business and in sticky negotiations. He knew a good deal about Hungary and about Nazi Germany. He had good relations with the Americans—he was a graduate of the University of Michigan. He had spent time in Palestine and had observed Jewish immigrants there who had escaped Nazi persecution. Most important, perhaps, he was imaginative, fearless, and driven to save as many lives as possible.

Wallenberg was introduced to Iver Olsen, representative of the War Refugee Board in Stockholm, by a close friend who was a Hungarian Jew living in Stockholm. Olsen and the board generally were urging neutral countries to do what they could in Hungary to save Jewish lives. After the chief rabbi of Stockholm made an urgent request to the Swedish government, King Gustav of Sweden made a personal appeal to Admiral Horthy at the end of June to save the remaining Jews. Wallenberg was only too eager to get personally involved. Olsen negotiated with the Swedish government and obtained its permission: Wallenberg was appointed as secretary of legation in the Swedish mission in Budapest. The Swedish Foreign Office indicated that Wallenberg would be available for any War Refugee Board assignments in Hungary. He arrived in Budapest on July 9 carrying two knapsacks, a windbreaker, a sleeping bag, and a revolver, all of which he would use over the next months.[35]

Two days earlier the War Refugee Board had cabled its representative in Stockholm that Wallenberg should find out what inducements would be most effective to stop the deportations and the killing. The board could make money available at neutral banks for use after the war or, in part, even in local currency now. Iver Olsen was given an initial fund of fifty thousand dollars to use at his discretion. The board suggested that Wallenberg explore with the Hungarian government the exemption of a number of categories of Jews from the deportations and that he present to the board any other proposals that he thought effective.[36]

Even before Wallenberg began to produce and distribute new types of Swedish protective documents on a much larger scale, international pressure against the Hungarian government escalated. On May 26 the United States suggested to the Cardinal Secretary of State that Pope Pius XII remind the Hungarian authorities and people of the moral values involved and the spiritual consequences of persecution and murder of helpless men, women, and children. One month later the Pope sent a telegram to Horthy, appealing to the regent to save many unfortunate people from "further pain and sorrow." The next day President Roosevelt warned that "Hungary's fate will not be like that of any other civilized nation . . . unless the deportations are stopped." After WRB prompting, the president of the International Red Cross also protested the deportations in letters to Horthy in early July. As historian Randolph Braham has noted, the Nazis' deteriorating military situation was at least as important as these appeals in convincing Horthy to part ways with his government—the risk of antagonizing the Allies became greater than that of alienating the Germans. The messages demonstrated that the western world had a real interest in the fate of the Jews in Hungary and that Hungary's treatment at the peace table might depend in part on how it treated the Jews.[37]

Horthy ended the discussion of the deportations at the Crown Council meeting of June 26 by exclaiming:

> I shall not tolerate this any further! I shall not permit the deportations to bring further shame on the Hungarians! Let the Government take measures for the removal of Baky and Endre [two key anti-Semitic officials in the ministry of the interior]. The deportation of the Jews of Budapest must cease!

The government, however, temporized and informed the Germans of the various offers to rescue or protect the Jews in Hungary. Hungary would not accept them without Germany's consent. Only the deportations from Budapest were delayed.[38]

For a brief period it appeared that the Hungarian and German authorities would reach a compromise. Veesenmayer recommended and Hitler agreed that the Hungarian government could accept specific offers by the Swiss, Swedes, and Americans to take limited numbers of Jews as long as Horthy would allow the rest of the deportations to take place quickly. But, when Horthy demanded the recall of the German occupation forces and the dismissal of the Sztojay government, Hitler blocked the move. Veesenmayer warned the regent that Germany had enough power in Hungary to guarantee a "correct" policy. Horthy nonetheless accomplished part of his objective in August with the dismissal of the prime minister and the minister of the interior.[39]

The War Refugee Board jumped upon the new-found willingness of the

Hungarian government to allow the emigration of all who had entry permits to another country. The board requested the neutral nations to inform Germany and Hungary that they would accept *all* Jews permitted to emigrate. The board also urged the British government to join the American offer but warned that the U.S. would proceed regardless of British action. The British asked for additional time to consider the "larger problems," especially that of accommodations. After several days the British government expressed its readiness to cooperate "to the extent of British resources." The board was not satisfied with this response and proceeded with its unilateral offer through the Red Cross. Several weeks later Great Britain associated itself with the American position. American consuls in Switzerland, Spain, and Portugal were authorized to issue up to 5,000 immigration visas, to refugee children from Hungary who reached these countries. The State Department also authorized visas for Hungarian relatives of American citizens and resident aliens. Unfortunately, German opposition prevented virtually all Jews from leaving Hungary or traveling through German-controlled territory.[40]

Not trusting the suspension of the deportations, however, Wallenberg fortunately continued to issue Swedish papers and move thousands of Budapest's Jews into houses under Swedish protection. Swiss and Red Cross representatives followed his example, and the War Refugee Board and Jewish organizations provided essential financial support. Under the circumstances, this was the most effective method of saving lives. Some 50,000 Jews were thus sheltered from later deportations.[41]

In October Horthy belatedly tried to extricate Hungary from the Axis and, at the same time, avert a Russian occupation. Since Germany had to intervene anyway to shore up its military position, the Nazis took the opportunity to resume the Final Solution. After making Horthy a virtual prisoner and installing an anti-Semitic puppet government, German representatives tried to round up the Jews of Budapest. But, even with the aid of pro-Nazi Hungarians, this was no longer a simple task. The Russians were approaching, and the activities of Wallenberg and company had brought protection to many. Wallenberg continued to work his magic, threatening German officers in Budapest with war crimes trials. Moreover, the rail route to Auschwitz was now blocked. The Nazis had to turn to a forced march of Jews in the direction of Austria. Partly because of negotiations in Switzerland involving the War Refugee Board (discussed below), 18,000 Jews were left in Vienna for labor there. Many thousands of others died on the march, but many fewer than Auschwitz could have disposed of. Most of the Jews of Budapest survived in spite of all of the efforts of Eichmann and company.[42]

The Joel Brand affair, one of the best known episodes in the Hungarian Jewish tragedy, aptly demonstrates the virtual impossibility of Allied negotiations with Germany for the release of Jews. In April 1944, Adolf Eichmann summoned a little-known young Hungarian Jew named Joel Brand to offer him a deal. Eichmann would release one million Jews in exchange for certain goods from the Allies, including ten thousand trucks. Brand should go abroad, establish contact with the western powers, and place the offer before them. Brand would be accompanied by Andor Grosz, a converted Hungarian Jew who had previously worked for German military intelligence, Hungarian military intelligence, and various other agencies, including Hungarian Jewish organizations. Although Brand was not informed of Grosz's mission, Grosz was now carrying out the SS's wish to establish a bridge to the west for possible peace negotiations. The authority for the move came from Himmler himself. Typical of Himmler's exaggeration of the power of American Jews, the Reich Führer SS suggested that Brand contact the American ambassador to Turkey, Laurence Steinhardt, who was Jewish.[43] If the Jews had great influence over Allied policy, as Himmler thought, then they presumably would have made a deal to spare their Hungarian brethren.

Brand was detained for a while in Istanbul because he lacked an entry visa. American vice consul Leslie Squires and AJJDC representative Reuben Resnik interviewed him there and quickly became suspicious. They feared that Germany was seeking primarily to drive a wedge between Russia and the west. (The SS promised to use the goods they hoped to obtain only on the eastern front.) After the Turks released Brand and Grosz, the British arrested both of them, in Palestine and Syria respectively. Brand was confined in Cairo and prevented from returning to, or communicating with, Hungary. Meanwhile, the deportations from Hungary to Auschwitz proceeded at the rate of ten to twelve thousand per day.[44]

The British Foreign Office and Colonial Office were united in rejecting the Brand offer, the Foreign Office regarding it as equivalent to a German request to suspend military operations. The Colonial Office found that negotiations with the Nazis might produce a German offer to unload even more Jews, which would lead to pressure on London to introduce an unmanageable number into Palestine. The Cabinet Committee on the Reception and Accommodation of Refugees and the War Cabinet rejected the Brand overture at the beginning of June. Washington, however, had to be informed, and there was some fear in London that the War Refugee Board might favor a deal with the Germans.[45]

The Brand offer did not go to the board directly but to the State Department. Undersecretary Stettinius quickly consulted Assistant Secretary of War John McCloy, who found the proposal "bizarre" and agreed with the British rejection. But, after consulting with the War Refugee Board, the State Department thought it worthwhile to delay an overt refusal. Perhaps the Germans would delay deportations as long as they thought there was a chance of a deal.

The board sent Bloomingdale's executive Ira Hirschmann to interview Brand and obtain further information. Hirschmann carried with him a letter written by FDR to him, authorizing Hirschmann to pursue all possibilities for saving the victims of Nazi persecution. At the same time, however, Ambassador

Steinhardt was informed that the U.S. could accept no offer without British and Russian consent. The real purpose of the delay and the Hirschmann mission, thus, was to induce the Nazis to wait rather than to deport Hungarian Jews immediately.[46]

Over British resistance, Hirschmann interviewed Brand in his cell in Cairo and found him sincere. Hirschmann concluded, as did officials of the Jewish Agency for Palestine, that Brand should be allowed to return to Hungary with some sign that the Allies might be interested. This might keep the door open without committing Britain and the U.S. to anything dubious. The British clearly did not agree, and, when the Russians were informed, Moscow found it neither permissible nor expedient to discuss such matters with the Germans. That meant that there was now a serious drawback—divisiveness among the Allies—even to going through the motions of negotiations. Brand remained under detention in Cairo.

The War Refugee Board at first joined Hirschmann in arguing that the Allies should try to spin out negotiations. The British ambassador to the United States, Lord Halifax, denounced this "interference" and described John Pehle as a would-be "twentieth century Daniel." But British and Russian objections and suspicions eventually swung even Pehle. When the Germans tried to reestablish contact with the Allies through Joseph Schwartz of the Joint Distribution Committee in Lisbon, Pehle opposed the meeting on the grounds that it might divide the Allies. The War Refugee Board gave up the idea of bartering goods for Jewish lives.[47]

Contrary to promises, the Nazis did not halt deportations while the Brand mission was in progress. The Hungarian government stopped the transports on its own in early July—and over German resistance. Moreover, the transcript of a 1947 conversation between a former SS official and a Hungarian Jewish leader, both closely involved in the negotiations, lends some support to those Allied officials who viewed the Nazi offer as a trick. The SS official, Kurt Becher, who dealt directly with Himmler on the Brand mission and two subsequent sets of negotiations for Jewish lives, quotes Himmler as saying "take what you can get [in the way of Allied goods]." But Himmler did not intend to give anything in exchange. Becher, who liked to think of himself as a soldier and a gentleman, claimed to have refused to have anything to do with such a swindle.[48] There is thus good evidence that Himmler was not yet willing to sacrifice the Final Solution for goods or for the possibility of negotiations with the west. The Allies, on their part, were certainly not willing to alienate the Russians (and perhaps inflame public opinion in Britain and the U.S.) for what seemed to be a highly dubious payment of ransom.

Becher subsequently had some success in arranging in Switzerland for the release of two groups totaling almost 1700 Hungarian Jews from German concentration camps without any Allied goods or payment in return. This episode showed that, by late 1944, Himmler's fanaticism had faded enough to allow at least the release of small numbers of Jews. At the same time, it also demonstrated Hitler's continuing opposition to sparing Jewish lives.

NEGOTIATIONS IN SWITZERLAND

The War Refugee Board, in the person of Roswell McClelland, its representative in Switzerland, was an important party in the negotiations which Kurt Becher carried out with AJJDC representative Saly Mayer in Switzerland. The Allies had ruled out both direct negotiations with the Nazis and the delivery of military supplies, but Mayer tried to interest Becher and, through him, Himmler in money. To help convince the German representatives that Mayer was serious, McClelland requested the WRB to supply him with a large sum of money that would be deposited in a blocked Swiss account.

By the end of October, Mayer enjoyed a credit of five million dollars provided by the War Refugee Board, but no money could be spent without McClelland's authorization. And McClelland was barred from making ransom payments. Nonetheless, the existence of the bank deposit and Mayer's skillful parrying of German demands at least dragged out the negotiations, temporarily protected the Jews of the Budapest ghetto from deportation, which resumed in Hungary in October 1944, and produced the release of 1,700 Hungarian Jews from the concentration camp at Bergen-Belsen and the diversion of 18,000 Hungarian Jews to Vienna instead of to Auschwitz.[49] In return, Mayer gave the Union of Orthodox Rabbis' representative Isaac Sternbuch about fifty-nine thousand dollars, which Sternbuch used to purchase tractors and coffee that were sent to Germany. This payment—partly ransom, partly additional bait— was made from other AJJDC funds without McClelland's knowledge and against War Refugee Board instructions.[50]

There were other negotiations in Switzerland that helped spare at least some Jews. Working partly in conjunction with high SS and RSHA official Walter Schellenberg, a pro-Nazi Swiss by the name of Jean-Marie Musy helped convince his friend Heinrich Himmler that American Jewish organizations might at least pay substantial sums to save the lives of Jews in German concentration camps. Musy began to negotiate with Isaac Sternbuch, who was asked to pay five million Swiss francs. In return, Germany would begin to send trainloads of Jews from the concentration camps to Switzerland. When Musy went back to Germany in mid-January 1945 to discuss the deal with Himmler, the Reich Führer SS told him about the other negotiations with Saly Mayer, about which Musy had known nothing. Himmler wanted to know whether Mayer was really in touch with the American government, which indicated that Himmler was interested at least as much in negotiations as he was in money or goods. Meanwhile, Himmler was busy working out a cover story to pass on to the Americans. He told Musy that Germany had put the Jews to use at hard labor and that naturally there was a high death rate among them. Germany had

had enough negative experience with Jews that it did not wish to keep the survivors; if the Americans wanted them, that was fine. But they could not be allowed to go to Palestine, since the Arabs rejected the Jews just as much as the Germans did.

Himmler's terms, however, were still strict. He not only wanted the equivalent of one thousand dollars per Jew but also insisted that Germany receive compensation in the form of tractors and heavy equipment. Musy tried to persuade Himmler that the Jewish question was a minor issue. The main thing, he argued, was to get negotiations with the west started. It appears from Himmler's notes that he was not immune to this argument.[51]

Musy went back to Switzerland, then back to Germany, then back to Switzerland once again. In the process he appears to have drifted away from Himmler's negotiating position. (It is also possible that Himmler changed his views as the German military situation deteriorated rapidly.) Musy was willing to accept five million Swiss francs, deposited in a bank account in his name. As a gesture of good faith, he had arranged for the transporting of 1,200 Jews to Switzerland. After WRB representative Roswell McClelland cleared the path with Swiss officials, the train of survivors from the Theresienstadt concentration camp arrived at Kreuzlingen on February 6. Musy promised additional trainloads after the five million Swiss francs were paid.[52]

There was never any question of paying Musy off. The only issue under discussion in Washington was whether the board could transfer the money to a blocked account in Switzerland and use the bank account balance to make Musy think that the deal was imminent. Unfortunately, rumors of the earlier negotiations (and payments) had raised suspicions, especially in Moscow. The risk of adverse Soviet reaction forced John Pehle's successor, General William O'Dwyer, to refrain from further endorsement of the blocked account deception. But American failure to pay was not necessarily the main reason why no further trainloads of Jews arrived in Switzerland. Hitler reacted violently when he heard about the negotiations and the train, and RSHA chief Ernst Kaltenbrunner obtained permission to prohibit the release of any more Jews.[53]

In Switzerland, Roswell McClelland found other ways to be effective. From his central vantage point in Bern he arranged to smuggle money into Nazi-occupied France, where resistance groups and welfare organizations provided shelter and support for Jews. He financed expeditions of refugees in France across the Pyrenees and into Spain. McClelland vigorously and frequently requested the assistance of the Swiss government and the International Red Cross in dealing with the Hungarian situation, with noticeable effect on their willingness to intercede on behalf of threatened Jews. Switzerland also became more open to admitting Jews as political refugees now that the United States was taking a more direct interest in them. The presence of observers from the IRC helped deter some concentration camp officials from carrying out last-minute orders to kill all prisoners. Through McClelland, the War Refugee Board and the private American organizations supplying funds also helped finance resistance elements in Slovakia, and within Germany itself, and sent food packages to thousands of concentration camp inmates who otherwise might not have survived. By 1945, German officials had grudingly agreed to receive and distribute some outside shipments of food.[54]

McClelland's activities, and those of other War Refugee Board representatives in Europe, clearly disrupted the efficiency of the Final Solution, even if they did not bring the program to a halt. David Wyman has credited the board with playing a crucial role in the saving of two hundred thousand Jews. The largest group was the approximately 120,000 Jews of Budapest who almost certainly would not have survived without the efforts of Wallenberg and others like him, backed by the board. In addition, the frequent warnings during 1944 that government officials in the satellite countries would be tried as war criminals if they cooperated with the German murder program undoubtedly helped save many thousands more. Yet McClelland himself wrote just after the end of the war that the successes were slight in relation to the fearful casualties.[55]

The main reason for the disparity was not the opposition that the War Refugee Board met in Europe—or back in Washington and even more in London—as unfortunate as that was. The Nazis had a program to exterminate Jews that had been refined by years of experience. That program continued until the men who gave the orders and those who carried them out changed their minds, or until the Allies intervened militarily. And even the frequent Allied threats during 1944 and 1945 to bring mass murderers to trial as war criminals did not deter most of those involved in the Final Solution.

BOMBING AUSCHWITZ

The Allies ruled out special military missions to rescue Jews and other civilians in concentration and extermination camps. Early in 1944 the War Department, in conjunction with British objections to the establishment of the War Refugee Board, had taken a stand against Allied military operations to rescue victims of Nazi persecution.[56] American military officials generally did not welcome additional responsibilities or demands on their resources. To defeat the Nazis as quickly and as thoroughly as possible was their overriding goal—and one that could be defended as humanitarian. As Roosevelt and the War Department had stated on a number of occasions,[57] if the Allies won the war quickly, that would end the suffering of much of Europe. Thus, various requests for the bombing of the rail lines leading to Auschwitz and the extermination camp facilities themselves never received a serious hearing in Washington in mid-and late 1944. Even the War Refugee Board hesitated to do battle on this issue.

The first requests for the bombing of the rail lines to Auschwitz reached the War Refugee Board in late June 1944. They had come from Jewish sources in Hungary, Slovakia, and Switzerland. John Pehle had doubts about the proposal. He had learned that bombing of rail lines accomplished only temporary disruption of German activities. Nonetheless, Pehle discussed the idea with McCloy on June 24. The War Department Operations Division rejected the proposal out of hand.

> The War Department is of the opinion that the suggested air operation is impracticable for the reason that it could be executed only by diversion of considerable air support essential to the success of our forces now engaged in decisive operations. The War Department fully appreciates the humanitarian importance of the suggested operation. However, . . . it is considerd that the most effective relief to victims of enemy persecution is the early defeat of the Axis, an undertaking to which we must devote every resource at our disposal.

A second request, this time endorsed by War Refugee Board representative Roswell McClelland, followed quickly on the heels of the first. The Operations Division advised the Civil Affairs Division to use the same basic answer.[58]

Benjamin Azkin and Lawrence Lesser of the WRB staff pressed the matter again in July, suggesting that the board take its case to the president. Lesser even wrote a draft of a directive from the president to the secretary of war, requesting an investigation of possible military operations to rescue civilians.[59] It is quite possible that, through Morgenthau, the matter did reach FDR. Through writer Edward T. Chase, McCloy has recently claimed that presidential aides Harry Hopkins and Samuel Rosenman asked McCloy to investigate the possibility of bombing death camps. McCloy recalls that the War Department General Staff and the air force operational commanders in Europe considered such ventures "of doubtful efficacy." He also claims that Hopkins and Rosenman subsequently told him of the president's view that the camps should not be bombed.[60] Whatever happened was enough to discourage Pehle, who informed Morgenthau in September that the board had decided against a new effort with the War Department.[61]

One possible influence on the board was the opposition of the American section of the World Jewish Congress, which wanted to avoid bombing attacks that would certainly kill many camp inmates. WJC representative Leon Kubowitzki suggested instead that the Polish underground send in parachute troops to destroy the gas chambers. Pehle could only point out the political and logistical difficulties that stood in the way of such an operation.[62]

Not until the Polish government in exile itself urged the board to support a bombing raid on Auschwitz did Pehle raise the matter again with McCloy in early October. McCloy's office did not respond. Pehle's last effort came in early November, after he had received the "Auschwitz Protocol"—the detailed description of the killing operations in Birkenau written by two Slovakian Jews who had escaped. Again, the Operations Division declined to undertake a long and risky mission to bomb a nonmilitary target.[63]

As historian David Wyman has pointed out in a trenchant article and again in his recent book,[64] the American Fifteenth Air Force, based in Italy, was already bombing the industrial areas around Auschwitz-Birkenau in an effort to destroy German oil supplies. On August 20, 127 Flying Fortresses bombed the factory areas of Auschwitz. Other raids struck there on September 13, December 18, and December 26. The argument that bombers would have had to be diverted from operations elsewhere was specious. It does not follow, however, that bombing the gas chambers could easily have been accomplished or, to follow Wyman, that successful bombing would have forced the Nazis to reassess the extermination program.[65]

The War Department had consistently struggled against outside efforts to make use of military personnel for nonmilitary purposes. If the military granted one request for assistance, however minor or meritorious, military officials feared that it would set an unfortunate precedent and encourage additional demands.[66] Those involved in the selection of bombing targets operated on certain assumptions. The main objective was to diminish the essential military equipment and supplies of the enemy, and the available number of planes was likely to remain small.[67] There was no way that men thinking along these lines were going to target the gas chambers at Birkenau, even if they knew about them.

It is impossible to demonstrate that the main opposition inside and outside the War Department to the proposals to bomb Auschwitz came from anti-Semites, and some of the key figures involved (e.g., McCloy)[68] clearly were not anti-Semitic. But they did not look at wartime planning and operations in terms of moral obligations to humanity. Their functions were limited by bureaucratic specialization. In the last analysis, War Department officials and the theater commanders (who eventually learned of the Auschwitz proposals) were judged on how effectively and rapidly they won the war. They knew that, and they resisted diversions from their task.

As far as the Nazi leaders were concerned, all of the evidence indicates that Hitler and most of those in charge of the machinery of destruction refused to be diverted, too. Even when the extermination camps in the east had to shut down because of the advancing Russian armies, the inmates could be (and were) shifted to the west and denied food. The Nazis had used execution squads before; they could use them again, if need be. They were less efficient than the gas chambers, and they used more manpower, but the Nazi regime had never bowed to economic and military constraints when it came to the Final Solution. Thus, as Henry Feingold once noted, it was in some ways easier for the Nazis to kill Jews than for the Allies to save them.[69]

The case for bombing Auschwitz and other death camps should not be overstated. It would have been a sign of Allied horror at Nazi genocide and Allied determination to do something about it, even at the risk of military and Jewish casualties. It would have forced high Nazi authorities to turn to less efficient means of murder, and it might have made some subordinates think twice about continuing their own role in the Final Solution of the Jewish question. It would have been humanitarian, and it should have been done, but it was no panacea.

ELEVEN

Roosevelt and the Refugees in the 1930S

Fifty years after his first presidential inauguration and many historical revisions later, Franklin Roosevelt has managed to retain the laurel bestowed upon him by biographer James MacGregor Burns: "Roosevelt was one of the master politicians of his time, certainly the most successful vote getter."[1] Burns and many others have marveled at FDR's political artistry, his almost instinctual ability to know and use to his own advantage men's values, fears, ambitions, and biases. With the adroitness of a sculptor, Roosevelt could chisel a coalition from the electorate, impart to it his goals and ideas, and smooth its rough edges with his humor, warmth, and unique charisma. "Conventions, primaries, elections, offices, constitutions, and opinion agencies" were his métier.[2]

Alternately a lion and a fox, according to Burns, FDR overpowered or outmaneuvered his political adversaries with a calculated cunning. This is not to suggest that the president always succeeded in getting his way with Congress or the entrenched government bureaucracy. Even Roosevelt's instructions could be found collecting dust beneath a pile of memoranda on the desk of a procrastinating official. Executive orders were only as effective as the president's ability to persuade officials to enforce a policy with which they might disagree.[3] And even the considerable patronage power of the president was not always sufficient to persuade recalcitrant congressmen that the risk of voting against FDR was greater than the punishment their constituents might mete out. Roosevelt was adept at picking his fights, spending his energy and resources on those he could most likely win. And, though he lost more than a few battles, he usually won the wars. Just as important was the impression the president left with the American people that he alone was in charge. For his ability to overcome opposition and inspire public confidence in himself and the New Deal, Nobel laureate Saul Bellow has assessed Roosevelt as "not an intellectual" but, unquestionably, "a genius in politics," an aptitude FDR manifested at the ballot box in four presidential elections.[4]

German Jews seeking sanctuary in the United States were not a large potential constituency nor were their advocates among American Jewry a disciplined phalanx of well-financed political operatives with a large political power base. Neither group could tip the political scales for a politician in search of a majority. Little wonder then that, on the matter of Jewish refugees, the politically astute Roosevelt was neither a lion nor a fox but, of necessity, a chameleon whose protean words and actions alternately enraged and elated American Jews as they have since puzzled historians.

Roosevelt's refugee policy, not unlike some of his economic policies, can best be understood as two policies: compliance with the restrictionist legislation in place since the 1920s and a symbolic humanitarianism extended to a suffering minority.[5] During his first two administrations, the most consistent quality of Roosevelt's policy toward European Jewry was his noninterference with the national quota system that Congress had passed in 1924. Roosevelt never failed to listen sympathetically to individual Jews and to Jewish organizations who petitioned the White House for relief of their coreligionists. But, even when FDR privately assured Jewish leaders that he would act to ease the suffering of their European brothers, he dissociated himself from public statements and other policies that singled out Jewish refugees for special assistance because they were targets of special abuse in Germany.

The president's dual course, largely charted by the political winds, was uneven. Often Roosevelt sought to deflect Jewish pressure from the White House. Between 1933 and 1936, FDR relied on the federal bureaucracy as a trapdoor through which to drop the nettlesome issue of refugees. The New Deal coalition had little to gain and much to lose by taking a stand on an issue that so aroused voters' moral, economic, and social sensibilities. The leniency in administrative procedures that visa applicants experienced after FDR's re-election bears the earmarks of a discreet White House initiative, designed to have a salutary but limited impact upon the flow of refugees. Even after his landslide victory, the president preferred such modest concessions to directly confronting the conflicting demands of refugee advocates and restrictionists. Rather, Roosevelt sought to defuse the issue with a call for an international forum on refugees in 1938. The other nations of the world were as little prepared for gestures of humanitarianism as the United States was, and little was accomplished. But the escalation of German persecution of the Jews, culminating in *Kristallnacht* on November 9, 1938, would not permit the White House to remain silent. With more symbol than substance, FDR denounced the persecution. By the eve of his bid for a third term in 1940, Roosevelt was confronting a war in Europe. The president was not alone in his fears that Nazi or Soviet agents might be infiltrating the United States camouflaged as refugees. This suspicion effectively put an end to any hopes that Roosevelt would finally throw open America's doors to a substantial number of European Jews.

The relationship of Franklin Roosevelt's Democratic party to the Jews long preceded his presidency. Prior to World War I, the Jewish bloc lacked coherence. After the war, Jewish voters frequently cast Republican ballots; in 1920, ten of eleven Jews elected to Congress were from the GOP. American Jews were also periodically attracted to third party movements in their search for a permanent political home, favoring socialist Eugene Debs with 24 percent of their votes in 1920 and the progressive Robert LaFollette with 17 percent in 1924. But, as an increasing number of naturalized immigrants went to the polls, being joined there by voters of second- and third-generation ethnic stock, the Jews began to bargain for a niche in a major party coalition. Most switched to the Democratic column. In 1928, Jews enthusiastically supported Al Smith at the polls. Smith's advisers included Belle Moskowitz, Joseph Proskauer, and Judge Samuel Rosenman, all familiar names to American Jewry. Two years later, six of eight Jews elected to Congress were Democrats. Much of Smith's Jewish support passed easily to Franklin Roosevelt.[6]

Roosevelt was no stranger to the Jews. In the New York State gubernatorial election of 1928, FDR received more votes from the Jewish community than did his Republican opponent, Albert Ottinger, a Jew, who spent much of the campaign defending himself against charges of insufficient piety lodged by Jews more observant than he. In 1932, Roosevelt got strong Jewish support, collecting at least three Jewish votes to every one of Hoover's. In 1936, Roosevelt got 96 percent of the votes in the nation's most Jewish ward in Chicago's Cook County.[7]

Despite the strong anti-Semitic overtones of the era, FDR did not hesitate to include Jews in his "Brains Trust" or to appoint Jews to public positions. He admired talent, wherever he found it, and he understood that those of humble roots often had a special commitment to social justice and a dedication to achieving it. With this profile in mind, Roosevelt requested a talent hunt:

> Dig me up fifteen or twenty youthful Abraham Lincolns from Manhattan and the Bronx to choose from. They must be liberal from belief and not by lip service. They must have an inherent contempt both for the John W. Davis's and Max Steurs [conservative corporate lawyers]. They must know what life in a tenement means. They must have no social ambitions.[8]

With many young and talented Jews being rejected by prejudiced firms in law and business, Roosevelt had little difficulty attracting individuals who knew "what life in a tenement" meant to work in the New Deal.

By 1935, the government was peppered with young, talented Jews such as Isador Lubin and Charles Wyzanski, Jr. (Labor), Robert Nathan (Treasury), Nathan Margold, Abe Fortas, Saul K. Padover, and Felix Cohen (Interior), Jerome Frank (Agriculture), David Lilienthal (TVA), and David K. Niles (WPA). While Roosevelt occasionally turned for advice to Justice Louis Brandeis, the elder statesman of progressivism, the president was much closer to Harvard Law professor Felix Frankfurter, to political confidant Benjamin Cohen, who drafted much of the New Deal's critical legislation, and to speechwriter Samuel Rosenman. The latter had joined Roosevelt while FDR was still governor of New York and was responsible, along with Raymond Moley, for the phrase "New Deal."

In his cabinet Roosevelt included Henry Morgenthau, Jr., highly respected on Wall Street, as head of the Treasury Department.[9]

Roosevelt did not capitulate to demands stoked by hatemongers, such as Father Charles Coughlin, William Dudley Pelley, and the leadership of the Ku Klux Klan, that he curb the number of Jews in his administration. Haters who referred to his administration as the "Rosenberg Administration" found FDR unruffled. Still, the master politician who had honed his instincts in the same New York Democratic party that included Tammany Hall never permitted his admiration for Jewish talent to cloud his instincts. FDR's Jewish appointments rarely exceeded the realities of the Democratic party's ethnic demography. Of 192 judicial appointments, Roosevelt gave 7 to Jews and 52 to Catholics. Only Morgenthau ever reached a cabinet-level position, and only Abe Fortas, at the Interior Department, reached the rank of an undersecretary. As historian Leonard Dinnerstein has observed, "one's fingers and toes" would be sufficient to count the number of Jews in policy-making positions in the Departments of State, War, Navy, and Commerce, the Federal Reserve Board, the Federal Trade Commission, the U.S. Tariff Commission, and the Board of Tax Appeals.[10]

Moreover, American Jewry could not convert these appointments, nor even their electoral support of Roosevelt, into sufficient pressure to persuade FDR to aid German Jewish refugees during the 1930s. Within weeks of his inauguration, Roosevelt was hearing from prominent Jewish friends and political cronies on the subject. While conversations with Irving and Herbert Lehman, and his personal favorite Felix Frankfurter, succeeded in getting FDR's attention, the results were less than dramatic. Roosevelt shunted the matter into the bureaucracy's hopper. When the refugee question became the subject of a tug-of-war between the State and Labor departments, Roosevelt treated Jewish pleas for a humanitarian gesture as he did all problems for which he had no comfortable solution—with distance.

Political scientists refer to Roosevelt's technique of policy making as "the prototype for the competitive management model."[11] Assessing Roosevelt as confident in his "political efficacy" and "comfortable in the presence of conflict and disagreement around him," they observe that Roosevelt "deliberately exacerbated the competitive and conflicting aspects of cabinet politics and bureaucratic politics" so he could manipulate the structure of relationships among subordinates and thereby "control and profit from their competition." Roosevelt especially used this technique in information gathering. Political scientist Richard Neustadt offers an anecdote from one of FDR's aides to elucidate the technique:

> He would call you in and he'd ask you to get the story on some complicated business, and you'd come back after a couple of days of hard labor and present the juicy morsel you'd uncovered under a stone somewhere, and then you'd find out he knew all about it, along with something else you didn't know. Where he got his

information from he wouldn't mention, usually, but after he had done this to you once or twice you got damn careful about your information.[12]

Roosevelt put his competitive technique to most effective use in decision making on policy issues. He "deliberately created 'fuzzy lines of responsibility, no clear chains of command, overlapping jurisdictions' in order to promote stimulating inter-departmental conflict which could and eventually did land in his lap."[13] Arthur Schlesinger, Jr., another Roosevelt biographer, remarked that, when it came to decision making, FDR's "complex administrative sensibility" was "forever weighing questions of personal force, of political timing, of congressional concern, of partisan benefit, of public interest." He liked to permit situations to "develop, to crystallize, to clarify; the competing forces had to vindicate themselves in the actual pull and tug of conflict; public opinion had to face the question, consider it, pronounce upon it—only then, at the long, frazzled end would the President's intentions consolidate and precipitate a result."[14] Though Roosevelt occasionally complained about entrenched bureaucracy, few presidents have equalled him in his ability to turn the bureaucrat's intractability to his own will when it was to his own political advantage.

In April 1933, FDR pursued the same restrictionist immigration policy as his Republican predecessor. He remained aloof as State Department officials such as Undersecretary William Phillips and Assistant Secretary Wilbur Carr tangled with Secretary of Labor Frances Perkins over the refugee issue in 1933. Though both sides sent documents and memoranda to the White House, there is no evidence that the president acted.

Instead, Roosevelt stood to the side and let the pugnacious bureaucrats nip at each others' heels until the attorney general could render an opinion on the legal issues involved, especially the controversial proposal to allow relatives and friends of a refugee to post bonds guaranteeing that the refugee would not become a public charge. In the end, FDR did not respond to New Dealer Perkins's call for a humane, generous refugee policy. He accepted State's strict enforcement of the LPC clause. State's policy enjoyed broad public support and the backing of increasingly important factions in the young New Deal's coalition such as the AFL. The fate of Roosevelt's economic programs and the political viability of the New Deal clearly took precedence over assisting foreign nationals in distress.

Between 1933 and 1936, FDR approached the refugee issue circumspectly. He offered a symbolic humanitarianism, continuing to meet with Jewish spokemen but largely in an effort to mollify the American Jewish community without making any promises. Jewish leaders, such as Rabbi Stephen Wise, recognized that stiff congressional opposition to refugee policy reform made Roosevelt wary of the issue. But without the assent of "General Headquarters," as Wise termed the White House, non-Jewish congressional advocates of reform, such as Senators Joseph T. Robinson (D-Arkansas) and Elbert Thomas (D-

Utah), were hesitant to raise the politically divisive issue. In the early summer of 1933, the American Jewish Committee and the American Jewish Congress were in rare agreement that a debate on the House floor "could lead to an explosion against us."[15] Wise, both popular and controversial because of his commitment to public protest on behalf of Jewish refugees, had long desired a private audience with Roosevelt. Not until January 1936, however, did the summons to Hyde Park finally come. The president greeted Wise warmly. Known for his monumental ego and pride in being a Washington insider, Wise was charmed by FDR. The rabbi's critics, especially those in the Yiddish press, argued that Wise was duped, co-opted by the wily Roosevelt. One prominent Yiddish journalist suggested that all FDR had to do was place his arm around Wise's shoulder and warmly intone his first name—"Steve, Steve"—and the rabbi was disarmed.[16]

Roosevelt enjoyed flattery—using it to manipulate others and receiving it as an expression of the admiration he craved. Even as he stroked others' egos, his own needed the nurture of those around him. He called each person on the White House staff as well as many of his visitors, such as Rabbi Wise, by their first names. He sometimes referred to himself as "Poppa." He liked to think of himself as father to many people besides his own children. He also answered to "Boss," "Skipper," and "Chief," all half-facetious terms of subservience which Wise and others used jokingly in FDR's presence. Wise also used them when referring to Roosevelt in correspondence, probably to indicate the flattering level of familiarity Roosevelt permitted him to enjoy.

Though Wise may have been even less immune than most to the Roosevelt charm, he did not fail to let Roosevelt know that the State Department's continued lack of cooperation was angering the American Jewish electorate. Using Felix Frankfurter as his pipeline to the Oval Office, Wise warned FDR that failure to act decisively on behalf of Jewish refugees might cause Jewish voters to switch to the Republicans in 1936. Others, such as Frankfurter and Herbert Lehman, continued to urge Roosevelt to speak out before November.[17]

When Roosevelt finally took public action, it was not to order modification of U.S. immigration policies or procedures. In August 1936, the president spoke out on the need to rebuild Palestine, the Jews' ancient homeland. The following month, he discussed with his cabinet the British intention of curbing the number of Jewish refugees admitted to Palestine. He urged the British not to close the Middle East safety valve. Still, despite the flurry of presidential inactivity regarding the quota system, by late 1936 the word probably reached officials at State that Roosevelt would appreciate some leniency on visa policy administration. By December 1936 refugees were experiencing an unusual easing of consular requirements, especially on matters of documentation and proof of support.

Roosevelt's ringing victory in the 1936 election—60.8 percent of the vote— was a mandate to continue the projects and policies of the first administration.

There is no evidence that FDR perceived his re-election as an opportunity to do more and send the Congress a comprehensive immigration reform bill. Public sentiment toward the Jews suggested that such an initiative would be politically risky. A 1937 poll conducted by the American Institute for Public Opinion indicated that 38 percent of those polled thought that anti-Semitism in the United States was increasing. Another poll conducted almost a year later revealed that, though 81 percent of the sample did not think there would be a "widespread campaign against the Jews in the U.S.," 48 percent did think that the persecution of the Jews in Europe was "partly" their own fault.[18] Even more important, though, by 1937 Roosevelt's own political capital was declining. His hold on Congress was tenuous at best. That summer a group of conservative Democratic senators broke with Roosevelt to join Republicans in an anti-New Deal bloc. Alienated by FDR's failure to balance the budget and to continue business's recovery, the coalition, which included Vice President John Nance Gardner, sought to frustrate Roosevelt's reform legislation and eventually carry the party away from the New Dealers.[19] Such political circumstances made it even more unlikely that FDR would take the political risk necessary to support liberalization of immigration restrictionism. But Germany's invasion of Austria in March 1938 raised issues that Roosevelt could not avoid. Austrian Jews almost immediately felt the sting of Nazi anti-Jewish policies. Jewish property was seized; some Jews were expelled from the country; still others were dragged off to concentration camps. Lines lengthened at American consulates.

At a cabinet meeting on March 18, 1938, Roosevelt asked his advisors whether the United States could aid Austrian political refugees; he did not single out the Jews for special mention though much of the Nazi abuse was directed at them. Recalling that the United States had been a haven for Germans during the last century, Roosevelt seemed to believe that the United States should again put out the welcome mat. He ordered the combination of German and Austrian quotas to give an increased number of Austrians a chance for an American visa from the unused portion of the German quota, which was considerably larger than Austria's. Roosevelt then asked the cabinet whether a bill he would initiate to increase the quota was likely to pass. Warned that it would not, FDR quickly abandoned the idea.[20] A battle in Congress always involved calling in favors and using up valuable patronage and personal credit. Experienced in legislative duels, the president chose not to fight when he could not win. And there is ample evidence that many congressmen would have been pressured to vote against the president. An Opinion Research Corporation Poll taken in March, the same month as the Anschluss, revealed that 75 percent of the respondents opposed the admission of "a larger number of Jewish exiles from Germany (17 percent were agreeable and 8 percent had no opinion).[21] Instead, FDR announced his intention of coaxing other countries to take from one hundred to one thousand Austrian families each. Any assistance to the Austrian families in need would lighten whatever burden the United States would eventually undertake.

Even those Jewish leaders pressing FDR hardest for action were acutely aware that there were political constraints on Roosevelt. Stephen Wise and others looked on with "amazement and horror" when Congressman Emanuel Celler introduced a bill into Congress that would suspend the quota provisions of the 1924 immigration law for refugee visa applicants. Referring to the bill as "almost . . . the work of an agent provocateur," Wise feared that an anti-immigration backlash would make impossible Roosevelt's intended liberal policies toward the Austrian Jews. The rabbi even quoted his "elevator lad," who said, " 'It is all right to take care of the Austrian Jews, but I cannot afford to give up my job for them.' "[22]

Several days after the cabinet meeting on March 18, the president responded to the entreaties of Morgenthau and ordered Sumner Welles to expedite the liberalization of immigration procedures. Welles was also instructed to appeal to Latin America to take some refugees.[23] Roosevelt wanted to go still further in internationalizing the refugee issue. He announced an invitation to other countries to join with the United States in establishing a special international committee to promote and support emigration from Germany and Austria. Roosevelt also suggested that, domestically, the government assist in mobilizing private organizations that could fund the emigration process. He signed a public appeal to the American people, reminding them of the American tradition of offering asylum to refugees. Roosevelt's only change in the draft Morgenthau prepared was to strike the words "religious" and "racial refugees" and to substitute "political refugees."[24] Even though he wanted to rescue the oppressed, Roosevelt reverted to his symbolic policy, an approach that would cost the United States government little and make few drains on his own political budget. If Hitler found it valuable to publicize the Jewish identity of his victims, Roosevelt found it equally expedient to obscure the religious identity of those he would see rescued.

Comfortable with the distance that the term "political refugees" afforded, FDR used it a second time in April. In New Deal style, the president turned an interfaith group of prominent Americans into the foundation of a new organization, the Presidential Advisory Committee on Political Refugees.[25] Roosevelt had again employed the "competitive management" approach that was so much a part of his personality. The PACPR was to be the liaison between whatever international committee was established, FDR's administration, and any private agencies concerned with immigration. Yet another agency had been created to wrestle with the Departments of State and Labor, offer the president information, compete for his ear, and manufacture the kind of creative chaos he thrived on.

The din that arose from Evian-les-Bains, where the international conclave on refugees met, was more the bluster and rhetoric of procrastination than the creative disharmony of competing interests, FDR's favorite tune. Few of the nations that attended came prepared to make a commitment to accept refugees. The only point of agreement was the establishment of a permanent Intergovernmental Committee on Refugees. If he had accomplished nothing else, FDR had at least made clear that he regarded the refugee issue as a matter of international humanitarianism and not a responsibility to be borne exclusively by the United States. As the IGCR commenced its duties under the leadership of Washington attorney George Rublee, Roosevelt could claim that he had placed the United States in a humanitarian role on the refugee issue, at least symbolically. But he could also be content that he had neither tampered with the nation's restrictionist policies nor cost himself the votes of the millions of Americans who continued to oppose the admission of refugees.

As usual, Roosevelt's political instincts were on target. Measures of public opinion suggest that even the limited hope his efforts offered refugees was more generous than that which the majority of Americans might have extended. A *Fortune* poll published the same month that the international conference convened reported that two-thirds of the respondents (67.4 percent) agreed that "with conditions as they are we should try to keep them [the refugees] out." Only 18.2 percent took Roosevelt's more moderate attitude that "we should allow them to come but not raise our immigration quotas." Far fewer, 4.9 percent of the sample, wanted to "encourage them to come even if we have to raise our immigration quotas." The other 9.5 percent were apathetic and did not know where they stood on the controversy.[26]

The shattering of glass in the cities and towns of Germany in November 1938, Kristallnacht, was heard in even the most apathetic American towns. Press coverage thrust the story before the American public and its reluctant president.[27] FDR was forced to respond. Still, the increasing unpopularity of a remilitarized Germany made Roosevelt's task easier. He could recall Ambassador Hugh Wilson "for consultation" and issue a strongly worded communique without apprehensions of a political backlash. Indeed, over 70 percent of those Americans polled on the recall of Wilson favored the move.[28] On November 15, FDR told reporters that he "could scarcely believe that such a thing could occur in twentieth century civilization."[29] Though he still did not modify the quota system, a generous Roosevelt did order the Labor Department to extend the visitors' visas of over 12,000 German Jewish refugees in the United States for another six months. So often had Roosevelt spoken the words and phrases that speechwriter Samuel Rosenman had written for him that the situation almost seemed reversed when Rosenman wrote, "I do not believe it either desirable or practicable to recommend any change in the quota provision of our immigration law."[30] Roosevelt could afford an act of generosity; more would be an extravagance he would not chance.

The day after his condemnation of the German rampage against the Jews, FDR met with PACPR's chairman, James G. McDonald, and two other members, Hamilton Fish Armstrong and George L. Warren. The three requested that Myron Taylor be sent to London as FDR's personal representative on refugee matters, thereby circumventing the unsympathetic ambassador, Joseph Kennedy. The ambassador had a tendency to act with flagrant disregard for the authority structure of the State Department and the wishes of the president. He believed a concern for European Jewry to be a misplaced humanitarianism that could be detrimental to the country's foreign policy toward Germany and Washington's relationship with London. McDonald, Armstrong, and Warren also asked for the president's support in a public appeal for funds or his sponsorship of a congressional appropriations bill to finance refugee resettlement. Finally, they urged Roosevelt to complete plans with the Dominican Republic to take advantage of Trujillo's offer to accept Jewish refugees.[31] Knowing quite well the prejudices of Joseph Kennedy, FDR had little hesitation in complying with all of the group's requests.

By late November, Roosevelt had become quite interested in finding alternative plans of refuge for the Jews. He saw colonization as an alternative to Palestine, which the British were jealously guarding. FDR hoped to raise private funds to purchase a sanctuary to accommodate over five million people and become the foundation of a permanent Jewish homeland.[32] Not unlike Lincoln who sought to remedy America's race problems by colonizing slaves and black freedmen abroad, FDR was hoping to relocate an unwanted population. Over the next two years, he considered locations in Africa, Asia, and even Alaska for his colonization plan. Any plan was open to consideration that avoided the public antagonism and congressional opposition that quota revision would likely entail.

After the elections of 1938, FDR could afford even less to antagonize Congress. Worsening economic recession and the anti-New Deal coalition of conservative Democrats and Republicans forged in 1937 had taken their toll at the polls. During the spring of 1938, Roosevelt launched an assault against New Deal opponents in party primaries. In a fireside chat he denounced these "Copperheads," a term borrowed from the Civil War era when it was used by Republicans to describe antiwar, ergo disloyal, Democrats.[33] He then barnstormed the country, speaking in behalf of Democrats loyal to the New Deal and attacking their opponents. But, except for the victories of Alben Barkley and Elmer Thomas in Kentucky and Oklahoma respectively, the trip was a failure. Candidates he supported lost in Georgia, South Carolina, and Maryland. In some states, such as Nevada and Colorado, the president actually avoided open fights with candidates he felt he could not beat. In the November elections, Republicans picked up eighty-one seats in the House, won eight seats in the Senate, and netted thirteen governorships. Despite their gains, the Republicans lost twenty-four of the thirty-two Senate elections. The New Deal was not moribund, but the Republican party was rising from the ashes of 1936. Controversial legislation on immigration was the last thing that most New Dealers in Congress wanted, and there is no evidence that FDR was prepared to take the attendant risks of supporting bills to expand quotas for the refugees.

While the president was thinking of which far-off land would prove both hospitable to the refugees and politically affordable to their benefactors, especially himself, the problem was brought to American shores. In May 1939, the president was presented with a crisis that could not be solved through his favorite technique of management and conflict: 933 passengers of the *St. Louis,* the majority of them Jewish refugees, were seeking a temporary home in Havana, Cuba. Over 700 of them had already applied for American visas, even securing affidavits of support. They wished to await their turn in Havana. When the Cubans denied permission for the ship to dock, the passengers telegrammed FDR for help, informing him that 67 passengers held American quota registration numbers. While diplomats stumbled over technicalities, the president left the telegram unanswered. The *St. Louis* returned to Europe, where only the extraordinary efforts of the Jewish Joint Distribution Committee prevented the passengers from returning to Germany and the likelihood of concentration camps. Roosevelt could have clipped the red tape with an executive order, but by so doing he would have created an extraordinary exception. The passengers adrift did not fit into any standard category—tourist, visitor, or visa-holding immigrant—and exceptions set precedents. The president would not take the risk of alienating the Cubans, perhaps his own State Department, and, most of all, the American public.

Similarly Roosevelt distanced himself from the humanitarian efforts of Senator Robert F. Wagner and Representative Edith Nourse Rogers to legislate refugee rescue. Their bill called for the transfer of 20,000 German children to the United States over a two-year period, in excess of the quota limit. Roosevelt's well-known response to an appeal for presidential endorsement was to scribble "File No Action" on the memorandum.[34] Once again the president accurately assessed the mood in Congress and, beyond that, among the public generally. The bill, emasculated by amendments, died in committee in the summer of 1939. Six months earlier George Gallup's pollsters had determined that 66 percent of the American people opposed the admission of 10,000 refugee children from Germany that year.[35] With another presidential election on the horizon and little amelioration of the hostility to immigrants, Roosevelt must have calculated the costs and benefits of his support. With the bill likely to lose, he could gain few supporters but lose many votes the following November by endorsing this compassionate but ill-fated and perhaps naive bill, votes that 20,000 youngsters arriving over a two-year period could not repay for many elections to come.

By the fall of 1939, FDR was preoccupied with the war in Europe and the politics of the homefront. The two converged in the threat of fifth column subversives. Throughout 1939 and 1940, the president and millions of other Americans feared that foreign subversives might be planted among the refugees by the warring powers, especially Germany and the Soviet Union. Now national security fears seemed an additional justification for restrictionism. While the president did not wish to alarm Americans unnecessarily, neither did he wish to lull them into a false security.

During the last months of 1939, in the light of national security fears, Roosevelt spoke with fresh enthusiasm about colonization as the only viable solution to the refugee problem. Colonization remained a solution that, when discussed in the abstract, provoked little public opposition, definitely an advantage with another presidential election coming. When Brandeis visited FDR in October 1939, Roosevelt raised the possibility of creating a new agency, a favorite New Deal tactic. This resettlement agency would be headed by Bernard Baruch. Brandeis, less than enthusiastic, commented that "Baruch would be more likely to consider colonization of Jews on some undiscovered planet than Palestine."[36] Roosevelt abandoned the agency idea but maintained an interest in large-scale resettlement schemes.

A month after Brandeis's visit, Roosevelt held extensive talks with Interior Secretary Harold Ickes on the use of Alaska as a refugee sanctuary.[37] Roosevelt was considering settling 10,000 individuals in Alaska, annually, for the next five years. Anticipating the criticism that such an endeavor might create a national enclave of Jews that might resist Americanization, the president had even considered limiting the proportion of Jews to 10 percent of the settlers. Early in 1940, an Alaska colonization act, the King-Havenner bill, was debated in Congress. Under the proposed legislation, refugees between 16 and 45 years of age who qualified for the new jobs that would be created in agriculture, forestry, fishing, mining, and fur farming could come to Alaska outside the immigration quota limits. Wives and children of the refugees would also be allowed to enter. In spite of the many economic benefits that the bill contained for the development of Alaska, the bill died in subcommittee for much the same reasons that the Wagner-Rogers bill failed to reach the floor. Public opposition was vocal, especially in Alaska. Immigration opponents in the forty-eight states saw it as a backdoor to America for refugees. Though Roosevelt was enthusiastic about the Alaska plan, once the bill was introduced the president backed away from it. Undersecretary of State Sumner Welles cautioned the president that the bill's passage would require new laws restricting immigration into the United States from the territory of Alaska. Again Roosevelt would have found himself locked in confrontation with congressional restrictionists. FDR withdrew to the sidelines, still intrigued by the idea of resettlement—especially in Africa.

In November 1940, Roosevelt won his controversial third term, scoring a decisive defeat by five million votes over Wendell Willkie. It was not an easy campaign for Roosevelt. As late as October 30, a Gallup poll showed Willkie about even with Roosevelt nationally and ahead of him in New York and other key states.[38] Some of FDR's supporters were wavering because New Deal economic measures had not banished the depression; others, because Roosevelt appeared to be steering the nation toward war in Europe. It was not an elegant campaign; it "spluttered to a surly finish," as Willkie charged that a third term would mean dictatorship at home and American boys dying on battlefields abroad.[39] Neither candidate ever promised American Jews major revision of the quota system or presented a fresh program for refugees. Nevertheless, Jewish voters supported FDR generously. The results of national surveys conducted by the American Institute of Public Opinion and by the National Opinion Research Center show that more than 90 out of every 100 Jews voted Democratic in 1940.[40]

Even more ironic, perhaps, than the large Jewish vote for Roosevelt was the president's reference to America's immigrant heritage in the brief prayer he offered in his "nonpartisan" election-eve radio talk:

> Save us from violence, discord and confusion; from pride and arrogance, and from every evil way. Defend our liberties, and fashion into one united people the multitudes brought hither out of many kindreds and tongues.[41]

The next morning fifty million Americans (the highest turnout in American history), including several million Jews, decided to stick with Roosevelt.

Like a sphinx on the American landscape, Franklin Roosevelt has mystified those who have sought to comprehend American refugee policy during the 1930s and beyond. Though none have judged him an anti-Semite, some have suggested that FDR "loved people only in groups and rarely fathomed the travail and agony of any single person."[42] Most agree that Roosevelt "loved the adoration and attention of people" and "played for his audience."[43] Historian Henry Feingold suggests that FDR was intellectually incapable of grasping the Jews' plight, a deceptively shallow individual who felt certain of his ability to get his way by "charm and manipulation." Indulging himself in psychological speculation, Feingold conjectures that Roosevelt had developed this aspect of his personality at Harvard, "where he felt a desperate need to be popular especially after invitations to the clubs of his choice eluded him. He tended to mute or otherwise obfuscate issues which did not directly enhance his popularity or were simply distasteful or entailed a price."[44] Such unsubstantiated interpretations seem unnecessarily convoluted and unilluminating. Roosevelt's response to the refugee situation was no more and no less than one might expect of any politician aware of the constraints upon his power.

That Roosevelt was a master politician is a piece of the common wisdom. What is perhaps less well understood is how Roosevelt's style of presidential leadership fueled the bureaucratic brush fires that consumed the refugee issue. Roosevelt's style, extolled by journalists and held up as a model by political scientists, was ideally suited to sustaining presidential power and prerogative in the era of bureaucratic government. It encouraged a controlled dissonance, a battle of bureaucrats that yielded the president information, allowing him several policy options from which to choose. FDR could pick over the remains of bureaucratic battles he had instigated or encouraged, sifting the data and mulling over the policy positions of the exhausted combatants. An issue without a vocal champion or great public support could not survive such battles. The plight of Jewish refugees was never a matter demonstrably critical to the national interest. It was a humanitarian issue of limited concern to most

Americans, as public opinion polls and congressional opposition to the Wagner-Rogers legislation amply demonstrate. Roosevelt wisely established a dual policy, one restrictionist and the other symbolically humanitarian. He eschewed confrontations that placed him in opposition to overwhelmingly public sentiment. Restrictionism, on the other hand, seemed very much in the public interest, especially in an era of economic depression. The result was that the issue of visas for Jewish refugees between 1933 and 1940 became bogged down in the bureaucratic machinery that FDR had mastered.

Would any astute occupant of the White House have behaved differently from FDR on the refugee issue? His actions were neither unusual for a president nor out of character for a politician aware of his limitations. It may well be that FDR's extraordinary ability to express compassion for the underdog, demonstrated often during the depression, has enticed historians into speculating about why he did not do more for European Jewry. Perhaps his unusually generous and warm relationships with many American Jews made his unwillingness to admit more refugees at his own political risk especially frustrating for Jewish leaders and more puzzling to many Jews in subsequent years than it should be. In the end, Roosevelt's abdication of leadership on the refugee issue might not be unusual or surprising if it were not inconsistent with others' inflated expectations of him. It is perhaps his own fault; he was so skilled in understanding and exploiting the political symbols and rituals to which American voters respond. His limitations politically, and perhaps personally as well, have yet to be fully accepted and understood by scholars and lay people alike.

TWELVE

Roosevelt and the Holocaust

To write about Franklin Roosevelt's reaction to the Nazi murder of approximately six million Jews is to engage in speculation. As far as is known, he said very little about it and wrote virtually nothing. It does not follow, however, that FDR was unconcerned or indifferent to Nazi mass murders of Jews.[1] Some of his comments and his actions during the late 1930s seem to indicate the contrary; he wanted to get Jews out of Germany before the murderers gained full sway.[2]

This complex master of the art of politics was at the same time loquacious and terse. He was outwardly gregarious but kept much to himself and often left associates and subordinates with sharply different impressions about his attitudes. Who else could keep both Breckinridge Long and Stephen Wise pacified at the same time? His calculated ambiguity may be proof of necessary political skills, but it makes life very difficult for historians of the Roosevelt presidency, whose problems are compounded by the absence of cabinet minutes (expressly prohibited by the president).

To judge Franklin Roosevelt's reaction to the Final Solution, we must first review his prior views on refugee policy, then calculate when he received information about the overall Nazi plan, and finally gauge any immediate or subsequent changes in his behavior. We must keep in mind that outside forces may have limited his ability to react in certain ways. Even a powerful president was not a free agent. But in the end we can assess FDR's attitudes only through his behavior.

In 1940, FDR reversed his previous view that the full German-Austrian quota (27,370) should be available for the many victims of Nazi persecution. Roosevelt did not simply turn visa policy over to the bureaucrats in the State Department. The evidence indicates that he gave the signal to tighten immigration regulations partly out of real concern for national security, partly out of recognition of political realities.

As early as September 6, 1939, he had requested that the attorney general instruct the FBI to take charge of all investigative work regarding espionage, sabotage, and violation of neutrality laws. Representatives of the FBI later held a series of conferences with local law enforcement agents throughout the country, stressing the seriousness of the danger and formulating detailed plans to cope with it. At one conference held in Washington on August 5–6, 1940, Attorney General Robert Jackson read a presidential statement about the danger of espionage, sabotage, and fifth column activity to representatives of forty-two state governments. The president condemned efforts during World War I in this field as inadequate and called for FBI direction of activity this time. Attorney General Jackson added that the Axis powers were now trying to weaken the U.S. as they had already weakened France before war had broken out in Europe.[3]

FDR's worries had been magnified in the spring of 1940. Already embarked upon an anti-Axis course in foreign policy, FDR had learned that an American code clerk named Tyler Kent, serving in the American embassy in London, had turned over to fascist sympathizers in London secret American-British diplomatic correspondence from 1938 on, including the Roosevelt-Churchill exchanges. The material quickly found its way to Rome and Berlin. Another by-product of the leak was that the Germans were able to crack the American codes, which then had to be changed. This was a psychological blow that struck the president hard. From this point on, FDR could hardly over-emphasize the fifth column danger.[4]

Another high-ranking official who shared this view of an endangered national security was former Assistant-Secretary of State George Messersmith, who had become ambassador to Cuba. Messersmith told Undersecretary Welles that the German conquest of France had gone so smoothly because French morale had alrady been undermined, not only by aliens but also by French citizens opposed to the government. Messersmith urged the president to take preventive measures against similar happenings in the U.S. and claimed that the American public would overwhelmingly support temporary sacrifice of civil liberties. Again, to Felix Frankfurter, Messersmith argued that the failure to restrict an insignificant minority had led to the breakdown of more than one European country. He advocated immediate controls over aliens and over certain native-born and naturalized Americans, whom he considered potentially even more dangerous.[5] With the administration's backing, Congress passed the Smith Act in June 1940, requiring all aliens to be registered and fingerprinted. Those who were presently or previously members of communist or fascist organizations could be deported. The Smith Act also made it a crime to advocate the violent overthrow of the government.[6]

Concern for security meant that the president was no longer willing to take many chances with foreign refugees. When a reporter asked the president how the American public's suspicions about aliens, particularly refugees, could be allayed, FDR in effect referred that task to private immigration organizations. But he defended the need to check refugees, because there were spies—voluntary and involuntary—among them. He specifically cited the German government's alleged threat to shoot the relatives of German Jewish refugees unless the latter agreed to work as spies for Germany.[7]

Precisely where the president obtained this information is uncertain. One possibility was Colonel William Donovan, who was receiving briefings and information from the British during the summer of 1940. British officials made no secret of their fears of a fifth column.[8] But FDR's source was more likely to have been Ambassador William Bullitt in France. In August 1940, having returned to the U.S., Bullitt gave a major foreign policy address backing the sale or lease of U.S. destroyers to Great Britain. In the course of this speech given to the American Philosophical Society in Philadelphia, Bullitt stated that war was coming to the U.S. and that the agents of the dictators were already preparing the way. He went on to describe how hundreds of communist and Nazi agents in France had transmitted the movements of the French army by short-wave radio to Germany. Bullitt then blamed the French for being even more hospitable to refugees from Germany than the United States was; allegedly, more than one-half of the spies captured in France were refugees from Germany. What is of particular interest about this diatribe is that both Undersecretary Welles and the president read Bullitt's speech beforehand. Welles went so far as to say that he approved every word of it. Two days after the speech the *New York Times* editorialized: "Our own history in the next few years will be happier if our people act now, in the spirit of Mr. Bullitt's warning."[9] Bullitt was an anti-Semite whose testimony on the issue of "refugee" agents might be doubted. But Roosevelt, Messersmith, Welles, and the *New York Times* were all reacting to the same fears. In fact, some of those most committed to an anti-Axis foreign policy, including the president, seemed most concerned about the danger of spies among the refugees.

The State Department could hardly show leniency to visa applicants in this atmosphere, nor did Breckinridge Long wish to. Circular telegrams went out in June, July, and September 1940 urging consuls to reject or at least suspend any visa application about which there was any doubt. One consul in Stockholm replied: "Very difficult, sometimes impossible [for] refugees here [to] satisfy us completely [regarding] past and potential future activities, criminal record, etc. . . . Result has naturally been delay and drastic reduction [in the] issuance [of visas] as envisaged [in] Department's telegraphic instructions [of] June 29."[10]

Even the privileged lists of intellectuals and labor leaders compiled by the President's Advisory Committee and other American organizations came under close scrutiny, which set off a prolonged political battle in Washington. Breckinridge Long told FDR that the emergency visa arrangements were being abused. Some of the applicants were not in entire accord with U.S. policy (i.e., too far to the left, in Long's view), and consular officers considered others not to be "of the desirable element." Moreover, the PACPR was submitting too many names. Long wanted to change the procedure by adding an additional check to weed out German agents and other undesirables and to cut down the number of names added in the future.

Roosevelt heard both sides, and, faced with conflicting testimony, he brought in Sumner Welles and Justice Department officials to help resolve the dispute. But Long eventually got what he really wanted—an interdepartmental visa review board in Washington that would scrutinize visa applications and weed out security problems. The restrictionists were bolstered further in June 1941 when the Congress passed a law enabling consuls to deny any kind of visa to anyone who would endanger public safety. After jurisdictional disputes broke out again in July between State and Justice, Hull consulted FDR, who decided that the basic responsibility on visas should remain with the State Department.[11]

Long's victory over McDonald was not accidental. The president also believed that security came before all else. When McDonald complained again to Eleanor Roosevelt, she spoke to her husband and brought back a message. FDR wanted the PACPR and the Intergovermental Committee to continue because of the future (not the present). The presidential committee should not be discouraged even if its nominees were not given visas, because sometimes investigations turned up information that made it necessary to refuse admission, and investigations had to be made.[12] This was, in effect, an endorsement of much of Long's position and a renunciation of the short-term changes in the immigration program that the president had advocated as late as October 1939.

Not all bureaucrats took the same view as Long. Taking advantage of a loophole in the immigration law for the Virgin Islands, Henry Hart of the Justice Department and Nathan Margold of Interior devised a plan in late 1940 to have the governor and legislature of the Virgin Islands admit refugees without visitors' visas. But Long and the State Department raised objections. Although Secretary of the Interior Harold Ickes backed the proposal, FDR came down on the other side.

> I yield to no person in any department in my deep-seated desire to help the hundreds of thousands of foreign refugees in the present world situation. The Virgin Islands, however, present to this Government a very serious social and economic problem not yet solved. If the Interior Department could find some unoccupied place . . . where we could set up a refugee camp without involving a small but highly difficult population problem now underway as in the case of the Virgin Islands, that would be treated with sympathy by the State Department and by me.[13]

When Margold persisted, the attorney general ultimately ruled the Virgin Islands plan illegal.[14]

Although Long was the administration's point man on the refugee issue, one must really speak of a State Department stance. Undersecretary Welles was free of Long's prejudices. But Welles, too, harbored deep suspicions about German government motives. In December 1940, he wrote to FDR that recent deportations of German Jews to unoccupied France indicated that the Germans were trying to "force our hand on the refugee problem."

> Were we to yield to this pressure all the evidence indicates that in the wake of the ten thousand Jews recently forced into France the Germans would drive on the French

the remaining Jews from Germany and the occupied territories, hundreds of thousands of persons, in the expectation that the French in turn would persuade this country and the other American republics to receive them. Information reaching us is conclusive that if we or the other American Republics yield to these blackmailing totalitarian tactics the Germans will inaugurate something approaching a "reign of terror" against the Jewish people. . . .[15]

The undersecretary believed that German persecution and deportation of Jews were primarily instruments to weaken the opponents of Nazi Germany. This indeed had been one aspect of German policy during 1938–39, but Welles and others now failed to perceive that Nazi policy had entered a new and more deadly phase. Assistant Secretary of State Adolf Berle, who had favored a formal American protest against German deportations of Jews to Poland in early 1940, found it "unhappy" but "necessary" in early 1941 to tighten the visa machinery, because the Russians and Germans were forcing some refugees to act as spies.[16] Lower-level State Department officials as well as Foreign Service officers abroad were hardly less diligent in protecting national security and eschewing risky humanitarian undertakings.

After December 1941 the idea of protecting national security remained a prime concern for FDR. The president approved the War Department's plan to intern the Japanese-Americans on the West Coast, and he urged Attorney General Francis Biddle to press criminal charges against his antiwar critics. He even wanted to get rid of alien waiters from Washington restaurants, where customers exchanged all too much confidential information about the war. As other scholars have noted, the war eroded the president's respect for due process and civil liberties.[17] In this context, it is easier to understand why FDR approved of the State Department's tighter visa regulations. Fairness to visa applicants was not even a remote presidential concern then.

Some in Congress were much more extreme. Senator Richard Reynolds of North Carolina announced in June 1941 that, if he had his way, he would, without the slightest hesitation, "build a wall about the United States so high and so secure that no single alien or foreign refugee from any country upon the face of the earth could possibly scale or ascend it."[18] Reynolds was more outspoken than most congressmen, but he was hardly alone on this issue. FDR certainly harbored no fondness for the isolationist Reynolds, but he had to work with an often-refractory Congress. A bill to extend the length of military service to eighteen months passed the House by only one vote in August 1941. The president did not want immigration to add to his foreign policy disputes with the Hill.

Obstructed for years by a strong isolationist faction in Congress, pilloried by right-wing extremists as "President Rosenfeld," depicted as being surrounded by Jews, well aware of a significant anti-Semitic current among the American public, and seeing the war as the greatest crisis in western history, FDR reacted as most realistic politicians would. He limited his visibility on Jewish issues partly in self-defense, partly in the hope that the public and Congress would be less likely to object to his defense and foreign policies.

As Roosevelt scholar Robert Dallek has observed, FDR wanted more than the support of a bare majority in Congress and among the public. If the United States entered the European war, it would need a broad, stable consensus, which was why the president waited for the other side to strike the first blow.[19] Conveniently, after the Japanese attack at Pearl Harbor, the German government came to the aid of its ally and declared war against the United States first. Hitler's foolhardy action eliminated the need for FDR to go to Congress and explain why the U.S. should work for the defeat of Germany, too. That did not stop former ambassador William Bullitt from telling people that the Roosevelt administration's emphasis on the European war as opposed to the Asian one was the result of Jewish influence.[20]

In actuality, considerations of strategy and propaganda during the war led Roosevelt to temper inclinations to do anything publicly on "Jewish" causes. In October 1942, knowing that political conditions in the Middle East and North Africa were sensitive and that the area was crucial to Allied military success, FDR thought it would be a good idea to have someone do a firsthand analysis on resettlement of refugees, which resulted in a tour of three and one half months for an American lieutenant colonel, Harold Hoskins, and an accompanying British officer. Among Hoskins's findings, reported back to the president in May 1943, were growing tensions between Arabs and Jews in Palestine and in the Middle East and North Africa generally:

> There is an ever-present Arab fear of American support for political Zionism with its proposed Jewish State and Jewish Army in Palestine. . . . *The experiences of British troops during their retreat in Burma are a grave and recent warning of the serious effects that a hostile, rather than friendly, native population can have on our military operations* [Hoskins's italics].

The primacy of the war effort dictated FDR's reaction. The president hastened to reassure King Saud of Saudi Arabia that no decision would be reached altering the basic situation in Palestine without full consultation of both Arabs and Jews.[21] He sent this message in spite of the fact that privately, to Morgenthau, FDR had talked about moving Arabs from Palestine to some other part of the Middle East to make room for additional Jews and an independent Jewish state.[22] This pro-Zionist solution was hardly an idea one could even raise publicly in the midst of an all-out war.

FDR also seemed quite sensitive to anti-Semitic currents in Spain and Latin America. When Gerardo Murillo, alias Dr. Atl, came out with the first booklet of a planned three-volume series entitled *Judios Sobre America (Jews over America),* J. Edgar Hoover sent a translated copy to the White House. The author claimed to demonstrate that FDR himself was of Jewish ancestry and that he had surrounded himself with Jewish advisors and cabinet members. Pictures even allegedly showed a physical resemblance between FDR, his family members, and various Jews. The president expressed the hope that the State Department and the Mexican government would be able to prevent publication abroad. The White House asked the attorney general to prevent publication and distribution in the U.S.[23]

When the president addressed the issue of war crimes, he avoided emphasizing the Nazi crimes against Jews. American Jewish organizations arranging a Madison Square Garden rally in July 1942 asked for a presidential statement to be read to the audience. FDR's response was "the American people not only sympathize with all victims of Nazi crime but will hold the perpetrators of these crimes to strict accountability in a day of reckoning which will surely come." Another presidential statement issued in August 1942 simply denounced barbaric crimes against civilian populations in Axis-occupied countries, particularly on the continent of Europe. FDR mentioned crimes carried out in many of the European countries, as well as in Japanese-controlled China and southeast Asia. Those involved in such behavior would eventually be brought to justice, he promised. According to presidential confidant Adolf Berle, Dutch government pressure as well as Berle's own feeling that the statement might deter crimes led to the presidential statement. Another presidential declaration was issued in October. Noting that the Axis crimes continued unabated, the president warned that the U.S. and other nations would bring the perpetrators before courts of law and that all war criminals would have to be surrendered at the end of the war.[24]

There is little question that the president was aware of the Final Solution by November 1942, if not earlier. Given Roosevelt's unwillingness to stir up additional trouble with Congress, certain lobbies, and Middle Eastern nations over European Jewry, he likely resisted believing the early reports of Jews being killed en masse in death factories. If Felix Frankfurter, a Jew, could not force himself to believe them,[25] why should FDR have been different? But the reports kept coming in. It strains credulity to think that Undersecretary Welles would have confirmed the information in Riegner's telegram of August 1942 and given Rabbi Wise leeway to make the information public without notifying the president of the situation.[26] And there were signs of minor shifts in policy, quite possibly as the result of the accumulated information. In the fall of 1942, the president did not hesitate to approve the admission, as a special case, of 5,000 Jewish children from France—no chance of spies there. But Sumner Welles, who had taken charge of the matter, took pains to avoid adverse publicity.[27]

A second indicator was Roosevelt's request to Congress in the Third War Powers Act for the power to suspend immigration laws in the interest of the war effort. The bill was introduced in November 1942, and Roosevelt lobbied personally with House speaker Sam Rayburn for the immigration provision only two days after Stephen Wise's press conferences on the Final Solution.[28] To be sure, the president's emissaries expressly denied, under hostile congressional questioning, that he intended to bring civilian refugees into the U.S., but one cannot rule out this possibility. What is clearer is that hostile congressional reaction and suspicion about the entrance of refugees, and the deletion of the provision from the bill, could only have strengthened FDR's inclination not to do battle publicly on behalf of European Jews.

Stephen Wise then asked the president to receive a delegation of Jewish leaders at the White House in early December as part of an international day of mourning (December 2) for European Jews. The Jewish leaders wished to give FDR specific information about the Final Solution. FDR did not wish to see the group and tried to avoid the meeting. He suggested that the delegation go to the State Department instead. Wise persisted, and, with the assistance of presidential advisor David Niles, he obtained an appointment for a small group of Jewish leaders with the president on Tuesday, December 8, at noon.²⁹

The president announced to the group that he had just appointed Herbert Lehman to head the new Office of Foreign Relief and Rehabilitation Operations. It gave him "sadistic satisfaction" to appoint a Jew to this post; "Junkers" would eventually have to go to Lehman on their knees and ask for bread. After Wise read the delegation's declaration and presented a detailed memorandum about the Final Solution, he appealed to FDR to bring the extermination program to the world's attention and "to make an effort to stop it." The president said that the government *was familiar with most of the facts,* but it was hard to find a suitable course of action. The Allies could not make it appear that the entire German people were murderers or agreed with Hitler's actions. He agreed to release another statement denouncing Nazi mass killings. When the delegation wanted some statement that it could release immediately, FDR authorized the re-release of his statement to July's Madison Square Garden rally, which, he said, had to be quoted exactly. That meant no specific emphasis of Nazi crimes against Jews. The delegation press release exceeded the president's instructions and quoted FDR as saying that he was shocked to learn that two million Jews had, in one way or another, already perished as a result of Nazi rule and crimes.³⁰

In his thank-you note to Niles afterward, Wise wrote that the "Chief" could not have been more "friendly and helpful," that he was "cordiality itself." Wise continued:

> The word he gave us will carry through the country and perhaps serve in some degre as warning to the beasts. . . . Thank God for Roosevelt. We ought to distribute cards throughout the country bearing just four letters, TGFR, and as the Psalmist would have said, thank Him every day and every hour.³¹

It is hard to escape the conclusion that Wise was more impressed by FDR's cordiality, his anti-Nazism, and his strong war leadership than any specific service to European Jewry. The president had not promised retribution against Germany or changes in refugee policy. And the United Nations Declaration of December 17, 1942, condemning the Nazis' "bestial policy of cold-blooded extermination," resulted more from pressure from the Polish government in exile and Winston Churchill's interest than anything the United States government did.

In early 1943, partly because of growing public pressure, the United States and Great Britain agreed to hold the Bermuda Conference to consider refugee assistance. But the early indications were that both governments would hold to their strict line that nothing could be done that might detract from the war effort. Moreover, the layers of visa committees in Washington had slowed visa approvals to a trickle. When a delegation of seven Jewish congressmen sought an appointment with the president to press their complaints on visas and related issues, again FDR tried to divert them to the State Department. Celler refused to accept that and promised an "off the record" session. They got their meeting at the White House on April 1.

White House secretary Edwin Watson subsequently informed Breckinridge Long that the delegation had criticized the voting of the military officials on the visa committees and had urged a simplification of the visa process. They also apparently pointed out the sharp decrease in the number of visas approved, and the president responded that perhaps visitors' visas would again be issued. In a follow-up meeting with Sumner Welles, Judge Joseph Proskauer of the American Jewish Committee, now also representing the Joint Emergency Committee on European Jewish Affairs, pressed for a Jewish delegation to attend the Bermuda Conference. That request was denied, and the Joint Emergency Committee itself was unable to obtain an audience with FDR before the conference, despite an urgent request.[32]

When Secretary of State Cordell Hull reported the results of the Bermuda Conference to the president, he posed a number of questions of "high policy," which needed presidential decisions. FDR agreed to the idea of moving a specific number of refugees from vulnerable locations to designated temporary havens, the costs to be shared by the U.S. and Great Britain. He rejected the idea of trying to bring refugees into the United States without compliance with the immigration laws or in excess of quota limitations. He advised against sending large numbers of Jews to North Africa and agreed that anything that would set off prolonged congressional debate should be avoided. FDR shared Hull's view that refugees should not be admitted to the U.S. as temporary visitors, which would be seen as an evasion of the quota laws.[33] That did not leave a great deal of room for action.

From 1940 until the middle of 1943, Franklin Roosevelt's behavior with regard to European Jewry showed general consistency. He undoubtedly regretted reported Nazi killings of Jews in Europe, but they did not affect him deeply enough to override his basic instinct: for domestic and foreign policy reasons, he could not allow the United States to be seen as giving Jews special leniency or assistance. Many millions of Europeans were suffering under Nazi rule, and Allied troops had their hands full with the Germans. It was not advisable—it was strongly inadvisable politically—to make a public issue of the Holocaust. It is significant that the two moves to relax tight immigration restrictions in the fall of 1942 were both supposed to go through quietly and that, when the immigration provision of Third War Powers Act became controversial, the president backed down.

If there was a deeper, more personal reason for presidential inaction, it may well lie in Roosevelt's upbringing and milieu. The president's mother was anti-Semitic, his half-brother even more so. The young Franklin Roosevelt absorbed some of this sentiment and only gradually grew out of it. By the time he reached the governorship of New York, he appreciated men and women of talent, whatever their background and descent. Steven Early, his friend and presidential press secretary, apparently did not. Some of FDR's best friends were anti-Semites.[34] If there was anyone aware of the influence of anti-Semitism in the United States, it was Franklin Roosevelt. He may have been overly sensitive to the danger of anti-Semitic reaction to American policies.

By the summer of 1943, three factors began to alter the president's attitude. The first was the improvement of the war situation. The invasion of Italy gave the Americans and British a toehold on the continent; the war on the eastern front was going better for the Allies. The war was far from over, but one could now confidently predict the outcome. The president began to take an interest in matters such as shipping food to suffering populations, but he ran into British resistance. He told Francis Pickett of the American Friends Service Committee that the worst conditions were in Poland and that he felt frustrated by the problem.[35] This was not yet a specific concern for the fate of European Jewry, but it was evidence of humanitarian concern.

The second influence, whose weight is difficult to measure, was a personal presentation of the horrors of the Final Solution. On July 28, 1943, at 10:30 A.M., the Polish ambassador, Jan Ciechanowski, and Jan Karski, a lieutenant in the Polish underground army, went upstairs in the White House to the president's study. Serving as a courier from the Polish underground, Karski had arrived in London with messages for the Polish government in exile, the Allied governments, and Polish Jewish leaders. One of his most important messages concerned the Final Solution:

> The unprecedented destruction of the entire Jewish population is *not* motivated by Germany's *military* requirements. Hitler and his subordinates aim at the total destruction of the Jews *before* the war ends and *regardless* of its outcome. The Allied governments cannot disregard this reality. The Jews in Poland are help-less. . . . Only the powerful Allied governments can help effectively.[36]

Roosevelt began to question Karski about German methods of political terrorism. Karski described mass arrests and concentration camps in Poland, some where mass murders were carried out daily. He went on to talk of his own clandestine visit to the Belzec extermination camp in 1942, where he entered disguised in the uniform of an Estonian guard. He saw hundreds of dead Jews packed into railway cars, which then were closed and moved outside the camp.

When the doors were opened, the corpses were removed and the bodies taken out and burned. He did not actually get to see the gas chambers themselves, which were enclosed and under tight security. Karski emphasized that there was no exaggeration in the accounts of how the Nazis were handling the Jewish question. Polish underground sources estimated the number of Polish Jews killed by November 1942 (when Karski left Poland) at 1.8 million, and the underground was convinced that the Nazis were out to exterminate the entire Jewish population. The president asked many other questions about various underground activities and, after an hour, said goodbye to Karski with a noncommittal comment. "Tell your nation we shall win the war."[37]

Five days before the Roosevelt-Karski meeting, Roosevelt had told Stephen Wise to "go ahead" with his plan for the relief and evacuation of Jewish refugees in Rumania and France. That was not quite evidence of presidential backing, although Wise certainly got the impression that FDR approved. Wise followed up his meeting with a letter to the president, who then took the initiative of inquiring with the Treasury Department (not the State Department) on the status of the proposal.[38] That inquiry led to the battle between Treasury and State, which resulted, ultimately, in the formation of the War Refugee Board.[39] The sequence of events suggests that Karski's presentation may have had an impact on the president's action and on initial approval of the rescue plan.

By far the most important factor inducing the president to take action was a changing public and congressional climate. One day after Congressman Will Rogers, Jr., Joseph Baldwin, and Senator Guy Gillette of Iowa introduced House and Senate resolutions calling upon the president to create a rescue commission to save the surviving European Jews from extinction, Undersecretary of State Edward Stettinius, Jr., who had replaced Sumner Welles, reported to high State Department officials that the president was convinced that not enough was being done on the Jewish refugee problem. FDR suggested establishing small offices in Algiers, Naples, Portugal, Madrid, and Ankara to assist Jews. There might also be another refugee camp and a small amount of money available for the purpose. But European Division chief Ray Atherton told Stettinius that the U.S. should avoid unilateral sponsorship of this type of activity, or it would be paying all the bills. Stettinius decided to refer the matter to Breckinridge Long, who was to consult Secretary Hull.[40] Whatever impetus FDR generated was quickly dissipated.

Growing cricitism of Long and the State Department in Congress and in the media made FDR aware of a political problem, in addition to a humanitarian one. Even then, it took the decisive intervention of Josiah DuBois relayed by Secretary Morgenthau to make FDR aware, in January 1944, that he had to take the refugee problem away from Long and the State Department or he would face a nasty political scandal. He took what action the Treasury Department contingent wanted but installed Secretary of War Henry Stimson on the War Refugee Board to curb possible impetuousness by Morgenthau and his subordinates.

It is extremely difficult to calculate whether a more active American refugee policy gained significant public support beyond the American Jewish community and liberal circles. There were still plenty of diehard opponents of immigration as well as of any diversion of effort on behalf of non-Americans. The most that one can say is that by 1944 there was less public and congressional resistance to the idea of a special government agency to look after the interests of victims of Nazi persecution.

FDR's willingness to support most of the proposals put forward by the War Refugee Board during 1944, including stern public warnings to the Hungarian government not to turn over its Jews to Germany, represented a significant reversal of earlier wartime policy. The most likely explanation for the turnabout is not that the president saw a chance to score political points during a presidential election year (since the political risks at least equaled the benefits) but that he was now confident about the outcome of the war and was willing to take some risks on behalf of a cause that he had neglected for some time. Still, there were limits to what the president would approve. The idea of bringing Jewish refugees into the United States outside the quota system and the usual immigration regulations obviously raised political as well as legal concerns, which troubled him. The stringent limitations on the refugee camp at Oswego, New York, demonstrate how sensitive the president was about giving European Jews a special status to enter the U.S.

It is true that President Roosevelt might have ordered the bombing of the gas chambers at Auschwitz-Birkenau. Even if he had wished to do so (for which there is no evidence), he must have been aware of the political risks. To send American pilots on a long and dangerous mission for the benefit of European Jews threatened with extinction might be justified morally. But would the American people understand it and approve of it? To override the stance of the War Department and to substitute his own moral impulse for official policy would carry grave risks for the president. If the requests for the bombing of Auschwitz reached him through McCloy, which is likely,[41] FDR shunned the potentially damaging political repercussions of a risky humanitarian strike. Only in retrospect does the efficacy of bombing Auschwitz and the moral imperative outweigh all else. It is instructive, however, to note that Winston Churchill, against the views of the Foreign Office and military, favored bombing Auschwitz but was unable to prevail.[42] When dealing with large bureaucracies, even chief executives are not all-powerful.

A comparison of Roosevelt's and Churchill's behavior makes it clear that the prime minister was far more concerned and motivated to make public statements on behalf of European Jewry. The same comparison, however, should make one beware of making the president the archvillain of American refugee policy. For despite Churchill and despite less unfavorable public opinion in Great Britain, British refugee policy toward European Jewry during the war was even less humanitarian than American refugee policy.

Although FDR was adept at manipulating government agencies and bureaucrats, he was to some degree the prisoner of bureaucratic government. A president could set general lines of policy in many areas and try to resolve conflicts and priorities. He could not continually supervise implementation of policy in more than one or two spheres, no matter how great his interest. Refugee policy during the depression, the era of Nazi expansion, and the world war could not command much of the president's time. Roosevelt had to depend upon the State Department and the War Department to carry out his foreign policy and military action against the Axis powers. He could force some officials to compete with each other. He could insert some of his own appointees into these agencies, New Dealers who understood his own goals and methods better than traditional civil servants and military officers. He could use Harry Hopkins and others as troubleshooters. But he could not carry out a radical purge of the bureaucracy, particularly not in time of war, without serious impairment of administrative efficiency and adverse political repercussions in Congress as well. All of this meant that the president had to operate in the bureaucratic world around him, however much he disliked it.

That world was stamped by certain traditions and nationalist values. Before 1933 the United States was far more the aloof isolationist seeking to insulate itself from the world's troubles than it was the defender of universal "human rights." Most American civil servants and military officers had received their training and experience in this pre-1933 world; they were not about to revolutionize their attitudes overnight. The institutional climate in the State and War departments, as well as in newer agencies such as the Office of War Information, was strongly opposed to active American assistance to European Jews. Proposed measures on behalf of European Jews frequently seemed to interfere with the normal functions of these agencies, and thereby with the success of the war effort. The fact that relatively few American officials could comprehend the extent and horror of the Final Solution only made it easier for them to pass on to other matters. Europe would always have its problems; the important thing now was to win the war.

The fluctuations in American refugee policy during the Roosevelt administration were determined in part by presidential initiatives but in part also by bureaucratic politics. The Labor Department's initiatives to loosen immigration regulations in 1933–34 contributed to the State Department's increased willingness to recognize affidavits from American citizens and residents pledging financial support for their European relatives. The transfer of the Immigration and Naturalization Service from Labor to Justice in 1940 weakened Labor's influence over refugee policy and facilitated the State Department's tightening of immigration regulations. The creation of the War Refugee Board in 1944 gave advocates of humanitarian measures a new foothold within the government and thus made possible a variety of life-saving measures in Europe.

The evidence presented in this book indicates that the president was quietly more liberal on the admission of Jewish refugees to the United States than the bureaucracy during the 1930s and approximately as restrictionist as the bureaucratic consensus during the 1940s. But, even when FDR chose to intervene personally in refugee policy as he did in 1938–39, he needed help to carry out his ideas. The history of American refugee policy between 1939 and 1945 indicates that most government agencies and officials were more efficient restrictionists than humanitarians.

The United States government did not match Adolf Hitler's single-minded frenzy to wipe out the Jewish "race" with corresponding determination to save those Jews who could be saved during the Holocaust. FDR's reluctance to engage himself directly in the cause of European Jewish refugees resulted first from his almost exclusive focus on the war itself, second from his perception of adverse political realities in the U.S. and in the west generally, and third from his dependence upon a bureaucracy largely unaccustomed to humanitarian initiatives.

There are always questions about how far a politician can be ahead of his own time and his own society and remain a successful politician. American refugee policy was one area where Franklin Roosevelt, so venturesome in other spheres, did not feel free to take on much additional risk.

NOTES

INTRODUCTION

1. Special Report IDS no. 317, June 16, 1943, National Archives (hereafter NA), Washington, Record Group (hereafter RG) 226, 37456. This document was declassified on October 9, 1985.

2. Bernard Wasserstein, *Britain and the Jews of Europe, 1939–1945* (London, 1979), 304–05.

3. Jewish National Committee (Warsaw) to Dr. Ignacy Schwarzbart, November 15, 1943, copy in Paul Baerwald Papers, Columbia School of International Affairs, New York.

4. This term has recently been used by David S. Wyman, *The Abandonment of the Jews: America and the Holocaust, 1941–1945* (New York, 1984), ix. Wyman applies the term to government, the public, and even American Jewry. The term's derivation goes back at least to Zygielbojm's suicide letters of May 1943: "By passive observation of this murder of defenseless millions and the mal-treatment of children and women, the men of these countries have become accomplices of criminals." Copy of letter in American Jewish Committee Archives, RG-1, EXO-29, Morris D. Waldman File, Poland 1944.

5. The phrase is Elie Wiesel's. See "Telling the Tale," *Dimensions in American Judaism* 2 (Spring 1968): 11, quoted by Saul S. Friedman, *No Haven for the Oppressed: United States Policy toward Jewish Refugees, 1938–1945* (Detroit, 1973), 143.

6. Arthur D. Morse, *While Six Million Died: A Chronicle of American Apathy* (New York, 1967), esp. 38–42.

7. David S. Wyman, *Paper Walls: America and the Refugee Crisis, 1938–1941* (Amherst, 1968), esp. 155–83.

8. Henry L. Feingold, *The Politics of Rescue: The Roosevelt Administration and the Holocaust, 1938–1945* (New Brunswick, N.J., 1970), esp. 15, 131–37, 158–59, 165.

9. Friedman, *No Haven*, esp. 139–54, 203–05.

10. Henry L. Feingold, "The Government Response," in *The Holocaust: Ideology, Bureaucracy, and Genocide: The San José Papers*, ed. Henry Friedlander and Sybil Milton (Milwood, N.Y., 1980), 247.

11. Wyman, *Abandonment*, esp. 9, 321–29.

12. Deborah E. Lipstadt, *Beyond Belief: The American Press and the Coming of the Holocaust, 1933–1945* (New York, 1986).

13. *American Jewry during the Holocaust*, ed. Seymour Maxwell Finger (New York, 1984); and David Kranzler, "Orthodox Ends, Unorthodox Means: The Role of the Vaad Hatzalah and Agudath Israel during the Holocaust," appendix 4-3, in *American Jewry.*

14. Haskel Lookstein, *Were We Our Brothers' Keepers? The Public Response of American Jews to the Holocaust, 1938–1944* (New York, 1986), 216.

15. Herbert A. Strauss, "Jewish Emigration from Germany: Nazi Policies and Jewish Responses" (I) and (II), in *Leo Baeck Institute Yearbook* 25 and 26 (1980 and 1981): 313–61 and 343–409.

16. Michael R. Marrus and Robert O. Paxton, *Vichy France and the Jews* (New York, 1983).

17. Irving Abella and Harold Troper, *None Is Too Many: Canada and the Jews of Europe, 1933–1948* (New York, 1983).

18. A. J. Sherman, *Island Refuge: Britain and Refugees from the Third Reich, 1933–1939* (Berkeley and Los Angeles, 1973).

19. Wasserstein, *Britain*, esp. 351–57.

20. Feingold, "The Government Response," 252.

21. John Higham, *Strangers in the Land: Patterns of American Nativism, 1860–1925* (New Brunswick, N.J., 1955). See also Higham's essays in *Send These To Me: Jews and Other Immigrants in Urban America* (New York, 1975).

22. Robert A. Divine, *American Immigration Policy, 1924–1952* (New Haven, 1957), 62–63; White House Press Release, September 8, 1930; A. Dana Hodgdon to Undersecretary of State Joseph P. Cotton, September 11, 1930; Cotton to Hodgdon, September 12, 1930; Secretary of State Henry L. Stimson to Secretary of Labor James J. Davis, November 21, 1930; and Assistant Secretary of State Wilbur J. Carr to J. P. Cotton, November 15, 1930, NA, RG 59, 150.062 Public Charge (hereafter PC) 8, 9, 44, 45 respectively. These documents also indicate that the State Department was concerned about possible criticism of the new interpretation of the public charge clause.

23. Louis D. Brandeis to Felix Frankfurter, April 29, 1933, Felix Frankfurter Papers, Box 29, Library of Congress (hereafter LC).

24. Frankfurter to Frances Perkins, April 27, 1933, Francis Perkins Papers, Columbia University.

25. "Bureaucracy," in H. H. Gerth and C. Wright Mills, *From Max Weber: Essays in Sociology* (New York, 1971), 224.

26. Herbert A. Strauss, "Jewish Emigration from Germany: Nazi Policies and Jewish Responses (II)," *Leo Baeck Institute Yearbook* 26 (1981): 359. David S. Wyman's modification of tabulations by Maurice R. Davie, *Refugees in America* (New York, 1947), 23–24, 27, in Wyman, *Paper Walls*, 218–19. This is roughly consistent with the National Refugee Service's estimate that almost 210,000 "Hebrew" immigrants and nonimmigrants entered the United States between 1933 and June 30, 1943. If we allow for another 2,000 Jews entering the U.S. between July 1, 1943, and the end of 1944, that would mean that there were roughly 38,000 non-Jewish refugees.

27. Abella and Troper, *None Is Too Many,* vi.

1. THE LABOR DEPARTMENT'S INITIATIVE

1. This conversation is referred to in a letter from Lehman to FDR, September 21, 1933, NA, RG 59, 150.01/2153. The White House usher's diary has no record of a visit to the White House on that date, but it is known that some confidential visitors were not listed there. Bruce Allen Murphy, *The Brandeis-Frankfurter Connection: The Secret Political Activities of Two Supreme Court Justices* (Garden City, N.Y., 1983), 254–55. On the other hand, it may have been a telephone conversation.

2. Cyrus Adler to Felix Warburg, March 24, 1933, Warburg Papers, Box 305, American Jewish Archives, Cincinnati, cited by Barbara Stewart McDonald, "United States Government Policy on Refugees from Nazism, 1933–1940" (Ph.D. diss., Columbia University, 1969), 46.

3. Felix Frankfurter to Raymond Moley, April 24, 1933, Frankfurter Papers, Box 137, LC; and Frankfurter to Moley, April 24, 1933 (different letter), Raymond Moley Papers, Folder 106/1, Hoover Institute, Stanford University. The first letter complained specifically that "the humane and courageous determination of the President taken two weeks ago last Friday [April 7]" had not been implemented. Frankfurter also wrote that Hull had agreed to the action at this cabinet meeting. The second letter offered proposals for "carrying out the President's thought . . . , the kind of moral gesture the President wanted to make." Although Frankfurter is a partisan source about Roosevelt, the specificity of his claim is convincing. He was in close touch with Frances Perkins during this period and probably heard her version of the events in cabinet. Charles E. Wyzanski, Jr., who was then solicitor of the Labor Department, stated that FDR referred the matter to Perkins and Hull. Wyzanski to Richard Breitman, August 12, 1982.

4. George Martin, *Madam Secretary: Frances Perkins* (Boston, 1976), 20–30, 34–37.

5. Frankfurter to Perkins, April 14, 1933; and Frankfurter to Moley, April 14, 1933, Moley Papers, Folder 106/1, Hoover Institute. The latter contains Frankfurter's handwritten comment that the drafts had been sent to FDR. For a similar and related communication from Frankfurter to FDR, see his telegram of April 16, 1933, NA, RG 59, Central Decimal File (hereafter CDF) 862.4016/586.

6. Max J. Kohler to Congressman Samuel Dickstein, May 3, 1933, American Jewish Committee Archives, RG 1, EXO-29, Waldman File, Immigration 1933.

7. Conference on Immigration Policy to Perkins, April 17, 1933, NA, RG 174, Frances Perkins: Immigration–General 1933.

8. This is implied by Perkins's rejoinder discussed in the next paragraph.

9. Jay Pierrepont Moffat Diary, April 20, 1933, Moffat Papers, Houghton Library, Harvard University. Wilbur Carr, too, wrote in his diary that Phillips had an "exciting" talk with Perkins in which she seems to have been "most unpleasant." Carr Diary, April 20, 1933, LC.

10. Martin, *Madam Secretary,* 37, 247.

11. See chap. 1, above. Charles E. Wyzanski, Jr., to Paul Freund, October 27, 1982, copy to Richard Breitman. Judge Wyzanski declined to reveal just how he learned of the 10 percent instruction. We may speculate that Felix Frankfurter was involved. Frankfurter had good contacts with a number of people inside the State Department and with Henry Stimson, who had been secretary of state in 1930. Wyzanski had been a Frankfurter student at Harvard Law School, and Frankfurter had recommended him to Perkins for the post of solicitor.

12. Bart Butler, Assistant Solicitor, to Stephen Early, April 20, 1933, NA, RG 59, 150.626J/3; and Moffat Diary, April 20, 1933, Houghton Library, Harvard.

13. NA, RG 59, 150.01/2110; and Carr Diary, April 21, 1933, LC.

14. HSC to Carr, April 24, 1933, NA, RG 59, 150.01/2110.

15. Perkins to Frankfurter, April 25, 1933, copy in Moley Papers, Folder 106/1, Hoover Institute; and Frankfurter to Perkins, April 29, 1933, Frances Perkins Papers, Columbia University.

16. Martin, *Madam Secretary,* 245–47.

17. MacCormack Memorandum for the Secretary, June 3, 1933, Frances Perkins Papers, III B/I 29, Connecticut College.

18. Interview with Judge Wyzanski, November 26, 1982. This was not Wyzanski's original impression, which was that MacCormack's banking experience had made him anti-Semitic. Wyzanski to parents, October 28, 1933. But he quickly learned otherwise.

19. D. W. MacCormack to Isador Lubin, August 23, 1933, with copy to Secretary Perkins, Perkins Papers, III B/I 20, Connecticut College.

20. Perkins Memorandum to MacCormack, August 24, 1933, Perkins Papers, III B/I 18, Connecticut College.

21. Hodgdon to Carr, June 23, 1933; and Instruction of July 6, 1933, NA, RG 59, 150.062 PC/590 1/2 and 150.062 PC/596.

22. "Special Instructions in Regard to Aliens Obliged to Leave the Country of their Regular Residence and Who Seek Escape from Conditions in that Country," September 5, 1933, NA, RG 59, 811.111 Regulations/1662; and Geist to Secretary of State, March 5, 1934, NA, RG 59, 150.626J/25.

23. Lehman immediately apprised James M. Warburg and Judge Julian Mack of what had taken place in the meeting with FDR. See Memo of Phone Call from JMW, September 14, 1933; and [memorandum of telephone call] from Mack, 2 P.M. [September 14, 1933], Felix Frankfurter Papers, Box 137, Germany 1933–1936, LC.Wyzanski heard from Perkins that Judges Cardozo, Lehman, Mack, and Proskauer also met with

the president around this time. Wyzanski to parents, January 12, 1934; Wyzanski to Freund, October 27, 1982. It is unclear whether this was a separate (unrecorded) meeting or whether the report was a garbled account of the Lehman-FDR meeting.

24. Hodgdon to Flournoy, September 28, 1933, NA, RG 59, 150.01/2145 1/2; Proskauer to Hull, September 22, 1933, NA, RG 59, 150.626J/26; and Irving Lehman to Franklin Roosevelt, September 21, 1933, NA, RG 59, 150.01/2153. The most revealing account, however, is Max Kohler to Alfred Cohen, September 22, 1933, Kohler Papers, Box 1, American Jewish Historical Society, Waltham, Mass. (hereafter AJHS). Judge Mack is credited with formulating the public charge bond arrangement in Wyzanski to Freund, October 27, 1982.

25. Hodgdon to Flournoy, September 28, 1933, NA, RG 59, 150.01/2145 1/2; and MacCormack's figure of 4,000 refugees in Kohler to Eugene S. Benjamin, December 12, 1933, Cecilia Razovsky Papers, Box 1, AJHS.

26. Wyzanski to parents, October 25, 1933.

27. Confidential Report by Judge Julian W. Mack: Memorandum of Washington Trip—October 30, 1933, American Jewish Committee Archives, RG 1, EXO-29, Waldman File, Germany–State Department Efforts 1933.

28. Wyzanski to parents, October 30, 1933.

29. Memorandum of January 22, 1934; modified slightly and issued as Instruction to Consuls, February 27, 1934, NA, RG 59, 150.01/2158 and 122.21/411F; and Carr to Hodgdon and Flournoy, October 31, 1933, Carr Papers, Box 10, LC.

30. Flournoy Memoranda of August 31, 1933 and November 14, 1933, NA, RG 59, 150.626J/17 and 150.01/2155.

31. Wyzanski to Secretary of Labor, November 3, 1933, copy in American Civil Liberties Union Archives, 1933, v. 597A, pp. 53–65, Mudd Library, Princeton University.

32. Wyzanski to parents, November 4, 1933; and Wyzanski to Freund, October 27, 1982.

33. The two departments had earlier discussed going to the attorney general. But Wyzanski was under the impression that FDR personally referred the decision to Cummings. Wyzanski to Breitman, August 12, 1982.

34. Attorney General Cummings to Secretary of Labor, December 26, 1933, NA, RG 174, Frances Perkins: Immigration–Public Charge Bonds.

35. Fletcher to Hodgdon, January 8, 1934; Wilkinson to Hodgdon, January 3, 1934; and Simmons to Carr, April 23, 1934, NA, RG 59, 150.01/2168 and 150.01/2211.

36. MacCormack Memorandum for the Secretary, January 26, 1934, NA, RG 59, 150.062 PC/677 1/2.

37. Wyzanski to parents, January 12, 1934. Handwritten notes of Perkins's conversation with Wyzanski in the margin of Cummings to Perkins, January 9, 1934, NA, RG 174, Frances Perkins–Immigration: Charge Bonds.

38. Wyzanski to parents, January 12, 1934; and Mack to Brandeis, January 9, 1934, Louis D. Brandeis Papers, University of Louisville Microfilm Series VI, Roll 100.

39. Perkins notes in margin of Cummings to Perkins, December 26, 1933, NA, RG 174, Frances Perkins–Immigration: Charge Bonds.

40. Wyzanski, "Immigration and the New Deal," February 4, 1934, Wyzanski Papers; Perkins to Mack, January 23, 1934; Mack to Brandeis, January 26, 1934, Brandeis Papers, University of Louisville Microfilm Series VI, Roll 100; Wyzanski Memorandum on the Admission of Refugees from Germany, February 10, 1934, Wyzanski Papers; Chart of Quota Immigration to the United States—1933–1942, National Refugee Service, August 23, 1943, based on releases of the Immigration and Naturalization Service, copy in Joseph Chamberlain Papers, Folder 32, YIVO Institute for Jewish Research, New York (hereafter YIVO).

41. Wyzanski to parents, January 24, February 2, 1934.

42. Edwin Mims, Jr., "German Refugees and American Bureaucrats," *Today*, January 20, 1934.

43. MacCormack Memorandum for the Secretary, January 12, 1934, NA, RG 174, Frances Perkins–Immigration: Charge Bonds. See also Chamberlain to May, April 17, 1934, cited by Stewart, "United States Policy," 198.

44. MacCormack Memorandum for the Secretary, January 26, 1934, NA, RG 59, 150.062 PC/677 1/2; and MacCormack Memorandum for the Secretary, January 12, 1934, NA, RG 174, Frances Perkins–Immigration: Charge Bonds.

45. NA, RG 59, 150.062 PC/669; 150.01/2211; 150.062 PC/687; and Max J. Kohler to Perkins, April 6, 1934, Felix Warburg Papers, Box 320, American Jewish Archives.

46. American Jewish Committee Archives, RG 1, EXO-29, Waldman File, German-Jewish Children's Aid, Report 2, April 12, 1934; MacCormack to Roger Baldwin, June 14, 1934; Baldwin to MacCormack, August 8, 1934; and Massey to Baldwin, August 11, 1934, American Civil Liberties Union Archives, vol. 691, Mudd Library, Princeton University.

47. Carr to Simmons, July 13, 1934, NA, RG 59, 150.01/2231.

48. Chamberlain to McDonald, August 25, 1934, James G. McDonald Papers, G-78, Chamberlain Folder, Columbia School of International Affairs; Coulter to Flournoy, September 4, 1934; and Simmons to Phillips, August 30, 1934, NA, RG 59, 150.626J/101.

49. Martin, *Madam Secretary*, 314–23; and *San Francisco Chronicle*, July 21, 1934, quoted in *ibid.* 323. See also Arthur Schlesinger, Jr., *The Coming of the New Deal* (Boston, 1959), 389-93.

50. Wyzanski to parents, July 23, 1934; and Martin, *Madam Secretary,* 323.

51. Simmons to Phillips, August 30, 1934, NA, RG 59, 150.626J/101; and Stewart, "United States Policy," 205–11.

52. Statement of Wilbur J. Carr before the Committee on Immigration of the House of Representatives, March 12, 1934, NA, RG 59, 150.01/2200; MacCormack to Representative Samuel Dickstein, March 10, 1934, copy in McDonald Papers, Chamberlain Folder, Columbia School of International Affairs; draft of Annual Report of Executive Committee Meeting, American Jewish Committee, January 5, 1935, Felix Warburg Papers, Box 320, American Jewish Committee Folder (b), American Jewish Archives; and quota immigration statistics in Geist to Secretary of State, July 19, 1934, NA, RG 59, 811.111 Quota 62/456.

53. Bowen to Cook, December 10, 1934; and Simmons to Carr, January 11, 1935, NA, RG 59, 150.062 PC/719.

54. MacCormack speech at Temple Ansche Chesed, January 25, 1935, copy in Frances Perkins Papers, III A/M 37, Connecticut College. See also MacCormack speech to HIAS, *New York Times,* March 4, 1935, cited by Stewart, "United States Policy," 196; and Minutes of Meeting of Committee on German-Jewish Immigration Policy, March 25, 1935, American Jewish Committee Archives, RG 1, EXO-29, Waldman file, Immigration 1934–35.

55. See chap. 2, above.

56. Minutes of Committee on German-Jewish Immigration Policy, November 4, 1935, Felix Warburg Papers, Box 330, National Coordinating Committee Folder, American Jewish Archives.

57. Wyzanski to parents, July 31, 1935.

58. Informal breakfast conference, November 6, 1935, Joseph Chamberlain Papers, YIVO.

59. Open letter of the Foreign Language Information Service, June 7, 1934, American Jewish Committee Archives, RG 1, EXO-29, Waldman File, Immigration 1934–35.

See also Perkins to Razovsky, July 24, 1934, Razovsky Papers, Box 1, AJHS. Wilbur Carr Memorandum, March 13, 1936, NA, RG 59, 150.01/2399; and Read Lewis Memorandum, November 16, 1936, American Civil Liberties Union Archive, vol. 890, pp.244–46, Princeton University. In 1938 Congress passed a bill sponsored by Representative Martin Dies, which incorporated some of the principal features of the Kerr bill. It, too, had failed to pass the first time around, despite lobbying efforts by some of the Jewish organizations. See joint letter of the American Jewish Committee, HIAS, and the National Council of Jewish Women, May 27, 1937, Felix Warburg Papers, Box 355, American Jewish Committee Folder, American Jewish Archives. On the content and the obstacles raised by restrictionists, see Stewart, "United States Policy," 250–53.

60. Harold Fields to Stephen Wise, January 29, 1937, Brandeis Papers, University of Louisville Microfilm Series VI, Roll 105.

2. GUARDIANS OF VISA POLICY

1. Waldo H. Heinrichs, Jr., "Bureaucracy and Professionalism in the Development of American Career Diplomacy," in John Braeman, Robert H. Bremner, and David Brody, eds., *Twentieth-Century American Foreign Policy* (Columbus, 1971), 132.

2. Ibid, 136. Katherine Elizabeth Crane, *Mr. Carr of State: Forty-Seven Years in the Department of State* (New York, 1960), 82–112, 121–26.

3. Interview with Howard Elting, Jr., December 27, 1983.

4. Wilbur J. Carr Diary, January 20, 1925, LC; and Heinrichs, "Bureaucracy and Professionalism," 133.

5. Carr Diary, October 19, 1919, LC; and Heinrichs, "Bureaucracy and Professionalism," 133.

6. Carr Diary, March 23, 1920, LC.

7. Joseph G. Grew, as quoted to Heinrichs, "Bureaucracy and Professionalism," 133.

8. Carr Diary, November 7, 1900, LC. Carr's desire for self-improvement and his feelings of inadequacy are discussed by Crane, *Mr. Carr of State,* 6–7.

9. Martin Weil, *A Pretty Good Club: The Founding Fathers of the U.S. Foreign Service* (New York, 1978), 46–49.

10. Heinrichs, "Bureaucracy and Professionalism," 119–206; Robert D. Schulzinger, *The Making of the Diplomatic Mind: The Training, Outlook and Style of United States Foreign Service Officers, 1908–1931* (Middletown, 1975), 52–78; Richard Hume Werking, *The Master Architects, Building the United States Foreign Service, 1890–1913* (Lexington, 1977), esp. 88–120; and Weil, *A Pretty Good Club,* 46–49.

11. Heinrichs, "Bureaucracy and Professionalism," 148.

12. Robert Wiebe, *The Search for Order* (New York, 1967), 295. See also Heinrichs, "Bureaucracy and Professionalism," 156.

13. The Rogers law was initially proposed in 1919 by Republican Congressman John Jacob Rogers of Lowell, Massachusetts, a member of the Foreign Affairs Committee and a leading proponent of foreign service reform. Heinrichs, "Bureaucracy and Professionalism," 158.

14. U.S. Congress, House, "Temporary Suspension of Immigration," House Report No. 1109, 66th Cong., 3d. sess., December 6, 1920, p. 10.

15. Crane, *Mr. Carr of State,* 269–70.

16. Carr to Alvey A. Adee, Second Assistant Secretary, Department of Labor, September 24, 1921, NA, RG 59, 150.01/544.

17. Thomas Bevan to the Secretary of State, May 6, 1925, NA, RG 59, 150.01/1305.

18. Secretary of State to Honorable Albert Johnson, Chairman, House Committee on Immigration, October 17, 1921, NA, RG 59, 150.01/649.

19. Carr to Albert Johnson, December 4, 1920, NA, RG 59, 150.01/15A.

20. Louis Marshall to Secretary of State, April 27, 1921, NA, RG 59, 150.01/617.

21. Carr Diary, August 9, 1924, LC.

22. Carr Diary, August 15, 1924, LC.

23. Carr Diary, February 22, 1934, LC.

24. HSC Memorandum for Mr. Hodgdon, September 8, 1930, NA, RG 59, 150.062 PC/3; Carr to Colonel D. W. MacCormack, June 15, 1933, NA, RG 59, 150.062 PC/586 1/2; and White House Press Release, September 8, 1930, copy in NA, RG 59, 150.626 J/no number.

25. White House Press Release, September 8, 1930, NA, RG 59, 150.626 J/no number. On the LPC clause, see Robert A. Divine, *American Immigration Policy, 1924–1952* (New Haven, 1957), 62–63.

26. Wilbur J. Carr to Cotton, November 15, 1930, NA, RG 59, 150.062 PC/45.

27. Carr to American Diplomatic and Consular Officers, April 24, June 24, 1931, NA, RG 59, 150.062 PC/149 and 219; and Stimson to Senator Royal S. Copeland, June 20, 1931, NA, RG 59, 150.062 PC/215.

28. Carr to Undersecretary of State William Castle, July 31, 1931, NA, RG 59, 150.062 PC/256.

29. Carr Diary, November 8, 1932, LC.

30. Crane, *Mr. Carr of State,* 306–08.

31. Carr Diary, November 8, 1932, LC.

32. Crane, *Mr. Carr of State,* 309.

33. Moffat Diary, April 20, 1933, Moffat Papers, Houghton Library, Harvard. See also Carr Diary, April 20, 1933, LC; Hodgdon to Carr, April 24, 1933, and attachment, "The Problem of Aliens Seeking Relief from Persecution in Germany," April 20, 1933, written by Carr, NA, RG 59, 150.01/2110.

34. Carr to Messersmith, June 1, 1933; and Carr to Hodgdon, June 6, 1933, NA, RG 59, 150.626J/92.

35. Hodgdon to Carr, June 22, 1933, NA, RG 59, 150.01/2120; and Instructions of July 6, 1933, NA, RG 59, 150.062 PC/596.

36. "Special Instructions in Regard to Aliens Obliged to Leave the Country of Their Regular Residence and Who Seek Escape from Conditions in That Country" [authored by Carr], September 5, 1933, NA, RG 59, 811.111 Regulations/1662.

37. Joseph Proskauer to William Phillips, July 18, 1933, NA, RG 59, 150.626J/no number; Phillips to Proskauer, August 5, 1933, NA, RG 59, 150.626J/no number; and Kohler to Hull, August 28, 1933, NA, RG 59, 150.626J/17.

38. Max Kohler to Proskauer, August 21, 1933, American Jewish Committee Archives, RG 1, EXO 29, Germany file, "State Dept. Efforts" Folder.

39. William Phillips Diary, October 30, 1933, William Phillips Papers, Houghton Library, Harvard.

40. Phillips Diary, August 10, 1936, Houghton Library, Harvard.

41. Phillips Diary, April 20, 1935, quoted in Shlomo Shafir, "The Impact of the Jewish Crisis on American-German Relations" (Ph.D. diss, Georgetown University, 1971), p. 162 n. 23.

42. Julian W. Mack to Rabbi Stephen S. Wise, October 17, 1933, Stephen S. Wise Papers, Box 105, AJHS.

43. Brandeis to Mack, January 24, 1934, Julian W. Mack Papers, Section XVI/93, Zionist Archives and Library, New York.

44. Simmons to Carr, February 16, 1934, NA, RG 59, 150.062 PC/669; and Simmons to Carr, February 23, 1934, NA, RG 59, 150.01/2169.

45. Carr's handwritten comment on Simmons's letter, February 19, 1936, NA, RG 59, 150.01/2385.

46. Crane, *Mr. Carr of State,* 314.

47. Carr Diary, June 6, 1934, LC.

48. Carr Diary, April 23, July 2, 3, 1936, June 24, 1937, LC.

49. See chapter five for a full discussion of Jewish efforts to influence FDR. Wise to Brandeis, January 26, 1936, Wise Papers, Box 106, AJHS; Wise to Frankfurter, March 2, 1936, Brandeis Papers, University of Louisville Microfilm Series, Section VI, Roll 103; Herbert Lehman to Felix Warburg, July 14, 1936, Herbert Lehman Papers, Special File, Felix Warburg Folder, Columbia School of International Affairs (hereafter CSIA). Unidentified newspaper clipping, August 14, 1936; Brandeis Papers; Mack to Brandeis, September 17, 1936, Brandeis Papers, University of Louisville Microfilm Series, Section VI, Roll 103.

50. The letter that Herbert Lehman received from FDR was drafted in the State Department, apparently by John Farr Simmons of the Visa Division at the request of Wilbur Carr. Roosevelt to Lehman, July 2, 1936, Official File (hereafter OF) 133A, Franklin D. Roosevelt Library, Hyde Park, N.Y. (hereafter FDRL). Roosevelt had simply asked the State Department to prepare a reply. FDR Memorandum for the State Department, June 17, 1936; and Carr to the President, with attached draft, June 27, 1936, NA, RG 59, 150.626J/208. The State Department issued no new instructions to consuls until December 1936.

51. Coulter to Carr and Carr's comment, November 30, 1936, NA, RG 59, 150.626J/242.

52. Wyman, *Abandonment of the Jews,* ix.

53. Crane, *Mr. Carr of State,* 316.

54. Crane, *Mr. Carr of State,* 328–29.

55. George Kennan, *Memoirs, 1925–1950* (New York, 1969), 66, cited by Stewart, "United States Policy," 59.

56. Messersmith Memorandum of Conversation with Goering, April 5, 1933, transmitted to Washington, April 6, 1933, copies in Messersmith Papers, Items 135–36, University of Delaware. See also Report of Continued Nazi Anti-Semitism in Messersmith to Secretary of State, March 31, April 3, 1933, copy in Messersmith Papers, Items 131, 133, University of Delaware.

57. Messersmith's alleged comment quoted in Max Kohler to Joseph Proskauer, July 12, 1933, American Jewish Committee Archives, RG 1, EXO-29, Waldman File, Germany—State Department Efforts.

58. Geist managed to secure the release from custody of the director of the B'nai B'rith and to gain protection for the Jewish Telegraphic Agency. See the report by a Jewish Telegraphic Agency correspondent in Mack Papers, XIV/84, Zionist Archives and Library; and Geist to Secretary of State, February 5, 1934, NA, RG 59, 150.626J/60.

59. Dodd to R. Walton Moore, June 21, 1934, Walton Moore Papers, Box 5, FDRL.

60. Billikopf to Mack, September 14, 1933, copy in Messersmith Papers, Item 298, University of Delaware.

61. Hyman Memorandum on the German situation, December 12, 1933, Felix Warburg Papers, Box 303, JDC Folder A, American Jewish Archives; Wise's comments at Administrative Meeting of the American Jewish Congress, September 23, 1933, Wise Papers, Box 87, AJHS.

62. See, particularly, Messersmith to Jay Pierrepont Moffat, May 20, 1933, Messersmith Papers, Item 180, University of Delaware. On Carr's views at this time, see Carr's Memorandum, Measures Considered with Respect to the Attitude of the United States toward the Jews in Germany, May 31, 1933, NA, RG 59, 150.626J/5.

63. Herbert A. Strauss, "Jewish Emigration from Germany: Nazi Policies and Jewish Responses (I)," *Leo Baeck Institute Yearbook,* vol. 25 (1980): 330–31; and Karl A. Schleunes, *The Twisted Road to Auschwitz: Nazi Policy toward German Jews, 1933–1939* (Urbana, 1970), 92–113.

64. Billikopf to Mack, September 14, 1933, copy in Messersmith Papers, Item 298, University of Delaware.

65. Messersmith to William Phillips, September 29, 1933, copy in Moffat Papers, vol. 3, Houghton Library, Harvard.

66. Kenneth Moss, "George S. Messersmith and Nazi Germany: The Diplomacy of Limits in Central Europe," in *U.S. Diplomats in Europe, 1919–1941,* ed. Kenneth Paul Jones (Santa Barbara, 1981), 115–18.

67. Messersmith's predictions began in the summer of 1933 and continued through the mid-1930s. See Billikopf to Mack, September 14, 1933, copy in Messersmith Papers, Item 298; Messersmith to Phillips, April 13, 1934, Item 364, Messersmith Papers, University of Delaware; Messersmith to Moffat, April 14, 1934, Moffat Papers, Houghton Library, Harvard; Messersmith to Phillips, August 18, 1934, Item 404; and Messersmith to Phillips, August 15, 1935, Item 552, Messersmith Papers, University of Delaware.

68. Messersmith's despatches and private letters to J. Pierrepont Moffat, chief of the Division of Western European Affairs, were often passed on to Undersecretary William Phillips, who as early as the fall of 1933 passed some of them directly to FDR. Moss, "Messersmith," 113. William Phillips wrote on August 14, 1934: "Since I have been away there has been no improvement visible economically in Germany; very few believe that the Hitler regime can carry on much longer." Phillips Diary, Houghton Library, Harvard. On State's recognition of Dodd's inadequacies, see, particularly, Wilbur Carr's Memorandum, June 5, 1935, Carr Papers, Box 12, LC. More generally on Dodd, see Robert Dallek, *Democrat and Diplomat: The Life of William E. Dodd* (New York, 1968); and Franklin L. Ford, "Three Observers in Berlin: Rumbold, Dodd, and François-Poncet," in Gordon A. Craig and Felix Gilbert, *The Diplomats, 1919–1939* (New York, 1965), 447–60. See also Robert Dallek, *Franklin D. Roosevelt and American Foreign Policy, 1932–1945,* (New York, 1979), 91–97.

69. Neville Laski to Cyrus Adler, September 5, 1934, with copy of Memorandum of Conversation with Messersmith, August 19, 1934, Felix Warburg Papers, Box 315, American Jewish Archives.

70. Messersmith to Moffat, June 13, 1934, Moffat Papers, Houghton Library, Harvard; and Laski to Adler, September 5, 1934, with Memorandum of Conversation with Messersmith, August 19, 1934, Felix Warburg Papers, Box 315, American Jewish Archives.

71. Mack to Brandeis, March 20, 1934; Brandeis to Mack, March 24, 1934, Brandeis Papers, University of Louisville Microfilm Series VI, Roll 100; Mack to FDR, December 2, 1935; and FDR to Mack, December 4, 1935, President's Personal File 2211, FDRL.

72. See, for example, Messersmith to Phillips, August 18, 1934; Messersmith to Secretary of State, November 23, 1934; Messersmith Papers, Items 404, 445, University of Delaware.

73. Mack to Brandeis and Frankfurter, August 18, 1935, reporting on conversation with Messersmith, Brandeis Papers, University of Louisville Microfilm Series VI, Roll 102. On the Olympics, see Messersmith to Phillips, August 21, 27, 1935; Dunn to Messersmith, November 20, 1935; and Messersmith to Dunn, December 4, 1935, Messersmith Papers, Items 546, 558, 616, 624, University of Delaware.

74. Messersmith to Phillips, March 13, 1936, Messersmith Papers, Item 670, University of Delaware.

75. General biographical information in "Trouble-Shooter in Berlin," *New York Times,* July 23, 1939; and obituary in *Cleveland Plain Dealer* March 4, 1955. J. Pierrepont Moffat wrote that Geist's political reporting and protection of American interests were both superlative. He urged that Geist remain in Berlin. Moffat to Messersmith,

November 1, 1934, February 12, 1935, Messersmith Papers, Items 435, 480, University of Delaware. On Messersmith's and Carr's view of Geist, see Carr Diary, April 24, 1936, LC. After a visit to Berlin, Undersecretary Phillips criticized Ambassador Dodd and praised Geist. Phillips Diary, December 22, 1935, Phillips Papers, Houghton Library, Harvard.

76. Geist to Moffat, June 9, 1934, August 10, 1934, Moffat Papers, vol. 5, Houghton Library, Harvard; and Geist to Secretary of State, July 28, 1934, NA, RG 59, CDF 862.4016/1410, "Situation of the Jews in Germany."

77. Geist to Moffat, September 15, 1934, Moffat Papers, vol. 5, Houghton Library, Harvard.

78. See chap. 1, above.

79. Messersmith expressed his feelings about the incident to James G. McDonald, who wrote it all down in his diary. McDonald Diary, April 2, 1933, copy in Felix Frankfurter Papers, Box 137, LC.

80. Messersmith, as quoted in Hodgdon to Carr, May 15, 1933, NA, RG 59, 150.626J/5.

81. Messersmith to Carr, July 5, 1933, NA, RG 59, 150.626J/14.

82. Billikopf to Mack, September 14, 1933, copy in Messersmith Papers, Item 298, University of Delaware.

83. Messersmith to Carr, July 5, 1933, NA, RG 59, 150.626J/14.

84. Messersmith to Carr, July 27, 1933; Dominion to Secretary of State, June 29, 1933, August 17, 1933, NA, RG 59, 150.626J/25, 150.626J/14, and /18; and Geist to Secretary of State, March 5, 1934, NA, RG 59, 150.626J/74.

85. Messersmith to Carr, Strictly Confidential, July 27, 1933, NA, RG 59, 150.626J/25.

86. The State Department's instructions of July 6, 1933 (Public Charge Provisions of the Law) and September 5, 1933 (refugees who had difficulty obtaining German documents required for American visa applications). See chap. 1, above.

87. Geist to Secretary of State, February 2, 5, 1934, NA, RG 59, 150.626J/56 and 150.626J/60.

88. See chap. 1, above.

89. Geist to Secretary of State, March 5, 1934, NA, RG 59, 150.626J/74.

90. William Ware Adams, "Current Immigration to the United States from the Consular District of Berlin," November 1, 1934; and Fletcher to Simmons, November 21, 1934, NA, RG 59, 811.111 Quota 62/468.

91. Wyman, *Paper Walls,* 156–66.

92. Report of Cecilia Razovsky, October 10, 1935, Felix Warburg Papers, Box 330, American Jewish Archives.

93. MacMaster to Clarence Pickett, November 23, 1934, American Friends Service Committee Archives, Philadelphia (hereafter AFSC), General File 1934: Letters from Germany; and Martin to Pickett, November 16, 1936, AFSC, General File 1937: Refugees.

94. Interview with Hermann Kilsheimer, September 3, 1983. Kilsheimer still had copies of the affidavits of support.

95. On the fluctuations of Nazi anti-Semitism, see Uwe Dietrich Adam, *Judenpolitik im Dritten Reich* (Düsseldorf, 1972), 115–24; and Schleunes, *Twisted Road to Auschwitz,* 113–32. On the decreasing rate of visa refusals, see C. P. Fletcher to Simmons, July 29, 1935, NA, RG 59, 811.111 Quota 62/483. Actually, the percentage of visa applicants refused means little by itself, because many potential applicants were placed on an LPC waiting list—their preliminary application was in effect deferred until economic conditions in the U.S. improved. See Geist to Secretary of State, September 10, 1934, NA, RG 59, 150.062 PC/704–05. For the fiscal 1934 statistics, see Fletcher to Simmons, July 29, 1935, NA, RG 59, 811.111 Quota 62/483. Herbert A. Strauss,"Jewish Emigration

from Germany: Nazi Policies and Jewish Responses (II)," *Leo Baeck Institute Yearbook* (1981): 359, gives a figure of 3,740 for calendar year 1934, which includes both Germans and Austrians. Our own statistics, based on consular records, indicate that nearly 5,000 individuals received immigration visas under the German quota in 1934. Of these visas, however, 861 were granted to native Germans who had already left the country, so only a little more than 4,000 German emigrants received visas from American consulates in Germany.

96. W. Ware Adams, "Current Immigration to the United States from the Consular District of Berlin, Germany," November 1, 1934, NA, RG 59, 811.111 Quota 62/468.

97. Messersmith to Phillips, August 21, 27, 1935, Messersmith Papers, Items 546, 558, University of Delaware.

98. Honaker to Dodd, September 30, 1935, NA, RG 84, Box 159, Stuttgart 1935.

99. Erhardt to Secretary of State, May 15, 1936, NA, RG 59, CDF 862.4016/1631. Erhardt said that it was entirely possible that Jews would fill the German quota by 1937 unless the United States took some action, such as reaching an agreement with the German government to take a set number of Jews, e.g., 13,000 per year. Carr's comment is in the margin of Simmons to Carr, June 27, 1936, NA, RG 59, 150.626J/205.

100. Unidentified newspaper clipping, August 14, 1936, Brandeis Papers; Mack to Brandeis, September 17, 1936, Brandeis Papers, University of Louisville Microfilm Series VI, Roll 103.

101. Feingold, *Politics of Rescue*, 16, claims that FDR ordered the State Department to extend to the refugees "the most humane treatment possible under the law." But Feingold's source is FDR's letter to Herbert Lehman of July 2, 1936, Of 133A, FDRL, which does not contain the quoted phrase. FDR Memorandum for the State Department, June 17, 1936, NA, RG, 150.626J/208. The State Department issued no new instructions to consuls until December 1936.

102. Huddle's conclusions are cited in Coulter to Carr, November 30, 1936, NA, RG 59, 150.626J/242.

103. Messersmith to Secretary of State, November 13, 1936, NA, RG, 150.01/2458.

104. Fletcher and Simmons to Coulter, November 28, 1936, ibid.

105. Coulter to Carr, November 30, 1936, NA, RG 59, 150.626J/242.

106. Visa Instruction, January 5, 1937, NA, RG 59, 150.626J/242.

107. One of the special assistants to the secretary of state did indeed happen to be Jewish. There is no evidence, however, that the appointment of this man, Leo Pasvolsky, had anything to do with the shift in policy. His field was international economic affairs, which was also Hull's main interest. Nonetheless, Brett's guess shows how Foreign Service personnel tried to "read" developments in the State Department and adapt their behavior accordingly.

108. Wiley to Brett, January 6, 1937; and Brett to Wiley, January 8, 1937, John Wiley Papers, Box 6, FDRL.

109. Riggs to John Farr Simmons, March 3, 1937; and John Farr Simmons to Riggs, May 14, 1937, NA, RG 59, 150.062 Public Charge/915 1/2.

110. Messersmith to Carr, January 18, 1937, personal, Messersmith Papers, Item 822, University of Delaware.

111. Jenkins to Secretary of State, August 3, 1937, NA, RG 59, 811.111 Quota 62/555; and Schneiderman to Wallach, June 4, 1937, American Jewish Committee Archives, RG 1, EXO-29, Waldman File, Immigration 1936–37.

112. Geist to Messersmith, November 1, 1937; and Messersmith to Geist, November 27, 1937, Messersmith Papers, Items 906–07, University of Delaware.

3. A WINDOW OF OPPORTUNITY?

1. The argument that Hitler's intention to wipe out the Jews was fixed early in his career has been championed by Lucy S. Dawidowicz, *The War against the Jews* (New

York, 1977). A recent formulation of the case, with new evidence, is Gerald Fleming, *Hitler and the Final Solution* (Berkeley and Los Angeles, 1984). See also the persuasive analysis in Shlomo Aronson, "Die dreifache Falle: Hitlers Judenpolitik, die Alliierten und die Juden," *Vierteljahrshefte für Zeitgeschichte* 32 (1984): esp. 35–36.

2. Schleunes, *Twisted Road to Auschwitz*, 125–26.

3. Ibid., 92–132.

4. Bernhard Lösener, "Als Rassereferat im Reichsministerium des Innern," *Vierteljahrshefte für Zeitgeschichte* 9 (1961): 264–313, cited by Schleunes, *Twisted Road to Auschwitz*, 128. Lösener was actually present during Hitler's monologue delivered to the bureaucrats, who were trying to agree on a definition of Jewishness for the Nuremberg Laws.

5. Adam, *Judenpolitik im Dritten Reich*, 159–77.

6. At the famous Hossbach conference of November 5, 1937. See *International Military Tribunal for the Trial of the Major War Criminals* (hereafter IMT) (Washington, D.C., 1949), vol. 25, doc. 386 PS.

7. *Documents on German Foreign Policy* (Washington, D.C., 1953) (hereafter *DGFP*), ser. D, vol. 5, doc. 579, pp. 783–85, cited by Strauss, "Jewish Emigration from Germany: Nazi Policies and Jewish Responses," 356; and Schleunes, *Twisted Road to Auschwitz*, 227–28.

8. Norman Bentwich Note on a Visit to Vienna, March 27–29, 1938, James G. McDonald Papers, General Correspondence, Bentwich Folder, CSIA.

9. Schleunes, *Twisted Road to Auschwitz*, 230.

10. Bormann, quoted in Schleunes, *Twisted Road to Auschwitz*, 225.

11. Yehuda Bauer, *My Brother's Keeper: A History of the American Jewish Joint Distribution Committee, 1929–1939* (Philadelphia, 1974), 243–44.

12. Detailed studies include Lionel Kochan, *Pogrom: 10. November 1938* (London, 1957); Hermann Graml, *Der 9. November 1938, "Reichskristallnacht"* (Bonn, 1958); and Rita Thalmann and Emmanuel Feinermann, *Crystal Night: 9–10 November 1939*, trans. Gilles Cremonesi (London, 1972).

13. This is particularly true of Adam's *Judenpolitik*, esp. p. 229 n. 146.

14. Feingold, *Politics of Rescue*, 52–53, 58, 66, 69–74. See also Stewart, "United States Policy," 351, 425–26.

15. Report by SS Oberscharführer Hagen on Jewish emigration, September 13, 1936, NA, RG 242, T-175/411/2936189-6194, reprinted in John Mendelsohn, ed., *The Holocaust*, vol. 5, *Jewish Emigration from 1933 to the Evian Conference of 1938* (New York, 1982), doc. 4. See also Eichmann/Hagen report, November 4, 1937, NA, RG 242, T-175/411/2936013-6068, reprinted in Mendelsohn, *The Holocaust*, vol. 5, doc. 6; and Circular of the Foreign Ministry, January 25, 1939, *DGFP*, ser. D, vol. 5, p. 931. This is also the conclusion of Strauss, "Jewish Emigration from Germany: Nazi Policies and Jewish Responses (I)," *Leo Baeck Institute Yearbook*, vol. 25 (1980): 347.

16. Riddleberger Memorandum Regarding General Goering's Views, August 11, 1938, in Wilson to Secretary of State, August 12, 1938, NA, RG 59, CDF 711.62/163.

17. *DGFP*, ser. D, vol. 4, doc. 271, pp. 338–40; and "Foreign Political Aspects of the Recent Anti-Semitic Measures of Germany," December 16, 1938, NA, RG 165, Box 1191, Germany 3500 Jews.

18. Wiley to Messersmith, June 8, 1938, Messersmith Papers, Item 1051, University of Delaware.

19. Geist to Secretary of State, December 15, 1938, NA, RG 59, 811.111 Quota 62/659.

20. Geist affidavit of August 28, 1945, IMT, vol. 28, p. 250, doc. 1759-PS.

21. "Nazi Paperwork for the Final Solution of the Jewish Question," paper presented at the annual meeting of the American Historical Association, December 28, 1983. Along these lines, see also Dawidowicz, *War against the Jews*, 137–38.

22. Hitler, as quoted in Dawidowicz, *War against the Jews,* 142.

23. Bullitt to Secretary of State, Personal and Secret for the President, September 19, 1939, NA, RG 59, CDF 740.00/2138, Confidential File. This document provides the text of a report on Hitler's speech of March 8 or March 9, supposedly delivered in Vienna on March 12 by State Secretary Wilhelm Keppler and one other German to Austrian officials. The substance of the information had been communicated to Washington in late March. See NA, RG 59, CDF 740.00/684, Confidential File. The September report provided the exact text and more details about the audience. The information was obtained by Otto of Hapsburg, who had extraordinary sources of information within the Austrian government. From other sources it can be confirmed that Hitler gave a speech on March 9, 1939, to the audience described by Otto of Hapsburg and that Keppler was in Vienna on March 12. Although there is no direct confirmation of this intelligence report, Gerhard Weinberg has accepted the account of the Hitler speech as probably authentic. See Weinberg, "Hitler's Image of the United States," *American Historical Review* 69 (1964): 1013, 1013 n. 27.

24. What Walter Laqueur, in *The Terrible Secret: Suppression of the Truth about Hitler's "Final Solution"* (Boston, 1980), has maintained about the early wartime period holds *a fortiori* before the war.

25. Wiley to Moffat, June 3, 1938, Moffat Papers, Houghton Library, Harvard; and Bauer, *My Brother's Keeper,* 225–26.

26. Feis to Frankfurter, March 22, 1938, Herbert Feis Papers, Box 33, LC.

27. *Newsweek,* April 4, 1938, pp. 10–11, cited by Stewart, "United States Policy," 272. Freud's passport was confiscated and his property threatened.

28. Feis to Frankfurter, March 22, 1938; and Feis to Cordell Hull, March 22, 1938, Feis Papers, Box 33, LC; and Moffat Diary, March 16, 1938, Moffat Papers, Houghton Library, Harvard.

29. Feis to Frankfurter, March 22, 1938, Feis Papers, Box 33, LC.

30. Wise to Brandeis, February 22, 1938, Wise Papers, Box 106, AJHS.

31. Messersmith to Geist, February 7, 1938, Messersmith Papers, Item 941, University of Delaware.

32. Messersmith wrote later that year to Felix Frankfurter: "The affidavit system does not have any basis in our immigration laws. It is a document which was devised through the ingenuity of consular officers in order that relatives and friends in this country should have an opportunity of aiding prospective immigrants for whom they were willing to take this obligation. . . . This affidavit system has worked out very well and is one of the most helpful factors of our immigration practice. . . . We [in the State Department] are deeply concerned that some extension of this affidavit system may be proposed to the Congress, and we believe that if it is, it will result in the doing away of the affidavit system altogether." Messersmith to Frankfurter, October 25, 1938, Frankfurter Papers, Box 83, Messersmith Folder, LC.

33. Moffat Diary, March 18, 1938, Moffat Papers, Houghton Library, Harvard; Messersmith to Hull, Moore, Moffat, and Shipley, March 18, 1938, NA, RG 59, CDF 840.48 Refugees/59; and Messersmith to Geist, November 7, 1938, Messersmith Papers, Item 1066, University of Delaware.

34. McLaughlin to Perkins, March 31, 1938, NA, RG 174, Assistant Secretary Charles V. McLaughlin: General Subject File, 1938–41, Immigration.

35. Visa Instruction of January 5, 1937, NA, RG 59, 150.626J/242. No subsequent instruction relaxing interpretation of the regulations has been found. There may, however, have been oral instructions issued.

36. Morgenthau Diaries, March 22, 1938, vol. 115, FDRL; and Harold L. Ickes, *Secret Diary: The Inside Struggle, 1936–39* (New York, 1954), vol. 2, pp. 342–43, as cited by Stewart, "United States Policy," 273.

37. Morgenthau Diaries, March 22, 1938, vol. 115, FDRL.

38. Ibid.

39. Chronological File, September–December 1938, American Jewish Committee Archives.

40. Moffat Diary, March 21, 22, 1938, Moffat Papers, Houghton Library, Harvard; and Welles to Morgenthau, March 23, 1938, Morgenthau Diaries, vol. 116, FDRL.

41. Hull to American Embassy, London, March 23, 1938, NA, RG 59, CDF 862.48 Refugees/A.

42. Feis to Frankfurter, April 4, 1938, Feis Papers, Box 33, LC.

43. Samuel McCrea Cavert Memorandum on White House Conference on Refugees, April 13, 1938, AFSC, General File 1938: Committees and Organizations—American Christian Committee for German Refugees; and Stephen Wise Memorandum, April 13, 1938, Brandeis Papers, University of Louisville Microfilm Series VI, Roll 106.

44. PACPR minutes, May 16, 1938, Wise Papers, Box 65, AJHS.

45. Moffat to Leland Harrison, June 1, 1938, Leland Harrison Papers, Box 28, LC; and Messersmith to Wiley, June 28, 1938, Messersmith Papers, Item 1012, University of Delaware.

46. S. Adler-Rudel, "The Evian Conference on the Refugee Question," *Leo Baeck Institute Yearbook* 13 (1968): 241–43.

47. Naomi Shepherd, *Wilfrid Israel: German Jewry's Secret Ambassador* (London, 1984), 133–34.

48. Adler-Rudel, "Evian," 245.

49. A. G. Brotman Report on the Evian Conference, July 6, 1938, American Jewish Committee Archives, RG 1, EXO-29, Immigration, Refugees—Evian; and Adler-Rudel, "Evian," 235–73.

50. See Frankfurter to McDonald, July 1, 1938, McDonald Papers, Frankfurter Folder, CSIA. Although Frankfurter did not use the term "New Deal," he did compare the step to the American government's intervention in the unemployment problem in 1933.

51. See Herbert Pell to Moffat, September 10, 1938, Moffat Papers, Houghton Library, Harvard.

52. Adler-Rudel, "Evian," 260.

53. Wiley to Messersmith, July 18, 1938, Messersmith Papers, Item 1017, University of Delaware; and Warren to Chamberlain, July 16, 1938, Joseph Chamberlain Papers, Item 461, YIVO.

54. Stewart, "United States Policy," 324, 326.

55. Henry L. Feingold, "Roosevelt and the Resettlement Question," *Rescue Efforts during the Holocaust: Proceedings of the Second Yad Vashem International Historical Conference, Jerusalem, April 8–11, 1974* (Jerusalem, 1977), 123–80.

56. Messersmith to Secretary of State, November 14, 1938, copy in Messersmith Papers, Item 1075, University of Delaware; and statement by FDR, November 15, 1938, reprinted in *Franklin D. Roosevelt and Foreign Affairs* (Clearwater, 1981), vol. 12, p. 83.

57. Shepherd, *Wilfrid Israel*, 147–49.

58. Messersmith to Secretary of State, November 17, 1938; and Messersmith to Welles, December 15, 1938, NA, RG 59, 150.01/2607 1/2 and 2617 1/2.

59. Press conference of November 18, 1938, quoted in Stewart, "United States Policy," 407–08.

60. Wise to Benjamin Cohen, November 17, 1938, Wise Papers, Box 64, AJHS; Minutes of PACPR, November 14, 21, 1938, copies in Wise Papers, Box 65, AJHS; and Moffat Diary, November 16, 1938, Houghton Library, Harvard.

61. Hull to FDR, November 22, 1938; and Hull (Moffat) to Taylor, NA, RG 59, CDF 840.48 Refugees/960A.

62. FDR Memorandum for the Undersecretary of State, November 26, 1938, OF 20, FDRL; Morgenthau to FDR; Bowman to FDR, November 21, 25, 29, 1938, President's Secretary's File, Box 177, FDRL.

63. Harry Hopkins Papers, Box 118, Refugee Problem, FDRL; and Morgenthau Diaries, January 24, 1938, vol. 106, FDRL.

64. Rosenman to FDR, filed December 12, 1938, President's Personal File, FDRL, cited by Stewart, "United States Policy," 391.

65. Arthur Murray to FDR, December 15, 1938, President's Secretary's File, Box 53, Great Britain, FDRL. See also David Reynolds, *The Creation of the Anglo-American Alliance, 1937–1941: A Study in Competitive Cooperation* (Chapel Hill, 1982), 47.

66. Jacob Landau Memorandum on Conversation with Messersmith, October 7, 1938, American Jewish Committee Archives, RG 1, EXO-29, Waldman File, Jewish Telegraphic Agency; and Messersmith to Geist, November 7, 1938, Messersmith Papers, Item 1066, University of Delaware.

67. Messersmith to Brandeis, October 24, 1938; and Messersmith to Geist, November 30, 1938, Messersmith Papers, Items 1054, 1084, University of Delaware; Moffat Diary, October 29–30, 1938, Houghton Library, Harvard; and *The Gallup Poll: Public Opinion, 1935–1971*, ed. George H. Gallup (New York, 1972), vol. 1, p. 12.

68. Messersmith to Morris, October 18, 1938, NA, RG 59, 811.111 Quota 62/616. Messersmith's attention to proper visa procedure is also revealed by his detailed instructions to Morris, September 10, 1938, NA, RG 59, 150.069/410, and by his praise when Morris was able to streamline the application procedure: Morris to Messersmith, November 30, 1938; and Messersmith to Coulter, December 20, 1938; and Messersmith to Morris December 22, 1938, NA, RG 59, 811.111 Quota 62/668.

69. Stewart, "United States Policy," 404; Hodgdon to Secretary of State, August 26, 1938; Alexander to Warren, August 29, 1938; Hull to American Consul, Berlin, September 1, 1938; and Messersmith to Geist, September 1, 1938, NA, RG 59, 811.111 Quota 62/595.

70. Geist to Secretary of State, September 8, 1938; and Hull to American Consul, Berlin, September 12, 13, 1938, NA, RG 59, 150.626J/482.

71. Knight to Visa Division, July 21, 1938; Alexander to Warren, May 14, 1938; Knight to Flournoy, May 18, 1938; and Bannerman to Warren, August 16, 1938, NA, RG 59, 150.062 PC/1056, 1062, 1063, 1074. Other evidence indicates that there were variations among consuls with regard to affidavits from nonrelatives. Razovsky to Shevell, November 14, 1938; and Razovsky to Taylor, February 9, 1939, Razovsky Papers, Box 2, National Coordinating Committee, AJHS.

72. Geist affidavit of August 28, 1945, IMT, vol. 28, doc. 1759 PS, p. 248. For a long time his efforts went unrecognized. But in 1954 the West German government awarded Raymond Geist its Commander's Cross of the Order of Merit for intervening with the highest officials in Nazi Germany on behalf of the victims of Nazi persecution and helping the latter to leave Germany. Geist was said to have acted "far beyond the bounds of the duties of his office" and "without consideration of potential personal disadvantages." Documents on Geist's service and award were kindly supplied by the embassy of the Federal Republic of Germany.

73. Stewart, "United States Policy," 405; and Messersmith to Warren, December 9, 1938, NA, RG 59, 811.111 Quota 62/595.

74. Pickett to Elkington, January 31, February 16, 1939, AFSC, Refugee Service 1939, Letters to Berlin; and Pickett Journal, February 17, March 1, 1939, AFSC.

75. Minutes of Refugee Committee, February 9, 1939, AFSC, Refugee Service 1939; and Messersmith to Geist, November 30, December 8, 1938, Messersmith Papers, Items 1084, 1093, University of Delaware.

76. Perkins to Messersmith, December 3, 1938, NA, RG 174, Frances Perkins, State

266   NOTES FOR PAGES 66–71

Department—1938; and Messersmith to Welles, December 15, 1938, NA, RG 59, 150.01/2617 1/2. On the subsequent fate of the Wagner-Rogers Bill and the Alaskan plan, see the excellent analysis by Wyman, *Paper Walls*, 75–115.

77. Wyzanski to Frankfurter, February 26, 1939, Frankfurter Papers, Box 113, Wyzanski Folder, LC; and Martin, *Madam Secretary*, 429.

78. Geist to Messersmith, December 5, 1938, Messersmith Papers, Item 1087, University of Delaware.

79. Messersmith to Geist, December 20, 1938, Messersmith Papers, Item 1099, University of Delaware.

80. Stewart, "United States Policy," 319–59; and Feingold, *Politics of Rescue*, 47–52.

81. Geist to Messersmith, January 22, 1939, Messersmith Papers, Item 1136, University of Delaware; copy of memoranda, February 1–2, in American Jewish Committee Archives, RG 1, EXO-29, Waldman File, Immigration/Refugees: European Situation, 1938–39; and Hull to Myron Taylor and George Rublee, February 8, 1939, NA, RG 59, CDF 840.48 Refugees/1384.

82. "There is some evidence to suggest that for Rublee and Welles and other State Department officials the issue by 1939 was not so much the extrication of the Jews from Germany, but rather the extrication of the Roosevelt Administration from the embarrassing position created by the Evian initiative." Feingold, *Politics of Rescue*, 68.

83. See, particularly, Geist to Messersmith, January 22, 1939, Messersmith Papers, Item 1136, University of Delaware; and Gilbert to Moffat, February 6, 1939, Moffat Papers, Houghton Library, Harvard.

84. Stewart, "United States Policy," 358; and Moffat Diary, December 19, 1938, Moffat Papers, Houghton Library, Harvard.

85. Robert Szold to Brandeis, April 19, 1939, Szold Papers, PEF, IX/14, Zionist Archives and Library, New York.

86. Moffat Diary, May 4, 1939, Moffat Papers, Houghton Library, Harvard. The German Trust, however, was not yet in existence, nor did it ever come into being. On the wrangling among German government agencies, see Rolf Vogel, ed., *Ein Stempel hat gefehlt: Dokumente zur Emigration deutscher Juden* (Munich, 1977), 265–80.

87. *DGFP*, ser. D, vol. 5, doc. 665, 933–36; and Schleunes, *Twisted Road to Auschwitz*, 253–54.

88. Conversation of Rolf Vogel with Schacht, January 16, 1970, in Vogel, *Ein Stempel*, 210; and *DGFP*, ser. D, vol. 5, pp. 919–25. On German opposition to Rublee's visit and to Schacht's initiative, see Vogel, *Ein Stempel*, 186–208.

89. Harold Tewell to Secretary of State, March 17, 1938, NA, RG 59, CDF 837.55J/ Confidential File, reprinted by Mendelsohn, *The Holocaust*, vol. 7, *Jewish Emigration: The St. Louis and Other Cases*, doc. 1, pp. 1–30. With reference to this despatch, one State Department official wrote: "This has been initialed for RA on the understanding that it will not become a part of the files of the Inter Govt. Committee. There are parts of it that it would be most undesirable for other than U.S. officials to see." Ibid., p. 31. Messersmith wrote: "The report discusses in a comprehensive manner a subject of great interest to the Department at this time. Mr. Tewell should be commended for his initiative in the submission of this thorough and timely report which has been given the rating of excellent." Ibid., p. 33. See also National Coordinating Committee for Aid to Refugees and Emigrants Coming from Germany to Dear Friends, June 15, 1939, AFSC, Refugee Service 1939: Committees and Organizations—Joint Distribution Committee.

90. Tewell to Secretary of State, May 9, 1939, NA, RG 59, CDF 837.55J/4, reprinted by Mendelsohn, *The Holocaust*, vol. 7, doc. 2, pp. 35–50.

91. German Embassy, Havana, to Foreign Office, May 11, 1939, reprinted (in German) in Mendelsohn, *The Holocaust*, vol. 7, doc. 4, pp. 88–89.

92. American Jewish Joint Distribution Committee to Dear Friend, June 15, 1939,

AFSC, Refugee Service 1939, Committees and Organizations: American Jewish Joint Distribution Committee.

93. German Embassy, Havana, to Foreign Office, May 25, 1939, in Mendelsohn, *The Holocaust,* vol. 7, doc. 4, pp. 102–03; Consul General Coert du Bois to Secretary of State, June 7, 1939, NA, RG 59, CDF 837.55J/39; telegram to President Roosevelt, May 29, 1939, NA, RG 59, CDF 837.55/19, in Mendelsohn, *The Holocaust,* vol. 7, doc. 9; and Morse, *While Six Million Died,* 274–75.

94. Morse, *While Six Million Died,* 280.

95. Coert du Bois Memorandum for the Files, May 29, 1939; and Wright Memorandum of Conversation, May 30, 1939, NA, RG 59, CDF 837.55J/39, in Mendelsohn, *The Holocaust,* vol. 7, doc. 3, pp. 59–61.

96. See, above all, Mendelsohn, *The Holocaust,* vol. 7, doc. 3, pp. 71–83. See also Berenson to Wise, June 14, 1939, Wise Papers, Box 91, AJHS.

97. Coert du Bois Memorandum for the Files, June 7, 1939, NA, RG 59, CDF 837.55J/39, in Mendelsohn, *The Holocaust,* vol. 7, doc. 3, pp. 85–86.

98. Morse, *While Six Million Died,* 282.

99. Ibid., 283–87; and Bauer, *My Brother's Keeper,* 279–80.

100. German Embassy, Havana, to Foreign Office, June 7, 1939; and Foreign Office Memorandum, July 4, 1939, in Mendelsohn, *The Holocaust,* vol. 7, doc. 4.

101. Wyman, *Paper Walls,* 75.

102. Ibid., 76–79, 87.

103. Ibid., 82.

104. Inglis to Balderston, July 19, 1939, AFSC, Refugee Service 1939, Refugee Children; and Warren to Messersmith, August 10, 1939, NA, RG 59, 150.01 Bills/151.

105. Morse, *While Six Million Died,* 268; and Stewart, "United States Policy," 527.

106. Messersmith to the Secretary, the Undersecretary, Moffat, and Achilles, January 23, 1939, NA, RG 59, 150.01 Bills/99.

107. Moffat Diary, May 25, 1939, quoted by Stewart, "United States Policy," 532.

108. Wyman, *Paper Walls,* 168–69.

109. The month-by-month totals of visas granted demonstrate the effects of the March 1938 presidential initiative upon the State Department and the consuls abroad. There is a noticeable increase in visas issued beginning in March 1938. In spite of occasional dips, the average number of visas issued from April 1938 until April 1939 is about 62 percent higher than the January–February 1938 level. The figures are: 1938—Jan., 1,321; Feb., 1,113; Mar., 1,614 Apr., 1,803; May, 1,191; June, 2,612; Jul., 2,098; Aug., 1,989; Sept., 2,012; Oct., 2,020; Nov., 2,086; Dec., 2,017; 1939—Jan., 1,798; Feb., 2,077; Mar., 1,991; Apr., 1,874. Data compiled from Hodgdon to Secretary of State, August 20, 1938; and Geist to Secretary of State, August 30, 1939, NA, RG 59, 811.111 Quota 62/596 and 62/754. It should be noted that the State Department's statistics on visas issued usually vary from the figures of the Immigration and Naturalization Service (INS) on immigrants admitted. Part of the reason is that not all visas are used. Sometimes the issuance of visas and the admission to the United States fall into different time periods.

INS data indicate that 17,868 immigrants came in under the German quota in fiscal 1938 (ending June 30, 1938) and that 32,759 were admitted in fiscal 1939. For the period July–December 1939, 12,415 were admitted to the U.S. National Refugee Service chart in Lawrence Klein to Reynolds, January 16, 1941, AFSC, Refugee Service 1941, Immigration Policies and Procedures.

110. Warren to Bryan, January 30, 1940, NA, RG 59, 811.111 Quota 62/769.

111. IGCR Committee Meeting on July 19, 1939—Excerpt, copy in Joseph Chamberlain Papers, YIVO.

112. Ibid. For a well-informed contemporary assessment of the British financial proposal and British Guiana, see Achilles to Moffat, July 28, 1939, Moffat Papers,

Houghton Library, Harvard. On the background to the presidential invitation, see also [McDonald] Memorandum of Conversation with Undersecretary of State Mr. Welles . . . August 23, 1939, Joseph Chamberlain Papers, YIVO.

113. [McDonald] Memorandum of Conversation with Welles, August 23, 1939, Joseph Chamberlain Papers, YIVO.

114. President's Advisory Committee on Political Refugees Memorandum to the President, September 26, 1939, Joseph Chamberlain Papers, YIVO.

115. George Warren to Chamberlain, September 28, 1939, Joseph Chamberlain Papers, YIVO.

116. Warren to Messersmith, November 4, 1939, NA, RG 59, 150.01 Bills/160; and Refugee Consultative Council, November 14, 1939, AFSC, Refugee Service 1939, Committees and Organizations, National Refugee Service.

117. Hull to American Embassy, Berlin, October 20, 1939, NA, RG 59, 811.111 Quota 62/735; and Non-Sectarian Committee for German Refugee Children, Minutes of December 17, 1939, AFSC, Refugee Service 1939, Committees and Organizations.

118. Non-Sectarian Committee, December 17, 1939, AFSC, Refugee Service 1939, Committees and Organizations; and Hull to American Embassy, Berlin, October 20, 1939, NA, RG 59, 811.111 Quota 62/735.

119. White House Press Release, copy of FDR's speech to the IGCR officers, October 17, 1939, copy in Hopkins Papers, Box 118, Refugee Problems, FDRL.

120. Moffat Diary, July 27, 1939, Houghton Library, Harvard.

121. Moffat Diary, October 23, 1939, Houghton Library, Harvard; Berle to FDR, October 23, 1939, President's Secretary's File, Diplomatic, Box 64, Palestine, FDRL; Robert Pell undated Memorandum on Intergovernmental Committee, NA, RG 59, CDF 840.48 Refugees/2122 Confidential File; and FDR to Secretary of State, March 3, 1940, President's Secretary's File, Diplomatic, Box 64, Palestine, FDRL. For later evidence of FDR's continued interest in long-term plans, see Dr. Alès Hrdlicka, Smithsonian Institution, to Mr. President, May 27, 1942, copy in NA, RG 59, 150.01/Bills 3-3045; and FDR to Undersecretary of State, December 4, 1939, President's Secretary's File, Diplomatic, Box 64, Palestine, FDRL.

122. White House Press Release and copy of FDR's speech to IGCR officers, October 17, 1939, copy in Hopkins Papers, Box 118, Refugee Problems, FDRL.

123. Lahousen affidavit, September 19, 1945, NA, RG 238, Lahousen folder.

124. Lahousen-Canaris Memorandum, September 14, 1939, reprinted in Helmuth Groscurth, *Tagebücher eines Abwehroffiziers 1938–1940: Mit weiteren Dokumenten zur Militäropposition gegen Hitler,* ed. Helmut Krausnick and Harold Deutsch (Stuttgart, 1970), 357–59.

125. NA, RG 242, Microfilm T-175, R 239, Frame 2728514.

126. *The Halder Diaries: The Private War Journals of Colonel General Franz Halder,* ed. Arnold Lissance (Boulder, 1976), 10–11.

127. NA, RG 242, Microfilm T-175, R 239, Frame 2728524-27; and express letter of September 21, 1939, in U.S. Chief of Counsel for the Prosecution of Axis Criminality, *Nazi Conspiracy and Aggression* (Washington, 1946–47) vol. 6, doc. 3363-PS, pp. 97–100.

128. Dawidowicz, *War against the Jews,* 154–55.

129. Groscurth Memorandum based on Briefing by Major Radke, September 22, 1939—Brauchitsch Conference with Heydrich (almost certainly on September 22, 1939), reprinted in Groscurth, *Tagebücher,* 361.

130. *Nazi Conspiracy and Aggression,* vol. 3, doc. 864-PS, pp. 619–21.

4. REFUGEES AND AMERICAN JEWRY

1. Finger, *American Jewry.* For a discussion of the commission's mission and the controversy that has surrounded it, see Lucy S. Dawidowicz, "Indicting American Jews," *Commentary,* June 1983, p. 43.

2. David Brody, "American Jewry, The Refugees, and Immigration Restriction (1932–1942)," in Abraham J. Karp, ed., *The Jewish Experience in America: Selected Studies from the Publications of the American Jewish Historical Society*, 5 (New York, 1969), 340.

3. Wyman, *Abandonment of the Jews*, 327–28.

4. Wiesel, "Telling the Tale," 9–12; Dawidowicz, "Indicting American Jews," 43; and Lookstein, *Were We Our Brothers' Keepers*, 216.

5. Joseph Brainen, as quoted by Brody, "American Jewry, The Refugees, and Immigration Restriction (1932–1942)," 321.

6. Moses Rischin, *The Promised City: New York's Jews, 1870–1914* (Cambridge, 1962), 104. The letter originally appeared in the *Yiddische Gazetten*, April 1894, and was translated by Harold Silver, "Some Attitudes of the East European Jewish Immigrants toward Organized Jewish Charity, 1890–1910" (M.A. thesis, Graduate School of Jewish Social Work, 1934), 219.

7. Nathan Glazer, "The Jews," in John Higham, ed., *Ethnic Leadership in America* (Baltimore, 1978), 19–35.

8. The standard work on the American Jewish Committee is Naomi W. Cohen, *Not Free to Desist: The American Jewish Committee, 1906–1966* (Philadelphia, 1972).

9. Nathan Glazer suggests that these terms, originally coined by Swedish sociologist Gunner Myrdal in his 1944 discussion of American black leadership, may be useful in describing patterns prevalent in other groups as well. Glazer, "The Jews," 20.

10. Cohen, *Not Free to Desist*, 33.

11. Henry L. Feingold, *Zion in America: The Jewish Experience from Colonial Times to the Present* (Boston, 1974), 217–19, and *A Midrash on American Jewish History* (Albany, 1982), 113–14.

12. There is no single outstanding study of the American Jewish Congress. But the best accounts of its activities are in works on Stephen S. Wise, its founder and guiding spirit. See Wise's autobiography, *The Challenging Years* (New York, 1949); and Melvin I. Urofsky, *A Voice That Spoke for Justice: The Life and Times of Stephen S. Wise* (Albany, 1982).

13. A good account of the founding of the American Jewish Congress and its participation in the Paris talks is in Melvin I. Urofsky, *American Zionism from Herzl to the Holocaust* (New York, 1976), 151–81.

14. Edward E. Grusad, *B'nai B'rith: The Story of the Covenant* (New York, 1966).

16. Moshe R. Gottlieb, *American Anti-Nazi Resistance, 1933–41: An Historical Analysis* (New York, 1982), 28–29.

16. Ibid., 28.

17. Rabbi Stephen Wise quoting Rev. John H. Holmes to Julian Mack, September 13, 1932, Wise Papers, Box 82, World Affairs—Germany, AJHS.

18. Telegram, Harold Debrest to FDR, March 8, 1933, NA, RG 59, CDF 862.4016/32.

19. I. Lehman to FDR, September 21, 1933, NA, RG 59, CDF 150.01/2153.

20. Jay Pierrepont Moffat to George A. Gordon, April 4, 1933, Moffat Papers, Houghton Library, Harvard.

21. Robert T. Bower and Leo Strole, "Voting Behavior of American Ethnic Groups, 1936–1944," Bureau of Applied Social Research, Columbia University (New York, 1948). See also Ronald H. Bayor, *Neighbors in Conflict: The Irish, Germans, Jews, and Italians of New York City, 1929–1941* (Baltimore, 1978), 147.

22. Leonard Dinnerstein, "Jews and the New Deal," *American Jewish History* 72 (1983), 461–76.

23. David Wyman describes in vivid detail how the activity of anti-Semitic demagogues contributed to the general opposition to anti-Semitism in the American population. See Wyman's *Paper Walls*.

24. The best book on this anti-Semitic activity is Leo P. Ribuffo, *The Old Christian*

Right: The Protestant Far Right from the Great Depression to the Cold War (Philadelphia, 1983), xi.

25. McWilliams, as quoted by Mike Landon, "Is There a Führer in the House?" *New Republic*, August 12, 1940, p. 212; and Wyman, *Paper Walls*, 14.

26. Herbert Stember, *Jews in the Mind of America* (New York, 1966), 54, 121.

27. Brody, "American Jewry, The Refugees, and Immigration Restriction (1932–1942)," 326.

28. Gottlieb, *American Anti-Nazi Resistance*, 29.

29. Ibid., pp. 29–31.

30. Moffat to Gordon, April 4, 1933, Moffat Papers, Houghton Library, Harvard.

31. Ibid.

32. Cordell Hull to George A. Gordon, March 26, 1933, in U.S. Department of State, *Foreign Relations of the United States* (hereafter *FRUS), 1933* (Washington, 1943), vol. 2, pp. 333–34.

33. Moffat to Gordon, April 4, 1933, Moffat Papers, Houghton Library, Harvard.

34. *New York Times,* March 27, 1933.

35. Gottlieb, *American Anti-Nazi Resistance,* 41–44.

36. Ibid. See also American Jewish Committee Archives, Minutes of Administrative Committee, April 1, 1933, in Minutes–Administrative Committee, 1933, American Jewish Congress File, Box 2, Folder 77. In this special report by Wise and Deutsch on their trip to Washington, the two say that Phillips led them to believe that Hitler agreed to a one-day boycott as a concession to his followers. Phillips and the State Department urged Wise and Deutsch not to make any statement that might worsen the situation.

37. Adler to Waldman, as quoted by Gottlieb, *American Anti-Nazi Resistance,* 42.

38. Ibid.

39. Memo of transatlantic conversation between Gordon and Phillips, March 31, 1933, *FRUS, 1933,* vol. 2, p. 342; telephone conversation between Gordon and Phillips, April 2, 1933, ibid., pp. 345–46; Gordon to Hull, April 4, 1933, ibid., pp. 350–51; and Hull to Gordon, April 5, 1933, ibid., p. 352.

40. *Jewish Daily Bulletin,* April 7, 1933.

41. Moffat to Gordon, April 4, 1933, Moffat Papers, Houghton Library, Harvard.

42. *New York Times,* March 21, 1933.

43. Gottlieb, *American Anti-Nazi Resistance,* 46.

44. Ralph Friedman to Cyrus Adler, March 22, 1933, American Jewish Committee Archives RG-1, EXO-29, Waldman Papers, Boycott Germany Folder.

45. *New York Times,* August 15, 1933. According to historian Moshe R. Gottlieb, Wise was unequivocally committed to the idea of a boycott. He feared, however, that if the timing were wrong the tactic could backfire and worsen the situation of German Jews. Gottlieb, *American Anti-Nazi Resistance,* 356 n. 4.

46. Wise to Frankfurter, Mack, and Brandeis [strictly confidential], May 23, 1933, Wise Papers, Box 109, Correspondence—Zionism, AJHS.

47. Ibid.

48. Wise to Mack, April 2, 1933, Wise Papers, Box 114, Correspondence—Zionism, AJHS.

49. Felix Frankfurter to Raymond Moley, April 24, 1933, LC. See chap. 1, n. 3.

50. Frankfurter to FDR, April 16, 1933, NA, RG 59, Social Matters, Race Problems file, CDF 862.4016/586 GC.

51. Raymond Moley to Frankfurter, April 28, 1933, NA, RG 59, Social Matters, Race Problems file, CDF 862.4016/586.

52. Hull to Frankfurter, May 6, 1933, NA, RG 59, Social Matters, Race Policy file, CDF 862.4016/586.

53. Cyrus Adler to A. Leo Weil, Jr., Esq., May 3, 1933, American Jewish Committee Archive, RG-1, EXO-29, Waldman File, Schacht Folder, 1933. See also American Jewish

Committee Archives, American Jewish Committee Executive Committee Minutes, June 5, 1933, vol. 6, pt. 1, p. 174.

54. Frankfurter to Proskauer, May 18, 1933, Frankfurter Papers, Box 137, LC.

55. Frankfurter to Frances Perkins, April 27, 1933, Part I, Box 4, Frances Perkins Papers, Columbia University.

56. Ibid.

57. Cyrus Adler to Abram C. Joseph, Esq., November 22, 1933, American Jewish Committee Archives, RG-1, EXO-29, Waldman File, Germany Folder.

58. Ibid.

59. American Jewish Committee Archives, American Jewish Committee Executive Committee Minutes, April 17, 1933, vol. 6, pt. 1, p. 128.

60. Proskauer to Brandeis, May 31, 1933, Brandeis Papers, University of Louisville Microfilm Series VI, Roll 99.

61. Proskauer to Wise, May 31, 1983, ibid.

62. "Dr. Stephen S. Wise," n.d., American Jewish Committee Archives, RG-1, EXO-29, Waldman File, Stephen S. Wise file.

63. Waldman to Rich, October 20, 1933, ibid.

64. Ibid.

65. Ibid.

66. The best description of the JLC's formation is George L. Berlin, "The Jewish Labor Committee and American Immigration Policy in the 1930's," in Berlin, ed. *Studies in Jewish Bibliography, History, and Literature in Honor of I. Edward Kiev* (New York, 1971).

67. Ibid., 50.

68. Yehuda Bauer, *American Jewry and the Holocaust: The American Jewish Joint Distribution Committee, 1939–1945* (Detroit, 1981), 23. The earlier period is covered in Bauer, *My Brother's Keeper.*

69. Bauer, *My Brother's Keeper,* 142.

70. McDonald's concern with the issue of Jewish refugees is best treated in the study by his daughter, Barbara McDonald Stewart, "United States Government Policy." It has since been published by Garland Press, 1981.

71. Bauer, *My Brother's Keeper,* 143; and Stewart, "United States Policy," 125.

72. R. Walton Moore, Memorandum for Moffat, March 16, 1934, as quoted by Stewart, "United States Policy," 138–39.

73. Wise to Brandeis, January 12, 1936, Wise Papers, Box 105, Correspondence—Zionism, AJHS.

74. Ibid.

75. Wise to Frankfurter, March 2, 1936 [personal and confidential], Brandeis Papers, University of Louisville Microfilm Series VI, Roll 103.

76. Excerpt from *The Jewish Day,* August 14, 1936, Brandeis Papers, University of Louisville Microfilm Series VI, Roll 103. See also Urofsky, *American Zionism from Herzl to the Holocaust,* 377.

77. Report of a Visit of Dr. Stephen S. Wise to President Roosevelt at Hyde Park, Mon. Oct. 5, 1936, Wise Papers, Box 68, Federal Government—Presidential, AJHS. In a cover letter, Wise told Frankfurter and Mack that this is almost a verbatim transcript; the cover letter is dated October 6, 1936; a separate cover letter was also sent to Brandeis.

78. Lawrence H. Fuchs, *The Political Behavior of American Jews* (Glencoe, Ill., 1956), 71–74.

79. Berlin, "The Jewish Labor Committee," 53.

80. Ibid., 53–54.

81. Wise to Frankfurter, March 30, 1938, Wise Papers, Box 109, Correspondence—Zionism, AJHS.

82. Ibid.

83. Schneiderman to Waldman, April 5, 1938, account of Executive Committee Meeting, American Jewish Committee Archives, RG-1, EXO-29, Waldman File, Immigration file 1938–39.

84. Frankfurter to Roosevelt, March 26, 1938, as quoted by Shlomo Shafir, "The Impact of the Jewish Crisis on American-German Relations, 1933–1939" (Ph.D. diss., Georgetown University, 1971), vol. 2, p. 706.

85. FDR to Herbert Lehman, March 28, 1938, OF 3186, FDRL; and Roosevelt to Irving Lehman, March 30, 1938, OF 3186, FDRL.

86. Herbert Lehman to FDR, March 28, 1938, OF 3186, FDRL; and FDR to Lehman, March 30, 1938, FDRL, also cited in Feingold, *Politics of Rescue*, 24. For the reaction of various groups, see Shafir, "Impact of the Jewish Crisis," vol. 2, pp. 713–15.

87. Feis to Frankfurter, April 4, 1938, Feis Papers, Box 33, LC.

88. Ibid.

89. Stephen Wise memo, April 13, 1938, Brandeis Papers, University of Louisville Microfilm Series VI, Roll 27. Minutes of the Second Session of PACPR, May 19, 1938; and Wise to Brandeis, April 21, 1938, Wise Papers, AJHS.

90. According to Barbara McDonald Stewart, a story circulated around Washington that the president had only appointed Baruch as one of the "Jewish representatives" to punish him for testimony Baruch had given a Senate committee investigating the New Deal. FDR knew that Baruch preferred being known as a great financier to being known as a leading Jew. Frankfurter wrote to the former Labor Department solicitor Charles Wyzanski, Jr., that "Messrs. Baruch and Morgenthau are preoccupied with saving their own hides and their own 'positions' in America and care next to nothing about the lot of Hitler's victims. Into your own private ears let me say that Mr. Justice Brandeis has characterized the attitude which Baruch revealed to him on the present Jewish situation as 'disgraceful.' These men are behaving precisely as did the rich and powerful Jews who helped bring on Hitlerism as a way of avoiding Bolshevism." Frankfurter to Wyzanski, April 18, 1938, Box 43, Frankfurter Papers, LC, and quoted in Stewart, "United States Policy," 285 n. 1. See Shafir, "Impact of the Jewish Crisis," vol. 2, 727–28.

91. Minutes of Second Session of the President's Advisory Committee on Political Refugees, May 19, 1938, Wise Papers, Box 65, AJHS; and Baruch to Hull, April 13, 1938, Cordell Hull Papers, Box 82, LC.

92. Minutes of the First Session of the President's Advisory Committee on Political Refugees, May 16, 1938, Wise Papers, AJHS; and Wise to Brandeis, May 17, 1938, Wise Papers, Box 106, Correspondence—Zionism, AJHS. See also Minutes of Third Session of PACPR, June 2, 1938, Wise Papers, AJHS; and Shafir, "Impact of the Jewish Crisis," vol. 2, 730.

93. S. Adler-Rudel, as quoted by Shafir, "Impact of the Jewish Crisis," vol. 2, 740.

94. Ibid., 741.

95. Paul Baerwald, Address to Annual Meeting of JDC, December 2–3, 1939, Paul Baerwald Papers, CSIA.

96. S. Adler-Rudel, as quoted by Shafir, "Impact of the Jewish Crisis," vol. 2, 741–42.

97. The American Jewish Committee came down firmly against the American Jewish Congress's proposed plebiscite. American Jewish Committee Archives, American Jewish Committee Executive Committee Minutes, May 11, 1938, vol. 7, pt. 1, pp. 89–103; Stroock to Wise, October 30, 1939, American Jewish Committee Archives, Chronological File, Sept.–Dec., 1939. For a brief history of the GJC from the American Jewish Committee's perspective, see appendix 4 to American Jewish Committee Executive Committee Minutes, January 20, 1940, vol. 7, pt. 1, pp. 159–67, American Jewish Committee Archives.

98. Memorandum, Wise to Lipsky and Shultz, June 7, 1938, Wise Papers, Box 68, AJHS.

99. Joseph C. Hyman to Isaiah Minkoff, July 28, 1939; and Minutes of the Executive Committee of the American Jewish Joint Distribution Committee, July 17, 1939, Archives of the Jewish Labor Committee, New York City.

100. Ibid.

101. Lewis L. Strauss, *Men and Decisions* (Garden City, New York, 1962), 110–13, and as quoted by Naomi Cohen, *Not Free to Desist*, 188.

102. Berlin, "Jewish Labor Committee," 60.

103. Wise to Perkins, January 7, 1937, Wise Papers, Box 65, Federal Government–Labor, AJHS.

104. Frankfurter to Billikopf, November 15, 1938, Frankfurter Papers, Box 25, LC.

105. Wise to David Niles, November 14, 1938, and postscript, probably written the following day, Wise Papers, Box 118, Zionism—Correspondence. AJHS.

106. Ben Green, "Report," December 19, 1938, AFSC, Refugee Service 1938, Germany: Reports.

107. *Congress Bulletin,* May 12, 1939, p. 4, and cited in Wyman, *Paper Walls,* 25.

108. Friedman, *No Haven for the Oppressed,* 98; and Urofsky, *A Voice That Spoke for Justice,* 307.

109. Urofsky, *A Voice That Spoke for Justice,* 310–11.

110. Cyrus Adler to Harry Schneiderman, September 3, 1939, American Jewish Committee Archives, Cyrus Adler Papers, Immigration Box 1936–39.

111. HS [Harry Schneiderman] to Adler, May 5, 1939, American Jewish Committee Archives, Adler Papers. See also Frederick A. Lazin, "The Response of the American Jewish Committee to the Crisis of German Jewry, 1933–1939," *American Jewish History,* 68 (March 1979): 304.

112. Efraim Zuroff, "Rescue Priority and Fund Raising as Issues during the Holocaust: A Case Study of the Relations between the Vaad Ha-Hatzala and the Joint, 1939 and 1941," *American Jewish History,* 68 (March 1979): 306.

113. Ibid., 311.

114. W. J. Bott to Hon. Franklin D. Roosevelt, January 22, 1939, NA, RG 60, 55789/979, Box 487.

5. THE FIFTH COLUMN THREAT

1. "Annual Quotas and Quota Immigrants Admitted," *Monthly Review,* Immigration and Naturalization Service, Department of Justice (Washington, D.C., 1939). The total listed for fiscal 1939 is 32,759. The excess over the quota level of 27,370 (for Germany plus Austria) results from the fact that some applicants received their visas in fiscal 1938 but arrived in the U.S. during fiscal 1939. Technically, the 5,389 persons came under the 1938 quota.

2. Wyman, *Abandonment of the Jews,* 132.

3. Richard Hofstadter, *The Paranoid Style and Other Essays* (New York, 1967), 3–40. See also David Brion Davis, "Some Themes of Countersubversion: An Analysis of Anti-Masonic, Anti-Catholic, and Anti-Mormon Literature," in Davis, ed., *The Fear of Conspiracy: Images of Un-American Subversion from the Revolution to the Present* (Ithaca, 1971), 9–22; and John Higham, *Strangers in the Land: Patterns of Nativism, 1860–1925* (New Brunswick, N.J., 1963), 7–8.

4. Higham, *Strangers in the Land,* 279–80.

5. Ibid.

6. American Jewish Committee Archives, American Jewish Committee Executive Committee Minutes, May 14, 1934, vol. 6, pt. 2, p. 285.

7. "Jews and Americanism," a report by Information and Service Associates, American Jewish Committee Archives, Chronological File, folder for May 1934.

8. American Jewish Committee Archives, American Jewish Committee Executive Committee Minutes, October 19, 1936, vol. 7, pt. 1, p. 15.

9. Walter Goodman, *The Committee: The Extraordinary Career of the House Committee on Un-American Activities* (New York, 1968), 3.

10. Ibid., 14.

11. Memorandum on Dickstein Resolution, American Jewish Committee Archives, Chronological File, folder for January–June 1937.

12. Forty-five percent of those questioned said Jewish businessmen were less honest than other businessmen. Therefore, the authors of the study concluded that "the impression of Jewish radicalism is far less definite than the impression of Jewish dishonesty." "Confidential Report on Investigation of Anti-Semitism in the United States in the Spring of 1938," American Jewish Committee Archives, Chronological File, folder for September–December 1938.

13. Henry Monsky, address at Detroit, July 3, 1939, as quoted in "Jewish Statements on Communism," American Jewish Committee Archives, Chronological File, folder for September–December 1939.

14. Friedman, *No Haven for the Oppressed,* 113.

15. *Fortune,* July 1940, in Hadley Cantril, ed., *Public Opinion: 1935–1946* (Princeton, 1951), 809.

16. Wyman, *Paper Walls,* 186–87.

17. Frank Knox, introduction to "Fifth Column Lessons for America" (Washington, 1940), as quoted by Richard Dunlop, *Donovan: America's Master Spy* (Chicago, 1982), 223–24.

18. Ibid.

19. Ibid.; and Bradley Smith, *The Shadow Warriors: OSS and the Origins of the CIA* (New York, 1983), 36–39.

20. J. Edgar Hoover, "Big Scare," *American Magazine,* August 1941, p. 24ff.

21. Visa Instruction of September 30, 1939, NA, RG 59, 811.11 Diplomatic/1442A.

22. Hull to American Embassy, Berlin, October 20, 1939, NA, RG 59, 811.111 Quota 62/735.

23. Messersmith to Warren, November 9, 1939, NA, RG 59, 150.01 Bills/160.

24. Samuel W. Honaker to Secretary of State, April 24, 1940; and attached, Honaker to Hodgdon, April 24, 1940; Robert C. Alexander to Warren, May 22, 1940, NA, RG 59, 811.111 Quota 62/807.

25. Circular Telegram to All Diplomatic and Consular Offices, NA, RG 59, June 29, 1940, 811.111 W.R./108A. On the background to this instruction, see, particularly, Breckinridge Long to Berle and Dunn, June 26, 1940, NA, RG 59, 811.111 W.R./107. Long observed that "we can delay and effectively stop for a temporary period of indefinite length the number of immigrants coming into the United States . . . by advising our consuls to put every obstacle in the way and to require additional evidence and to resort to administrative advices [sic] which would postpone the granting of visas."

26. Derry (Perth, Australia) to Secretary of State, August 2, 1940, NA, RG 59, 811.111 W.R./242; and DuBois (Havana, Cuba) to Secretary of State, October 15, 1940, NA, RG 59, 811.111 Cuba/166.

27. Hull to American Embassy, Berlin, September 11, 1940, NA, RG 59, 811.111 Germany/17. On the nature of Warren's guidance, see Pell to Secretary of State, September 6, 1940, NA, RG 59, 811.111 Refugees/260.

28. Diary, April 23, 1940, Adolf A. Berle Papers, Box 211, FDRL.

29. Diary, May 8, 1940, Berle Papers, Box 211, FDRL.

30. Messersmith to Secretary of State, June 21, 1940, NA, RG 59, 150.626 J/798.

31. *New York Times,* August 2, 19, 1940, cited by Feingold, *Politics of Rescue,* 129.

32. Henry Pol, "Spies among Refugees?" *Nation,* August 31, 1940. See the editorial and the article in the same issue.

33. Presidential Press Conference, June 5, 1940, *Complete Presidential Press Conferences of Franklin D. Roosevelt* (New York, 1972), vol. 15, pp. 495–96.

34. Henry L. Stimson Diaries, September 26, 1940, Roll 6, LC.

35. Memorandum re Cabinet Meeting, October 18, 1940, Henry L. Stimson Papers, Memos, Minutes, Notes, 1940–1945, Roll 127, LC.

36. Memo of Conference with Mr. McCloy, November 8, 1940, ibid.

37. *Complete Presidential Press Conferences,* vol. 15, May 21, 1940, pp. 352–53. See also Samuel Rosenman, ed., *The Public Papers and Addresses of Franklin D. Roosevelt* (New York, 1941), vol. 9, pp. 223–29.

38. *Complete Presidential Press Conferences,* vol. 15, May 21, 1940, pp. 352–53.

39. Conference on National Defense, May 30, 1940, *Complete Presidential Press Conferences,* vol. 15, pp. 420–21. Also quoted in Richard Polenberg, *One Nation Indivisible: Class, Race, and Ethnicity in the United States Since 1938* (New York, 1980), 43.

40. Diary, May 8, 1940, Berle Papers Box 211, FDRL.

41. J. Woodford Howard, *Mr. Justice Murphy* (Princeton, 1968), 207; and Polenberg, *One Nation Divisible,* 44.

42. Polenberg, *One Nation Divisible,* 44.

43. Steinhardt to Secretary of State, October 2, 1940; and attached, Hull to Steinhardt, October 8, 1940, NA, RG 59, 811.111 Refugees/397.

44. Steinhardt to Secretary of State, November 5, 1940, President's Secretary's File, Box 68, Russia 1937–40 Folder, FDRL. See also attached document, Welles to FDR, November 22, 1940.

45. Friedman, *No Haven for the Oppressed,* 126.

46. Office of Censorship, Daily Report, September 1942, NA, RG 59, 840.48 Refugees/3489. See also Warren memo attached to McDonald to Hull, March 13, 1942, James G. McDonald Papers, CSIA.

47. Morgenthau Diaries, vol. 693, pp. 217–18, FDRL.

6. BRECKINRIDGE LONG AND THE JEWISH REFUGEES

1. Long bunched "the communists, extreme radicals, Jewish professional agitators, [and] refugee enthusiasts" as his chief opponents. Breckinridge Long Diary, February 6, 1938, Box 5, LC. Such remarks seemed to confirm Long's anti-Semitism to scholars such as Henry Feingold. Feingold, *The Politics of Rescue,* 135.

2. Long Diary, February 15, 1941, Box 5, LC.

3. Henry Feingold now describes Long as less a hater of Jews per se than an old-timer in government, resentful of all the "new men" that Roosevelt brought to Washington. Rather than ideological, Long's anti-Semitism seems "a matter of gentility and class" to Feingold. He "rarely sees evidence of strident anti-Semitism" in Long's letters and diary. Feingold, "The Government Response," 268.

4. Wyman, *The Abandonment of the Jews,* 191.

5. Long Diary, December 9, 1940, September 4, 1941, Box 5, LC.

6. Breckinridge Long to Franklin D. Roosevelt, September 6, 1935, Breckinridge Long Papers, Box 115, LC.

7. Fred L. Israel, ed., *The War Diary of Breckinridge Long, Selections from the Years 1939–1944* (Lincoln, Nebraska, 1966), xxiv. See also Phillips Diary, August 1, 1935, Houghton Library, Harvard.

8. FDR to Long, June 18, February 22, 1936, Long Papers, Box 117, LC.

9. Long Diary, December 29, 1940. Box 5, LC.

10. Ibid., June 17, 1940, November 20, 1940; Long to FDR, September 18, 1940, NA, RG 59, 811.111 Refugees/260; and Presidential Press Conference, June 5, 1940, *Complete Presidential Press Conferences*. Roosevelt and Hull were receiving information that Soviet subversives were among the refugees. Steinhardt to Secretary of State, October 2, 1940, NA, RG 59, 811.111 Refugees/397; and Welles to FDR, November 22, 1940, attached to Steinhardt to Secretary of State, November 5, 1940, President's Secretary's File, Box 68, Russia 1937–40 Folder, FDRL.

11. Memorandum of Meeting in the Office of the Acting Secretary, Friday, July 26, 1940, on the Subject of Political Refugees, NA, RG 59, 811.111 Refugees/348.

12. Coulter to Welles, July 27, 1940; and, attached, Welles to Certain American Diplomatic and Consular Offices (Lisbon, Oporto, Marseilles, Bordeaux, London, Dublin), July 26, 1940, NA, RG 59, 811.111 Refugees/193; and Wyman, *Paper Walls*, 138.

13. Eleanor Roosevelt to Sumner Welles, September 6, 1940; and, attached, Karl Frank to Eleanor Roosevelt, August 30, 1940; and Welles to Eleanor Roosevelt, September 12, 1940, NA, RG 59, 811.111 Refugees/322.

14. Minutes of Fortieth Meeting of the President's Advisory Committee on Political Refugees (PACPR), September 18, 1940, Stephen S. Wise Papers, Box 65, AJHS.

15. Long to Coulter, September 14, 1940; and Coulter to Long, September 17, 1940, NA, RG 59, 811.111 Refugees/260.

16. Long to FDR, September 18, 1940; and Hull to McDonald, September 19, 1940, NA, RG 59, 811.111 Refugees/260.

17. McDonald and Warren to Hull, September 24, 1940, NA, RG 59, 811.111 Refugees/953.

18. Clarence E. Pickett to Evelyn Hersey, September 24, 1940, Committees and Organizations: American Christian Committee for German Refugees, AFSC Refugee Service, 1940, AFSC.

19. Long Diary, September 24, 1940, Box 5, LC.

20. Eleanor Roosevelt to FDR, September 28, 1940, OF 3186, FDRL.

21. FDR to Undersecretary of State, October 2, 1940, OF 3186, FDRL; Steinhardt to Secretary of State, October 2, 1940; and Long to FDR, October 3, 1940, NA, RG 59, 811.111 Refugees/397.

22. McDonald and Warren to FDR, October 8, 1940, OF 3186, FDRL.

23. Long Diary, October 10, 1940, LC.

24. McDonald to Frankfurter, October 10, 1940; and McDonald to Eleanor Roosevelt, October 10, 1940, in Franklin and Eleanor Roosevelt folders, James G. McDonald Papers, General Correspondence file, CSIA.

25. Minutes of PACPR Dinner Meeting, October 14, 1940, Folder 46, Joseph Chamberlain Papers, YIVO.

26. Ibid.

27. Breckinridge Long's Memorandum of a Conference at Luncheon, October 18, 1940, Long Papers, Box 211, LC.

28. Felix Cole to Secretary of State, October 24, 1940, NA, RG 59, 811.111 Refugees/705.

29. Howard K. Travers to Avra Warren, October 26, 1940, NA, RG 59, 811.111 Quota 64/153.

30. Minutes of Forty-first Meeting of PACPR, October 30, 1940, Wise Papers, Box 65, AJHS; and Long to Welles, November 8, 1940, Long Papers, Box 211, LC.

31. Long Diary, November 22, 1940, Box 5, LC.

32. Ibid.

33. Ibid.

34. Memorandum for the Secretary of the Interior, December 18, 1940, OF 3186, FDRL.

35. Pat Frank to [?], December 5, 1940, marked confidential, American Jewish Committee Archives, RG-1 EXO-29, Waldman File, U.S. Government, State Department, Folder 1937–40.

36. Hull to FDR, December 16, 1940; attached press release entitled "Political Refugees," December 18, 1940; and article by Herbert Agar, "Our State Department," NA, RG 59, 811.111 Refugees/733.

37. Forty-second Meeting of PACPR, December 19, 1940, Wise papers, Box 65, AJHS.

38. Agar, "Our State Department."

39. Circular Telegram to Certain Diplomatic Missions and to All Consular Offices except Those in France, Belgium, The Netherlands, Germany, and Italy," June 5, 1940; Biddle to Long, June 20, 1941, NA, RG 59, 811.111 W.R./359 1/2; *New York Times,* June 19, 1941; and Morse, *While Six Million Died,* 300.

40. Biddle to Hull, June 21, 1941; attached, especially, Atherton to Moore, August 8, 1941, NA, RG 59, 811.111 W.R./391; and 55 Statute 252, Public Law 113, 77th Congress.

41. *New York Times,* June 25, 1941; and RWF to Coulter and Warren, May 29, 1941, NA, RG 59, 811.111 W.R./415. See also RWF to Long, June 3, 1941; Long to Jackson, June 4, 1941, NA, RG 59, 811.111 Committees/3; Jackson to Hull, June 11, 1941, NA, RG 59, 811.111 Quota/2443; Clarence Pickett Journal, June 9, 1941, AFSC; and *Department of State Bulletin,* September 10, 1944, pp. 277–78. Several items that refer to the work of the Appeals Committee appear in the Papers of Joseph Chamberlain and the National Refugee Service Papers (NRS) at the YIVO Institute for Jewish Research. The relevant Joseph P. Chamberlain documents are numbered 3379 and 3340-44; NRS 570. See also Travers to Long, August 4, 1942, Long Papers, Box 212, LC; and Wyman, *Abandonment of the Jews,* 129–34.

42. Pell to Taylor, March 2, 1941, March 7, 1941, March 11, 1941, April 5, 1941, Myron Taylor Papers, FDRL. See also Minutes of the President's Advisory Committee on Political Refugees, April 14, 1941, Chamberlain Papers, YIVO.

43. Messersmith to Hull, June 28 1941, NA, RG 59, 811.111/2275.

44. Long to Adolf Berle and James C. Dunn, June 26, 1940, NA, RG 59, 811.111, W.R./107, copy also in Long Papers, Box 211, LC.

45. Long to Warren, December 23, 1940, Long Papers, Box 211, LC.

46. Memorandum, Long to Welles, July 1, 1941, Long Papers, Box 211, LC.

47. Ibid.

48. Long Diary, April 20, 1943, Box 5, LC.

49. Long Diary, August 30, 1942, Box 5, LC.

50. *PM,* February 11, 1941.

51. Long Diary, September 12, 1942, Box 5, LC.

52. Long Diary, March 19, 1943, Box 5, LC.

53. *FRUS, 1943,* vol. 1, pp. 146–47. An excellent description of the selection process appears in Malcolm Mark Rossman, "Bermuda Conference: Recourse to Rescue" (M.A. thesis, City College of the City University of New York, 1971).

54. *FRUS, 1943,* vol. 1, pp. 146–47.

55. Independent Jewish Press Service, May 21, 1943. See also *From Evian to Bermuda* (New York, 1943), 16; and Rossman, "Bermuda Conference," 67–68.

56. Long to Wise, April 13, 1943, Long Papers, Box 203, LC.

57. Ibid.

58. Dickstein to FDR, April 2, 1943, OF 3186, FDRL.

59. Roberts to FDR, April 8, 1943, OF 3186, FDRL.

60. Seymour to Hull, April 13, 1943, NA, RG 59, 548.G1/19.

61. Hayter to Brandt, April 2, 1943, NA, RG 59, 548.G1/13.
62. Long to Law, April 7, 1943, Long Papers, Box 203, LC.
63. Murray to Welles, April 19, 1943, Long Papers, Box 203, LC.
64. Draft of Letter of Guidance, April 13, 1943, Long Papers, Box 203, LC.
65. U.S. Congress, Senate, 78th Cong., 1st sess., *Congressional Record*, 3434.
66. Long Diary, April 20, 1943, Box 5, LC.
67. Wise to FDR, April 28, 1943, President's Personal File 3292, FDRL; and Long to Warren, January 7, 1944, Long Papers, Box 212, LC.
68. Dodds to Long, June 16, 1943, Long Papers, Box 203, LC.
69. *New York Times*, May 4, 1943.
70. U.S. Congress, House, 78th Cong., 1st sess., *Congressional Record*, 4044–47.
71. Long Diary, May 7, 1943, Box 5, LC.
72. Long to Welles, May 14, 1943, Long Papers, Box 203, LC.
73. Long Diary, June 23, 1943, Box 5, LC.
74. Ibid.
75. *Contemporary Jewish Record*, October 1943, 503–04; Long Memo of Conversation with Bergson and Hirschmann, September 1, 1943, Long Papers, Box 5, LC; and Wyman, *Abandonment of the Jews*, 149–50.
76. U.S. Congress, House, Committee on Foreign Relations, *Hearings on Resolutions Providing for the Establishment by the Executive of a Commission to Effectuate the Rescue of the Jewish People of Europe on H. Res 350 and H. Res 352*, 78th Cong., 1st sess., 1943, p. 23.
77. Memo, Dr. Slawson to Gottschalk, December 21, 1943, American Jewish Committee Archives, RG-1, EXO-29, Waldman Papers, Immigration/Refugees/Rescue, 42-48. See also Proskauer to Long, December 28, 1943, same file and folder. Statistics vary, and estimates of Jewish refugees admitted between January 1933 and June 30, 1943, are sometimes cited as high as 210,000. See Introduction, n. 26.
78. *New York Times*, December 8, 1943, cited by Feingold, *Politics of Rescue*, 236.
79. *FRUS, 1943*, vol. 1, p. 226.
80. For Long's testimony, note 76, above. Morse, *While Six Million Died*, 96.
81. Long Diary, January 24, 1944, Box 5, LC.

7. A MESSAGE TO RABBI WISE

1. Christopher R. Browning, "A Reply to Martin Broszat Regarding the Origins of the Final Solution," *Simon Wiesenthal Center Annual* 1 (1984): 127, persuasively argues that Hitler gave authorization for a plan to be drawn up. Gerald Fleming, *Hitler and the Final Solution* (Berkeley and Los Angeles, 1984), 44–45, demonstrates that somewhat later that year Hitler avoided an explicit order for the killing of Jews but orally stated his wish that it be done.
2. *Trial of the Major War Criminals before the International Military Tribunal* (Nuremberg, 1947–49): vol. 26, pp. 266–67, doc. 710-PS.
3. Rudolf Hoess, *Commandant of Auschwitz* (New York, 1959), 135, 173, 197.
4. Hoess, *Commandant*, 175–76.
5. On the deportations, see Raul Hilberg, *The Destruction of the European Jews* (New York, 1984), vol. 2. On Wolff, see Martin Broszat, "Hitler und die Genesis der 'Endlösung': Aus Anlass der Thesen von David Irving," *Vierteljahrshefte für Zeitgeschichte* 25 (1977): 766. Himmler's telephone log confirms that he spoke with Wolff about Wolff's visit to Berlin. See NA, RG 242, T-84, R 25/0270523. The conclusion that Hitler was involved follows Broszat, cited above.
6. Hoess, *Commandant*, 197-200. Some additional details of the Himmler visit are available in Himmler's chief counselor's appointment book, July 17, 1942, NA, RG 242, T-581 (Hauptarchiv), R 39A, no frame number; and I. G. Farben Wochenbericht

13. 7.—26. 7. 1942, copy in NA, RG 238, NI 14551. Höss repeated Himmler's comment to Adolf Eichmann. See Jochen von Lang, ed. *Eichmann Interrogated: Transcripts from the Archives of the Israeli Police,* trans. Ralph Manheim (Toronto, 1983), 83.

 7. Hoess, *Commandant,* 198.

 8. NA, RG 242, T-175, R 122/2647914.

 9. Koppelmann passed on Schulte's formulation. It first appears in written form in Gerhart Riegner's telegrams to Washington and London on August 8, 1942. See also notes 15 and 20, below.

 10. For more details on Schulte's mission, see Walter Laqueur and Richard Breitmann, *Breaking the Silence* (New York, 1986), 1–8, 118–33.

 11. Interviews with Riegner, February 10, 1983, May 30, 1984.

 12. Walter Laqueur, "The Mysterious Messenger and the Final Solution," *Commentary,* March 1980, p. 55. In an interview on February 10, 1983, Riegner confirmed that what Laqueur had published about the industrialist in this article was accurate.

 13. Riegner's letter of August 4, 1942, to Guggenheim, which Riegner graciously made available. Guggenheim's letter of introduction for Riegner, dated August 6, 1942, is in NA, RG 84, Geneva Confidential File 1942, 110.2. Interviews with Riegner, February 10, 1983, May 30, 1984.

 14. Interviews with Riegner, February 10, 1983, May 30, 1984.

 15. Elting Memorandum, August 8, 1942, re conversation with Riegner, NA, RG 84, Geneva Confidential File 1942, 110.2; and Elting to Secretary of State, August 10, 1942, NA, RG 59, CDF 862.4016/2234.

 16. Harrison to Secretary of State, August 11, 1942, NA, RG 59, CDF 862.4016/2234; and Friedman, *No Haven for the Oppressed,* 131. The State Department summary passed to the OSS is in NA, RG 226, Entry 4, Box 1, Despatches from Neutral Posts, 11 Aug. 1942.

 17. Memos in NA, RG 59, CDF 862.4016/2233 Confidential File.

 18. Huddle to Elting, August 21, 1942, NA, RG 84, Geneva Confidential File 1942, 110.2; Squire to Riegner, August 24, 1942; and Riegner to Squire, August 26, 1942, Geneva Confidential File 1942, 800.

 19. *Complete Presidential Press Conferences,* vols. 19–20, no. 842.

 20. Interviews with Riegner, February 10, 1983, May 30, 1984. British reaction is discussed extensively by Martin Gilbert, *Auschwitz and the Allies* (New York, 1981), 59. A copy of Silverman's telegram to Wise went to the State Department: NA, RG 59, CDF 740.00116 E. W. 1939/553.

 21. Untitled document in French marked "From R," undated; Elting's Political Notes, August 13, 1942 (which contain a translation of Riegner's document); undated report on Czechoslovakia, marked "from R;" Elting's Political Notes, August 17, 1942, NA, RG 84, Geneva Confidential File 1942, 800; and Donald Lowrie to Tracy Strong, August 10, 1942, attached to Elting to Harrison, August 11, 1942, NA, RG 84, Geneva Confidential File 1942, 800.

 22. Huddle's handwritten comment on Sholes to Harrison, August 31, 1942, NA, RG 84, Bern Confidential File 1942, Basel Folder, 800; and Squire to Secretary of State, September 15, 1942, NA, RG 84, Bern Confidential File 1942, Geneva Political Reports Folder, 800.

 23. Squire's Political Notes, September 12, 1942, NA, RG 84, Bern Confidential File 1942, 800; Harrison's memorandum, September 10, 1942, Leland Harrison Papers, Box 33, LC; and Huddle's marginal comment on Squire's Political Notes, September 8, 1942, NA, RG 84, Bern Confidential File 1942, Geneva Political Reports, 800.

 24. Wise to Welles, September 2, 1942, NA, RG 59, CDF 840.48 Refugees/3080. On Welles and Hull, see Dallek, *Franklin D. Roosevelt and American Foreign Policy,* 149, 421. On Welles and Eleanor Roosevelt, see Weil, *A Pretty Good Club,* 130. At a

cabinet meeting Hull told President Roosevelt that groups in the south would object to a change in the status of German Jewish refugees from "enemy aliens" to "friendly aliens," an objection which blocked the change. Hull later told Stephen Wise of this incident. See Wise to Bernard Baruch, July 13, 1943, Baruch Papers, vol. 62, R-2, Mudd Library, Princeton University.

25. Wise to Welles, September 2, 1942; Atherton to Welles, September 3, 1942, NA, RG 59, CDF 840.48 Refugees/3080; and Rosenblum to Wertheim, September 8 and 9, 1942, American Jewish Committee Archives, RG-1, EXO-29, Waldman File, Poland 1942. See also Wise to Nahum Goldmann, September 4, 1942, cited in Urofsky, *A Voice That Spoke for Justice,* 319.

26. Schenkolewski and Tress to McDonald, September 3, 1942; and McDonald's secretary to Mrs. Franklin D. Roosevelt, September 4, 1942, James G. McDonald Papers, PACPR Folder, CSIA; Agudath Israel cable, September 4, 1942, Stephen Wise Papers, Box 82; and Wise to Frankfurter, September 4, 1942, Wise Papers, Box 109, AJHS.

27. For sharp criticism of Wise, see Friedman, *No Haven for the Oppressed,* 142–45. The inaccurate charge that Wise withheld the Riegner cable from the Orthodox leaders (until the end of the war!) is made in Joseph Friedenson and David Kranzler, *Heroine of Rescue,* (Brooklyn, 1984), 87; and David Kranzler, "Orthodox Ends, Unorthodox Means: The Role of the Vaad Hatzalah and Agudath Israel during the Holocaust," *American Jewry during the Holocaust* (New York, 1984), Appendix 4–3, p. 3.

28. Rosenblum to Wertheim, September 8 and 9, 1942, with summaries of the two meetings of Jewish leaders, American Jewish Committee Archives, RG-1, EXO-29, Waldman File, Poland 1942. This contemporary evidence definitively refutes Friedenson, Kranzler, and others (see note 27, above). Some details of the joint meetings of Jewish organizations were also published several months later: "The Tragedy of European Jewry," *Bulletin of the World Jewish Congress,* January 1943, p. 1.

29. Wyman, *Abandonment of the Jews,* 54–55, correctly points out that, if Wise was wrong to withhold the information from the press, the other Jewish leaders at the early September meetings were equally guilty (if not more so). Wise had told them of the Riegner telegram, and they had not given their word to the undersecretary of state to refrain from publicity. The members of the PACPR, Felix Frankfurter, Dean Acheson, Henry Wallace, and Harold Ickes were also informed.

30. Wise to Frankfurter, September 16, 1942, reprinted by Carl Hermann Voss, ed., *Stephen S. Wise: Servant of the People; Selected Letters* (Philadelphia, 1969), 250–51; Wise to Perlzweig, September 17, 1942, Wise Papers, Box 92; Wise to Mack, October 6, 1942, Wise Papers, Box 115; excerpt from Morgenthau's speech of March 20, 1947, Wise Papers, Box 117, AJHS.

31. Cox to Ciechanowski, September 14, 1942, Oscar Cox Papers, Box 6, FDRL.

32. Wise to Bakstansky, September 29, 1942, Wise Papers, Box 104, AJHS.

33. Taylor's general mission was to persuade the Pope to exercise moral leadership and to refrain from any pressure for a compromise peace. See President's Secretary's File, Box 71, Vatican: Myron Taylor, FDRL; Lichtheim despatch in NA, RG 84, Bern Confidential File 1942, 840.1 Jews.

34. Copy of the Lichtheim-Welles despatch in NA, RG 84, Bern Confidential File 1942, 840.1 Jews. On this episode, see Gilbert, *Auschwitz and the Allies,* 64–65, 71.

35. On the request for the Vatican's confirmation of reports, see Wyman, *Abandonment of the Jews,* 49; Memorandum of Conversation of September 25, 1942 . . . ," President's Secretary's File, Box 71, FDRL; Taylor to Maglione, September 26, 1942, Taylor Papers, Box 1, 1942, LC; Welles to Taylor, October 21, 1942, Taylor Papers, Box 1, 1942, LC; and Tittman Report of Audience with Pope, January 5, 1943, copy in William Donovan Papers, Box 102A, vol. 5, U.S. Army Military History Institute, Carlisle, Pa.

36. Hitler's speech was monitored and translated in the U.S. See NA, RG 165, Box 1193, Germany 3700. Excerpts are quoted by Morse, *While Six Million Died*, 6–7.

37. Welles to Harrison, October 5, 1942, NA, RG 84, Bern Confidential File 1942, 840.1 Jews; and RG 59, CDF 740.00116 E. W. 1939/600A.

38. Harrison to Welles, October 6, 1942, NA, RG 59, CDF 740.00116 E. W. 1939/601; Harrison to Squire and Huddle to Squire, October 6, 1942, NA, RG 84, Geneva Confidential File 1942, 800; Wise to Mack, October 6, 1942, Wise Papers, Box 115; and Wise to Frankfurter, October 9, 1942, Wise Papers, Box 109, AJHS.

39. White House press release in OF 5152, FDRL.

40. Letters and interviews with Riegner. Documents Submitted to His Excellency . . . Leland Harrison, October 22, 1942, NA, RG 84, Bern Confidential Correspondence 1942, 840.1 Jews. The name Eduard Schulte is found in a source appendix for the document about the Final Solution.

41. Squire to Harrison, October 29, 1942, NA, RG 84, Bern Confidential File 1942, 800; Harrison to Welles, October 24, 1942, NA, RG 84, Bern Confidential File, 840.1 Jews; and Harrison to Welles, October 31, 1942, NA, RG 84, Bern Confidential File 1942, 840.1 Jews.

42. Squire to Riegner, November 4, 1942; Riegner to Squire, November 5, 1942, NA, RG 84, Geneva Confidential File 1942, 800; and interview with Riegner, February 10, 1983.

43. Squire to Secretary of State, October 29, 1942; Squire to Harrison, October 29, 1942, NA, RG 84, Geneva Confidential File 1942, 800; and Harrison to Welles, October 31, 1942, NA, RG 84, Bern Confidential File 1942, 840.1 Jews.

44. Biographical information about Burckhardt is from Riegner and in Wilhelm Kosch, *Biographisches Staatshandbuch: Lexicon der Politik, Presse, und Publizistik* (Bern, 1963). The Hitler-Burckhardt meeting is described by Burckhardt in *Mein Danziger Mission* (Zurich, 1960), 341–48.

45. Squire to Harrison [November 7, 1942], NA, RG 84, Bern Confidential File 1942, 840.1 Jews; and Squire to Harrison, November 7 and 9, 1942, NA, RG 84, Geneva Confidential File 1942, 800.

46. Squire to Harrison, November 9, 1942, NA, RG 84, Geneva Confidential File 1942, 800. See also Squire to Harrison, November 23, 1942; and Riegner Memorandum of Meeting with Burckhardt, November 17, 1942, NA, RG 84, Geneva Confidential File 1942, 800.

47. Wyman, *Abandonment of the Jews*, 51, 363, has verified Wise's account. "Wise Says Hitler Has Ordered 4,000,000 Jews Slain in 1942," *New York Herald Tribune*, November 25, 1942; and State Department Report of December 15, 1942, cited in Memorandum on the Bermuda Conference, February 22, 1944, War Refugee Board Records, Box 3, FDRL.

48. In the AP article printed in the *Herald Tribune* (see note 47 above), Wise is described as saying that he had learned through sources confirmed by the State Department of the Nazi extermination campaign. On the reaction of State Department officials, see Eddy to Gordon and attached, December 7, 1943, NA, RG 59, CDF 862.4016/2251. The standard State Department response to inquiries about Wise's information was to refer the questioners to Rabbi Wise or to various published articles. State also pointed out that, in referring to unofficial publications, "the Department assumes no responsibility for the accuracy of statements contained therein." McDermott to *The Christian Century*, November 25, 1942, NA, RG 59, CDF 740.00116 E. W. 1939/656; and E. Wilder Spaulding to Murphy, January 18, 1942, NA, RG 59, CDF 740.00116 E. W. 1939/685.

49. Memorandum on the Bermuda Conference, February 22, 1944, War Refugee Board Records, Box 3, FDRL.

50. Wertheim, Held, Goldstein, Wise, Monsky, and Rosenberg to Mr. President, December 8, 1942, and attached memoranda, OF 76-C, FDRL.

51. On Frankfurter's reaction to Jan Karski's information about the killings of Jews, see Laqueur, *Terrible Secret,* 3.

52. Adolph Held's description of the meeting is quoted in detail by Monty N. Penkower, *The Jews Were Expendable: Free World Diplomacy and the Holocaust* (Urbana, 1983), 85–86.

53. On Roosevelt and the Third War Powers Act, see Message of the President of the United States, November 2, 1942, 77th Cong., House of Representatives, *House Documents,* vol. 16 (Washington, 1943), doc. 882; and Wyman, *Abandonment of the Jews,* 56–58.

54. On FDR's conference with Wallace and Rayburn, which is not mentioned in Wyman, see Wallace Diary, November 26, 1942, p. 1995, Columbia Oral History Collection, Columbia University, cited in Dallek, *Franklin D. Roosevelt and American Foreign Policy,* 446.

55. On the advice that FDR was receiving on the Jewish problem around this time, see Richard Breitman, "The Allied War Effort and the Jews, 1942–43," *Journal of Contemporary History* (January 1985): 141–43.

56. Winant to Secretary of State, December 7, 1942, NA, RG 59, CDF 740.00116 E. W. 1939/660 and 692.

57. Wasserstein, *Britain,* 174. The British draft declaration is in NA, RG 59, CDF 740.00116 E. W. 1939/664.

58. Reams to American embassy, London, December 10, 1942, NA, RG 59, CDF 740.00116 E. W. 1939/674A.

59. State Department Press Release, December 16, 1942, copy in NA, RG 59, CDF 740.00116 E. W. 1939/749.

60. Racynzski to Biddle, December 9, 1942; and Biddle to Secretary of State, December 18, 1942, NA, RG 59, CDF 740.00116 E. W. 1939/712.

61. *Bulletin of the World Jewish Congress,* January 1943, no. 4, pp. 10–11.

62. Warren to Greene, September 18, 1939, NA, RG 59, 150. 626J/678.

63. Berle to EU [European Division], February 17, 1940; Berle to the Secretary, February 23, 1940; Long to EU, February 23, 1940; Hickerson to Berle, February 26, 1940, NA, RG 59, CDF 862.4016/2172 and 2198.

64. Here I follow Robert O. Paxton, *Vichy France: Old Guard and New Order, 1940–1944* (New York, 1975), esp. 46–49.

65. Roswell McClelland, "An Unpublished Chapter in the History of the Deportation of Foreign Jews from France in 1942," unpublished manuscript kindly furnished by Roswell McClelland. See also Notes on an Interview with Marshall Petain, August 6, 1942, NA, RG 84, American Consulate Geneva, Confidential File 1942, 800.

66. *FRUS, 1942,* vol. 1, p. 465.

67. Welles to Paul Baerwald, August 19, 1942; Moses Leavitt to James Vail, August 19, 1942; Hugh Cumming to American Friends Service Committee, August 22, 1942; AFSC, General File (hereafter GF) 1942: France—Relief and Refugees, Children's Transport. See also Welles to James G. McDonald, August 19, 1942, NA, RG 59, CDF 840.48 Refugees/5732.

68. Tuck to Secretary of State, August 26, September 11, 1942, *FRUS 1942,* vol. 2, pp. 710–13.

69. Long Diary, September 12, 1942, Box 5, LC; and Atherton to Welles, September 3, 1942, NA, RG 59, CDF 840.48 Refugees/3080.

70. Statement by George L. Warren, September 14, 1942, AFSC, GF 1942: France— Relief and Refugees, Children's Transport.

71. Long Diary, September 12, 1942, Box 5, LC; Warren Statement, September 14, 1942, AFSC, GF 1942: France—Relief and Refugees, Children's Transport; Memoran-

dum on Telephone Conversation with Dr. Schwartz on September 22, 1942; and Frawley to Noble, September 25, 1942, AFSC, GF 1942: France—Relief and Refugees, Children's Transport; and Hull to Tuck, September 28, 1942, *FRUS, 1942*, vol. 2, p. 713.

72. H. J. Resolution 345, 77th Cong. 2d sess. The bill was referred to the Immigration and Naturalization Committee. Hull to Tuck, September 28, 1942, *FRUS, 1942*, vol. 2, p. 713; and Welles to McDonald, October 2, 1942, McDonald Papers, Welles Folder, CSIA.

73. Marrus and Paxton, *Vichy France and the Jews*, 266, 269; Tuck to Secretary of State, October 3 and 9, 1942, *FRUS, 1942*, vol. 2, pp. 714–15; and Samuel McCrea Cavert Memorandum on Refugee Children Project [late October 1942], AFSC, GF 1942: France—Relief and Refugees, Children's Transport.

74. Summary of press conference in Radio Bulletin No. 244, October 15, 1942, copy in NA, RG 84, American Embassay Vichy, Confidential File 1942, 840.1.

75. Report by Burritt Hiatt, based on information telephoned by Tuck to Marseille, October 23, 1942, AFSC, GF 1942: France—Activities Log of B. Hiatt; and Marrus and Paxton, *Vichy France and the Jews*, 267.

76. Estimate of 350 in Marrus and Paxton, *Vichy France and the Jews*, 267; and 200 in Wyman, *Abandonment of the Jews*, 133, who also mentions Welles's involvement. On the Visa Division, see Hull to American Embassy, Madrid, January 5, 1943, NA, RG 59, 811.111 Refugees/2072A.

77. Hull to American Legation, Bern, December 3, 1942, and attached, NA, RG 84, Bern Confidential File 1942, 840.1 Refugee Children. Bauer, *American Jewry and the Holocaust*, 263, goes so far as to assert that most of these children were saved. Between 5,500 and 6,000 Jewish children were kept underground throughout the occupation, but another 8,000 to 10,000 children were sent to Auschwitz.

78. NA, RG 242, T-175, Roll 94/2615330 and Roll 103/2625558.

79. Himmler to Müller, December 1942 (the day was left bank), NA, RG 242, T-175, Roll 103/2625557.

80. Himmler to Ribbentrop, January 29, 1943, NA, RG 242, T-175, R 68/2584330–31.

81. See express letter of September 23, 1943, NA, RG 242, T-175, R 658/no frames. On Bergen-Belsen, see Gilbert. *Auschwitz and the Allies*, 261, 271, 289.

82. Winant to Secretary of State, November 14, 16, 1942, NA, RG 59, CDF 862.5151/2386.

83. Hull to American Legation, Bern, November 24, 1942, NA, RG 84, Basel Confidential File 1942, 820.02/811.11.

8. WAR PROPAGANDA AND THE JEWS

1. Minutes of the meeting are quoted extensively in Gerald Fleming, *Hitler and the Final Solution* (Berkeley and Los Angeles, 1984), 101–04.

2. H. R. Trevor-Roper, ed., *Blitzkrieg to Defeat: Hitler's War Directives, 1939–1945* (New York, 1971), 117; and Peter Calvocoressi and Guy Wint, *Total War: Causes and Courses of the Second World War* (Harmondsworth, 1972), 356.

3. Translations of German broadcasts were compiled and distributed in the State Department. They may be found in NA, RG 59, CDF 740.0011 European War 1939. On other German propaganda in the Arab world, see J. Rives Childs to Secretary of State, July 21, 1942, copy in NA, RG 226, 19434; and Military Attaché Report on Attitude of Moslem World toward United Nations, August 15, 1942, copy in NA, RG 226, 20457.

4. Bracht to Himmler, September 17, 1942; and Himmler to Bracht, September 23, 1942, NA, RG 242, T-175, R 58/2573260-64.

5. Murray to Berle, Welles, and Hull, December 1, 1942, NA, RG 59, 740.0011 E. W. 1939/26651.

6. Parker Memorandum of Conversation, December 22, 1942, *FRUS, 1942,* vol. 4, pp. 557–58.

7. Morgenthau Presidential Diaries, December 3, 1942, Morgenthau Papers, Box 5, pp. 1200–03, FDRL.

8. Reams to Hickerson and Atherton, December 9, 1942, NA, RG 59, 740.00116/694; and Reams Memorandum of December 10, 1942, ibid., both cited by Morse, *While Six Million Died,* 33–34.

9. Patton letter and Darlan report in NA, RG 331, Film 71D, File 091.

10. Hull Memorandum of Conversation with Halifax, December 9, 1942, NA, RG 59, CDF 740.0011 E.W. 1939/26620.

11. Stimson Diaries, December 27, 1942, vol. 41, Roll 8, LC.

12. See chap. 8, above.

13. Welles to Biddle, July 6, 1942; and FDR to Sikorski, July 3, 1942, NA, RG, 84, Box 2748, 711 (Jewish atrocities).

14. Biddle to Secretary of State, August 13, 1942, NA, RG 84, Box 2748, 711 (Jewish atrocities).

15. Memorandum to Secretary of State Hull, July 30, 1942, *FRUS, 1942,* vol. 1, pp. 46–47.

16. Adolf Berle Diary, August 18–20, 1942, Berle Papers, FDRL; and OF 5152, War Crimes Commission, FDRL. See also *FRUS, 1942,* vol. 1, p. 59.

17. See chap. 7, above.

18. Caught in Germany after the German declaration of war against the United States, this group was interned by the Germans at Bad Nauheim and later exchanged for German citizens similarly caught in the U.S. The military attaché was Colonel William D. Hohenthal.

19. Study of War Propaganda, March 6, 1942, NA, RG 165, Box 1185, Germany 2900–2950.

20. Jewish Telegraphic Agency Memorandum, December 7, 1942, American Jewish Committee Archives, RG-1, EXO-29, JTA Overseas News Agency Folder 1940–43.

21. NA, RG 208, E-1, Box 3, Meetings 4, Committee on War Information Policy.

22. NA, RG 208, E-1, Box 3, Motion Pictures 1943.

23. Wasserstein, *Britain,* 182.

24. Wasserstein, *Britain,* 176; and Monty N. Penkower, "The Bermuda Conference and Its Aftermath: An Allied Quest for 'Refuge' during the Holocaust," *Prologue,* vol. 13, no. 3 (1981): 146, 148.

25. Wasserstein, *Britain,* 180–81.

26. Copy in NA, RG 59, CDF 840.48 Refugees/3633.

27. Wasserstein, *Britain,* 184–85; and *FRUS, 1943,* vol. 1, pp. 134–37.

28. Murray to Berle, Welles, and Hull, February 18, 1943, NA, RG 59, CDF 840.4016/68; and Murray Memo of March 1, 1943, NA, RG 59, 740.0011 European War 1939/28375.

29. War Refugee Board Memorandum of February 22, 1944, summarizing Visa Division memoranda related to the Bermuda Conference, War Refugee Board Records, Box 3, FDRL.

30. Matthews to Secretary of State, February 20, 1943, *FRUS, 1943,* vol. 1, p. 138; Achilles to Welles, March 4, 1943, NA, RG 59, CDF 740.00116 E. W. 1939/848; Long's draft with Long to Welles, February 22, 1943, Long Papers, Box 212, LC; and final text in *FRUS, 1943,* vol. 1, pp. 140–44.

31. Wise to FDR, March 4, 1943, President's Personal File 5029, FDRL; Morse, *While Six Million Died,* 46–47; Feingold, *Politics of Rescue,* 175–76; and *New York Times,* March 2, 1943.

32. Press Release, March 3, 1943, McDonald Papers, General Correspondence, State Department Folder, CSIA.

33. Hull Memorandum of Conversation, March 22, 1943, *FRUS, 1943,* vol. 3, pp. 28–32.

34. *Parliamentary Debates,* Fifth Series, vol. 126, House of Lords, March 23, 1943, pp. 856–57; and Rossman, "Bermuda Conference," 58–61.

35. Minutes of Joint Committee on European Affairs, March 29, 1943, American Jewish Committee Archives, from Manson Files, Abba Hillel Silver Papers, Temple Archives, Cleveland; and Minutes of PACPR, March 30, 1943, McDonald Papers, PACPR Folder, CSIA, both cited by Penkower, "Bermuda Conference," 155.

36. It is unclear whether Eden slipped and said 60,000 rather than 30,000 or whether Hopkins got the number wrong in his notes of the meeting. Sixty thousand would have exceeded the White Paper limits by 31,000. Hopkins Memorandum of Conversation, March 27, 1943, *FRUS, 1943,* vol. 3, pp. 38–39; and Harvey Diary, April 25, 1943, quoted by Wasserstein, *Britain,* 34.

37. Views of the Government of the United States Regarding Topics Included in the Agenda for Discussion with the British Government, Long Papers, Box 203, LC. This document was given to the delegates on April 13, 1943. War Refugee Board Memorandum of February 22, 1944, Box 3, FDRL; and *New York Times,* April 3, 1943, p. 1.

38. Confidential Memorandum for the Chairman, April 20, 1943, Long Papers, Box 203, LC, cited by Rossman, "Bermuda Conference," 93–98; and War Refugee Board Memorandum of February 22, 1944, summarizing Visa Division memoranda on the Bermuda Conference, War Refugee Board Records, Box 3, FDRL.

39. Dodds to Long, April 24, 1943; Hull to Dodds, April 28, 1943, *FRUS 1943,* vol. 1, pp. 164, 172; Joint Chiefs of Staff to Secretary of State, April 26, May 7, 1943, *FRUS, 1943,* vol. 1, pp. 296–97, 299; and Wasserstein, *Britain,* 194–95.

40. Wasserstein, *Britain,* 205-15; and Penkower, "Bermuda Conference," 167–70.

41. Marnie Schauffler to Clarence Pickett *et al.,* June 11, 1943, AFSC, Refugee Service Files, Committees and Organizations: U.S. State Department; Dodds to Long, April 24, 1943; Hull to Dodds, April 28, 1943, *FRUS, 1943,* vol. 1, pp. 164, 172; Joint Chiefs of Staff to Secretary of State, April 26, May 7, 1943, *FRUS, 1943,* vol. 1, pp. 296–97, 299; and Wasserstein, *Britain,* 194–95.

42. The United States formally associated itself with British efforts to persuade Bulgaria to allow Jews to leave. See Harrison to Secretary of State, June 24, 1943, NA, RG 59, 840.48 Refugees/3905. On the Red Cross complaints, see International Red Cross to American Legation, Bern, May 5, 1944, NA, RG 84, Box 336, 840.1 Jews. On Welles's meeting with Halifax, see Welles Memorandum of Conversation, June 24, 1943, NA, RG 59, 840.48 Refugees/3913.

43. See the German documents in Mendelsohn, *The Holocaust,* vol. 7, doc. 17, esp. pp. 173, 181, 197. Minister Harrison reported from Bern that German secret police agents were turning back Jewish travelers from the Bulgarian-Turkish border. Harrison to Secretary of State, June 24, 1943, NA, RG 59, 840.48 Refugees/3905.

44. See the treatment in Wasserstein, *Britain,* 215-17.

45. Minutes of the Meeting of the American Delegation, April 25, 1943, quoted by Rossman, "Bermuda Conference," 160–61; and War Refugee Board Memorandum of February 22, 1944, summarizing Visa Division memoranda on the Bermuda Conference, War Refugee Board Records, Box 3, FDRL.

9. ON A BROAD HUMANITARIAN BASIS

1. For additional details in these areas, readers should consult Wyman, *Abandonment of the Jews,* 143–77, 193–206; Penkower, *The Jews Were Expendable,* 122–47; Finger, ed., *American Jewry during the Holocaust:* and Lipstadt, *Beyond Belief,* 197–217.

2. Squire to Harrison, January 20, 1943; Lichtheim and Riegner to Wise, January 19, 1943; and Huddle to Squire, January 26, 1943, NA, RG 84, Bern Confidential File 1943, 840.1 Jews. See also Harrison to Secretary of State (for the Undersecretary), January 21, 1943, NA, RG 59, CDF 740.00116 E. W. 1939/753.

3. Memorandum of January 25, 1943, NA, RG 59, CDF 860C.4016/644 1/2.

4. See Chaps. 7 and 8, above.

5. Hull to American Legation, Bern, February 10, 1943, NA, RG 59, CDF 740.00116 E. W. 1939/753 Confidential File.

6. Welles to Harrison, personal, October 5, 1942; Harrison to Squire, strictly confidential, October 6, 1942, NA, RG84, American Legation, Bern, Box 5, Confidential File, 840.1, and American Consulate, Geneva, Confidential File 1942, 800.

7. I here agree with Wyman, *Abandonment of the Jews,* 81.

8. Squire to Harrison, March 10, March 18, 1943; and Harrison to Squire, March 22, 1943, NA, RG 84, Bern Confidential File 1943, 840.1 Jews.

9. Squire to Harrison, March 24, 1943, NA, RG 84, Bern Confidential File 1943, 840.1 Jews.

10. Harrison to Squire, April 22, 1943, NA, RG 84, Bern Confidential File 1943, 840.1 Jews.

11. Harrison to Department, April, 20, 1943, NA, RG 84, Bern Confidential File 1943, 840.1 Jews; and Hull to American Legation, Bern, April 27, 1943, NA, RG 84, Bern Confidential File 1943, 840.1 Jews.

12. Welles to Wise, April 27, 1943, Wise Papers, Box 82, AJHS.

13. Die Lage der deportierten Juden in Transnistrien [December 1942], NA, RG 242, T-175, R 663/no frame; Bauer, *American Jewry and the Holocaust,* 339–44; and Hava Eshkoli, "The Transdnistrian Plan: An Opportunity for Rescue or a Deception," in Finger, *American Jewry during the Holocaust,* Appendix 4–6.

14. Bauer, *American Jewry and the Holocaust,* 346–47; and Eshkoli, "The Transdnistrian Plan." The Rumanian trial balloon eventually became known in the west and received a great deal of publicity in February 1943. By this time the Germans had already killed the plan. There were not many in the United States who knew in 1943 that the newspaper stories were inaccurate, that the plan was dead and that the widely advertised price listed by the Committee for a Jewish Army (For Sale to Humanity: 70,000 Jews, Guaranteed Human Beings at $50 a Piece) was a tiny fraction of what the real total had been. But historians ought to know this and ought to point it out. See, however, Feingold, *Politics of Rescue,* 181–82; and Wyman, *Abandonment of the Jews,* 86–87, 93, 98–99.

15. Bauer, *American Jewry and the Holocaust,* 347; and Eshkoli, "The Transdnistrian Plan."

16. On the objections to ransom, see chap. 7, above. On British reaction to mass emigration to Palestine, see chap. 8, above.

17. Penkower, *The Jews Were Expendable,* 127; Welles to Wise; and Riegner to Wise, April 20, 27, 1943, Wise Papers, Box 82, AJHS.

18. The World Jewish Congress plan was a version, much scaled down, of the earlier Rumanian proposal for the 70,000 Jews. On British opposition to relief shipments to occupied Europe, see Penkower, *The Jews Were Expendable,* 123.

19. Record of Meetings on the Question of Relief through the Blockade [April 1943], NA, RG 59, CDF 840.48/6115; and Pickett Journal, April 12, 1943 (conversation with FDR) and June 15, 1943 (conversation with Francis Sayre about FDR-Churchill conversation), AFSC. The latter states: "The President did his best to persuade Churchill but without success. Churchill was adamant in saying that nothing must interfere with the military effort and that this probably would. The public reason is that Germany would probably interfere, but the actual reason is not that. It is Churchill's insistence on the primacy of the military consideration."

20. [Meltzer] Memoranda of Conversations, July 16, 30, 1943, NA, RG 59, CDF 840.48 Refugees/4074 and 4211.

21. Fleming, *Hitler and the Final Solution,* 66–67, 79, 113, 137–39.

22. Stephen Wise, *Challenging Years: The Autobiography of Stephen Wise* (New York, 1949), 193–94. According to these memoirs, the proposal dealt with Poland and Hungary. Contemporary documents, however, clearly indicate that the Rumanian and French schemes (as well as one in Slovakia) were the ones under consideration. See Wise to FDR, July 23, 1943, copy in NA, RG 59, CDF 840.48 Refugees/4212. For recapitulations of events, see Paul to Secretary Morgenthau, August 13, 1943; and Jewish Evacuation, December 13, 1943, Morgenthau Diaries, vol. 688, FDRL. See also Monty N. Penkower, "Jewish Organizations and the Creation of the War Refugee Board," *The Annals of the American Academy of Social and Political Science* (July 1980): 130.

23. [Hull] Memorandum on Jewish Refugee Evacuation Plan, July 19, 1943; Brandt to Feis, August 3, 1943; Feis to Secretary, August 4, 1943, marked urgent; and Hull to American Legation, Bern, August 6, 1943, NA, RG 59, CDF 840.48 Refugees/4012 and 4212 and 862.4016/2269. Meltzer told Treasury official Josiah DuBois that he had been *instructed* by the State Department to say that the State Department had no comments to make on the proposal but that it would not object to Treasury issuing a license. Paul to Secretary Morgenthau, August 13, 1943, Morgenthau Diaries, vol. 688, FDRL. See also Jewish Evacuation, December 13, 1943, Morgenthau Diaries, vol. 688, FDRL.

24. Hull to American Legation, Bern, September 17, 1943, NA, RG 59, CDF 840.48 Refugees/4502A.

25. Berle to Hull, September 16, 1943, NA, RG 59, CDF 840.48 Refugees/4502.

26. Auszug aus dem Stenogramm uber die Sitzung des Ministerrates, November 17, 1943, NA, RG 242, T-175, R 660/no frame.

27. NA, RG 59, CDF 862.4016/2292.

28. Details are covered in Wyman, *Abandonment of the Jews,* 181–82; and Penkower, *The Jews Were Expendable,* 130–33. The State Department's letter to Treasury was on December 6, 1943. For Treasury's reaction and DuBois's naming of Atherton and Murray, see Jewish Evacuation, December 13, 1943, Morgenthau Diaries, vol. 688, FDRL. On Long, Wyman, *Abandonment of the Jews,* 181, is accurate.

29. Winant to State Department, December 15, 1943, NA, RG 59, CDF 840.51 Frozen Credits/12144, quoted in Wasserstein, *Britain,* 247.

30. On the distinction between the earlier plan for 70,000 Jews and the scaled-down proposal for 5,000, see Eshkoli, "The Transdnistrian Plan."

31. Pehle's suggestion, of course, was by no means the first time that this idea had been raised. The Gillette-Rogers Resolution, then before Congress, contained the same notion, and some Jewish organizations had suggested the idea earlier.

32. Jewish Evacuation, December 18, 1943, Morgenthau Diaries, vol. 688, FDRL.

33. Morgenthau Diaries, December 19, 1943, vol. 688, FDRL. On Cox's previous efforts, see Wyman, *Abandonment of the Jews,* 183. Twice during the meeting of December 19, Cox stated that Roosevelt favored the idea of a refugee commission but that the State Department had opposed it.

34. Wyman, *Abandonment of the Jews,* 184–85, is quite inaccurate on Morgenthau's intention to go to Hull only. See Morgenthau Diaries, December 19, 1943, vol. 688 (p. 128), December 20, 1943, vol. 688 (p. 169), FDRL.

35. Jewish Evacuation, December 20, 1943 (10:30 A.M.), Morgenthau Diaries, vol. 688, FDRL.

36. DuBois Memorandum for the Files, December 18, 1943, Morgenthau Diaries, vol. 688, FDRL; and interview with Josiah DuBois, October 12, 1982. DuBois declined to reveal the name of his friend in the State Department, but Hiss is listed in the memorandum. Donald Hiss was the brother of Alger Hiss.

37. [Luxford] Memorandum for the Files, December 20, 1943; Jewish Evacuation,

December 20, 1943 (2:25 P.M.), and December 23, 1943, Morgenthau Diaries, vol. 688, FDRL; and Morgenthau statement, according to DuBois, interview of October 12, 1982. The quote from Paul is from the minutes of December 23, 1943.

38. Interview with Josiah DuBois, October 12, 1982.

39. Interview with Josiah DuBois, October 12, 1982. There is independent evidence that DuBois used very strong language. Just before the meeting with FDR, Morgenthau told the rest of the Treasury group (in the absence of DuBois): "I think we have covered it all, and DuBois will have the last worry that I am not going to be tough." Paul said, "I told him to keep his mouth shut." Morgenthau Diaries, January 15, 1944, vol. 694, FDRL.

40. Interview with John Pehle, September 3, 1982. See chap. 7, above.

41. Kades to Morgenthau, August 11, 1943; Bergson Memorandum, July 16, 1943; and Kades to Morgenthau, July 10, June 21, 1943, NA, RG 65, Entry 198, Box 212 (Pehle Papers).

42. Report to the Secretary on the Acquiescence of this Government in the Murder of the Jews, January 13, 1944. This document has been published by Michael Mashberg, "Documents Concerning the American State Department and the Stateless European Jews, 1942–1944," *Jewish Social Studies*, vol. 39 (Winter–Spring 1977): 163–74. Mashberg, however, attributes the report to Paul. The original copy in the possession of Josiah DuBois makes clear that Dubois drafted the report. Pehle and Paul later had a hand in editing it. Draft of executive order in War Refugee Board Records, Box 27, vol. 1, FDRL.

43. Pehle Memorandum for the Secretary's Files, January 16, 1944, Morgenthau Diaries, vol. 694, FDRL.

44. Luxford Memorandum for the Files, January 20, 1944, War Refugee Board Records, Box 27, FDRL.

45. Wyman, *Abandonment of the Jews*, 209, 213.

46. Morgenthau Diaries, January 15, 1944, vol. 694, FDRL; Morse, *While Six Million Died*, 92; Stettinius Memorandum of Conversation with Morgenthau, January 26, 1944, Stettinius Papers, Box 724, University of Virginia; and Pehle Memorandum for the Files, February 1, 1944, War Refugee Board Records, Box 28, vol. 3, FDRL. The War Department's two top candidates for the post were General William Haskell and Commissioner of Immigration Earl Harrison, but War Department officials found Pehle acceptable. See Patterson to Stimson, January 27, 1944; Amberg to Stimson, January 26, 1944, Robert P. Patterson Papers, Box 169, Refugee Committee Folder, LC; and Stimson to Morgenthau, January 27, 1944, NA, RG 107, Box 14, Treasury Folder. The quote from Paul is in Paul to Jerome Frank, February 4, 1944, copy in War Refugee Board Records, Box 28, vol. 3, FDRL.

47. Friedman Memorandum re Cable to Missions, January 26, 1944; and Pehle Memorandum for the Files, January 31, 1944, War Refugee Board Records, Box 30 and 28, FDRL. The quotation comes from Morse, *While Six Million Died*, 324, but Morse did not learn the source. DuBois said that it was Dunn who made the remark. Interview of October 12, 1982. Weil, *A Pretty Good Club*, 144–47, considers Dunn the most influential figure in the department after the forced departure of Sumner Welles. DuBois described Dunn as "basically an anti-Semite."

48. Department to American Embassy, London, January 25, 1944; Morgenthau to McCloy, January 28, 1944, copies in War Refugee Board Records, Box 28, vol. 3, FDRL.

49. Moose to Secretary of State, February 16, 1944, copy in War Refugee Board Records, Box 33, FDRL.

50. McCloy to Morgenthau, February 6, 1944, copy in War Refugee Board Records, Box 25, vol. 3, FDRL.

51. Pehle Memorandum for the Files, January 31, 1944, War Refugee Board Records, Box 28, vol. 3, FDRL; and Charles P. Taft to Dear Ambassador, February 10,

1944, Taft Diaries, Box 4, LC.

52. Friedman Memorandum re Cable to Missions, January 26, 1944. War Refugee Board Records, Box 30, FDRL; Minutes of State Department meeting on War Refugees, January 28, 1944, Charles P. Taft Papers, Box 3, LC; and Pehle Memorandum for the Files, February 1, 1944, War Refugee Board Records, Box 28, vol. 3, FDRL.

53. Raynor to Pehle, February 5, 1944, with attached British Memorandum, War Refugee Board Records, Box 30, FDRL.

54. DuBois-Pehle Memorandum for Stettinius, February 10, 1944, War Refugee Board Records, Box 25, vol. 3, FDRL.

55. Memorandum on [WRB] Accomplishments since February 2, 1944, Ira Hirschmann Papers, Box 1, FDRL; and Memorandum for Record, 23 June 1944 on Proposed Air Action to Impede Deportation of Hungarian and Slovak Jews, NA, RG 107, Records of the Office of the Secretary of War, ASW 400.38.

56. War Refugee Board to American Embassy, London, February 9, 1944, copy in Stettinius Papers, Box 745, War Refugee Board Folder, University of Virginia; and Developments during the Week of March 13–18, 1944, Ira Hirschmann Papers, Box 1, FDRL.

57. Lesser to Pehle, February 2, 1944, War Refugee Board Records, Box 17, FDRL.

58. Copy in War Refugee Board Records, Box 30, Measures Directed toward Halting Persecution, FDRL.

59. War Refugee Board Staff Conference, February 23, 1944, War Refugee Board Records, Box 27, vol. 1, FDRL; Pehle Memorandum for the Files, February 23, 1944, War Refugee Board Records, Box 33, FDRL; Raydon Memorandum for the Files, February 29, 1944; Hackworth to Stettinius, February 26, 1944; Reams to Dunn, February 26, 1944; and Dunn to Stettinius, February 28, 1944, Stettinius Papers, Box 745, War Refugee Board Folder, University of Virginia.

60. DuBois Memorandum for the Files, March 2, 1944, War Refugee Board Records, Box 27, vol. 1, FDRL.

61. Taylor Personal to the President and Memorandum to the President, March 3, 1944, copies in Stettinius Papers, Box 250, London Mission–Refugees Folder, University of Virginia.

62. Pehle Memorandum for the Files, March 6, 1944, War Refugee Board Records, Box 30, Measures Directed toward Halting Persecution, FDRL; and Stettinius to Early, March 6, 1944, President's Secretary's File, Box 177, Refugees, FDRL.

63. Morgenthau Diaries, March 7, 1944, vol. 706, FDRL.

64. Taft Memorandum of March 10, 1944, Taft Diaries, Box 4, LC; Stettinius Memorandum for Early, March 8, 1944, President's Secretary's File, Box 177, FDRL; Stettinius to Early, March 8, 1944, Early Papers, Box 18, Stettinius Folder, FDRL; Pehle Memorandum for the Files, March 9, 1944, War Refugee Board Records, Box 30, Measures Directed toward Halting Persecution, FDRL; and Stimson Diaries, March 9, 1944, vol. 46, Roll 8, LC. At this time the British continued to oppose a denunciation of German atrocities against Jews as well as War Refugee Board spending for relief in Rumania and France. See Gilbert, *Auschwitz and the Allies,* 178.

65. Pehle Memorandum for Mr. Stettinius, March 10, 1944, Stettinius Papers, Box 745, War Refugee Board Folder, University of Virginia: Tully Memorandum for the President, March 8, 1944; DJB Memorandum for the President, March 22, 1944; Statement by the President of the United States, President's Secretary's File, Box 177, Refugees, FDRL.

66. Hamblet (London) to Control Desk OWI (New York), March 24, 1944, NA, RG 208, Entry 359, Box 116, Refugees-Policy.

67. DuBois Report to the War Refugee Board, March 6, 1944, private papers of Josiah DuBois. Interview with Dubois, October 12, 1982.

68. Wyman, *Abandonment of the Jews,* 263.

69. On Stimson, see Henry L. Stimson and McGeorge Bundy, *On Active Service in Peace and War* (New York, 1948); and Elting Morrison, *Turmoil and Tradition: Henry L. Stimson* (New York, 1960).

70. Stimson Diaries, March 9, 21, 1944, vol. 46, Roll 8, LC; interview with Pehle, September 3, 1982; Lesser and DuBois Conversation with Clarence Pickett, April 4, 1944, Pickett Journal, AFSC; and Pehle to Leonard Ackerman, April 13, 1944, War Refugee Board Records, Box 1, Ackerman Folder, FDRL.

71. Pehle to Stimson, March 29, 1944; Pehle Memorandum for the President; Stimson to Pehle, March 31, 1944; Stimson to Morgenthau and Hull, March 31, 1944, NA, RG 107, Box 14, War Refugee Board Folder.

72. Pickett Journal, April 4, 17, 1944, AFSC; and Stimson Diaries, May 8, 1944, vol. 47, Roll 9, LC.

73. Pehle Memorandum to Hull, Morgenthau, and Stimson, May 20, 1944, Morgenthau Diaries, vol. 532, FDRL; and Stettinius to Hull, January 8, 1944, with copy of Hull to American Embassy, January 3, 1944, NA, RG 59, CDF 840.48 Refugees/4735.

74. Undated Friedman Memorandum [May 27, 1944], War Refugee Board Records, Box 49, Conversation with Other Agencies Folder, FDRL; History of the War Refugee Board, vol. I, pp. 232–33, FDRL and private possession of George Lesser; Pehle to McDonald, June 9, 1944, with copies of FDR to the Congress of the United States, June 12, 1944, and FDR to Murphy, June 9, 1944, James G. McDonald Papers, War Refugee Board Folder, CSIA. According to Ruth Gruber, at the time a special assistant to Secretary of the Interior Ickes, Ickes proposed in cabinet that the refugees be sent to the Virgin Islands. See Ruth Gruber, *Haven: The Unknown Story of 1000 World War II Refugees* (New York, 1984), 13.

75. History of the War Refugee Board, vol. I, pp. 234–35.

76. Ibid., 235–37. For interesting accounts of these refugees' experience in Oswego, see Gruber, *Haven;* and Wyman, *Abandonment of the Jews,* 268–76.

77. See chap. 7, above.

78. Pehle Memorandum for Stettinius, March 10, 1944, Stettinius Papers, Box 745, War Refugee Board Folder, University of Virginia. See also Morse, *While Six Million Died,* 345–46.

79. History of the War Refugee Board, vol. I, pp. 247–49; and interview with Josiah DuBois, October 12, 1982. DuBois's account diverges from Wyman, *Abandonment of the Jews,* 279; and Morse, *While Six Million Died,* 346. Morse gives the number of Polish Jews in the Vittel group as 238; the official WRB history lists 239.

80. History of the War Refugee Board, vol. I, pp. 250–62; and Morse, *While Six Million Died,* 347.

81. Berle Memorandum of Conversation, May 31, 1944, Berle Diary, May–August 1944, Berle Papers, Box 216, FDRL; and Briggs to Secretary of State, June 19, 1944, War Refugee Board Records, FDRL. On the Hungarian rescue efforts, see chap. 10, above.

82. Berle to Pehle, March 28, 1944; Pehle to Berle, May 2, 1944; Berle to Pehle, June 3, 1944, NA, RG 59, 811.111 Refugees/2191; Lesser Memorandum of Conference in Berle's Office, June 3, 1944, War Refugee Board Records, Box 10, Issuance and Reissuance of Visas, FDRL; and Travers to Berle, July 15, 1944, NA, RG 59, CDF 811.111 Refugees/2196.

83. See Chap. 2, above.

84. Pehle to Morgenthau, November 3, 1944, Morgenthau Diaries, vol. 696, FDRL; McCloy Memorandum for the President, October 20, 1944; FDR to Stimson, October 18, 1944, NA, RG 107, Box 14, White House Correspondence 1944–45; and Memo for the Record, March 20, 1945, NA, RG 319, ABL 383.7.

85. For the report, see McClelland to Pehle, October 12, 1944, War Refugee Board

Records, Box 6, Extermination Camps, FDRL. For the Vrba-Wetzler saga, see Gilbert, *Auschwitz and the Allies,* 191–98, 231–39.

86. Virginia Mannon Memorandum to Files, November 22, 1944; and Davis to Pehle, November 23, 1944, War Refugee Board Records, Box 6, German Extermination Camps Folder, FDRL; McCloy to Stimson, December 20, 1944; Stimson to McCloy, December 21, 1944, NA, RG 107, Box 14, War Refugee Board Folder; Lipstadt, *Beyond Belief,* 265–66; and interview with Pehle, September 3, 1982.

87. "Gallup Finds Most Believe Atrocity Tales[!]" and "Genocide," *Washington Post,* December 3, 1944. See also Lipstadt, *Beyond Belief,* 347–48.

10. THE WAR REFUGEE BOARD IN EUROPE

1. An often-overlooked fact is that during 1943 the Swedish government tried to persuade Germany to allow the emigration of all Norwegian Jews and Dutch Jews and some remaining Polish Jews to Sweden. The German government flatly refused. See Johnson to Secretary of State, April 13, 1943, excerpt in NA, RG 226, Entry 145, Box 2, Folder 26. This incident highlights the infeasibility of all of the proposals made in the United States during 1943 for negotiations with Germany, either directly or through neutral nations, for the release of Jews. See Wyman, *Abandonment of the Jews,* 88, 97, 115. Even if the War Refugee Board had been created earlier, it would not have led to successful negotiations with Germany.

2. On Hitler's last will and testament, see John Toland, *Afolf Hitler* (New York, 1976), 1211–14.

3. For more detailed treatment, see, particularly, History of the War Refugee Board; and Wyman, *Abandonment of the Jews,* 209–307.

4. Haim Avni, *Spain, the Jews, and Franco* (Philadelphia, 1982), 73–77; and Clarence Pickett conversation with Carlton Hayes, April 23, 1942, Pickett Journal, AFSC.

5. The Refugee Problem in Spain, April 21, 1942, unsigned memorandum, Carlton Hayes Papers, Box 6, Refugee Organizations, Columbia University.

6. Carlton J. H. Hayes, *Wartime Mission in Spain,* 1942–1945 (New York, 1945), 3–10.

7. Ibid., 5–7, 10.

8. Pickett conversation with Hayes, April 23, 1942, Pickett Journal, AFSC.

9. Hayes Memorandum for the President on the Refugee Problem in Spain, May 3, 1943, Hayes Papers, Box 3, Memoranda to FDR, Columbia University; and Hayes to Secretary of State, May 31, 1943, Report on the Refugee Problem in Spain, NA, RG 59, CDF 840.48 Refugees/3894.

10. Hayes Memorandum for the President on the Refugee Problem in Spain, May 3, 1943, Hayes Papers, Box 3, Memoranda to FDR, Columbia University; Avni, *Spain, the Jews, and Franco,* 103; and Wriggins to Kullman, April 19, 1943, AFSC, Refugee Service Files, Spain 1943: Correspondence with Europe.

11. Avni, *Spain, the Jews and Franco,* 103–07; and [Blickenstaff] Confidential Report, August 19, 1943, NA, RG 169, E-124, Box 36, Refugees-Spanish, OFRRO Subject File.

12. Avni, *Spain, the Jews, and Franco,* 116–17.

13. See chap. 8, above.

14. Makinson to Secretary of State, March 1, 1943, NA, RG 59, CDF 840.48 Refugees/3695; and Hayes to Secretary of State, September 29, 1943, NA, RG 59, CDF 840.48 Refugees/4523.

15. R. Brandin Memorandum, June 28, 1943, Hayes Papers, Box 6, Refugee Organizations, Columbia University.

16. Joseph Schwartz to Hayes, May 28, 1943; Hayes to Schwartz, June 9, 1943; Schwartz to Hayes, July 29, 1943, NA, RG 84, American Embassy, Madrid 1943, vol. 23.

17. Hayes to Secretary of State, September 25, 1943; Memorandum of Conversation with the Foreign Minister, September 20, 1943, NA, RG 59, CDF 840.48 Refugees/4551; Hayes to Secretary of State, November 9, 1943; and McDonald to Latimer, November 5, 1943, NA, RG 59, CDF 840.48 Refugees/4809. In *Wartime Mission in Spain,* Hayes estimated that 16,000 Frenchmen were transported to North Africa during 1943. In his report to the State Department of May 31, Hayes cited a total of 25,000 to 30,000 undocumented refugees who had entered Spain since November 1942. NA, RG 59, CDF 840.48 Refugees/3894. The American Friends Service Committee estimated in March 1943 that there were 12,000 potential visa applicants to the U.S. in Spain. Marnie Schauffler to James Vail *et al.,* March 1, 1943, AFSC, Refugee Service 1943, Committees and Organizations: U.S. State Dept. All of these statistics are roughly consistent. The total number of refugees minus the French and minus several thousand of other Allied nationalities (some of whom were Jews) would leave the stateless, most of whom were Jews.

18. History of the War Refugee Board, vol. I, p. 112, FDRL.

19. Hayes, *Wartime Mission in Spain,* 206–25. Wyman's comment, *Abandonment of the Jews,* 226, that the battle over Spanish wolfram was already won certainly does not apply at this time.

20. History of the War Refugee Board, vol. I, p. 112, FDRL; and Hayes to Secretary of State, February 3, 1944, NA, RG 59, CDF 840.48 Refugees/5110.

21. JBF [Friedman] Memorandum on Discussion of Proposed Cable to Ambassador Hayes, February 14, 1944, War Refugee Board Records, Box 25, Spain Folder, FDRL.

22. Charles P. Taft Diaries, February 16, 1944, Taft Papers, Box 4, LC; War Refugee Board to Hayes, March 23, 1944, NA, RG 59, CDF 840.48 Refugees/5279 Confidential File; Undated Memorandum [on Ambassador Hayes], War Refugee Board Records, Box 25, Spain Folder, FDRL; and History of the War Refugee Board, vol. 1, pp. 113–15, FDRL.

23. Wyman, *Abandonment of the Jews,* 225.

24. History of the War Refugee Board, vol. 1, pp. 117–19; Undated Memorandum [on Ambassador Hayes], War Refugee Board Records, Box 25, Spain Folder, FDRL; and Lieutenant Gerhart Memorandum for the Assistant Chief of Staff, G-2, May 3, 1944, NA, RG 319, Box 945, MID 383.7.

25. James Mann Memorandum, Conversations in Spain with Ambassador and Others [late June 1944], War Refugee Board Records, Box 71, FDRL; and Pehle Memorandum of Conversations with Hayes [July 20, 1944], War Refugee Board Records, Box 25, Spain, FDRL.

26. James Mann Memorandum, War Refugee Board Records, Box 71, FDRL.

27. Ibid.; and interview with George Lesser, May 11, 1982.

28. Avni, *Spain, the Jews, and Franco,* 173.

29. See Braham, *Politics of Genocide,* vol. 1, pp. 39–75.

30. Summary Report of the Activities of the War Refugee Board with Respect to the Jews in Hungary (hereafter Summary Report—Hungary), p.1, War Refugee Board Records, Box 34, FDRL.

31. Ibid., 1–3.

32. On this statement, see chap. 9, above.

33. Braham, *Politics of Genocide,* vol. 1, pp. 386–415; vol. 2, pp. 596–615; and State Department Special Interrogation of Carl Berthold Franz Rekowski, September 17 and 19, 1945, NA, RG 226, XL 25105.

34. Summary Report—Hungary, 4–6, 9, 14.

35. Per Anger, *With Raoul Wallenberg in Budapest: Memories of the War Years in*

Hungary, trans. David mel Paul and Margareta Paul (New York, 1981), 46–50; Grossman Memo to War Refugee Board, January 10, 1945, War Refugee Board Records, Box 34, Hungary 1, FDRL; and Laura Margolis to James Mann, January 12, 1945, War Refugee Board Records, Box 16, Mann Folder, FDRL.

36. Pehle Memorandum for the Members of the War Refugee Board, July 15, 1944, NA, RG 107, ASW 400.38 Jews.

37. Summary Report—Hungary, War Refugee Board Records, Box 34, pp. 9a–14, FDRL; and Braham, *Politics of Genocide,* vol. 2, pp. 754, 1070–72.

38. Braham, *Politics of Genocide,* vol. 2, pp. 755–63.

39. Ibid., vol. 2, pp. 766–69.

40. Summary Report—Hungary, War Refugee Board Records, Box 34, pp. 17–25, FDRL; Report of the War Refugee Board for the Week of August 7–12, 1944, copy in NA, RG 165, Box 2802; and Pehle to Stettinius, July 29, 1944, War Refugee Board Records, Box 70, Hungarian Offer, FDRL.

41. Anger, *With Raoul Wallenberg,* 55–60.

42. See Braham, *Politics of Genocide,* vol. 2, pp. 1057–95. For further details on Wallenberg, see John Bierman, *Righteous Gentile: The Story of Raoul Wallenberg, Missing Hero of the Holocaust* (New York, 1981).

43. Braham, *Politics of Genocide,* vol. 2, pp. 942–45.

44. Mendelsohn, *The Holocaust,* vol. 15, pp. 85–132. Braham, *Politics of Genocide,* vol. 2, pp. 946–49; and Bauer, *American Jewry and the Holocaust,* 394–95.

45. Gilbert, *Auschwitz and the Allies,* 217–19.

46. McCloy to Stettinius, June 10, 1944, Stettinius Papers, Box 742, War Department–McCloy Folder, University of Virginia; Gilbert, *Auschwitz and the Allies,* 225; and Hirschmann Memorandum to Ambassador Steinhardt, June 22, 1944, copy in NA, RG 107, ASW 400.38, July 20, 1944.

47. Hirschmann Memorandum to Steinhardt, June 22, 1944, NA, RG 107, ASW 400.38, July 20, 1944; Pehle Memoranda for the Files, July 8, 1944; and Pehle to Stettinius, July 27, 1944, War Refugee Board Records, Box 70, Joel Brand Proposal, FDRL. See also Gilbert, *Auschwitz and the Allies,* 242–44.

48. Mendelsohn, *The Holocaust,* vol. 15, doc. 5, pp. 57, 66. See also Gilbert, *Auschwitz and the Allies,* 228–29, on British reaction to the offer. On Becher's self-image, see McClelland's report to O'Dwyer, August 2, 1945, in Mendelsohn, *The Holocaust,* vol. 16, doc. 4, p. 45.

49. For details, see Bauer, *American Jewry and the Holocaust,* 408–28.

50. Ibid., 429.

51. Musy to Himmler, November 18, 1944; and Himmler Niederschrift, January 18, 1945, NA, RG 242, T-175, R 118, 2643519–21.

52. Roswell McClelland, Confidential Memo, February 6, 1945, private papers of Roswell McClelland; and Warren to Grew, February 15, 1945, copy in Stettinius Papers, Box 745, War Refugee Board Folder, University of Virginia.

53. Warren to Grew, February 19, 1945, copy in Stettinius Papers, Box 745, War Refugee Board Folder, University of Virginia. According to Kurt Becher, Himmler said that Hitler became aware of newspaper articles about the train and forbade any further release of Jews. Independently, Musy said that Schellenberg cited Hitler's opposition to the release of Jews. Mendelsohn, *The Holocaust,* vol. 16, doc. 1, p. 2; and doc. 2, p. 23. See also Bauer, *American Jewry and the Holocaust,* 430.

54. For a summary, see McClelland Report, August 2, 1945, reprinted in Mendelsohn, *The Holocaust,* vol. 16, doc. 4, pp. 10–59.

55. Wyman, *Abandonment of the Jews,* 285; and McClelland Report, August 2, 1985, reprinted in Mendelsohn, *The Holocaust,* vol. 16, doc. 4, p. 59.

56. See chap. 9 above. Wyman, *Abandonment of the Jews,* 291–93, has also stressed this point.

57. Feingold, "The Government Response," 256; and Wyman, *Abandonment of the Jews*, 292. See also FDR's reaction to the Bermuda Conference decisions, *FRUS, 1943*, vol. 1, pp. 177–79.

58. McClelland to War Refugee Board, June 24, 1944, and attached documents; Pehle Memorandum for the Members of the War Refugee Board, July 15, 1944, NA, RG 107, ASW 400.38 Jews; and Wyman, "Why Auschwitz Was Never Bombed," *Commentary*, October 1980, p. 39.

59. Lesser suggested a memorandum to the president that would raise anew the issue of military operations to save civilian lives. Lesser Draft Memorandum for the President, July 13, 1944, War Refugee Board Records, Box 34, Hungary Folder I, FDRL.

60. Edward T. Chase, "Why We Didn't Bomb Auschwitz," *Washington Post*, May 21, 1983.

61. Wyman, "Why Auschwitz," 40.

62. Leon Kubowitzki to Ernest Frischer, Czechoslovakian Government in Exile, August 2, 1944, War Refugee Board Records, Box 4, Censorship Intercepts Folder, FDRL. Kubowitzki and the World Jewish Congress feared that Allied bombing of camp inmates would give the Nazis a chance to claim that the Allies, not the Nazis, were responsible for previous killing. Pehle Memorandum for the Files, August 11, 1944, War Refugee Board Records, Box 34, Hungary I Folder, FDRL.

63. Pehle to McCloy, October 4, 1944, NA, RG 107, ASW 400.38 Jews; and Wyman, "Why Auschwitz," 40.

64. Wyman, "Why Auschwitz," 41–44, and *Abandonment of the Jews*, 298–303.

65. Wyman, *Abandonment of the Jews*, 304.

66. Ibid., 293.

67. Bombing Objectives, Office of Economic Warfare, October 18, 1943, NA, RG 169, Entry 146, Box 886.

68. See chap. 8, above.

69. Feingold, *Politics of Rescue*, 307.

11. ROOSEVELT AND THE REFUGEES IN THE 1930S

1. James MacGregor Burns, *Roosevelt: The Lion and the Fox* (New York, 1956), xi.

2. Ibid.

3. The classic discussion of the power to persuade is in Richard E. Neustadt, *Presidential Power: The Politics of Leadership* (New York, 1960), 42–63. More recently, political scientist James David Barber has described FDR as an active-positive president, who used "a variety of styles, moving flexibly among a number of modes of political action." According to Barber, such a president regards his style as a "bag of tools, not a way of life." James David Barber, *The Presidential Character: Predicting Performance in the White House* (Englewood Cliffs, 1972), 211.

4. Saul Bellow, "In the Days of Mr. Roosevelt," *Esquire*, December 1983, p. 532.

5. The importance of symbolic politics is best described by Murray Edelman, *The Symbolic Uses of Politics* (Urbana, 1964). Recent scholarship suggests that FDR's tax policies, for example, were really two: "one a revenue workhorse, the other a symbolic showpiece." See Mark H. Leff, *The Limits of Symbolic Reform: The New Deal and Taxation, 1933–1939* (Cambridge, 1984), 2–3.

6. Lawrence H. Fuchs, *The Political Behavior of American Jews* (Glencoe, 1965), 99–107; Samuel Lubell, *The Future of American Politics* (New York, 1956), 36–37; Mark R. Levy and Michael S. Kramer, *The Ethnic Factor: How American Minorities Decided Elections* (New York, 1973), 103; and Henry L. Feingold, " 'Courage First and Intelligence Second': The American Jewish Secular Elite, Roosevelt, and the Failure to Rescue," *American Jewish History* 72 (June 1983), 426–27.

7. Burns, *Roosevelt: The Lion and the Fox,* 104; Lawrence Fuchs, "American Jews and the Presidential Vote," *American Political Science Review* 49 (1955): 385–401; and Dinnerstein, "Jews and the New Deal," 474.

8. Jerrold Auerbach, *Unequal Justice: Lawyers and Social Change in Modern America* (New York: 1976), 187.

9. Dinnerstein, "Jews and the New Deal"; and Feingold, "'Courage First and Intelligence Second,'" 443–44.

10. Dinnerstein, "Jews and the New Deal," 475.

11. Alexander George, *Presidential Decisionmaking in Foreign Policy: The Effective Use of Information and Advice* (Boulder, 1980), 148–50.

12. Neustadt, *Presidential Power,* 150.

13. George, *Presidential Decisionmaking in Foreign Policy,* 150.

14. Schlesinger, *Coming of the New Deal,* 528.

15. Wise to Frankfurter, June 6, 1933, Wise papers, Box 109, Correspondence—Zionism, AJHS.

16. Simon Weber, interview with Alan M. Kraut, August 17, 1983.

17. Report of a Visit of Dr. Stephen S. Wise to President Roosevelt at Hyde Park, Mon. Oct. 5, 1936 [verbatim transcript, according to Wise's cover letter to Frankfurter, October 6, 1936], Wise Papers, Box 68, Federal Government—Presidential File, AJHS.

18. Hadley Cantril, ed., *Public Opinion, 1935–1946* (Princeton, 1951), 381–82.

19. James T. Patterson, *Congressional Conservatism and the New Deal: The Growth of the Conservative Coalition in Congress, 1933–1939* (Lexington, 1967), 160–63.

20. Morgenthau Diaries, March 22, 1938, vol. 116, FDRL; and Ickes, *Secret Diary,* vol. 2, pp. 342–343. See also Stewart, "United States Policy," 273.

21. This poll was conducted by the Research Opinion Corporation in March 1938. It is cited in Charles Herbert Stember *et al., Jews in the Mind of America* (New York, 1966), 148. A later Opinion Research Corporation poll, commissioned by the American Jewish Committee in May 1938 revealed that 82 percent of the polling sample opposed increased immigration of Jewish refugees. See Chronological File, September–December 1938, American Jewish Committee Archives.

22. Wise to Frankfurter, March 30, 1938, Wise Papers, Box 109, Correspondence-Zionism, AJHS.

23. Moffat Diary, March 21, 22, 1938, Moffat Papers, Houghton Library, Harvard; and Welles to Morgenthau, March 23, 1938, Morgenthau Diaries, vol. 116, FDRL.

24. Morgenthau Diaries, March 18, 1938, vol. 116, FDRL.

25. Samuel McCrea Cavert, Memorandum on White House Conference on Refugees, April 13, 1938. AFSC, General File 1938, American Christian Committee for German Refugees.

26. Stember, *Jews in the Mind of America,* 145.

27. Lipstadt, *Beyond Belief,* 98–109.

28. Cantril, *Public Opinion,* 382.

29. Statement by President, November 15, 1938, reprinted in *Franklin D. Roosevelt and Foreign Affairs* (Clearwater, 1981), 2d ser., vol. 12, p. 83.

30. Rosenman to FDR, December 12, 1938, President's Personal File, FDRL.

31. Wise to Benjamin Cohen, November 17, 1938, Wise Papers, Box 64, AJHS; Minutes of PACPR, November 14, 21, 1938, Chamberlain Papers, YIVO; and Moffat Diary, November 16, 1938, Houghton Library, Harvard.

32. FDR Memorandum for the Undersecretary of State, November 26, 1938, OF 20, FDRL; Morgenthau to FDR; and Bowman to FDR, November 21, 25, 29, 1938, President's Secretary's File, Box 177, FDRL.

33. Burns, *Roosevelt: The Lion and the Fox,* 360–61.

34. Morse, *While Six Million Died,* 268; and Stewart, "United States Policy," 527.

35. Stember, *Jews in the Mind of America*, 149.

36. Brandeis discussion with FDR quoted in Alpheur Thomas Mason, *Brandeis: A Free Man's Life* (New York, 1946) and cited in Shafir, "Impact of the Jewish Crisis on American German Relations, 1933–39," vol. 2, p. 970.

37. Harold L. Ickes, *The Secret Diary of Harold L. Ickes*, vol. 3, *The Lowering Clouds, 1939–1941* (New York, 1954), 56–57. See also Wyman, *Paper Walls*, 102.

38. Cantril, *Public Opinion*, 600–19.

39. Burns, *Roosevelt: The Lion and the Fox*, 451.

40. Fuchs, *The Political Behavior of American Jews*, 101.

41. Prayer quoted by Burns, *Roosevent: The Lion and the Fox*, 451.

42. Paul Conkin, *The New Deal* (Arlington Heights, 1967), 5; and Feingold, "The Government Response," 255.

43. Feingold, " 'Courage First and Intelligence Second,' " 456.

44. Conkin, *New Deal*, 10–11, 14–15; and Feingold, " 'Courage First and Intelligence Second,' " 457.

12. ROOSEVELT AND THE HOLOCAUST

1. Wyman, *Abandonment of the Jews*, 312–13, admits the problem posed by lack of clear evidence of Roosevelt's views. This does not prevent him from labeling FDR as insensitive and indifferent. See also ibid., xi, 103.

2. See chap. 3, above.

3. Copy in Attorney General Jackson to Secretary of War, August 1, 1940, NA, RG 107, Fifth Column Correspondence. See also Department of State, Division of Current Information, Radio Bulletin no. 185, August 5, 1940, copy in NA, RG 107, Records of the Office of the Secretary of War.

4. Breckinridge Long Diary, May 22, June 22, 1940, LC, cited and discussed in Joseph Lash, *Roosevelt and Churchill, 1939–1941: The Partnership That Saved the West* (New York, 1976), 137.

5. Messersmith to Welles, May 22, 1940, Messersmith Papers, Folder 1360, University of Delaware; and Messersmith to Frankfurter, May 31, 1940, Frankfurter Papers, Box 83, Messersmith Folder, LC.

6. See chap. 5, above.

7. Presidential Press Conference, June 5, 1940, in *Presidential Press Conferences*, vol. 13–14. See chap. 5, above.

8. Dunlop, *Donovan*, 210–11; and Wasserstein, *Britain*, 84–102.

9. Bullitt's speech is reprinted in *New York Times*, August 19, 1940. Information about Welles and Roosevelt is in Bullitt's memorandum, August 12, 1940, reprinted in Orville H. Bullitt, ed., *For the President, Personal and Secret: Correspondence between Franklin D. Roosevelt and William C. Bullitt* (Boston, 1972), 499. Bullitt had earlier, well before the fall of France, written FDR much the same thing—that large numbers of Jewish refugees in France were spying for Germany. See Ted Morgan, *FDR* (New York, 1986), 498–99.

10. Circular telegram of September 19, 1940, NA, RG 59, 811.111 Refugees/260; Johnson to Secretary of State, September 28, 1940, NA, RG 59, 811.111 Refugees/376;

11. Secretary of State's Memo, July 26, 1941, NA, RG 59, 811.111 War Regulations/366A.

12. Eleanor Roosevelt to McDonald, March 2, 1941, Eleanor Roosevelt Papers, Box 1612, FDRL.

13. FDR Memorandum for the Secretary of the Interior, December 18, 1940, OF 3186, FDRL.

14. Feingold, *Politics of Rescue*, 155–56.

15. Welles to Mr. President, December 21, 1940, NA, RG 59, CDF 840.48 Refugees/2352.

16. See chap. 5, above. Berle Diary, March 5, 1941, Berle Papers, FDRL.

17. Dallek, *Franklin D. Roosevelt*, 334–35.

18. *Congressional Record*, June 5, 1941.

19. Dallek, *Franklin D. Roosevelt*, 277, 285, 267.

20. Frankfurter Telephone Conversation with Secretary of War Stimson, June 16, 1943, transcript in Stimson Papers, Roll 127, LC.

21. Hull to FDR, May 7, 1943; Undated Summary of Colonel Hoskins's Report on the Near East; Welles to the President, June 14, 1943; Roosevelt to King Saud, June 15, 1943, President's Secretary's File: Confidential File, Box 13, State Department 1943, FDRL.

22. Morgenthau Presidential Diaries, December 3, 1942, Box 5, FDRL.

23. Memo to Watson and President, December 2, 1942; Early to Welles, December 4, 1942; Welles to Early, December 12, 1942, President's Secretary's File: Confidential File, State Department, FDRL.

24. The comment of July 1942 is quoted in Jewish Delegation Press Release, December 8, 1942, American Jewish Committee Archives, RG-1, EXO-29, Waldman Papers, Germany/Nazism/American Jewish Congress. For the other statements, see OF 5152; White House Press Release, October 7, 1942; and Berle Diary, August 18, 1942, and attached Statement of the President of the United States, Box 214, FDRL.

25. Laqueur, *Terrible Secret*, 3, 237.

26. See chap. 7, above.

27. See chap. 7, above.

28. See chap. 7, above.

29. Watson Memorandum, November 30, 1942; Watson comment about FDR's reaction, December 1, 1942; Wise to Dear Boss, December 2, 1942, OF 76-C, FDRL; Wise to Niles, December 2, 1942, Wise Papers, Box 181, AJHS; and Welles to Watson, December 4, 1942, OF 76-C, FDRL.

30. Held's account of meeting, pt. 3, sec. 1, no. 15, Jewish Labor Committee Archives, quoted by Penkower, *The Jews Were Expendable*, 85–86; and Jewish Delegation Press Release, December 8, 1942, copy in American Jewish Committee Archives, RG-1, EXO-29, Waldman Papers, Germany/Nazism/ American Jewish Congress.

31. Wise to Niles, December 9, 1942, Wise Papers, Box 181, AJHS.

32. Watson to Long, April 1, 1943, and attached documents, OF 3186, FDRL, copy also in NA, RG 59, 811.111 Refugees/4–143. See also Celler's report in Meeting of the Joint Emergency Committee on European Jewish Affairs, April 10, 1943, American Jewish Committee Archives.

33. *FRUS, 1943*, vol. 1, pp. 177–79.

34. Morgan, *FDR*, esp. 23, 37, 47, 275, 445.

35. Pickett Journal, April 12, June 15, 1943, AFSC.

36. Jan Ciechanowski, *Defeat in Victory* (Garden City, 1947), 179–80. Nowak's message is reprinted in Laqueur, *The Terrible Secret*, 232.

37. Ciechanowski, *Defeat*, 182; and Laqueur, *Terrible Secret*, 231, 236.

38. Wise to the President, July 23, 1943, and handwritten comment on Meltzer memorandum, Proposed Arrangement for Relief and Evacuation of Refugees in Rumania and France, July 30, 1943, NA, RG 59, CDF 862.4016/2286 and 840.48 Refugees/4211. On August 10, 1943, Wise reported confidentially and off the record about the evacuation plan to the Joint Emergency Committee for Jewish Affairs, stating that the government had approved the plan. American Jewish Committee Archive, RG-1, EXO-29, Waldman File, Joint Emergency Committee.

39. See chap. 9, above.

40. Meeting of the Undersecretary with the Assistant Secretaries, Political Advisors, and Geographic Division Heads, November 11, 1943; Stettinius to Long, November 11, 1943, Stettinius Papers, Boxes 732, 215, Meeting with Asst. Secretaries Oct. 1943 and Long Folders respectively, University of Virginia.

41. See chap. 10, above.

42. Gilbert, *Auschwitz and the Allies,* esp. 267–76.

BIBLIOGRAPHICAL NOTE

This study relies heavily upon the records of American government agencies. To describe the debates and directions in refugee policy, we had to follow a paper trail laid by numerous departments and offices, which in most cases led us to the National Archives (NA), the Washington National Records Center, which is an annex of the National Archives at Suitland, Maryland, and the Franklin D. Roosevelt Presidential Library (FDRL) in Hyde Park, New York. Of the utmost importance were the records of the Department of State (Record Group 59), particularly, in the Central Decimal File, file numbers 740.0011, European War 1939; 740.00116, European War 1939; 837.55J; 840.48; 840.48 Refugees; and 862.4016, all at the National Archives. At Suitland we found file numbers 150.01, 150.062 Public Charge, 150.069, and 150.626J (Jews) of greatest value for the debates over regulating immigration during the 1930s. Complementing these State Department records, but less complete, were the Labor Department records at the National Archives (Record Group 174) and a segment of the Frances Perkins Papers in the Connecticut College Library, New London. Also useful were the Francis Perkins Papers at Columbia University. The late Charles E. Wyzanski, Jr., former solicitor general in the Labor Department, provided access to his private correspondence during his term in office, which helped to complete the picture of Labor's refugee policy. For the period after 1940, when the Immigration and Naturalization Service was transferred to the Justice Department, there are documents about the transfer and subsequent interagency battles still in the possession of the Justice Department.

The original records at Suitland of American consulates, legations, and embassies in the European countries (Record Group 84) provided a level of detailed information about Jewish emigration and Nazi persecution of Jews not always contained in the State Department's Central Decimal File. Unfortunately, records for the American consulates in Germany survive only through 1935. But records of the nearby posts, especially in Switzerland and France, have a good deal of useful information on later developments in Germany and German-controlled territories as well as on refugee emigration generally.

Foremost among our sources at the FDRL were the Records of the War Refugee Board, the Henry Morgenthau, Jr., Diaries, Presidential Diaries, and Roosevelt's Official File 133A. Among the many other useful collections there, we should single out the Eleanor Roosevelt Papers, the Harry Hopkins Papers, the Samuel Rosenman Papers, the Adolf Berle Papers, the Oscar Cox Papers, the Ira Hirschmann Papers, the John Wiley Papers, the R. Walton Moore Papers, and the Myron Taylor Papers.

The Records of the Office of the Secretary of War (Record Group 107) in the National Archives contain a good deal of information regarding the military's stance toward refugee policy during the war, especially during the tenure

299

of the War Refugee Board. The diaries of Secretary of War Henry L. Stimson (originals at Yale, microfilm copies at the Manuscript Division of the Library of Congress), the Robert P. Patterson Papers at the Library of Congress (LC), and the Charles P. Taft Diaries (LC) add substantially to the official records.

The following record groups in the National Archives contain intelligence reports from American and Allied sources regarding Nazi persecution of Jews: RG 165, Records of the War Department General and Special Staffs (Suitland); RG 226, Office of Strategic Services (NA), Plain Number, L, XL files and Entry 4; and Record Group 319, Records of the Army Staff (Suitland). Record Group 208 (Suitland) provides useful details about the Office of War Information's treatment of Nazi atrocities against Jews. Other less essential caches of war-related refugee records are in RG 56 (NA), RG 169 (Suitland), and RG 331 (Suitland).

At the American Jewish Historical Society on the campus of Brandeis University, the extensive Stephen S. Wise Papers gave us great insight into the interaction of American Jewish leaders with government officials throughout the Roosevelt years. Also extremely useful (for Jewish activity in the 1930s) were two smaller collections, the Cecilia Razovsky Papers and the Max J. Kohler Papers. The records of the American Jewish Congress, however, are thin and disappointing. Much richer, especially for understanding American Jewish efforts in the 1930s, were the Felix Warburg Papers at the American Jewish Archives (AJA) in Cincinnati. Since the completion of our manuscript, the AJA has also acquired the papers of the World Jewish Congress. These should be useful in future studies.

The Zionist Archive and Library in New York City contains the small but important Julian W. Mack Papers and Robert Szold Papers. We profited greatly from the huge Morris D. Waldman File in the American Jewish Committee Records, as well as the minutes of the executive committee. Sometime after we finished our research, these records were transferred to the YIVO Institute for Jewish Research, New York, where they are complemented by the Joseph Chamberlain Papers, the files of the National Refugee Service, and a complete set of the minutes of the President's Advisory Committee on Political Refugees.

The papers of the Jewish Labor Committee in New York, still in that agency's possession, provide a thorough description of the debate among Jewish organizations over the boycott issue in the 1930s. The B'nai B'rith records in Washington, D.C., offer details on the virulent debates among Jewish organizations over various strategies and tactics for influencing American policy.

The Society of Friends (Quakers) is not a Jewish organization. Nonetheless, one of the most important private collections, both for the 1930s and 1940s, is the archive of the American Friends Service Committee (Philadelphia), whose leaders and refugee experts were active in Europe and the United States. Among the records of the AFSC, the Frances Pickett Journal supplements the lower-level records in the General File and the Refugee Service File. Also of some use were the records of the Unitarian Field Service at the Harvard Divinity School Library.

The Manuscript Division of the Library of Congress possesses the private papers of numerous prominent individuals involved in refugee policy. Two of the best collections there are the Wilbur J. Carr Papers and the Breckinridge Long Papers. The Cordell Hull Papers are disappointing, but the Laurence A. Steinhardt Papers offer the unusual views of an American Jewish diplomat abroad. The papers of Supreme Court Justice Louis D. Brandeis (originals at the University of Louisville, microfilm copy at LC) and presidential advisor and Supreme Court Justice Felix Frankfurter show their behind-the-scenes lobbying efforts. The Harold Ickes Papers and Diaries offer the view of a non-Jewish cabinet member sympathetic to Jewish refugees. The papers of American minister in Switzerland Leland Harrison and presidential envoy Myron Taylor also have some useful material.

The Sol Bloom Papers and the Emanuel Celler Papers in the New York Public Library give useful details on the match between an American Jewish congressman who was an apologist for the State Department and one of State's severest critics. Somewhere in between was Samuel Dickstein, whose papers are in the AJA in Cincinnati.

At Harvard University's Houghton Library, the papers and diaries of Jay Pierrepont Moffat and William Phillips offer inside views of life and policy making in the State Department during the 1930s. At Columbia University we used the Carlton J. H. Hayes Papers to check on refugee problems in Spain during the war. There is useful material in the Columbia University Oral History Collection from Frances Perkins, Henry A. Wallace, James P. Warburg, Joseph Proskauer, George Rublee, and others. We also used the James G. McDonald Papers to great advantage; less important were the Paul Baerwald Papers and Herbert H. Lehman Papers. These last three collections were formerly part of the Columbia School of International Affairs Archive.

At the University of Virginia, the Edward R. Stettinius, Jr. Papers gave us considerable information about developments within the State Department during 1943 and 1944. At the University of Delaware, the George S. Messersmith Papers provided perceptive observations of developments in American refugee policy and Nazi persecution of Jews during the 1930s. At Georgetown University, we consulted the Robert F. Wagner Papers for information about Senator Wagner's role, especially in the Wagner-Rogers Bill.

At Princeton University's Seeley G. Mudd Library, we used the Bernard Baruch Papers and the records of the American Civil Liberties Union, which showed considerable interest in refugee policy. At the U.S. Army Military History Institute at Carlisle Barracks, Pennsylvania, the William J. Donovan Papers contain relevant intelligence reports as well as information about Allied refugee policies.

INDEX